The Citizenship Education Program and Black Women's Political Culture

Southern Dissent

UNIVERSITY PRESS OF FLORIDA

Florida A&M University, Tallahassee
Florida Atlantic University, Boca Raton
Florida Gulf Coast University, Ft. Myers
Florida International University, Miami
Florida State University, Tallahassee
New College of Florida, Sarasota
University of Central Florida, Orlando
University of Florida, Gainesville
University of North Florida, Jacksonville
University of South Florida, Tampa
University of West Florida, Pensacola

The Citizenship Education Program and Black Women's Political Culture

DEANNA M. GILLESPIE

Foreword by Stanley Harrold and Randall M. Miller

University Press of Florida
Gainesville · Tallahassee · Tampa · Boca Raton
Pensacola · Orlando · Miami · Jacksonville · Ft. Myers · Sarasota

Publication of this paperback edition made possible by a Sustaining the Humanities through the American Rescue Plan grant from the National Endowment for the Humanities.

Copyright 2021 by Deanna M. Gillespie
All rights reserved
Published in the United States of America

First cloth printing, 2021
First paperback printing, 2023

28 27 26 25 24 23   6 5 4 3 2 1

Library of Congress Cataloging-in-Publication Data
Names: Gillespie, Deanna M., author. | Harrold, Stanley, writer of
    foreword. | Miller, Randall M., writer of foreword.
Title: The Citizenship Education Program and black women's political
    culture / Deanna M. Gillespie ; foreword by Stanley Harrold and Randall
    M. Miller.
Other titles: Southern dissent.
Description: Gainesville : University Press of Florida, [2021] | Series:
    Southern dissent | Includes bibliographical references and index.
Identifiers: LCCN 2021007604 (print) | LCCN 2021007605 (ebook) | ISBN
    9780813066943 (cloth) | ISBN 9780813057866 (adobe pdf) | ISBN 9780813080239 (pbk.)
Subjects: LCSH: Citizenship Education Program—History. | African American
    women civil rights workers—History. | African American women—Political
    activity—History. | White supremacy movements—United States—History.
Classification: LCC E185.97.C83 G55 2021 (print) | LCC E185.97.C83
    (ebook) | DDC 305.48/896073—dc23
LC record available at https://lccn.loc.gov/2021007604
LC ebook record available at https://lccn.loc.gov/2021007605

The University Press of Florida is the scholarly publishing agency for the State University System of Florida, comprising Florida A&M University, Florida Atlantic University, Florida Gulf Coast University, Florida International University, Florida State University, New College of Florida, University of Central Florida, University of Florida, University of North Florida, University of South Florida, and University of West Florida.

University Press of Florida
2046 NE Waldo Road
Suite 2100
Gainesville, FL 32609
http://upress.ufl.edu

To my family

Contents

List of Illustrations ix

Foreword xi

Acknowledgments xiii

List of Abbreviations xvii

Introduction 1

1. "We're Going to Learn Together": Groundwork on Johns Island, South Carolina, 1948–1957 12

2. "New Outposts in the Growing Movement": Citizenship Schools in South Carolina and Alabama, 1958–1961 33

3. "Bring This Community Leadership Program to Your Town and County": Groundwork in Southeastern Georgia, 1960–1961 52

4. "Say It Is for Citizenship": Citizenship Education in Southeastern Georgia, 1961–1964 72

5. "We Shall Overcome Today": Groundwork in the Mississippi Delta, 1961–1963 93

6. Freedom Days: Citizenship Education in Mississippi, 1963–1965 118

7. "So Much Taking Place . . . So Rapidly": Citizenship Education in Mississippi and Alabama, 1965–1967 141

8. The Citizenship Education Program's "Second Phase," 1966–1969 163

Epilogue 183

Notes 189

Bibliography 241

Index 253

Illustrations

Figure 1. Bernice Robinson with Johns Island citizenship school students   29

Figure 2. Ethel Grimball with Wadmalaw Island student   37

Figure 3. Allene Brewer with Edisto Island citizenship school students   38

Figure 4. Citizenship Education Program teacher training group   78

Figure 5. Dorothy Cotton, Annell Ponder, and Septima Clark   84

Figure 6. Dorothy Cotton leading literacy education session   170

Figure 7. Septima Clark guiding student's hand   171

Map 1. The South Carolina Lowcountry   14

Map 2. Georgia's First Congressional District   58

Map 3. The Mississippi Delta   94

Map 4. Alabama's Black Belt counties   146

Foreword

The black civil rights movement of the 1950s and 1960s was the most important American social movement during the last century. Based on a long struggle for black freedom in America, dating back to the seventeenth century, it mobilized thousands of black activists and their white allies, gained the right to vote for black men and women, and ended de jure racial segregation in public schools and colleges, parks, doctors' offices, stores, and many public and private places, among other advances. It also opened elective office to black men. And it produced great black leaders—among them Martin Luther King Jr., Bayard Rustin, James Farmer, Ralph Abernathy, Bob Moses, Andrew Young, and John Lewis.

The black civil rights activism moved along two fronts of legal challenges and direct action against racial discrimination. Such landmark U.S. Supreme Court decisions as *Brown v. Board of Education of Topeka, Kansas* (1954) struck down the principle of "separate but equal" that had provided constitutional cover for Jim Crow laws and white power for generations. At the same time, well-publicized direct action campaigns such as protest marches, boycotts, and sit-ins provided constant pressure to end racial discrimination in transportation, education, and public services, spaces, and facilities of all kinds, and to get equal access to private businesses such as lunch counters and restaurants, motels and hotels, and amusement parks and movie theaters. Such action mobilized tens of thousands of people to protest social wrongs and force change. It also led to the passage of such major congressional legislation as the Civil Rights Act of 1964 and the Voting Rights Act of 1965.

Much of that story of civil rights has focused on the leadership roles of men. But the dynamics and direction of civil rights activism owed much to the leadership and work of black women. During the 1950s and 1960s, for example, they helped desegregate schools, organized and sustained boycotts and sit-ins, marched, arranged and attended rallies, gave speeches, and lobbied public officials. Examples abound. Clara Luper emerged as a leader in desegregating the University of Oklahoma starting in 1958 and gained prominence in that state as a sit-in organizer. Rosa Parks helped lead the Montgomery, Alabama, branch of the National Association for the Advancement of Colored People (NAACP) and won lasting fame for refusing to give up her seat on a Montgomery city bus to a white man in 1955, which inspired the Montgomery bus boycott. Ella Baker encouraged the creation of the Student Non-Violent Coordinating Committee (SNCC) and a more aggressive direct action approach to protesting. Fannie Lou Hamer became a leading civil rights orator who organized Mississippi's Freedom Summer and led voter registration efforts. And there were many others.

In her cogent study, *The Citizenship Education Program and Black Women's Political Culture,* Deanna Gillespie brings to the fore the many black women involved in citizenship education and voter mobilization across the South. In doing so, she demonstrates that the civil rights movement went well beyond the mass demonstrations, speeches, and legislation that garnered so much public attention in newspapers and on newscasts. In regard to citizenship education, it involved women as local organizers and leaders in an effort throughout the South to gain the right to vote for African Americans. Doing so, Gillespie argues, was "subversive work in the Jim Crow South."

As Gillespie emphasizes, the Citizenship Education Program was important for both black and women's rights, on the latter count because the formal enfranchisement of women in the Nineteenth Amendment in 1920 did not enfranchise black women in the South until blacks organized to get it and the Voting Rights Act of 1965 provided federal protection for it. Her close study of the Citizenship Education Program and the many women engaged in it as teachers is an insightful reminder that it took more than rallies, marches, speeches, court rulings, and legislation to promote and gain black rights. It took the persistent day-to-day labor of thousands of black women teaching others how to read and write so as to be able to pass literacy tests and exercise political influence.

By telling that story, Gillespie's book is a welcome addition to the *Southern Dissent* series.

Stanley Harrold and Randall M. Miller
Series Editors

Acknowledgments

I began this project when I was looking for a fresh start. I'd been a social worker for ten years, working in south Atlanta and then moving into a job that took me all over Georgia. I talked with local groups about schools, health and welfare services, employment and job training, safety, and justice, and we discussed their future plans. The work convinced me that any meaningful change required a reckoning with history. In 2001, I left my job to study the past. When I met Kitty Sklar at SUNY-Binghamton, she looked me in the eye and said, "You must come here." So I did. She believed that this social worker could be a historian, and I decided to believe it too. Kitty consistently supported this project and gave me space to work out ideas while keeping my feet firmly grounded in women's history. Tom Dublin, John Stoner, Jean Quataert, Arleen De Vera, and David Hacker asked challenging questions and refined my thinking about citizenship, gender, race, and region.

This project has been a calling card. I met Kat Charron over a southern breakfast and found a kindred spirit who generously pointed me where her work had not gone. Fellow Citizenship Education Program (CEP) scholar David Levine kindly shared research notes. Todd Moye, Stephanie Shaw, Ann Short Chirhart, Françoise Hamlin, and Marcia Synnott read and commented on parts of this work as it took shape. Charles Payne and Carol Strickland provided an early boost of confidence, and reviewers at the *Journal of Southern History* refined my analysis of the Mississippi Delta. I am profoundly grateful to Stanley Harrold, Randall Miller, Sian Hunter, and reviewers at the University Press of Florida for their enthusiasm and support.

Thanks to Southern Christian Leadership Conference staff members and archivists who saved those boxes of CEP records and to Dorothy Cotton and former CEP teachers who graciously shared their stories. Cynthia Lewis and Elaine Hall at the King Center and Kathy Shoemaker and

Courtney Chartier at Emory University were invaluable guides. Thanks also to archivists at the Wisconsin Historical Society and Charleston's Avery Research Center for assistance with images.

This work would not be possible without significant support. Research fellowships and travel grants while at SUNY-Binghamton gave me time and resources to pore over documents and find the story. A Presidential Semester Incentive Award at the University of North Georgia reignited this project in the fall of 2016, and a course release approved by UNG's College of Arts and Letters sustained forward momentum. UNG's Department of History, Anthropology, and Philosophy paid for original artwork, and many thanks to Bruno Berry for creating maps for this book. Special thanks to Jeff Pardue and Chris Jespersen for their dogged support.

My life's paths led to the best people around. Friendships forged at Mount Holyoke College more than thirty years ago get better with age. Many thanks to these uncommon women: Amy Alvarez, Debby Arnold, Nancy Benton, Clara Beshoar, Bridget Blitz, Jen Boulais, Aimee Boulanger, Amy Brown, Carrie Enquist, Minnie Rajwar, and Jo-Ann Shyloski. At SUNY-Binghamton, Andie DeKoter, Greg Geddes, Denise Lynn, Mary Weikum, Gaylynn Welch, and Melyssa Wrisley helped this temporarily misplaced southerner feel at home in frozen upstate New York. In Fall 2009, I joined UNG's Department of History, Anthropology, and Philosophy, home to some of the best storytellers and teachers that I know. Thanks especially to Mary Carney, Phil Guerty, Ric Kabat, Jonas Kauffeldt, Johanna Luthman, Sara Mason, Clay Ouzts, and Ben Wynne. Finally, to students who listened to my stories about Septima Clark, the Highlander Folk School, and citizenship schools: your interest convinced me that someone might read this book.

Thanks to Jack and Cyndi Smith, Mason and Michelle Berryman, and Marie Abercrombie, who gave me food, coffee, and a bed as I came through on research trips, cleverly hiding impatience for the final product. When I left my job for uncharted territory, my parents, Ken and Nancy Gillespie, stifled concerns to listen, encourage, and advise—all in equal measure. They've endured many thinking-out-loud sessions, and I'm glad that they're seeing the fruits of this labor. Bill, Amanda, Ellie, Emma, and Sam are a source of inspiration and strength. I started this project when the girls were born, and it is finally seeing the light of day as they graduate from high school.

Lastly, thanks to all family representatives that I met through Georgia's Family Connection. We were reviving a War on Poverty–era belief that lasting change depended on partnerships with the people who raised families in local communities. So we invited family representatives to our tables. These women were—and are—fierce advocates who cut through bureaucratic jargon, asked questions, challenged status quo, and taught me about fairness, justice, and equity. They embodied a continuous line of southern women's leadership, the same line running through the Citizenship Education Program. I put this project on a shelf in 2008. The election year of 2016 called me back. I am honored to tell this story of these people dedicated to the vision of one nation, under God, indivisible, with liberty and justice for all.

Abbreviations

AMA	American Missionary Association
ASCS	Agricultural Stabilization and Conservation Service
CCCV	Chatham County Crusade for Voters
CDGM	Child Development Group of Mississippi
CEP	Citizenship Education Program
CIO	Congress of Industrial Organizations
COFO	Council of Federated Organizations
CORE	Congress for Racial Equality
DCIFVO	Dallas County Independent Free Voters Organization
DCVL	Dallas County Voters League
LCFO	Lowndes County Freedom Organization
MFDP	Mississippi Freedom Democratic Party
MFLU	Mississippi Freedom Labor Union
MSSC	Mississippi State Sovereignty Commission
NAACP	National Association for the Advancement of Colored People
OEO	Office of Economic Opportunity
PDP	Progressive Democratic Party
SCLC	Southern Christian Leadership Conference
SCOPE	Summer Community Organization and Political Education
SERF	Selma Emergency Relief Fund
SGCV	Southeastern Georgia Crusade for Voters
SNCC	Student Non-Violent Coordinating Committee
SRC	Southern Regional Council
UCBHM	United Church Board of Homeland Missions
VEP	Voter Education Project
VISTA	Volunteers in Service to America

Introduction

The air was already heavy and warm. Morning breezes kept the room at a comfortable temperature, but handheld church fans at each seat hinted at the warmer afternoon ahead. As workshop participants finished a traditional southern breakfast, a few conversed with friends from home while others made small talk with new acquaintances. Still others gazed out the windows at the Dorchester Academy's wide lawn. For some, the live oaks and Georgia pines seemed a world away from rural hometowns scattered across the South. They looked forward to the beach field trip where they planned to collect seashells and gather sand in Coca-Cola bottles for friends and family back home.[1]

Promptly at nine o'clock, Dorothy Cotton walked to the chalkboard at the front of the room and asked them to take their seats. She opened the session with a prayer and group singing. As the last notes faded, she asked, "What is a citizen?" They carefully considered the question. The first to respond said, "Someone who doesn't break the law." Others picked up on this idea, adding, "Following the Ten Commandments" and "If you treat your neighbor right." Cotton patiently encouraged responses and waited for the moment. It happened in every workshop. One of the students mentioned the Constitution. Cotton beamed and asked, "What is this Constitution?" and sparked "intense dialogue." One hundred years after passage of the Fourteenth Amendment, the gathered adults were reminded, or learned for the first time, that "all persons born or naturalized in the United States . . . are citizens of the United States and the state wherein they reside. No state can breach or privilege this." Cotton emphasized the last phrase: *"No state can breach or privilege this."* For southern African Americans, this information radically altered their relationship to the state.

On this morning, "they learned and accepted that there [was] something called the 'supreme law of the land,' and an amendment that says no state can breach this." As the discussion continued, participants "started to get a new awareness of their own power."[2]

Between 1961 and 1970, similar discussions marked the opening of the Southern Christian Leadership Conference's (SCLC) teacher training workshops for the Citizenship Education Program (CEP). From its origins on the South Carolina coast in 1957, the CEP spread to every southern state by 1969. Gathering in churches, living rooms, beauty shops, and community centers, citizenship school teachers, mostly black women, taught friends and neighbors to read and write. This was subversive work in the Jim Crow South because reading, writing, and calculating was empowering. Literate black men and women gathered their own information, figured fair compensation for a hard day's work, and registered formal complaints, and they walked up courthouse steps, faced white courthouse clerks, and took literacy tests for voter registration. In the segregated South, teaching literacy for political action could crack the foundation of white supremacy. Citizenship school teachers were well aware of this potential and nurtured the individual transformations that sowed seeds for collective action. CEP students practiced ABCs in lessons designed to spark discussion about the very meaning of citizenship. Blending traditions of participatory democracy and a deeply rooted gendered political culture, CEP students and teachers enacted a citizenship that was more than an abstract status conferred by the state. "First-class" citizens acted in service to self, family, community, and nation. CEP classes became gathering spaces where local people discussed, organized, and demanded change. From these makeshift classrooms, they contributed to the groundswell for social justice.

This book tells the citizenship school teachers' story. These women are not new to the civil rights narrative. In photographs of mass meetings, they are there, singing, praying, and giving hard-earned money to support the cause. When organizers recall direct action campaigns, these women are there, marching, cooking, brewing pot after pot of strong coffee, and opening their homes to field staff and volunteers. In news reports about violence that kept pace with non-violent action, these women are there as well, mourning the dead, comforting the injured, and nursing their own wounds. There was a tie that binds, and for many southern African American women, that tie was the Citizenship Education Program. Like the contrast dial on an old television, this book brings their work into sharp focus.[3]

This is not the first study to reveal CEP teachers at work. The program originated through a partnership between local leaders on the South Carolina coast and the Highlander Folk School. In 1961, the SCLC assumed administrative responsibility for the newly renamed Citizenship Education Program. As a result, the program has been incorporated into studies of these supporting institutions.[4] Memoirs by civil rights organizers document CEP teachers' leadership and participation in local campaigns.[5] Recent trends in civil rights historiography shed further light on the citizenship schools. Beginning in the 1990s, historians shifted the spotlight from charismatic male leaders to broaden perspective on the civil rights movement, directly challenging gendered characterizations of women as supporters and followers.[6] Within this scholarship, Katherine Mellen Charron's biography of CEP founder Septima Clark provides the most comprehensive assessment of citizenship school teachers' reach and impact.[7] At the same time, local histories reframed a top-down narrative that privileged civil rights organizations and the federal government. These historians advanced not one mass movement but a framework of "civil rights movements" where collective momentum from "a web of local struggles" generated the groundswell for political, social, and economic reform. These studies often captured CEP teachers' leadership and activism before the movement arrived and after a local campaign ended.[8] The CEP's emphasis on literacy as a strategy for social change has drawn attention from education scholars. In this field, David Levine's work represents the most comprehensive study of the program's blend of literacy education and political empowerment.[9]

Across the South, local women integrated CEP teaching into ongoing community service, which helps explain why this region-wide mass mobilization remained largely hidden from view. Everyone and no one knew about CEP classes, which creates a problem when trying to piece the puzzle together because, as historian Tiyi Morris wrote about Mississippi's Womanpower Unlimited, "this is simply what black women did; without fanfare or expecting praise." Much of this community work went undocumented; however, in the CEP, teachers submitted attendance reports to receive monthly stipends. These reports along with teachers' correspondence and surveys were transferred to the King Center and Emory University. Thus the CEP offers a rare opportunity to "render the invisible visible."[10] Still, there are gaps. CEP reports document extensive activity in South Carolina, but local teachers' attendance records and correspondence are missing in archival collections. Attendance records, surveys, and program reports from late 1965 to early 1969 are scant compared to previous years. Existing records tell incomplete stories because teachers who wrote lengthy narratives were the exception. The majority recorded brief comments in limited space provided on CEP forms. Oral history interviewing filled in some gaps, and a few former teachers graciously shared their stories. I found details about others in secondary sources, oral history collections, and local newspapers. U.S. Census and vital records and newspaper articles shed further light. I located more details in organizational records as varied as the Student Non-Violent Coordinating Committee (SNCC) and the Mississippi State Sovereignty Commission.

The Citizenship Education Program and Black Women's Political Culture assembles these fragments to reveal an expansive story of black women's grassroots activism, adding to scholarship that reframes a standard narrative of the civil rights movement.[11] The CEP fits into a familiar Montgomery-to-Memphis timeframe, but alters the perspective to highlight lesser-known people and places. In the same year as the U.S. Supreme Court's landmark decision in *Brown v. Board of Education*, the citizenship school idea was born in discussions between Johns Island community activist Esau Jenkins, Charleston schoolteacher Septima Clark, and Highlander Folk School director Myles Horton. A month after a citywide bus boycott ended in Montgomery, Charleston beautician Bernice Robinson opened the first citizenship school on Johns Island. As television cameras followed Freedom Riders into Alabama and Mississippi in the spring of 1961, the CEP relocated to the SCLC's Atlanta office. In 1962, with attention focused on Albany, Georgia, the program took root across the state in Savannah, eventually spreading to rural counties across the First Congressional District. Later that year, local women organized CEP classes in the Mississippi Delta just as SNCC organizers moved into the region. By the following year, CEP classes opened in Mississippi's southeastern corner. As college students attracted national attention during Freedom Summer, CEP teachers and students staffed multiservice community centers and registered voters for the Mississippi Freedom Democratic Party (MFDP). By the end of that summer, CEP veterans were among the MFDP delegates on the national stage at the Democratic National Convention. The following spring, Martin Luther King Jr. led marchers out of Selma. Cameras trained on King did not notice CEP teachers organizing in his wake. Into the late 1960s, local people adapted and applied CEP lessons in new battles for political empowerment and economic and social justice. Focusing on the CEP contributes to a broader understanding of where, when, why, and how the movement happened.

Centering on the CEP also expands our understanding of who organized and who led. As Septima Clark explained, "The teachers we need in a Citizenship School should be people who are respected by the members in the community, who can read well aloud, and who can write their names in cursive writing." These criteria cast a wide net and pointed to black women as primary agents. When southern state legislatures passed segregation laws in the late nineteenth century, teaching remained one of the few professions open to black women. Within separate school systems designed to reinforce racial inferiority and second-class citizenship, black teachers told and retold stories of resistance and achievement.[12] The CEP drew on this role and these traditions. CEP teachers differed in age, experience, education, social class background, and occupation; however, teaching was familiar work, rooted in a gendered political culture nurtured over generations. Across the South, schoolteachers came out of retirement to organize CEP classes while the program attracted teachers forced out of public schools in post-*Brown* purges. Beauticians mobilized community networks and opened classes in independently owned businesses. Association with the SCLC brought the program into black churches and tapped into churchwomen's networks. Recent high school graduates inspired by young people sitting at lunch counters organized CEP classes. Still others had simply grown "sick and tired of being sick and tired."[13] The CEP welcomed this diverse group, mobilizing leaders and community networks in support of the broader movement. The flexible criteria for teachers coupled with a structured workbook, supporting materials, and schedule provided a blueprint that was transferred from one community to the next.

The CEP always operated on two levels: institutional and local. *The Citizenship Education Program and Black Women's Political Culture* intertwines these narratives. Program administrators, first at Highlander and later at the SCLC, set policies, designed and led training workshops, recruited local teachers, crafted materials, and managed finances. CEP expansion within a rapidly changing landscape required ongoing revision and refinement, a process also taking place at the local level as CEP teachers and their students adapted and interpreted program lessons. Using a case study approach, *The Citizenship Education Program and Black Women's Political Culture* examines groundwork in areas with concentrated CEP activity as well as the dynamic interactions between local people and organizations. Time and place mattered because communities and states crafted the narratives of slavery, Reconstruction, "redemption," and Jim Crow segregation in different ways. CEP classes fit into local histories that teachers had helped, and were helping, to shape. In addition, the movement arrived at different times and in different ways so that in some places, CEP classes provided the impetus for local action, while in others, CEP teachers sustained and intensified momentum from local campaigns. Their work centered on common goals: improving literacy, increasing black voter registration, and mobilizing friends and neighbors. How they went about this work depended on local context.

The program name serves as analytical threads woven throughout the book. The first thread is Citizenship. In CEP classes, teachers and students claimed and enacted first-class citizenship, broadly defined. Local classes prepared southern black people to confront political systems hardened through decades of rigid enforcement. Since the late nineteenth century, the federal government consistently deferred suffrage questions to states, lending tacit support for complex voter registration laws. In southern states, poll taxes, literacy tests, grandfather clauses, and frequent registration renewal functioned as designed. Punctuated with extralegal violence and harassment, laws effectively purged black voters and blocked registration into the twentieth century. African Americans won an important victory in 1944 with the U.S. Supreme Court's decision in *Smith v. Allwright* to end all-white state primaries. In the late 1950s, the CEP tapped into a groundswell pushing to remove remaining obstacles to black voter registration. In classes, teachers reinforced a Reconstruction-era understanding of "suffrage as a collective, not an individual possession." First-class citizenship, like freedom in the post–Civil War South, "would accrue to each . . . individually only when it was acquired by all of them collectively."[14]

Registration and casting a ballot were important markers of first-class citizenship, but CEP lessons extended beyond voter registration. By the end of a three-month course, students gained "an all-around education in community development." According to program lessons, first-class citizens practiced non-violence, paid taxes, and were safe drivers. They had "first rate handwriting," were polite, and demonstrated "good manners."[15] CEP teachers were expected to teach and model these behaviors. The CEP spread across the South, in part because the program echoed racial uplift ideas of the early twentieth century. Couched in an ideology of bourgeois respectability, the CEP posited that African Americans became "first class citizens" through education, behavior, and presentation. Each individual reflected on the entire community, and it took all to counter racist stereotypes that underpinned segregation. The CEP mobilized several thousand people who agreed with the underlying argument.[16] Direct action campaigns are a significant part of civil rights history and rightfully so. The CEP was a different strategy that mobilized a different group of people. Although some teachers and students participated in sit-ins, picket lines, and marches, situating CEP classes in the center of the narrative shifts our view into private spaces where seemingly more moderate leaders tapped into older ideology to mobilize communities.

Read another way, this seemingly moderate approach proposed a radical redefinition of citizenship. Citizenship was not simply a performance for white approval. Citizenship was active and collective, and CEP lessons empowered African Americans to claim all that had been long denied and to remove markers of inferiority imposed through racial segregation.[17] Collective action fundamentally shifted the power that maintained white supremacy. When local people mastered "first rate handwriting," they replaced an X, their "mark" that signified both illiteracy and a loss of identity, with a name that denoted personhood. They mastered basic arithmetic to break the bonds of dependence and figure for themselves. With information about federal entitlements, they laid claim to health services, education, and financial security for their families. From CEP classes, teachers and students pressured local governments to extend sewer lines, install street lights, pave roads, and build playgrounds. These additions improved health and safety, but most of all, these projects removed the visible differences between white and black neighborhoods.[18] These tensions between a class-based bourgeois ideology and the radical potential of an empowered black electorate run through the CEP narrative.

The next narrative thread is Education. In the CEP, education was used for social change, which likewise had a long history in southern states. Into the late nineteenth century, black teachers, mostly women, fully understood the radical potential of an educated African American electorate in the segregated South, and across the region, they reached beyond classrooms to engage entire communities in their efforts to "lift the race."[19] Professionally trained educators were not the only teachers. Mothers, grandmothers, aunts, and neighbors passed on lessons that guided black children through Jim Crow's unforgiving rules. They taught the Bible on Sunday mornings and carried the message through the week. Theirs was a political culture built on family and community, constant struggle, and the unshakable belief in human dignity and a just and better day.[20] Citizenship schools were built on these foundations. Teaching was "women's work," and through the

CEP, local women stepped into a recognizable role and adopted a gendered identity clothed in respectability, providing some cover for the political nature of their work and challenging charges of rabble-rousing by civil rights workers.[21]

Foregrounding the CEP reframes our view of education history. Before emancipation, southern lawmakers constructed legal codes that punished those who taught enslaved people. After the Civil War, access to formal education was a tangible symbol of freedom, and across the South, freedpeople sought assistance from the federal Freedman's Bureau and northern philanthropic institutions to build schools. When assistance was not forthcoming, they pooled resources and built their own. The schoolhouse was contested space in the late nineteenth century as southern lawmakers established separate and decidedly unequal school systems, systems that endured well into the twentieth century.[22] The CEP reveals their legacy. The *Brown* decision promised access for school-age black children but did not extend to adults too old for school. CEP teachers moved into this breach. Teachers shared stories of elderly students who held pencils for the first time and practiced writing until they could sign their names without snapping the lead and tearing the paper. Before attempting literacy tests for voter registration, CEP students read newspapers and letters from family members for the first time.

Infused with principles of participatory democracy, the CEP transformed the very nature of education. Meeting twice a week for three months, local teachers "started where the people are," constructing lessons from their students' daily experiences, an approach that stood in stark contrast to experiences outside of the classroom. In these protected spaces, teachers and students cast off identities assigned to them through Jim Crow segregation and intentionally crafted a new identity. They were not "apathetic" or "lazy" or "unable to learn" as racist education and political systems claimed. Instead, teachers and students defined their priorities; analyzed complex relationships between economics, politics, and social inequality; and proposed solutions to locally defined problems. Leaders emerged and communities were organized. They were first-class citizens with "a new awareness of their own power." Social movements require collective action born out of individual transformation and CEP teachers created spaces for this to happen.[23]

The final narrative thread is Program. Operating a region-wide program required structure, resources, and administration. Citizenship schools evolved at the Highlander Folk School and this period has received the most scholarly attention. In late 1960, Highlander director Myles Horton balked at administering the rapidly expanding program and sought a new institutional home for the schools. Beginning in the summer of 1961, CEP teachers organized under the auspices of the SCLC. The SCLC looms large in civil rights historiography with president Dr. Martin Luther King Jr. serving as the primary focal point. King's emergence from the Montgomery bus boycott to his assassination in Memphis established the time frame for early organizational studies and for the entire movement. Situating King in the center of the organization emphasizes interpersonal relationships and politics within King's inner circle and the SCLC's involvement in direct action campaigns. The CEP represented a different approach, and the SCLC's male ministers tended to view the program as a kind of woman's auxiliary. Gendered biases obscured the program's reach and impact, an interpretation sustained by historians who dismissed the program as a limited experiment in voter registration or used CEP staff members Septima Clark and Dorothy Cotton as foils to illustrate sexism within the organization.[24]

Centering the CEP acknowledges the gendered politics within the SCLC but draws different conclusions about the program's significance. Andrew Young served as the CEP's first director at the SCLC, and as he was drawn into King's inner circle, black women maintained the expansive network of local classes. A funding stream from the Field Foundation, along with the SCLC leaders' ambivalence, shielded the program from competitive internal politics and granted the CEP staff members relative autonomy. Septima Clark, Dorothy Cotton, Bernice Robinson, and Annell Ponder secured financial support, recruited teachers, designed lessons and training workshops, and expanded the SCLC's reach across the South. The program depended on personal relationships, meaning these women spent much of the decade on the road. Securing staff salaries and teachers' stipends required detailed reports culled from an avalanche of attendance records, correspondence, and surveys from local teachers.

Through their efforts, Clark, Cotton, Ponder, and Robinson sustained a program that added critical skills and tools for a generation of community leaders. For local teachers, foundation-funded stipends were economic lifelines independent of white employers and anointed community work with a wage, elevating it above uncompensated volunteer activity. With this financial support, hundreds of African American women developed and honed teaching, organizing, and political action skills. In South Carolina, Georgia, Mississippi, and Alabama, high-performing teachers served as area supervisors, mentoring new recruits and managing local networks.

Beginning in the mid-1960s, local women leveraged community leadership experience, including the CEP, to earn positions in federal anti-poverty programs and to run for elective office. In doing so, they infused CEP principles, practices, and values into local agencies and politics.

The program ebbed and flowed in different places at different times, and so this book traces the CEP's trajectory through a series of case studies focused on the places with the highest concentration of CEP activity.[25] The first two chapters retrace program development in the South Carolina Lowcountry. In these formative years, synergy between local leaders and the Highlander Folk School set the foundation for a program that would extend across southern states. Chapters 3 and 4 follow the program's growth and decline in southeastern Georgia where Savannah's direct action campaign fueled interest in voter registration, which in turn provided an opening wedge to expand the urban movement into surrounding counties. The next three chapters move into more familiar territory in civil rights historiography. Foregrounding the CEP reframes the much-studied Mississippi movement, highlighting local teachers' groundwork before Freedom Summer and extending the narrative beyond the MFDP challenge of 1964. Chapter 7 reframes the voting rights campaign in Selma, shifting attention from the Edmund Pettus Bridge to the CEP teachers and local leaders who adapted to federal civil rights legislation. Chapter 8 draws on a limited source base to examine CEP activity after 1966, when financial resources ran dry and uneasy coalitions fractured just as local teachers confronted a resurgent conservative movement waging political war on federal reform. The last chapter describes how this looked and felt on the ground as CEP teachers struggled to sustain the movement they had helped to build.[26]

This outline implies more order than you will encounter in the narrative. Social movements rarely follow linear paths along uncomplicated timelines. The CEP did not stop in one place before starting in another. For this reason, narrative threads overlap throughout the text. Each two-chapter case study begins with "Groundwork" to describe local context and explain how the CEP integrated into this context. The subsequent chapter examines the trajectory of the CEP in that place. You will also encounter a lot of names in the text. Several thousand people came through the CEP. Some teachers organized classes for several years, and others organized only one class. Some submitted lengthy detailed reports, while others wrote only a sentence or two. At the risk of overwhelming readers, I identify teachers by name to "render the invisible visible." Finally, local teachers rarely removed "CEP hats" when they engaged in other community organizing or political action activities, complicating efforts to define neat and clean starting and ending points. Throughout the text, I use the term "CEP teacher" or "CEP supervisor" to denote people who were active in the program as determined by a monthly salary or attendance rosters and correspondence. "CEP veteran" denotes a local person with experience in the CEP.

These are not uncomplicated stories of progress, but in the retelling, we can more fully understand why "the movement" remains unfinished. This is the story of the civil rights movement as a woman's movement, not because CEP teachers prioritized what might be defined as feminist goals but because the program tapped into a deeply rooted gendered political culture. This is a story of the time, energy, resources, and talent needed to generate and sustain this kind of wave, and it is a story of internal and external forces that can limit potential and pull it apart. CEP teachers and their students confronted legal, political, and social systems and demanded to be treated with dignity and respect. Across the South, they experienced economic and physical reprisals for their work. They celebrated federal legislation to end segregation and struggled to sustain optimism as promises eroded. Through their work, they advanced a vision of a more perfect union where active citizens exercise power to influence and shape decisions and policies that directly affected their lives. In the microcosm of makeshift classrooms, CEP teachers created democratic spaces that changed the way people saw themselves and their neighbors, where they got "a new awareness of their own power."

1

"We're Going to Learn Together"
Groundwork on Johns Island, South Carolina, 1948–1957

On January 7, 1957, Charleston beautician Bernice V. Robinson closed her shop early. She prepared a light supper for her mother, gathered up books and papers, and waited for her brother's car. Together, they crossed the bridge to Johns Island, arriving at the Progressive Club for the seven o'clock meeting. Robinson collected her materials and walked into the back room. She looked around, made sure that tables and chairs were in place, and waited. Soon, ten women and four men gathered in the small space. Robinson greeted them and invited each to take a seat, all while fighting her own nerves. The last chair scooted into place and Robinson set down some ground rules. "I'm not going to be the teacher," she said. "We're going to learn together. You're going to teach me some things, and maybe there are a few things I might be able to teach you, but I don't consider myself a teacher."[1] With that, Robinson opened the first citizenship school.

The class marked the culmination of a three-year experiment. Between 1954 and 1957, television news cameras filmed angry crowds outside southern schools and African Americans who walked rather than rode buses in Montgomery, Alabama. On the South Carolina Sea Islands, another revolution was under way as Esau Jenkins taught his bus passengers to memorize sections of the state constitution. Armed with this knowledge, some passed the literacy test and registered to vote. In the summer of 1954, Charleston schoolteacher Septima Clark invited Jenkins to a workshop at the Highlander Folk School, where director Myles Horton was looking for a place to test a community leadership program. Jenkins impressed Horton, and the feeling was mutual. By the next summer, Jenkins requested assistance to move his bus lessons into a school where black residents could learn to read and write.²

It fell to Septima Clark and Bernice Robinson to make the plan work. In 1974, Horton remembered having some ideas but "the burden fell on Septima." Clark has received the lion's share of attention. She told her story in a 1962 autobiography and in a first-person narrative published in 1979. In the late 1970s, Charleston city officials honored Clark's contributions, opening the Septima P. Clark Day Care Center and renaming a portion of the crosstown expressway.³ Scholars searching for "invisible southern black women leaders in the civil rights movement" found Clark in the 1980s, and in 2009, Katherine Mellen Charron's biography became the definitive work on Clark's life and work.⁴ Bernice Robinson has received less attention in comparison. In his 1998 autobiography, Horton credited Robinson, "more than Septima or I or anybody else," with "develop[ing] the methods used by Citizenship Schools."⁵ Robinson rarely addressed her "exclusion," explaining that she did not want to "sound off" about "facts [that] were not properly recorded." "Then too," she added, "very rarely does anyone interview me." In the late 1970s, Robinson began to "crow a little," and as she remembered it, "Esau dreamed about the idea . . . [and got] the wheels in motion, but it was left to me to make it a reality."⁶

In interviews and first-person narratives, Clark and Robinson connected dots to draw straight lines to the citizenship school program. This chapter reexamines that groundwork. Clark and Robinson crafted the program born out of class, gender, and racial segregation. A trained schoolteacher, Clark brought classroom experience and ties to an extensive network of civic clubs and organizations. Robinson was part of this network, where she honed organizing skills by watching and doing. Clark's position in the public school system left her vulnerable to economic reprisal, but Robinson's independently owned beauty shop shielded her as she engaged in political organizing. Both Robinson and Clark were steeped in a gendered political culture that called black women into a life of service, and they infused these ideals into all aspects of the citizenship school program.

Esau Jenkins and Myles Horton also played critical roles. Growing up on Johns Island shaped Jenkins's views on political power and injustice, the potential of collective action, and the devastating legacy of generational poverty and illiteracy. Just as Clark and Robinson embodied gendered expectations of a life of service, Jenkins embodied a black manhood forged in the 1940s when an intense focus on the ideals of freedom and democracy

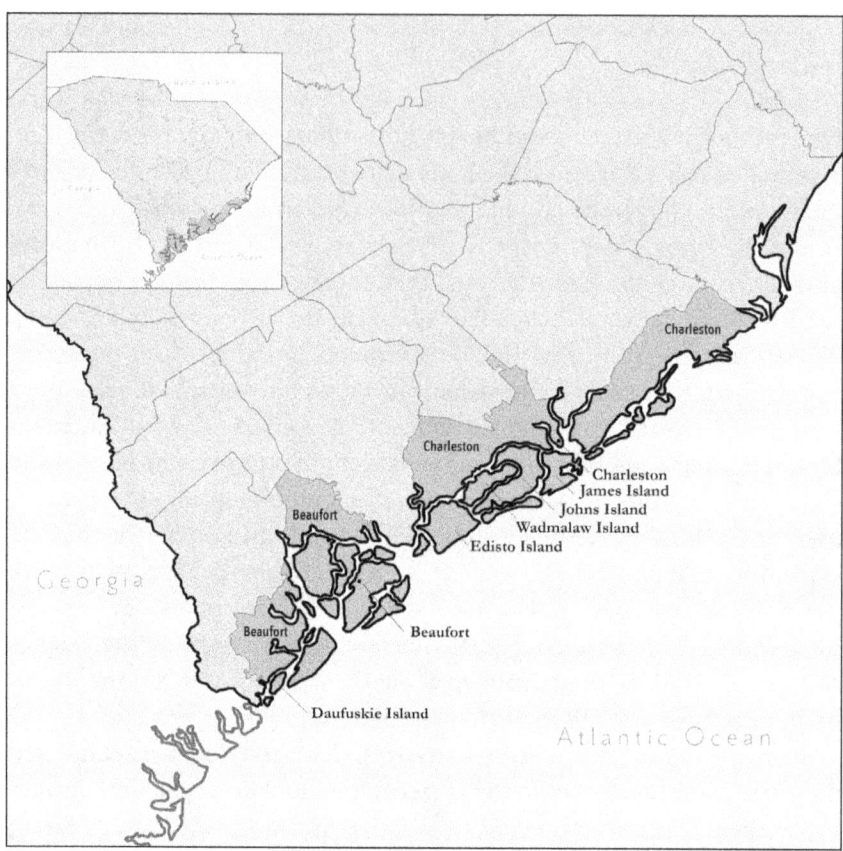

Map 1. The South Carolina Lowcountry. © Bruno Berry.

created openings for direct challenges to segregation.[7] Myles Horton was that rare breed of white southern progressive, using integrated workshops in Highlander's retreat-like setting to create a world as it "ought to be." Horton was the link to private foundations that paid travel expenses, salaries, and stipends to support experimentation, relationship building, and eventual collaboration and synergy. The citizenship school program emerged from these entangled roots.[8]

Early Influences

Septima Poinsette Clark and Bernice Violanthe Robinson grew up in Charleston, and although they were cousins, their paths did not cross, perhaps because Clark's mother had initially fancied Robinson's father, only to watch her sister walk down the aisle with him.[9] Early experiences shaped their approaches to work and community service. Born in 1898, Clark was the older of the two by sixteen years. She grew up in one of the city's working-class neighborhoods where white ethnic workers lived next door to black families. Appearance mattered and, as historian Katherine Charron described, Clark's mother, Victoria Poinsette, "struggled mightily . . . [with] her desire for a middle-class lifestyle on a working-class budget." Septima Clark learned early lessons in respectability from her mother, who insisted that her daughters not play with the children of unmarried interracial couples, not holler down the street, and always have "something to do" when the Poinsette boys had friends over to the house. Education was the path to economic stability and middle-class respectability, Clark's parents believed, and so Clark spent her first three school years with "people [who] constituted a sort of upper class." She transferred to public school and graduated from Burke Industrial School. Teaching conferred a coveted status and respectability and in the early twentieth century remained one of the few professions open to black women. While the state of South Carolina deemed her eighth-grade education good enough to teach black children in a country school, Clark's teachers and her mother insisted on more. Clark enrolled at Avery Institute, earning a licentiate of instruction, the equivalent of two years of college education.[10]

Clark began her teaching career as the South Carolina state legislature wove a complex web of segregation laws, often enforced through extralegal violence. Within this evolving system, poorly resourced segregated schools on abbreviated academic calendars were intended to blunt and discourage intellectual development, curiosity, and aspiration. In Charleston, public school officials reserved the city's classrooms for white teachers and dispatched black teachers to surrounding rural areas. These young women were some of the first black professionals to bridge the gap between the city and the neighboring barrier islands.[11] In the fall of 1916, eighteen-year-old Clark accepted her first teaching position at Promise Land School on the southern end of Johns Island. She later admitted "[knowing] little about these islands or the people" except for "weird tales" she had heard before accepting the position.[12] Clark confronted the realities of rural teaching standing inside a two-room "log cabin style [school]" with "a fireplace at one end" and "uncomfortable, back-breaking benches." On school days, up to 132 children crowded in from up to eight miles away. The island operated on agricultural rhythms so that Clark and her teaching partner did not see all of their students until late November, and many were out again by late

February.¹³ The teaching partner quit after six months but Clark forged ahead, believing that she had signed on for a "life of service." Necessity was the mother of invention: Clark used dry cleaners' bags to record her students' "stories of their country right around them, where they walked to come to school, the things that grew around them, what they could see in the skies." She tacked up the bags and turned the stories into reading and spelling lessons.¹⁴ Through improvisation, her students taught her about the island, and she taught them that their experiences had value.

Clark compared the island and its people to her home in Charleston and found the former lacking. "Living conditions . . . were very crude," she recalled, and from her perspective, many black islanders "led listless, indifferent lives" and "cared little . . . about improving themselves." Fraternal and civic organizations might "improve the lot," but island folk remained wedded to "superstition" and "the most primitive culture," she concluded, reflecting her contemporaries' views that rural black folk, the "less fortunate," must be improved.¹⁵ Racial uplift was a blend of economics, education, character, and respectability. Teachers acted as missionaries while organizations, clubs, and associations served as the infrastructure for this uplift work. Clark developed a "warm affection" for Johns Islanders through a "varied and entertaining" social life but never fully discarded early assessments of the "primitive culture" that needed to be "lift[ed] to a better life."¹⁶

In 1919, Clark accepted a position at Avery and returned to Charleston to a different kind of training ground. Clark threw support behind the NAACP chapter's campaign to place black teachers in the city's public schools. As white school officials insisted that "cooks and the laundresses didn't want their children taught by Negro teachers," Clark and her students joined an "army of volunteers" at mass meetings and canvassed for signatures from the very cooks and laundresses upheld as supporters of the current policy. When the state legislature moved to overturn the board's policy, local officials relented and hired black teachers in time for school opening in the fall. The campaign was valuable experience for Clark. She learned how to listen, mobilize, and mentor.¹⁷ The next year, she accepted a better-paying position thirty-five miles up the coast. Marriage to a navy man took her out of South Carolina. She returned eight years later, widowed with a young son. Clark started over at Promise Land School, where the grass was mowed and stoves replaced open fireplaces, but she saw "little if any progress . . . in raising the educational and cultural standards" in the overcrowded school. Once again, Clark threw herself into her work, teaching children during the day and tutoring adults at night.[18] A job offer in the state capital took her out of the Lowcountry for the next eighteen years.

Bernice Robinson was following a different path. She grew up in one of Charleston's all-black working-class neighborhoods, the youngest of James and Martha Robinson's nine children. Jimmy Robinson laid brick and tile, and Mattie took in sewing. Where Victoria Poinsette saw a teaching credential as a ticket into middle-class respectability, the Robinsons made sure their children mastered a skilled trade that afforded a measure of economic independence in a society where legal segregation stunted access to professional occupations. Robinson also learned about community service from her parents' examples. Before dawn each morning, black women left Sumter Street and its adjoining courts to cook and clean in white families' homes, and every morning their children ate breakfast in Mattie Robinson's kitchen.[19]

In contrast to Clark's teaching aspirations, Robinson later recalled feeling that she did not have "any control over the destiny of [her] life in certain aspects." She graduated from Burke High School after ninth grade, the highest grade then available for black students, and followed an older sister to New York. When the sister fell ill, Robinson returned to Charleston, married, and was left alone with a daughter when her husband abandoned them during the Depression years. Out of necessity and a desire for better opportunities, Robinson returned to New York and landed a job in the garment district where the money was good but "not *steady*." To support herself and her daughter, Robinson took beauty school classes at night and opened a shop with a friend. She got her first taste of political action when she registered to vote and "mail[ed] out cards and letters to [a local assemblyman's] constituents."[20]

Gendered expectations brought Robinson and Clark back to Charleston in the summer of 1947. Their parents were not well and needed their daughters at home. The cousins reentered a city transformed by a steady stream of federal dollars. Beginning in the wartime years, workers flooded into Charleston's naval yard and harbor at a pace that continued unabated into the postwar years.[21] Economic opportunity did not cross the color line, however. Clark secured a teaching position and Robinson "went from job to job trying to get [her] salary back up." She passed the federal civil service exam and languished on the naval yard's waiting lists. She eventually found work in an upholstery shop. After living in New York, Robinson bristled at sitting in the "little buzzards' roost" at movie theaters and avoided restaurants where she anticipated rude treatment. She rode the city bus but "it used to gall me every time . . . I had to sit in the back," she remembered. Clark shared this experience on a different bus, forced to give up her seat for white men heading to the naval yard. In 1954, Robinson and her brothers cleaned out the garage and installed sinks and dryers, getting Robinson off the bus and back in the beauty business.[22]

Clark and Robinson connected in the postwar surge of political activity. In the early 1940s, NAACP membership had soared, and organizers established a new state conference in 1942. Two years later, a statewide Progressive Democratic Party (PDP) swelled to 45,000 members with chapters across the state. In 1944, the PDP focused on black political participation, challenging South Carolina's all-white delegation at the 1944 Democratic National Convention and backing PDP founder Osceola McKaine's bid for U.S. Senate. From across the state, prospective black voters filed complaints about county clerks who manipulated literacy and good character tests to reject registration applications.[23] In 1946, NAACP attorneys took up PDP secretary George Elmore's case. Two years after the U.S. Supreme Court's decision in *Smith v. Allwright*, Charleston-based federal judge J. Waties Waring's ruling in *Elmore v. Rice* ended the state's all-white primary with the judge declaring, "It is time for South Carolina to rejoin the Union."[24] NAACP and PDP registration drives resulted in 4,360 newly registered black voters in Charleston County, and more than 30,000 black citizens cast ballots in the Democratic primary.[25]

Postwar momentum carried into the 1950s, and Clark and Robinson met regularly at NAACP meetings. From her position on the executive board, Clark grew disillusioned with the chapter's approach to political organizing. Despite optimistic predictions, black voters failed to sway the mayoral election in 1951 and were disappointed again when three black candidates lost in state elections the following year. The literacy test administered at a registration office open only three days a month during daytime work hours posed an insurmountable obstacle. Black voters needed to understand the political process, Clark believed, and a "greatly divided" NAACP board was ill equipped for the task. Robinson disagreed. Serving as chapter secretary and membership coordinator, she believed "we really started making something out of the Charleston branch" under Arthur "Joe" Brown's leadership. Membership tripled to over one thousand as the branch focused on voter registration. City officials responded by appointing black police officers, initiating a slum clearance program, and running sewer lines into black neighborhoods. Officials balanced these concessions with measures to shore up the status quo, including cutting city council seats from twenty-four to twelve and requiring citywide elections for all council members.[26]

Clark and Robinson worked through formal and informal networks to address community issues. At her shop, Robinson balanced hair appointments with political activity, calling, "If you get too hot under [the dryer], just cut her off and come out" as she hurried out the door. The NAACP was her ticket to state, regional, and national conferences where she learned "to organize . . . to get people to register."[27] Clark sought other outlets through women's clubs and organizations. She served on the Metropolitan Council of Negro Women and was chairperson of the segregated Young Women's Christian Association (YWCA). In 1955, her civic work led back to Johns Island when Clark convinced her Alpha Kappa Alpha (AKA) sorority sisters to organize an immunization drive to stem the spread of diphtheria. Clark had earned local islanders' trust, so they boarded buses bound for the Health Department in Charleston where ninety-seven children "took the shot," she reported.[28] For both Robinson and Clark, formal organizations served as critical components for social change. Associations, benevolent societies, and civic and professional clubs brought people together, created consensus, and mobilized resources to address specific issues. Organizers committed to service emerged from these networks.

The View from Johns Island

Johns Islander Esau Jenkins shared this faith in formal organizations and served with Clark on the NAACP executive board. In the early twentieth century, members of a "Talented Tenth" had theorized that respectable black men would "lift the race," with respectability demonstrated through education, behavior, and occupation.[29] Born and raised in the rural South, Jenkins was a different kind of race man, claiming respectability through individual acts of resistance born out of the injustice of racial segregation and poverty. According to Jenkins, he dropped out at fourth grade because "the school we had here wasn't encouraging to go to." He married at seventeen and grew cotton on the family's four-and-a-half-acre plot where he set himself apart from poor black farmers like his father. One season, Jenkins calculated the anticipated payment from their harvest, and his father warned, "The white folks never like that." "Well, I'm not figuring for the white folks . . . I'm figuring for my own benefit," Jenkins replied. He showed his calculations to the white supervisor who, according to Jenkins, "realized that he made a mistake."[30] In the late 1930s, Jenkins urged Johns

Islanders to organize after a white man shot and killed a black man who accidentally ran over the white man's dog.[31] Jenkins's brand of race leadership came with risks, and by 1945, Jenkins severed economic ties with island landowners, opening a fruit stand in Charleston and starting a bus business to transport black workers and high school students into the city. Economic independence created space for political organizing and replaced the formal education that was fundamental in earlier constructions of black male leadership.[32]

In the late 1940s, Jenkins organized a local Progressive Club, "emphasiz[ing] . . . 'progressive,' which [means] look upward, do something better." Members had to do two things: register to vote and pay twenty-five cents in monthly dues. The dues paid bonds and other court fees. Voter registration, on the other hand, was part of a long-term plan to harness the power of Johns Island's black majority.[33] Jenkins built the new political organization on the island's social institutions and cultural traditions. The club met at a local praise house. African Americans had purchased land and lumber for Moving Star Hall in the 1910s, and forty years later, it remained "black space" where congregants made the rules. "The Rebel Time" was not a distant past as black residents remembered fathers, mothers, and grandparents born into slavery. Enslaved people on the Sea Islands had blended English, French, German, and African phonetics to obscure messages passed among black folk. A century later, their distinct Gullah dialect survived.[34] Gatherings at Moving Star Hall preserved these cultural traditions rooted in resistance. "The door are open for each and every one," John Smalls explained. "If you want to speak, anything you want to say, you got the opportunity." Within a segregated society determined to inscribe racial inferiority, "you can feel yourself in that hall," Janie Hunter explained. Congregants established the Moving Star Society, collecting ten-cent contributions to "tend the sick and bury the dead." Moving Star gatherings countered daily reminders of second-class citizenship, replacing it with a communal-based citizenship where each citizen was responsible to the whole.[35]

Progressive Club meetings melded tradition with contemporary concerns about economic security and political empowerment. Club members encouraged sharecroppers "to save . . . enough to buy small lots and build homes for themselves."[36] In 1950, while NAACP attorneys filed suit on behalf of parents in South Carolina's Clarendon County, Jenkins circulated a petition for a consolidated four-year high school and buses for black students.[37] The club's voter registration efforts bore fruit in 1954 when the local magistrate expected to lose white voters' support for being "too lenient" with black residents. After he asked for Jenkins's help, Jenkins brokered a deal. If he agreed to "treat them better, make them realize they're human beings when they come to court," Jenkins would campaign for the judge. On Election Day, 99 percent of black voters cast ballots for the embattled magistrate, while white votes split among other candidates. The victory was evidence of the power of collective action and solidified Jenkins's position as an influential power broker.[38]

Political organization took on new urgency in the postwar years. In 1950, Johns Island was home to 4,004 residents. Sixty percent of black farmers owned land, but things were changing. Faced with wartime labor shortages, white farmers had mechanized, a trend that continued in the postwar years, encouraged by federal farm agents teaching modern efficient techniques. Pressured to increase yield, African American farmers mechanized, but as the Reverend G. C. Brown observed, their small plots were "no comparison with white farms."[39] Black farmers grew a variety of vegetables that provided year-round income, but cotton still paid better even though it was seasonal. As a result, black farm families depended on wages earned on white-owned "plantations." In the laying-by time between fall harvest and spring planting, "they go into a hardship," Jenkins observed.[40] As Sea Island farmers struggled, timbermen bought and cleared Hilton Head Island, and Charleston-area developers turned their gaze to neighboring James Island. Interest in oceanfront property raised taxes and placed a premium on land once deemed undesirable. Across Charleston County, black farmers gave in and sold, reducing their overall number from 867 in 1954 to 268 just five years later.[41] With "nothing much ... to do here but cut cabbages or run a tractor," young people read the signs and left, Brown explained. Developers moved in and whittled remaining farms into smaller plots.[42]

More of the island's black workers commuted into Charleston on Jenkins's bus. Among the passengers, Alice Wine stood out. Like many Johns Islanders, Wine had limited formal schooling; she had walked seven miles to school for three years and quit. She married a neighboring farmer's son at eighteen and raised seven children while helping to chop and crate cabbages for the "Columbia truck." By the fall of 1948, Wine worked as a maid in Charleston, but at home, her husband's throat cancer was "far advanced." Lee Grant Wine died in November and at forty-two years old, Alice Wine was a widow.[43] Wine remembered her mother's stories about black people going "to see Judge Beckett and they vote," which may have influenced her next move. "I was on the bus," she recalled, "and Mr. Jenkins said ... 'I want to carry you down to register.'" She insisted, "I cannot read this hard thing," but Jenkins convinced her to try. "My tongue so heavy until I couldn't pronounce the words," she told him. He explained, "The hard word is the things for you to learn."[44] She memorized the required section of the state constitution, and when it was her turn at the registration office, she "read those things just like I been know 'em." When she came out, Jenkins called, "Miss Wine, you get it?" "Yes, sir," she replied. Wine's success bolstered her confidence in herself and in Jenkins, later describing him as "a wonderful conqueror."[45]

Jenkins extended voter registration lessons for everyone on the bus. Before arriving in Charleston, he pulled into a vacant lot. Passengers took out sheets of paper and fell silent. For thirty minutes, they listened as Jenkins reviewed the state constitution and voting procedures. Empowering black folk to register came at a price as one landowner blocked Jenkins's trucks and buses from entering his property, costing Jenkins "sixty dollars, . . . eighty dollars a day."[46] Reprisals also took a toll on Jenkins's family when school officials at Haut Gap High School reneged on a teaching position for one daughter and blacklisted the other.[47]

As Jenkins's daughters' experiences demonstrated, black schoolteachers were prime targets for white politicians and employers intent on blunting civil rights activities. In May 1954, the U.S. Supreme Court declared segregated schools to be unconstitutional. In response, the South Carolina legislature took aim at the "subversive" NAACP and required all public employees to submit lists of organizations where they held memberships. Within two years, fifty-five Citizens Councils organized across the state, and the combination of state laws and local intimidation reduced NAACP branches from eighty-four to thirty-one.[48] Shielded from the backlash, Robinson invited teachers and nurses to "have their [NAACP] membership cards come to [her] house." In the direct line of fire, Clark refused to renounce her membership, reasoning that if white schoolteachers could join "the KKK . . . and the White Citizens' Council," she could join the NAACP. The Charleston Board of Education disagreed and did not renew her teaching contract, erasing her "long build-up" for retirement. "Unwilling to supinely accept this summary discharge," Clark appealed to the NAACP. Correspondence to "the national office just caught dust," and the state office was distracted "integrating a golf course," she bitterly recalled.[49]

Making Connections at Highlander

By the time of her dismissal, Clark was making regular trips to the Highlander Folk School in Monteagle, Tennessee. During her first visit in 1954, she applied her teaching experience and helped to draft a pamphlet for local school districts considering desegregation plans.[50] The project reflected the folk school's new direction. Into the early 1950s, Highlander had been an integral part of the Congress of Industrial Organizations' (CIO) efforts to build a southern labor movement. When the anti-communist Red Scare put labor organizations under intense scrutiny, the CIO purged suspected and confirmed communists, pressuring Horton to ban communists from Highlander. Horton refused and the CIO withdrew financial support. With school desegregation cases winding through federal courts, Horton shifted gears. A lifelong southerner, he acknowledged that a federal court decision would not change beliefs and customs overnight. Instead, "each community would determine the extent to which integration is a reality."[51] Horton refashioned Highlander workshops into a rare opportunity for southern black and white leaders to discuss the ruling and develop solutions. A new direction required new funding streams, and Horton turned to private philanthropy. In 1953 and 1954, the Chicago-based Marshall Field Foundation awarded grants for the workshops to bring local people like Clark to Highlander. At the same time, Horton secured a three-year grant from the Emil Schwarzhaupt Foundation for experimental community leadership projects. Horton later reflected that the flexible Schwarzhaupt grant "was the most valuable grant Highlander received."[52] Private funding detached Highlander from labor organizations, but the new emphasis put the folk school in the crosshairs of southern politicians intent on stopping civil rights reform.

The new workshops integrated Horton's philosophy about education and social change. At Highlander's retreat-like setting, Horton and his staff removed "artificial barriers" constructed by local and state segregation laws so that participants "liv[ed], play[ed], and work[ed] together" in fully integrated workshops, enacting "the democratic society which the South could become."[53] They ditched traditional role-playing exercises that Horton dismissed as "games or . . . playing around" and encouraged participants to talk about their experiences. They did not need experts because they *were* the experts, and solutions emerged from these discussions. Horton summed up, "Our job is . . . to help people take over their own lives." Highlander workshops radically challenged assumptions about citizenship and education, embracing Progressive Era beliefs that political and economic power emanated from the group and collective action lifted all boats. Horton's approach also upended public education practices where students were passive recipients, drilling in rote memorization exercises. At Highlander, Horton and his staff taught through questions, encouraging participants to formulate answers and determine next steps.[54]

Clark's visit drew Horton's attention to the South Carolina Lowcountry as fertile ground for a community leadership program. Clark served as an important liaison in these early months, introducing Horton and his wife, Zilphia, in Charleston's social and civic organizations and recruiting for Highlander workshops. A month after her first visit, Clark invited Jenkins to Monteagle, hoping "a . . . workshop would do for him what it had done for [her]." Jenkins made a favorable impression when he announced bold plans to run for school board trustee.[55] By the start of the next year, the route from Monteagle to Charleston was well worn. In February, Horton hired Clark to make regular reports as he continued his own visits, and that summer, Clark stayed busy transporting Johns Island volunteers to Monteagle. Back on Johns Island, Jenkins made good on his promise, mobilizing support for his school board bid through churches, the local Citizens Club, and the Progressive Club. On Election Day, 192 of the 200 registered black voters selected Jenkins.[56] Jenkins's near win "scared the mischief out of . . . the white folks" who rewrote the rules to appoint, rather than elect, future school board trustees. African Americans also responded, coordinating trips to the registration office in order to arrive in pairs "so as not to arouse suspicion." When Horton visited a month later, Jenkins boasted, "It took 10 years to get the first 200 registered," he said, "but 50 had registered" since his program started. The next month, Clark returned for a Citizens Club meeting and reported "sixty-four registrants since the February meeting."[57]

Citizens Club meetings quickly became the center for political action and for Horton's "general adult education program." "Everything is discussed," he reported to Schwarzhaupt, "farm problems, school problems, health and world affairs," and conversations continued "long after the meetings were held." Jenkins retained his singular focus on black voter registration. Armed with the ballot, voters could wield enough power in black-majority districts to make noticeable and lasting change. From Jenkins's perspective, open discussions were not as useful as a leader, like himself, simply telling people what to do. Horton agreed with the result but disagreed on the process. By March, Horton and Jenkins were at loggerheads.

After "several hours on 2 different occasions," Horton concluded that Jenkins was "beginning to understand the need for developing other people as leaders," but Jenkins kept proposing meetings and "did not indicate that he understood how the meetings could be used for leadership directly or indirectly."[58] From Jenkins's perspective, Horton moved too slowly with a lot of talk about "getting people active" and a "leadership training program" and no substantive plan or tangible results.[59]

Clark intervened with a set of skills tailored to the situation. She knew how to organize, she translated abstract ideas into practical terms, and while she valued discussion, she also knew how to guide process toward results. She invited Jenkins and the Hortons to her home and directed the "long session." Jenkins remained committed to electing a black representative on the school board. Harkening to the earlier NAACP petition drive, Clark proposed a survey. Going door to door would give people a task and generate widespread support, she explained. Jenkins volunteered his daughter Marie to conduct the survey. Clark countered. She knew local men from her teaching days and felt sure that they would help. If this initiative was going to succeed, they needed "all the help possible," she reminded Jenkins. Jenkins eventually agreed, though Horton noted, "Septima is still trying to convince Esau that she knows what she is talking about . . . and has a genuine interest in the island."[60]

Jenkins admitted, "My ideas . . . have changed in many ways. . . . Giving others something to do . . . is very important," but Clark was not entirely convinced of the conversion. In May, over 250 people gathered for a Citizens Club meeting where Clark joined Jenkins, a high school teacher, an insurance agent, and an undertaker at the head table. The Reverend J. T. Enwright moderated and "each speaker pointed out the value of the ballot." It was "a packed house" and attendees "listened attentively and gave hilarious applause," Clark reported, but when no one asked questions, she decided, "The next thing to do is to get those tongues loosened up." Clark returned in September with Bernice Robinson. The Reverend Robert Wagner's wide-ranging sermon on union organizing, Supreme Court decisions, and the church's failings on civil rights dominated the three-hour meeting. Wagner "was friendly" but "has very little of worth to tell those people," Clark concluded. When Jenkins followed and "talk[ed] too long," she observed, "some of the people got angry and walked out."[61] It would take more time to land on a strategy that upended a speaker-listener meeting format.

That summer, Clark urged Robinson to attend a Highlander workshop on the United Nations. Robinson had attended her first workshop the previous summer, writing to Horton that it "was one of the most wonderful experiences" and offering pragmatic advice. "Selling the United Nations is all right," she wrote, but "sell Highlander because you are putting into action and working it out." Robinson accepted Clark's invitation and throughout the first week, she watched films, listened to presentations, and mingled with political scientists and economists.[62] Jenkins arrived for the second week when conversations again focused on the United Nations. At the close of the workshop, Horton asked participants how they planned to enact Highlander's lessons. "I need to get my people registered to vote," Jenkins told the group. "They got to read a part of the Constitution and they don't know how to read." Makeshift literacy lessons were helping, but "I need a school," he insisted. At the end of two weeks of discussion, Robinson perked up at this concrete, easily understood, locally defined problem. "I thought, 'Yeah . . . People can't read,'" Robinson recalled. When asked, "What are we going to do about this situation on Johns Island?" Horton offered conditional support. "Let me see if I can find some money," he said. "You try to find a place and we'll see where we go from there."[63]

Johns Island's First Citizenship School

Jenkins immediately got to work, starting at the public schools, but "the principal was afraid . . . the school authorities would frown on that; he wasn't willing to risk it." Jenkins approached the Methodist minister and ran into the same problem because the preacher's wife taught school. After two dead ends, Jenkins turned to Highlander, and in late 1956, Horton extended a loan for the Progressive Club to purchase a "dilapidated school house." Club members repaired the building and set up a grocery store, quickly repaying Highlander's loan with store profits. Freed from the debt, club members received annual dividends of twenty-five to thirty dollars. Like Moving Star Hall, the club belonged to black residents, and profits stayed on Johns Island. The store occupied the front room of the schoolhouse, and Jenkins and Clark decided that the two back rooms would be ideal for adult literacy classes because the store was easily accessible, black residents routinely gathered there, and passersby could not "peep in" from the road.[64]

Horton, Clark, and Jenkins planned the school for December to February, the laying-by time for field workers. Delays in securing a location pushed the start date to January. They were ready to identify a teacher and Robinson was their first choice. She did not have formal teaching credentials, but she understood the Highlander approach and they trusted her. More importantly, because Robinson was a regular at Johns Island meetings, local residents knew her and trusted that she was not "high-falu-tin" and "try[ing] to make fun of them." Finally, as Horton later pointed out, black beauticians like Robinson "owned their own businesses [and] didn't depend upon whites for their income." Robinson, however, did not share their confidence and insisted, "I never been no teacher and I'm not going to be a teacher." Horton and Clark had readied their response. For the citizenship schools to work, they did not need "a certified teacher . . . working by a straitlaced curriculum." Instead, they wanted "a community worker who cares for the people." Ultimately, they argued, "Either you do it or we don't have a school."[65] Robinson relented and accepted the assignment.

If she was going to teach, she needed students, so Robinson made the rounds to local churches. In January, she opened the first class with fourteen students. Clark was away on a fund-raising trip, so Robinson was on her own and she improvised. She had borrowed reading materials from sisters-in-law who taught elementary school but quickly concluded that the materials were too childish for her adult students.[66] She pulled out the voter registration application and asked students to read it and sign their names. When they struggled, she wrote each name on poster board, distributed pencils, and encouraged each student to trace his or her name. Pencils snapped as hands accustomed to manual labor adjusted to a different kind of work.[67] Based on this assessment, Robinson determined that three students "had to start from scratch" and eight could "read a little but very poorly." Robinson adapted Highlander's participant-centered approach and asked what they wanted to learn.[68] They wanted to register to vote, but more than that, they wanted skills and knowledge for everyday activities. They wanted "to read a newspaper, . . . to read the Bible, . . . to know how to fill out an application blank . . . [and] to get a money order so they could order things by catalog." They wanted to read letters from family members "rather than have . . . the white people they worked for to read them." Literacy was the foundation for political empowerment, but Robinson's students also translated these skills in practical terms that would sharpen boundaries between work and family life and sever ties that sustained dependence and reinforced second-class status.[69]

Over the next few weeks, Robinson scrambled for materials. Clark's nephew worked at the post office and smuggled out a money order book. Robinson stayed up copying the forms so she could return the book by the next morning. In class, she copied the form onto the blackboard and helped students fill in blanks. When men in the class requested help with math skills, she gathered up newspaper ads. "If two pounds of beans are forty-nine cents, and you want four pounds of beans, how much will it be?" she asked and demonstrated how to calculate the answer.[70] She handwrote an enlarged version of Jenkins's worn voter registration application. Students read sections of the state constitution and "drill[ed] . . . on spelling and pronunciation and . . . the meaning of the words." Robinson interspersed films and music from Highlander to "break . . . monotony." Continuing to improvise, she requested copies of the United Nations Declaration of Human Rights and set a goal for "each to be able to read and understand the entire thing before the end of the school."[71] By the third week, they settled into a routine. Students took turns opening class with a devotional and Robinson collected their homework. Reading came next, followed by math. She wrote enthusiastically, "They really want to learn and are so proud of the little gain they have made so far."[72] Creating a curriculum from students' needs would become the hallmark for the citizenship school program.

Her students' enthusiasm helped ease the pressure of a hectic schedule. Class met twice weekly from seven o'clock until nine o'clock. On those nights, Robinson closed her shop early and she and Mattie ate a light dinner. A neighbor sat with Mattie while Bernice caught a ride to the island. She got home late, paid the sitter, and worked on new lessons. Between classes, she assembled materials, copied forms, transcribed documents, and gathered examples. Highlander paid expenses for travel and materials, but not sitters' fees. In between classes, Robinson worked extra hours to catch up on sewing projects and hairdressing appointments. Compensation came from her students. Within a few weeks, sixty-five-year-old Anna Vastine, who had signed with an X, recognized her printed name for the first time. "I had goose pimples all over me," Robinson recalled. "It really meant something."[73]

Robinson's lessons reached more than her fourteen students. When teenage daughters accompanied their parents and snickered from the corner of the room, Robinson distributed public speaking materials and instructed each girl to prepare a lesson. Pushed out of their comfort zone, some fidgeted, covered their mouths, and played with their hair, and then it was their parents' turn to snicker. Robinson soothed bruised egos, and soon the girls took turns reading and presenting information to the class. Robinson incorporated sewing and crochet lessons, passing on practical and marketable skills learned at her mother's side. Esau Jenkins visited regularly,

Figure 1. Bernice Robinson (*standing*) and Johns Island citizenship school students, ca. 1957. Courtesy of Wisconsin Historical Society, WHS-3234.

freeing Robinson for sewing lessons while he guided the adult students. Lessons carried over into the Progressive Club store, as Horton observed during a February visit. While Robinson held class on one side of a partition, "some 30 or 40 young men and a sprinkling of older people" milled around "listening in on the entire class." Robinson paid particular attention to one person. Jenkins's first student, Alice Wine, worked the register in the Progressive Club store, and when Robinson noticed Wine counting on her fingers, she intervened. Laying out toothpicks and matchsticks, she taught Wine how to subtract "without those sticks."[74]

Clark visited in late February, and Robinson was anxious to see how a trained schoolteacher would teach the class. To her relief, Clark "took words out of the Constitution, . . . divided each word into syllables and practiced pronouncing them" in the same way that Robinson had.[75] Clark set to work assembling a student workbook from Robinson's lessons and materials gathered at the school board, the League of Women Voters, and other civic groups. Edited passages served as reading and writing exercises, and taken as a whole, the workbook was a primer on the political and economic rights of "first class citizens." Students learned that they were entitled to public services such as health screenings and Social Security. On the Sea Islands, these services helped to ensure physical well-being, addressed concerns about the spread of disease, and provided a basis for economic stability. Clark's materials reinforced that first-class citizens filed tax returns, requested property tax assessments, and paid taxes on time to avoid penalties. For Johns Island landowners, paying taxes on time prevented foreclosure of property that was both home and the basis for family economic stability. To practice handwriting skills, students wrote formal letters that established relationships with elected officials. Clark encouraged students to write "when [the officials] do something that is good" because "it is very important to encourage them."[76]

After his February visit, Horton remarked, "I am not easily impressed because I have seen so many educational ventures flop, but I was impressed to hear the people there talking about integrating the schools and voting while Bernice corrected homework." Robinson's students did more than talk; they learned. "They could read and write their own names, and they could do arithmetic," Robinson reported. Although students were prepared to register, they decided to wait until the following year when state law required all South Carolina voters to renew their registrations. When citizenship school graduates went to the registration office, they all passed, received certificates, and returned "fairly shouting!" Clark recalled.[77] Robinson and Clark organized another class in December with similar results. The newly registered voters became ambassadors for the citizenship school program.

* * *

By early 1958, Horton, Clark, Robinson, and Jenkins judged their experiment in citizenship education to be a success and laid plans for additional classes. The program had evolved through intentional groundwork that linked progressive approaches to education and participatory democracy, traditions of racial uplift and black women's community leadership, and cultural practices on the Sea Islands. The first citizenship school was rooted in a specific time when postwar economic opportunities raised aspirations but bypassed African American workers, when postwar political organizing laid groundwork for continuing challenges to Jim Crow, and when state and local governments mounted resistance intended to blunt reform. The school was also rooted in a specific place defined by both isolation and generational poverty and rich cultural heritage that preserved traditions of mutual aid and social institutions. Robinson and Clark forged a program that adapted the Highlander approach to Sea Islands life, where the structure evolved from student requests and operated in tune with community rhythms. For Johns Islanders, direct influence over content and discussion topics mirrored gatherings at Moving Star Hall where every voice mattered.

Emphasis on voter registration ensured that classes accomplished Esau Jenkins's main goal, but citizenship school classes did more. The evolving pedagogy blended practical approaches to education honed by black schoolteachers like Clark and the Highlander approach that transformed the meaning and purpose of education. Crafting materials based on student requests preserved Myles Horton's belief in group-centered education where solutions to social problems emerged from discussion and debate. Class discussions designed to encourage questions and discussion meant that literacy education was a strategy for social change, rather than a process of rote learning that discouraged and blunted creativity and intellectual curiosity.

The resulting citizenship school curriculum reflected an internal tension that would define the program. Clark and Robinson infused materials with their construction of first-class citizenship. In the back room of the Progressive Club, students learned to read and write so that they could register to vote, to become first-class citizens. Lessons derived from student requests but also imparted information about required taxes, public services, and federal entitlement programs. The skills and information gathered in the citizenship school classroom provided a foundation for political empowerment and economic security. The practical lessons imparted other messages as well, preparing students to become what Clark would describe as "discerning and participating citizens of a Southern state."[78] Citizenship schools were training grounds for first-class citizens who met specific criteria that included literacy, manners, financial responsibility, and active engagement in community uplift.

They created the program as storm clouds gathered. In 1953, Mississippi senator James O. Eastland spearheaded creation of the Senate Internal Security Sub-committee to root out "subversives." Horton was called before the committee as citizenship schools got under way. Federal officials struck at Highlander's weak spot. In February 1957, the Internal Revenue Service revoked Highlander's tax-exempt status, making it impossible for the institution to receive grant funds. A lengthy legal defense threatened to siphon resources away from residential workshops and other programs. Armed with letters of support, Horton appealed the decision and the IRS restored Highlander's tax-exempt status.[79] Optimistic that they were back on solid ground, Clark, Robinson, Horton, and Jenkins initiated steps to implant citizenship schools in more communities.

2

"New Outposts in the Growing Movement"

Citizenship Schools in South Carolina and Alabama, 1958–1961

News of registered black voters on Johns Island spread south to Wadmalaw Island, and community leaders decided to investigate. On Wadmalaw, black residents made up 85 percent of the island's population, so more registered voters could make a noticeable difference.[1] Juanita Grimball took the lead. She knew Esau Jenkins through family connections; his daughter Ethel was married to Grimball's nephew.[2] In early 1958, she crossed Bohicket Creek for a meeting at the Johns Island Progressive Club where Jenkins narrated a silent film about the Highlander Folk School. At the end of the meeting, Grimball invited him to repeat the performance at her church. Two hundred people gathered for the show and got "a real thrill" from Jenkins's narration. Septima Clark answered questions from eager participants, distributed Highlander pamphlets, and left "exceedingly encourage[ed]."[3]

Over the next two years, local leaders trained at Highlander returned home and organized citizenship schools in Charleston and on Wadmalaw, Edisto, and Daufuskie Islands. Expansion across the South Carolina Lowcountry marked a new phase in the Johns Island experiment.[4] Bernice Robinson and Septima Clark turned improvised materials and methods into a structured program with a standard workbook and training workshop. Their work was informed by the Lowcountry experience infused with respectability politics where education and behavior served as the basis for claims to citizenship rights. Local women from Charleston and the Sea Islands became role models for future citizenship school teachers to emulate. Experienced teachers qualified for supervisor positions when they demonstrated expertise with the citizenship school model. As supervisors, they both passed on the citizenship school method of linking literacy and political action and served as an example for local women embodying the role of citizenship school teacher.

As the program took shape, Robinson and Clark became ambassadors into the South Carolina up-country and northern Alabama. Clark's visits to Huntsville were an early test in unfamiliar territory. Organizing citizenship schools in a region where African Americans were a distinct minority and communities fractured along class lines tested Clark's ability to build relationships necessary for program implementation. Expansion into new areas also revealed the potential and the limitations of materials and teacher training workshops designed by and for Lowcountry teachers.

Clark and Robinson did this work as state officials took aim at Highlander and its director, Myles Horton. By the late 1950s, Jim Crow segregation was under siege on multiple fronts. The U.S. Supreme Court's decision in *Brown v. Board of Education* led to massive resistance against school desegregation plans, most noticeably in Little Rock, Arkansas, in the fall of 1957. Two years earlier, Rosa Parks's refusal to give up her seat on a Montgomery city bus led to a year long boycott in the "Cradle of the Confederacy." In both cases, federal intervention upheld rights to equal access and accommodations. Southern legislators interpreted civil rights victories as evidence of communist infiltration, and in this climate, Tennessee state officials charged Horton with fomenting "community unrest and chaos."[5] As the 1950s came to a close, Horton and the Highlander staff battled to keep the folk school open. With debates raging in courtrooms and committee hearings, the citizenship school program took on increased importance as private foundations' investments kept Highlander afloat. Horton, however, worried that the rapidly expanding program would overwhelm other folk school programs, putting him at odds with Clark and Robinson's expansion efforts.

Expanding the Citizenship School Idea in the Lowcountry

Outreach to Wadmalaw predated Juanita Grimball's visit. Jenkins had initiated contact four years earlier when county officials merged Johns Island and Wadmalaw Island into one voting precinct. In March 1955, Horton made his way to Wadmalaw and "found conditions similar to those on Johns Island." By May, Jenkins was "working quietly" with a fledgling political action group.⁶ Six months later, Clark traveled to Wadmalaw and addressed a congregation gathered for Sunday morning service. She lived in Charleston, she acknowledged, but she knew about the islands through her work on neighboring Johns Island. In her remarks, she highlighted Charleston's active NAACP chapter and recent federal court decisions and pointedly asked, "Can you sit there and fail to register? To vote? Or refuse to join the NAACP?" Clark's questions and invitation to Highlander were met with "loud amens," but four months later she reported, "Slow going on Wadmalaw."⁷ Horton and Clark invited Wadmalaw leaders to a series of one-day workshops, but when plans fizzled, Horton conceded that local leaders needed the immersive "residential experience" at Highlander.⁸

Three years later, the Wadmalaw Improvement Committee offered a new opportunity. Following the film presentation, Jenkins returned with a voting machine for a crash course on South Carolina's election laws. Vote for only one gubernatorial candidate, he instructed, and vote for exactly ten representatives "so your vote can count." Do not follow a white man's advice; he was likely to "tell you to vote for somebody who won't help you," Jenkins advised. That same summer, Juanita Grimball and Jenkins's daughter, Ethel Grimball, made the trip to Highlander.⁹ Ethel Grimball was no stranger at the folk school. A trained schoolteacher, Grimball had formed an immediate bond with Clark, and in 1955, Clark and Horton unsuccessfully rallied support when Grimball lost a teaching position due to "her civic activities and the civic activities of her father." Shut out of public schools, Grimball put her sewing skills to use at The Citadel in Charleston.¹⁰ The citizenship school program blended teaching expertise and political organizing skills, and Grimball jumped at the chance to organize a class.

In December, Grimball opened Wadmalaw Island's first citizenship school at the Presbyterian church. Clark and Horton had recruited Robinson out of concern that a trained teacher would establish a hierarchical relationship and undermine community leadership development. In some ways, schoolteacher Grimball represented an early departure from this model; however, her community work ensured that she was not seen as "high falutin.'" As Clark and her peers demonstrated in the early twentieth century, black schoolteachers were expected to be adept community leaders and organizers. The teaching credential conferred status and authority; the individual teacher earned respect through community work. Grimball embodied this role before opening her citizenship school. She grew up on Johns Island, married into a prominent family on Wadmalaw, and was actively involved in community affairs. Her friends and neighbors also knew that unjust laws kept Grimball out of the public schools, a decision that impacted the island's schoolchildren and the broader community. They gathered at the Presbyterian church because they trusted Grimball to do this "woman's work."[11]

On Wednesdays and Thursdays for three months, Grimball's twenty-six students hurried home from work, ate a quick supper, and walked to the church where they crowded into the nine-by-six-foot space. Most students were forty to fifty years old, and for these day laborers, the citizenship school was a long-awaited opportunity to overcome the limitations of rural segregated schools. Grimball used the voter registration application to replicate Robinson's practical exercises. Students practiced handwriting by filling in blanks on the form, practiced reading with copies of the state constitution, and mastered cursive writing to sign "legibly."[12] Grimball adapted the curriculum to suit her teaching style. "Individual instruction is essential," she believed, assigning an elementary-level reader for "adult beginners" and a "veteran's reader" for more advanced students. Following Robinson's lead, Grimball incorporated sewing and crochet lessons into citizenship school meetings.[13] Since these skills were viewed as women's work, Grimball taught the lessons to female students in the class. As Grimball's and Robinson's experiences showed, these lessons were more than an opportunity to learn a new hobby. Seamstress work offered an important gendered avenue for black women to earn money in a constricted segregated economy.

Her students' motivations varied as much as their abilities, and like Robinson, Grimball adapted lessons to meet students where they were. Arthur Jenkins qualified to vote under property and tax requirements, and with Grimball's instruction, he improved his math skills. Twenty-five-year-old Anderson Mack, on the other hand, started at the beginning, with Grimball guiding his hand to teach cursive writing. One young man brought his Bible and asked for extra help to "conduct prayer meetings for his people." On school nights, the class served as his congregation as he "wrestled with . . . the Scriptures." Grimball's students quickly applied their citizenship school lessons. By April 1959, twenty-four of the twenty-six students were registered voters. They organized the Board of Concerned Members of Wadmalaw Island and ran a successful campaign to elect a former student to the voting precinct executive committee.[14]

Citizenship schools extended farther south when Allene Brewer opened a class at the Presbyterian church in Edisto Island's Larimer community. Black residents made up the majority on Edisto, and in Clark's estimation,

Figure 2. Ethel Grimball (*right*) with Wadmalaw Island student, ca. 1958. Photograph by Ida Berman, © Karen Berman.

they "were not as backward perhaps as those on Wadmalaw."[15] Brewer was a social worker and minister's wife, steeped in the same call to service that Clark answered at Promise Land School. Esau Jenkins's son Abraham remembered Brewer as "quite a community person . . . instrumental in so many little things that you don't hear much about." She and her husband, the Reverend U. L. Brewer, served as officers of the Edisto Island Voters Association and attended civic club meetings on neighboring islands and in Charleston. Discussion of citizenship schools at a North Charleston meeting stoked Brewer's interest. She learned more at a Highlander workshop and opened a citizenship school in December 1958. Her thirty-eight students spanned two generations, ranging in age from twenty-one to seventy-six years old. Likely influenced by her social work training, Brewer immediately set to work creating community in her classroom. In an early session, she distributed citizenship school workbooks, pieces of cloth, needles, and thread. With her guidance, students crafted book bags that became part of a collective identity. Brewer assessed ability and organized groups so that students could learn from each other. When lessons

Figure 3. Allene Brewer (*standing, in sweater*) with Edisto Island citizenship school students, ca. 1958–1959. Courtesy of Wisconsin Historical Society, WHS-51401.

wound down, students often stayed for a "little social session." Like Grimball and Robinson, Brewer incorporated sewing and crochet lessons into her classes. When the three-month school ended, thirty-four students registered to vote. Women from the class gathered for the sewing circle that continued to meet weekly.[16]

Grimball and Brewer influenced Clark's concept of both the citizenship school program and local teachers. Both Grimball and Brewer retained elements of Robinson's class and tested the program's flexibility by adapting it to suit their personalities and expertise. Clark's confidence in Grimball and Brewer rested on personal relationships, the women's professional training in education and social work, and their active involvement in churches and community organizations. Grimball and Brewer lived on the islands, but in Clark's view, they were not "backward." They modeled a construction of first-class citizenship grounded in education, respectability, and community service. Their ability to recruit and retain students signified adult residents' desire to lay claim to long-denied or inadequate basic education. Their participation also showed an agreement with the program's premise about first-class citizenship and black women's leadership in uplift efforts. Local folk like Anderson Mack attended the Sea Islands schools because they wanted to overcome deficits in formal education and because they agreed that first-class citizens were literate. Literacy served as the basis for laying claim to long-denied rights, signified most directly in successful voter registration.

In the fall and winter of 1958, schools were under way on Wadmalaw and Edisto Islands and in Charleston. In October, Mary Lee Davis traveled from North Charleston to neighboring James Island for a series of workshops that brought the Highlander approach to the Lowcountry. Clark's and Jenkins's descriptions of citizenship schools got her attention. Davis ran a beauty shop and was increasingly disturbed by the "dilapidated shacks" and "slum dwellings" left behind after the city's token gestures at infrastructure improvements. A run-down neighborhood was bad for business, she explained. Registered residents could "assert some power" and "get the eyes and ears of the politicians."[17] Davis offered to organize a class, and Bernice Robinson stepped in to teach. Domestic workers spread the word and for two evenings a week from mid-December to mid-March, seventeen students ranging in age from fifteen to fifty-two gathered in Davis's shop. Robinson tailored lessons to students' priorities, crafting a chart that explained how city government officials made decisions and how and when local people could influence this process. At the end of the three-month class, twelve students earned attendance certificates and five registered to vote.[18]

After the start of the new year, Clark carried news of the citizenship school program nearly one hundred miles south to Daufuskie Island, a barrier island only accessible by the mail boat that ran three times a week. This was Clark's third visit, and it was sunny and calm when she climbed aboard for the nearly two-hour trip. Church deacon Isaiah Graves and his wife, Sylvia, served as hosts, and that evening, Clark inquired about potential "interest in voting and working together to get the things they needed and wanted." Buoyed by positive response, Clark set out the next morning and chatted easily with people she met. That evening, twenty-five gathered at Mary Fields School, where Clark carefully tailored her message to the audience. "Have you been thinking about how hard it is to get here?" she asked, highlighting a sharp decline in the island's population from 320 to 141 in only three years. "No work . . . but a little oyster factory open during the winter season" coupled with isolation drove young people into Charleston and points north, Clark reasoned. Attendees agreed that transportation was their "number 1 problem," and Clark suggested writing to local and state officials. Nods of agreement created an opening. "A letter from tax payers who are registered voters will carry more weight," she advised. They needed to get "the book" and register people. "Who is the leader in this community?" Clark asked, and all pointed to Viola Bryan.[19] It took some encouragement before Bryan agreed. The groundwork laid, Clark offered to organize citizenship schools and left with assurances that Sylvia Graves and schoolteacher Frances Jones would come to Highlander.[20]

By February 1959, four citizenship schools were wrapping up in Charleston and on the Sea Islands. A total of 106 students completed the three-month classes, 60 earned attendance certificates, and 56 registered to vote. The schools' influence spread beyond the makeshift classrooms. When registration offices opened during the first week of each month, citizenship school teachers took "anyone, man or woman," to register. Folk school graduates organized residential seminars where participants discussed "cooperatives, driver education, social security, today's cash crop, income taxes, and health services."[21] Two months after Clark's visit, Viola Bryan shared news. "The letters has [sic] been signed by each voters and taxes [sic] payers on the island," and Gov. Ernest F. Hollings's office sent "a very encouraging letter," she wrote, concluding, "The whole community joins us in saying thank you." Clark returned to Daufuskie in late May to finalize preparations for a citizenship school. Highlander had a "new outpost in the growing movement."[22]

From Experiment to Program

Program expansion prompted discussions about funding and structure. As early as October 1958, Myles Horton had written to Maxwell Hahn at the Marshall Field Foundation with a proposal. "A project . . . shows promise of developing into something that might well be spread through the South," he began, emphasizing that the Sea Islands citizenship schools had seeded "a year-round pattern of citizenship education evolved by the people themselves." Monthly meetings, residential conferences, and recreation, health, and civic projects ensured that momentum did not wane after three-month classes ended. The program required a reliable funding source, which a three-year grant from Field would provide.[23] Funding came through in January, and Clark, Robinson, and Horton turned attention to program administration. Based on the Lowcountry experience, they agreed to recruit only African Americans as teachers because as Horton acknowledged, "Whites would . . . take over by force of habit." Teachers should be at least twenty-one years old, have some high school education, and be able to "read well aloud" and "write legibly on the blackboard." They needed to know, or be willing to learn, voter registration procedures and public services in their community.[24] The criteria intertwined threads of education and community work. Citizenship school teachers adopted a recognizable identity carried over from segregated schools where teachers were instructors, mentors, information brokers, and community organizers. Citizenship schools extended this role to community leaders who did not have formal credentials. Horton, Clark, and Robinson acknowledged that local people needed support to do this work. To offset class-related expenses, Horton allocated fifty-dollar stipends for teachers operating biweekly classes for up to three months. Clark and Robinson finalized plans for a week-long workshop designed as orientation and immersive training. Participants got practical advice about recruiting students and organizing a classroom, and a quick introduction to the program's "learn by doing" method with time reserved for practice.[25]

Robinson and Clark revised the workbook in time for citizenship schools opening in the fall. Workbooks established the program as an offshoot of the Highlander Folk School. Lessons blended Horton's ideas about participatory democracy and community leadership development and Clark's and Robinson's practical approach to literacy education. A brief description of Highlander served as a reading exercise and an introduction to a "new kind of school" that promoted tolerance across race, religion, and an urban-rural divide. Highlander's "Official Statement of Policy" came next, affirming that democratic citizenship rested on "freedom of thought and religion, to equal rights to a livelihood, education and health; to equal opportunity to participate in the cultural life of the community and to equal access to public services."[26] In recitations, students practiced literacy skills and claimed a broad set of rights. Reading and writing exercises followed, but this was not an elementary primer with exercises about "dogs, cats, bunnies, chickens," Clark insisted, "Not one exhortation to 'Come Muff, see Puff.'" Instead, Clark and Robinson altered few of the materials from the first Johns Island class, ensuring that students "learn[ed] by doing something of real practical value to [them]."[27]

Voter registration continued to be a primary focus, and workbook lessons and classroom instruction guided students through a rehearsal of the process. Clark and Robinson reprinted South Carolina's election law so that students read and interpreted: "Registration that is good and valid in the year 1957 shall be good and valid until May 1, 1958, and thereafter registration that is good and valid in the year immediately preceding any year of general registration shall continue to be good and valid only during the first four months of the year of general registration. The registration of voters for each new ten-year period may begin on September first preceding the new registration year, and all certificates issued during such period shall be good for voting and jury duty for the next ensuing ten-year period."[28] Convoluted language might frustrate students with limited skills, but that was the point. County registrars required prospective black voters to read, write, and interpret parts of the state constitution, and registrars employed their own discretion in evaluating responses. The workbook retained practical exercises where students practiced handwriting using the voter registration application, and the lesson served as a dry run for an eventual meeting with the county registrar. In makeshift classrooms among friends and neighbors, adult students gained confidence to pass the test and were equipped to recognize unfair practices.[29] One-page descriptions informed students about required taxes, social security, and public health services, concluding with Robinson's exercises in filling out a mail order blank and a money order. Working with materials that were directly relevant to their daily lives, Clark estimated that citizenship school students learned basic literacy skills in eighty hours, eighteen hours less than traditional adult literacy programs.[30] Altogether, the citizenship school workbook served as a guide for the fundamentals of literacy and the practices of first-class citizenship.

The workbook and class discussions projected optimism that change was possible and within grasp. Armed with literacy skills, black citizens could successfully register to vote. Citizenship schools and Highlander workshops sowed seeds at the grass roots, and increasing black voter registration suggested that the Lowcountry was fertile soil. There were silences in the workbook and in reports about the Sea Islands experiments, however. Workbook lessons reinforced, rather than challenged, racialized constructions of citizenship that allowed white southerners to claim full citizenship rights without challenge while African Americans' rights, particularly poor and rural African Americans, were conditioned on education, behavior, and presentation. Citizenship school lessons also failed to acknowledge that in the Jim Crow South, education and presentation did not automatically translate into voter registration and equal treatment.

Program Expansion during the Red Scare

Intensifying attacks on Highlander threatened to undermine the citizenship program as legislators took aim at organizations and institutions advocating an end to segregation. The 1953 congressional inquiry was the opening salvo in a prolonged effort to shutter the folk school. In February 1959, Tennessee state legislators launched an investigation into Highlander's "alleged subversive activities." Committee members held hearings and pored over financial records, property deeds, and attendance lists, searching for ties between Highlander and a web of "subversive" organizations and activists.[31] They targeted Horton, who acknowledged his affiliation with the organizations and individuals identified by the committee but denied direct ties to the Communist Party. Committee members were most confounded by Highlander's purpose, noting that although the school purported to "preserv[e] local culture and customs," "very few" local residents had "set foot on the grounds." Instead, Highlander staff were spending time on "some sort of voting registration activity on an island." According to the committee members, Highlander's racially integrated programs proved Horton's intent to sow "community unrest and chaos" in "a meeting place for known Communists and fellow travelers." Based on these findings, state officials moved to revoke Highlander's charter.[32]

Clark and Robinson were drawn into the legal battle during a workshop in late July. Horton was away in Europe, so Clark served as host and supervisor. It had been a long week and as she relaxed during a film screening, police officers shattered the calm, herding participants into the hall and ordering Clark to "put that film out." Although state officials wanted to close Highlander for violating segregation ordinances, the federal *Brown v. Board of Education* ruling gave Horton grounds to challenge these charges. They hit on another strategy and ordered a search for alcohol, which would violate the dry county's local ordinance. Ignoring Clark's assurances that there was nothing to find, they rummaged through buildings while the Reverend Solomon S. Seay, Sr., from Montgomery led choruses of "We Shall Overcome." Officers finally emerged from Horton's basement with a cobweb-covered jug, claiming they had found moonshine. They arrested Clark, who passed time at the Grundy County jail quietly singing to herself until two local white teachers posted bail money. She returned to Highlander close to midnight and saw guests off the next morning.[33]

Intended to halt Highlander programs, the raid had the opposite effect. Six weeks later, more than sixty people from eight states gathered to learn about "the citizenship school idea." They were a diverse group of ministers, social workers, church leaders, beauticians, storekeepers, mechanics, and housewives, and by the end of the week, they were equipped to organize local classes.[34] The raid deepened Clark and Robinson's commitment to citizenship schools and to Highlander. In between folk school workshops and meetings, they were in perpetual motion on recruiting trips. In the spring of 1959, Robinson spread the word across South Carolina's up-country from Anderson to Spartanburg and Greenville. Amidst negative publicity, she assured Horton, "It doesn't disturb me at all" and pledged to "keep the ball rolling." Clark hit the road in June, making personal appeals in Aiken, Columbia, Cheraw, and Sumter. Throughout the first half of 1959, reflecting their belief in the power of organizations and networks, Clark and Robinson introduced the citizenship school model at meetings of the Council of the Southern Mountains, the South Carolina Council on Human Rights, and the South Carolina Adult Education Coordinating Council.[35] Outreach and professional networking made Clark and Robinson the faces of the citizenship school program and Highlander more broadly.

Sea Islands citizenship schools moved on their own momentum. Classes on Wadmalaw and Edisto Islands and in North Charleston enrolled 131 students. On Johns Island, teachers opened a second school in the Promise Land community where Clark had begun her teaching career nearly sixty years earlier. By the start of 1960, their efforts contributed to a 300 percent increase in black voter registration on Johns Island. In March, Allene Brewer submitted a detailed report from Edisto Island. She augmented the citizenship school workbook with maps, pictures, filmstrips, and new exercises in "letter writing and the Bible" and the "history of our country and progress of the Negro." Students enjoyed "Singing School" where they learned together or one student taught the others, and this "helped people to take their minds off of themselves and center them more on one another." Brewer nurtured community engagement beyond the makeshift classroom and schedule. Local women continued to gather for a weekly sewing class, and Brewer arranged field trips to meetings on neighboring Sea Islands and in Charleston to "broaden their view outside of themselves and their community." At the close of the school, Brewer estimated that eighty of one hundred newly registered voters were "influenced [by the] efforts of the adult school directly or indirectly." Brewer's students spread the word door to door to encourage registration that added up so that in 1960, two hundred black residents were registered on Edisto Island, an increase of 160 in two years.[36]

Student testimonials reinforced lessons that linked literacy education, political empowerment, and community leadership. For Ms. Finney on Johns Island, the citizenship school made up for inadequate instruction in the island's segregated schools. "Since I come to this school, I learn much more than all my school days cause I never learned to print . . . and I've learned to print now," she wrote. Edisto Island student Ms. Vanderhorst agreed. "Since I started attending it, I can read better," she wrote, adding, "I also registerd [sic] and vote it help me be a better citizen."[37] Individual achievement sowed seeds for collective action to address deeply rooted political, social, and economic inequality. Lula Bligen and Solomon Brown put new skills to use as officers in the Edisto Island Voters Association. Brewer's students' "each one, get one" campaign encouraged Tony Daise to spread the word about voter registration and transport people to the polls on Election Day. Ethel Grimball's student Anderson Mack organized to establish mail delivery to individual homes, open a kindergarten program, improve roads on Wadmalaw, and open a new community center with fellow students.[38]

Citizenship Schools in Northern Alabama

Buttressed by promising results on South Carolina's coast, Clark tested the program in northern Alabama. In March 1960, she contacted Chessie Harris who was "single-handedly combatting juvenile delinquency" by taking in "neglected Negro children" in Huntsville. At Clark's invitation, Harris brought "a carload of men and women" to Highlander and asked Clark to visit. During her two-week stay, Clark got to know local folks by replicating Horton's method of "walk[ing] around . . . just talking and talking to people." Informal conversations convinced thirty-three people to attend Highlander workshops during the summer.[39] Clark returned several times, but despite these regular visits, Clark confided to Horton, "All the people are strangers to me. . . . So different from the island people." Negative publicity about Highlander dogged her, and she hoped that "they . . . learn to believe in me."[40] Clark's reflections put factors contributing to success on the Sea Islands into sharp relief. On Johns Island, Clark was not among "strangers." She had spent much of her professional life connected to the island and its people. They knew her and she knew them, forming the basis of a trusting relationship. Citizenship schools emerged out of ongoing activity and three years of intense effort. In northern Alabama, citizenship schools would be part of an effort to seed collective action. As Clark made inroads in northern Alabama, she warned Horton that "more time must be spent with the potential leaders" and these recommendations had funding ramifications because building relationships "takes constant hammering."[41]

Early suspicion and mistrust dissipated, and by the end of the summer, thirty-three volunteers participated in Highlander workshops, which, in Clark's view, built a "substantial bridge" capable of "span[ning] the communist gossip." Highlander graduates fueled local organizing, and Clark returned in July for a mass meeting called by the Madison County Voters League. She invited Reverend Seay to drive up from Montgomery to hear plans to put a black candidate on the ballot and endorse candidates running for commission seats in the upcoming fall election. These were plans ambitious for the "penniless organization," and Clark observed that "not one of them knew anything about the government of their city or how to preside at a meeting." Seay's impromptu lesson clarified election procedures, helping to reinforce the value of a connection to Highlander and its resources.[42]

Clark's reports continued to draw contrasts between northern Alabama and the South Carolina Lowcountry. Esau Jenkins's motivations for political organizing stemmed from demographics; black people were in the majority, and in this context, increased voter registration could shift the balance of political power. In Madison County, Alabama, African Americans made up just over 18 percent of the population. In Huntsville, the percentage dropped to 13 percent, and as a result, African Americans held a precarious position in this part of the state. Voter registration and political organization could galvanize support behind a common agenda, but securing gains depended on favorable relationships with the white majority. Fractures opened, dividing city and county leaders largely along class lines as each competed for influence and support. "The city people . . . will not listen to a county leader," Clark wrote to Horton. She recommended working with "one rooted in the lives of the city people and [another] rooted in the lives of the county people." As Clark observed, black professionals were acutely aware of risks posed by involvement with communist-tainted Highlander and civil rights activities. "Degree crazy" local people looked to this professional class for leadership, and with economic ties to white employers, Clark concluded that "there was no way in the world" this group would organize citizenship schools.[43] She found a receptive audience with Huntsville-area ministers, likely influenced by the successful bus boycott in Montgomery less than two hundred miles to the south. There, the Reverend Martin Luther King Jr. and the Montgomery Improvement Association preached a gospel of non-violence and transformed civil rights action into a moral cause. Madison County ministers mobilized congregations, and by December, two citizenship schools were under way in Huntsville, another met in nearby Farley, and two more opened in New Market, enrolling a total of 115 students. By the following February, eighty-six students registered to vote.[44] Success in northern Alabama pointed to the possibility of transplanting citizenship schools in vastly different areas across the South.

A New Relationship with the Southern Christian Leadership Conference

Alabama schools got under way while Horton confronted festering problems. The pending legal case kept a cloud of uncertainty over the school's future. Horton was also increasingly concerned about the citizenship schools' impact on the folk school's mission to serve as an incubator. Once local programs were under way, Highlander's "job [was] to get out of the way before we [were] run over," he later reflected. When legal challenges and financial uncertainty forced cancellation of workshops on "The Role of Highlander in the South" and "Community Leadership Development," Horton determined that the citizenship school program "was swamping Highlander" and accelerated efforts to transfer ongoing administration to another home. With citizenship schools operating in Alabama and the Sea Islands and expanding into southeastern Georgia and western Tennessee, Horton looked for a way out. He pledged support through the first quarter of 1961 but declared that "it was not sound . . . to continue financing field programs."[45] In January, Horton outlined a revised policy whereby Highlander would train teachers and supervisors and transfer administration to "initiating organizations" that would recruit teachers, provide supervision, and cover operating costs. The policy would redefine Clark's and Robinson's roles, emphasizing outreach and training and limiting direct supervision of local schools.

In Horton's opinion, an organization like the Southern Christian Leadership Conference (SCLC) was an ideal home for the citizenship school program, and he opened negotiations with them in the fall of 1960.[46] This marked Horton's second attempt to establish ties with the SCLC. In September 1957, Highlander's twenty-fifth anniversary celebration brought Martin Luther King Jr. to Monteagle.[47] A year later, the SCLC's executive director, Ella Baker, attended a weeklong workshop on the heels of a massive voter registration drive. Fashioned on the Reverend Billy Graham's popular revivals, the Crusade for Citizenship aimed to double the number of black registered voters in southern states by 1960 through evangelical-style appeals that linked registration and Christian duty. Drawing on her extensive organizing experience with the NAACP, Baker launched the crusade in February 1958 with mass meetings and prayer vigils in two dozen southern cities. Enthusiasm waned as the SCLC struggled to turn the one-day event into a sustained campaign. The following fall, Baker recommended a new strategy to mobilize "religious bodies, civic and fraternal organizations (composed of women, especially)" in support of a "literacy project" to "reduce functional illiteracy." This kind of project could equip people with "the basic tools (reading and writing)" and prepare them "for effective social action." This would be a call to action for black women, Baker argued, because it opened "a 'respectable' channel for helping the cause." That same month, she attended a Highlander workshop and formed an instant connection with Clark. At the SCLC, despite King's endorsement of Baker's plan, the "literacy project" failed to take shape.[48]

The SCLC was more receptive in the fall of 1960 when Horton tried again. Earlier that spring, groups of college students took seats at whites-only lunch counters and refused to move. The "sit-in movement" spread across the South, and by April, student leaders organized the Student Non-Violent Coordinating Committee (SNCC), pulling Baker away from the SCLC and capturing national attention.[49] Presidential politics also influenced the SCLC's decisions. After Democratic candidate John F. Kennedy pledged federal action on voting rights if elected, King moved to align the SCLC with the prospective president's agenda, creating an opening for Horton.[50] In October, Horton met with newly appointed executive director Wyatt T. Walker and public relations director James Wood to outline plans to expand citizenship schools through SCLC affiliates. A month later, Wood and Horton hammered out a deal whereby the SCLC would pay Septima Clark's salary, making her "available to SCLC on a full time basis," and local SCLC affiliates would cover costs for prospective teachers attending Highlander workshops. Horton introduced Wood to L. B. Moore from the Marshall Field Foundation, and the three informally agreed on plans for the SCLC to "take over ... the leadership training program in its entirety" after a year.[51]

Wood sold the plan to the SCLC board in an argument that echoed Baker's points. Citizenship schools "offered many advantages," he explained, because the SCLC gained "a proven curriculum" in a program run "by well qualified persons" in "a facility that is established and working."

Most important, Wood stressed, "There is no initial layout of monies."[52] According to former Highlander staff member Anne Lockwood Romasco, King was skeptical, concerned that accusations of communism that swirled around Highlander and Horton could be turned on King and the SCLC. In addition, although citizenship schools presented a solution for voter registration, the program was an uncomfortable fit because the schools had not originated within the black church. In early December, Horton and Lockwood made a second trip to Atlanta, where King "spent about four hours going over the costs and every detail," eventually endorsing the program.[53]

Clark, Horton, and Robinson set to work, refining the teacher training workshop to incorporate insights from experienced teachers from the South Carolina coast and northern Alabama. The discussions revealed program founders' and early teachers' consensus about the links between education and citizenship. Local teachers shared recruiting strategies, emphasizing the importance of assuring potential students that a "lack of formal education is a misfortune and not a disgrace, and that it is possible to learn, even after they are adults." Subsequent discussions clarified the program's purpose. Robinson led off, asserting, "Until [African Americans] are registered voters, and can read and write and participate in public affairs, they aren't living up to their obligations." Voter registration was a marker of first-class citizenship, but the comment pointed to something more. First-class citizens were obligated to be educated and actively engaged. Citizenship schools went beyond basic literacy instruction, as Huntsville teacher Robert C. Adams emphasized. "In a business meeting, our people ... don't know how to put a motion at the right time," he explained. This had real consequences because "there were times if they'd known what to do, they could have had some rights." Allene Brewer confirmed points about voter registration and political engagement, but she also highlighted lessons in "making change, keeping bills paid, ... sending off a money order, and writing letters." These were critical skills for first-class citizenship, she argued, because people who could do these things broke bonds of dependence.[54] The discussion revealed the internal tensions within the citizenship schools. Robinson, Brewer, and Adams spoke in terms like "should" and "must," echoing earlier rhetoric of a middle-class bourgeois respectability and racial uplift; however, embedded within these "musts" and "shoulds" was a belief that education held the promise of tangible economic opportunities and community advancement.

The revised workshop added structure to teacher training and fueled further expansion. Between October 1960 and June 1961, local teachers organized fifty-four schools in southeastern Georgia and western Tennessee, on the South Carolina Sea Islands, and in Huntsville and Montgomery in Alabama. Over 1,500 people attended classes and 713 citizenship school students registered to vote. Program staff set an ambitious goal to reach "some 90,000 unqualified potential voters" by June 1962. Horton carried through with plans to limit Highlander's role to training teachers. In January 1961, he declared the Sea Islands program "independent [from Highlander's] guidance, instruction, and financial backing," and in Huntsville, students pooled resources to sustain classes, agreeing to "contribute $2 to cover the costs of rent, equipment, etc." in one class and moving other classes into private homes to cut expenses.[55] Highlander's five-day workshops drew attendees from southeastern Georgia, signaling growing momentum in this area.[56]

* * *

Between 1958 and 1961, citizenship schools expanded beyond Johns Island and became an official program. Citizenship school teachers in Charleston and on Edisto and Wadmalaw Islands mobilized communities and contributed to a groundswell sweeping across the Sea Islands. Teachers like Allene Brewer and Ethel Grimball directly influenced the materials and lessons that would be transferred to new communities as well as the criteria and expectations for local teachers. Individual transformation planted the seeds for collective action, just as Clark, Robinson, Horton, and Jenkins had envisioned. Measurable gains in voter registration and successful community improvement projects attracted more resources. Northern Alabama served as the program's first testing ground outside of the Sea Islands, and Clark's work exposed the critical importance of groundwork to build trust and impart the program's broader principles and purpose.

Program expansion proved to be a double-edged sword as Myles Horton welcomed long-term foundation funding but grew increasingly concerned about the citizenship schools' impact on other folk school programs. Horton's desire to restrict Highlander's involvement increasingly stood at odds with Clark's and Robinson's calls for more field visits and direct interaction with local teachers and supervisors. Horton's decision to limit Highlander's involvement to training teachers changed the program focus and shifted responsibility to local leaders. Shallow roots in northern Alabama withered as teachers and students struggled to sustain the program. On the Sea Islands, extensive groundwork and leadership development sunk firmer roots. Citizenship schools and voters' leagues met regularly into the 1960s, and Esau Jenkins opened a "voter information center" where monthly sessions served as community forums about services available through the Social Security office and the Health Department and sustained "the Highlander spirit."[57]

Sea Islands organizers built on groundwork laid, in part, through citizenship schools and the SCLC stood ready to take over program administration at the same time that Bernice Robinson's outreach to southeastern Georgia established a new outpost. Between October 1960 and June 1961, citizenship school teachers organized twenty-one classes in thirteen counties across Georgia's First Congressional District. Six hundred and thirty people enrolled in the classes and 110 registered to vote. These figures signaled a new phase in the program's evolution. In southeastern Georgia, citizenship schools would keep pace with a dynamic movement in urban Savannah and provide the opening wedge for political organization in surrounding rural counties with local black women at the forefront of these efforts.

3

"Bring This Community Leadership Program to Your Town and County"

Groundwork in Southeastern Georgia, 1960–1961

On the morning of May 8, 1960, Bernice Robinson turned onto the coastal highway and drove out of Charleston. After stops in nearby Frogmore and Beaufort, she followed the highway south to Savannah, arriving in the early afternoon. She had little to show from her first trip the previous fall and hoped for better results. On this visit, Robinson met with W. W. Law, president of the city's NAACP branch. It had been three years since the first Johns Island class, and she spoke confidently about citizenship schools. Law was interested and introduced her to Hosea Williams, who was co-ordinating voter registration activities through the Chatham County Crusade for Voters (CCCV). When Williams told Robinson about the CCCV's survey of registered black voters and a registration drive already under way, Robinson saw an opening and shared information about citizenship schools. At Williams's invitation, she stayed for an afternoon mass meeting and departed optimistic about possibilities.[1]

The spring meeting set the stage for citizenship school expansion into southeastern Georgia.[2] By the time Robinson arrived, NAACP-organized mass meetings, sit-ins, and economic boycotts had galvanized Savannah's black community. Partnering with Highlander opened a new stream of funding, materials, and support. Under Williams's leadership, citizenship schools filled a unique niche within a complex constellation of activities. In contrast to direct action strategies, the schools met out of public view, opening another entry point for black residents to join the movement. Black women's community networks mobilized and expanded their role to include literacy education and voter registration. Citizenship schools delivered basic literacy education into rural counties where segregated public schools were perpetually under-resourced. In Savannah and surrounding counties, black women organized classes that set the foundation for a region-wide network.

Program expansion in southeastern Georgia played out against changes at Highlander. By early 1961, with citizenship schools organizing in new locations, Myles Horton was exploring options to turn full-time program administration over to another organization to return the folk school to its original purpose of training local people and seeding a variety of new programs. At the same time, private foundations began to back away as persistent legal challenges hounded Horton and Highlander, adding urgency to discussions about transferring the citizenship school program. Septima Clark and Bernice Robinson, architects of the citizenship schools, became bargaining chips in negotiations with the Southern Christian Leadership Conference (SCLC). Reverberations reached into Savannah and stoked rivalry between Williams and the city's NAACP branch leadership.

The Savannah Movement before the CEP

When Bernice Robinson arrived in Savannah, the city was swept up in civil rights demonstrations. On the Sea Islands, postwar political organizing, traditions of mutual support, and connections to urban Charleston laid groundwork for citizenship schools. In Savannah, civil rights demonstrations in the spring of 1960 set the stage. The demonstrations tapped deep roots of organized protest. In 1906, black leaders sustained a nearly yearlong boycott of the city's streetcars, delaying passage of city ordinances until 1907. A decade later, black Savannahians organized an NAACP chapter and successfully blocked plans to relocate a red-light district into their community. When the chapter lapsed into inactivity during the Depression years, the Young Men's Civic Club launched a voter registration drive in 1938.[3] In the early 1940s, the Reverend Ralph Mark Gilbert rebuilt the NAACP chapter, directing voter registration drives, boycotts of downtown stores, and protest marches from the pulpit of First African Baptist Church. Young people joined the NAACP Youth Council, and in 1941, fifty Savannah State College students were arrested after refusing to move from whites-only seats on a city bus. Six years later, Youth Council president W. W. Law organized students in a protest of the city's segregated schools, and three years after that, Law was president of the NAACP branch, directing voter registration campaigns and organizing classes to "drill the people" on the required literacy test.[4] White backlash in the late 1940s and throughout the 1950s curtailed NAACP activities but did not destroy the infrastructure.

That infrastructure reignited in the spring of 1960 from sparks lit in Greensboro, North Carolina. On February 1, four black students who were enrolled at North Carolina Agricultural and Technical College refused to move from a whites-only lunch counter in the downtown Woolworth's store. From there, sit-ins "swept like brush fire," and in Savannah, the next generation of NAACP Youth Council members was ready. They faced new penalties as state lawmakers hurriedly amended trespassing laws, empowering police to arrest "sit-downers" and extending sentences to up to eighteen months' imprisonment and a $1,000 fine. Gov. Ernest Vandiver assured anxious Georgians that "the full resources of the state would be available to end any demonstrations [and] that local law enforcement could handle any such situations." In early March, a group of white Savannahians made additional preparations, organizing a Citizens Council chapter.[5] NAACP Youth Council members were determined to join the regional movement and secured support from the city's branch. The day before the annual Saint Patrick's Day celebration, three black students sat at the lunch counter in Levy's Department Store and held their ground as the waitress refused service. City police moved in and charged the trio with violating the "just passed state law."[6]

Former student activist Otis S. Johnson recalled that the sit-in released "the sense of injustice that was bubbling up" and jolted a citywide network into action.[7] When "sit-downers" appeared in court, black residents crowded into the small courtroom and overflowed into the hallway while another "sizeable crowd" gathered outside police headquarters. Judge George E. Oliver's declaration that Savannah was "a place of law and order" and a pledge to fine "those of either race causing any further trouble" failed to quell the movement. Within a week, police had arrested twenty-five "sit-downers."[8] Black doctors and businessmen posted bail while Law organized a campaign aimed at the city's shopping district, calling for picket lines, a boycott, and continued sit-ins at nightly mass meetings held at Bolton Street Baptist Church.[9]

Black women played critical roles in the movement. When ministers balked at hosting mass meetings because, as Law recalled, they "didn't want their church bombed" or they believed that "this is not saving souls," NAACP Women's Auxiliary members "with[held] their money from the collection plate" and spoke with ministers "in most uncertain terms." One by one, they opened the door to "Brother Law." The women's intervention ensured links between regular religious worship and political action. Johnson remembered, "We went to Sunday School at 10, 11–11:30 was morning service, then you came home and got something to eat, then you went to the NAACP meeting, went back and got a snack, went to church meeting.... So all day was church, you just put the NAACP in between." The Women's Auxiliary solved another problem when Mercedes Wright organized a committee to cull black residents' names from the city directory. They divided their new directory alphabetically and distributed copies among the committee members. After mass meetings, NAACP leaders passed on news and instructions to Virginia Mack, who relayed information to members who, in turn, called people in their assigned section. "That's how the word would get around," Law recalled.[10] This structure reinforced a gendered hierarchy where black men were in the public eye while black women's work took place out of public view. Local radio personality Bernita Bennette was an exception, routinely inviting local leaders to share updates on her programs, *Brunch with Bernita* and *Tomorrow's Leaders*.[11]

Hosea Williams later recalled his impatience with the NAACP's focus on direct action. "We [can] picket all we want. We [can] picket the courthouse. . . . We can sit-in, we can walk-in, we can kneel-in," he agreed, but "We are going to have to control our share of politics." A separate organization could effectively coordinate voter registration activities, he argued.[12] NAACP registration director John M. Brooks threw support behind the plan, and the local chapter created the CCCV, appointing Williams as director in early April 1960. Law allocated NAACP funds so that the CCCV would not "bog itself down in fundraising," setting strict rules to use funds for "actual registration and voter activities."[13] Williams had his own organization under Law's watchful eye.

Williams had always been an uneasy fit in Savannah's black urban middle class. He grew up across the state in rural Attapulgus near the Florida line. After serving in World War II, he used the G.I. Bill to earn a master's degree at Atlanta University. He married Juanita Terry and they moved to Savannah, where he worked for the U.S. Department of Agriculture and she taught at Spencer Elementary School. By 1960, Williams was a self-described "social climbin', middle class Negro." NAACP membership served as a marker of this status, but Williams chafed in Law's shadow. At mass meetings and on the radio, Williams built support for the CCCV through a personal narrative of daily humiliations and constant battle with Jim Crow.

He did not grow up in Savannah's middle class, he reminded audiences. Williams talked frankly about his unmarried parents and watching his grandparents toil "like slaves," beginning and ending the workday when "you cain't see your hand [in front of] your face." He recalled walking to school and moving aside for the school bus. "Every day . . . probably just my imagination, those white kids would spit on us or throw rocks at us, holler, and call us niggers," he recalled. Williams acknowledged that he no longer walked those dirt roads. He and Juanita were, by all accounts, middle class: two paychecks, professional employment, and a home in one of the city's best black neighborhoods; however, he could not "escape black America." He had money but still had to tell his young sons, "Naw, you cain't have a Coke and sandwich" when they went downtown. When the boys cried, Williams "couldn't tell 'em the truth [because] the truth was they was black and they didn't 'low black people to use them lunch counters." Williams described how he "picked the two kids up" and vowed to "bring 'em back someday." Reporter Archie Whitfield remembered Williams's speeches at the East Side Theater. "Man, you could just feel the tension in the place," he recalled. "You could see that he was recounting the experience of every black person in there."[14]

Through the CCCV, Williams expanded voter registration activities and mobilized new support for the growing movement. In June, funeral director Sidney A. Jones donated space for the CCCV's new office. NAACP funds kept the office open six days a week, and from this hub, Williams organized a base that Otis Johnson later described as "a cohort of real street level, grassroots kind of folk," many engaged through visits to pool halls in the city's segregated neighborhoods. Morris Brown College graduate Emogene Stroman accepted a job as the CCCV's full-time secretary. While Williams was the CCCV's public face, Stroman mastered the state's voter registration laws and doled out practical advice that demystified the process. She printed leaflets and prepared kits for block workers, led efforts to organize precincts, and recruited volunteers to transport prospective voters to the courthouse.[15] Stroman's work at the CCCV caught Bernice Robinson's attention, and in July, Stroman attended a citizenship school training workshop, "contributing much as a panelist," Robinson noted.[16]

Early Citizenship Education in Savannah

Highlander and the CCCV forged a relationship born out of necessity. The same month that Stroman attended the workshop, Highlander's executive council voted to appeal a lower court's decision to close the school. Horton split his attention between the ongoing court battle and sustaining funding streams. Savannah held the most promise, and Horton urged Robinson to intensify outreach because they needed "programs growing out of the Sea Island project as soon as possible."[17] Robinson returned to Savannah and in a whirlwind day, she and Stroman compiled a list of prospective Highlander participants and visited with CCCV board members to drum up support. Septima Clark and James Macanic accompanied Robinson on a return trip, and Clark confirmed, "Literacy is the immediate need."[18] In late November, Williams made his first trip to Monteagle and found acceptance that eluded him in the NAACP. Clark was impressed with Williams's "art of questioning" that "brought out many facets of the program that we took for granted" and recommended a "closer working relationship" with this "outstanding community leader." Horton and Williams agreed to open citizenship schools "on Highlander's terms," including materials for local schools and stipends for teaching-related costs.[19] Williams had resources independent of the NAACP, and Horton had tangible evidence of the program's expansion.

In the first week of December, Clark phoned the Williams home and was "shocked" at the news that classes had not started. Echoing earlier advice to Esau Jenkins, Clark advised Williams to delegate and "get some leaders trained to do some of the things you are forced to do now."[20] By the end of the month, citizenship schools were under way. On the west side, thirty students attended Stroman's classes at the CCCV office while Williams opened a school on the east side of town. Stroman and Williams determined that a schedule suited to Johns Island farm laborers was not a good fit in urban Savannah. Attendance at in-town classes was inconsistent throughout December, and after the first of the year, they consolidated and moved the class to Butler Presbyterian Church. At the end of three months, attendance had improved and forty-eight students registered to vote. In urban Savannah, citizenship schools served a broader purpose. Makeshift classrooms were intimate spaces, a rarity in an urban environment and within a local movement built on public demonstrations. Stroman's and Williams's students continued to gather after the school's three-month time frame because as they told Clark, "The 'Each one Teach one' idea" caught on and "has drawn us closer together." They were planning a family social "to know each other" and believed they "developed something wonderful."[21]

Juanita Williams enlisted help from high school student Carolyn Roberts for a citizenship school in the Burroughs-Canebrake community. Located

58 · The Citizenship Education Program and Black Women's Political Culture

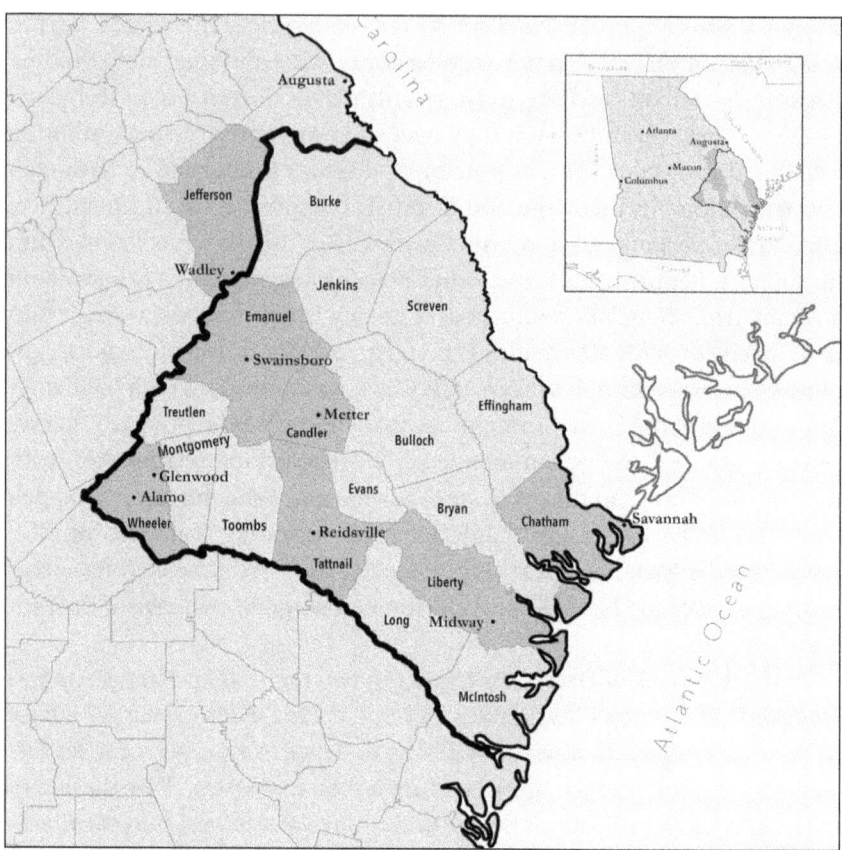

Map 2. Georgia's First Congressional District, ca. 1960. © Bruno Berry.

outside the city limits in rural Chatham County, Burroughs-Canebrake was more like Johns Island than urban Savannah. Citizenship schools were needed because as Hosea Williams reported, "Only about one in ten is employed. . . . The average child stops school at about the sixth or seventh grade." Residents owned "a lot of land, good land," which was proving to be a double-edged sword because as on the Sea Islands, "the white people would like to get hold of the land," he wrote. From December to March, thirty-two students, ranging in age from eighteen to sixty-five, attended classes at the local school. Although winters were relatively mild in southern Georgia, a "worn out wood stove" proved inadequate and during cold snaps, half of the class stayed home. At the end of three months, Hosea Williams reported that twenty-six students registered to vote and twenty students organized a laundry cooperative "to develop some type of industry of their own . . . to give them some jobs and bring some money into the area." For the students, citizenship school lessons illuminated a path to political empowerment and economic stability for individual families and for the entire community. Williams credited the school with inspiring "the first time any initiative has been shown by Negroes in this area."[22] Between October 1960 and February 1961, citizenship schools like the one in Burroughs-Canebrake operated alongside other voter registration activities, resulting in nine thousand newly registered African American voters.[23]

Early Citizenship Education in Southeastern Georgia

Williams believed that citizenship schools could be an opening wedge into rural counties, and on evenings and weekends he crisscrossed the nineteen counties in Georgia's First Congressional District.[24] In these trips, Williams confronted different histories of segregation and resistance. In black-majority coastal counties, black voter registration rates were as high as 50 percent, largely as a result of local initiatives like the one in Liberty County, where local people organized an NAACP chapter in the early 1950s and elected sawmill owner Ralph Quarterman as president. With support from black school administrators, teachers taught night school where residents could earn a high school diploma and learn to "read the material and get their voter registration cards" and "conduct their own business." Coupled with relatively moderate county leadership, these efforts opened the door for African American registration, and by 1958, they accounted for over half of the county's voters.[25] In the spring of 1960, Quarterman tested the strength of this black electorate in his bid for a commissioner-at-large position. He liked his chances. The sawmill business offered protection from direct economic reprisal, and a number of black voters had similar protection through federal employment at Fort Stewart, a military base sprawling across Liberty County and neighboring Long County. On Election Day, "the largest percentage of voters to participate in an election in Liberty County" flooded polling places. White voters united behind one candidate and Quarterman lost by 722 votes.[26] By the time of Williams's visit, Quarterman served as W. W. Law's vice president of the state NAACP.

Rural inland counties told different stories. In the 1940s, state laws blunted protest and voter registration activities in urban Savannah while Klan night riders did the work in outlying areas and memories of organizers like Dover Carter, Isaac Nixon, and Robert Mallard remained fresh. In 1946, Carter organized an NAACP chapter in Montgomery County, and within two years, six hundred African Americans registered to vote. Ignoring threats, Carter transported black voters to cast ballots in the state's 1948 Democratic primary. At the same time, Nixon voted in neighboring Toombs County. Klansmen Johnnie Johnson and his brother-in-law Thomas Wilson assaulted Carter, and that same evening, Nixon was shot on his front porch, managing to accuse Johnson and his brother Jim before he died. Two months later, an all-white jury acquitted the Johnson brothers, and by early 1949, the NAACP helped the Carter family move north. Citizenship school teacher Greta Rhynes remembered northern-born Robert Mallard, who married a local girl and opened "civil rights classes" in rural Tattnall County, and she remembered his ambush in November 1948. When the Mallards came home from church, "these people lay in wait along the road and dragged him out of his car and killed [him]," she recounted. According to Rhynes, Mallard's murder served the intended purpose because civil rights organizing "died right down . . . and didn't flare up again until the 1960s."[27]

Memories of these events likely influenced the outcome of a more recent statewide voter registration drive. Ahead of 1957 state elections, Atlanta NAACP branch president John H. Calhoun united NAACP chapters, the Masonic Lodge's Georgia Voters League, and the Georgia Teachers and Education Association (GTEA) into one "non-partisan, political organization." He divided the state into ten districts, engaged organizers in more than seventy of the state's 159 counties, and urged local leaders to set aside "old rivalries, partisan politics, and personal differences" for all-out door-to-door registration drives. In October, Calhoun documented a net gain of five thousand voters, or 3 percent, across the state. Calhoun pointed to two reasons for disappointing results: "General lethargy on the part of potential voters" and the state's "legal purges for failure to vote in two years," which forced organizers to expend energy and resources just to "hold ground already gained."[28]

Williams believed that citizenship schools might address what Calhoun called "general lethargy." In intimate spaces out of the public eye, friends and neighbors could organize communities and urge voter registration. In December, Williams drummed up support with an invitation that read like a carnival barker's advertisement. "We have a NEW program and NEW ways of carrying out this program that will make you the most honored and respected leader in your county by both black and white citizens," Williams pledged. The program represented "modern leadership" and was something "that all good people have wanted for years." Williams closed with an urgent call: "BE THE FIRST TO BRING THIS COMMUNITY LEADERSHIP TO YOUR TOWN AND COUNTY."[29] Fifty-four representatives from five counties gathered in early January to hear Myles Horton outline Highlander's offer, and by the end of the meeting, they united as the Southeastern Georgia Crusade for Voters (SGCV). Using Chatham County as a model, SGCV affiliates agreed to identify ten to twelve local people to serve as teachers and supervisors and to cover costs associated with local schools and teacher training workshops.[30]

David J. Norwood spearheaded efforts in Tattnall County. A veteran of the Georgia Voters League, he had canvassed the county and knew that few black residents could pass the literacy test. A revised test adopted in 1958 only made the questions harder.[31] Norwood recognized that Highlander's offer would address this problem, and he knew who to ask to teach local classes. He and the Ealeys attended church together, so Norwood knew that their twenty-one-year-old daughter Pearlie was back at home. Norwood told her about the citizenship school program and urged her to go to Highlander. The invitation came as Pearlie Ealey was at a crossroads. In 1955, she had graduated as valedictorian at Collins Colored High School and moved to Cincinnati to live with an aunt and uncle because, as she recalled, "there were no jobs around here and I was tired of picking cotton." Living in Cincinnati took her out of cotton fields and into domestic work, but she was homesick. By 1957, her father had suffered several strokes and was unable to work so she came back home. "I did domestic work and things like that," she recalled. "I did work in tobacco a little, but . . . I wasn't picking any more cotton." In 1960, her father passed away and Ealey was deciding whether to stay in Collins or return to Cincinnati. In February 1961, she joined a ten-member, four-county contingent of prospective teachers and supervisors for a teacher training workshop at Highlander.[32]

At the workshop, Ealey and fellow participants learned "the citizenship school method" directly from Bernice Robinson, who passed on recruiting strategies and methods to assess adult students' skills, teach basic literacy in the context of voter registration, and relate lessons to students' everyday lives. Co-leader James L. Macanic encouraged teachers to get students out of the classroom to political and civic meetings. After Ealey and the others departed, Robinson and Macanic assessed this first group recruited through Williams's expanded SGCV network. Macanic noted that participants needed "fundamental training in simple subjects such as reading, writing, and spelling," though some "are better prepared than the others." Robinson recommended "more training for the four men recruited as supervisors," acknowledging that "being known" in their home counties would "serve well for recruiting."[33]

Like Septima Clark's earlier outreach into northern Alabama, expansion into rural southeastern Georgia tested the citizenship school program. On the Sea Islands, Clark and Robinson recruited teachers through personal relationships and Lowcountry networks. They shared common bonds with Ethel Grimball and Allene Brewer. All had professional training, and all were active members of civic associations, dedicated to community service, and steeped in a politics of respectability. Robinson's outreach to Savannah took her into unfamiliar territory, but she had forged relationships with Williams and Stroman before they arrived at Highlander. In contrast, the rural southeastern Georgia volunteers were strangers. Compounding the problem, Williams did not know the teachers and supervisors either. The southeastern Georgia contingent started from a different point as well. Sea Islands teachers were active in local civic organizations and brought professional skills and expertise to citizenship classes. Teachers recruited from rural southeastern Georgia would develop expertise by doing, which required a different level of support. In addition, they came from counties where the NAACP had failed to take root and the SGCV was attempting to plant new seeds.

Robinson's comments about the Georgia supervisors highlighted different interpretations of the citizenship school's purpose, differences rooted in gendered and racialized constructions of leadership. Williams grafted citizenship schools onto a growing region-wide network modeled on the NAACP. As a result, he conflated the role of citizenship school supervisor with director of a county-level political action group. In Williams's view, and the view of men recruited into the SGCV, this public position was reserved for a race man. Teaching, on the other hand, was "women's work" that happened behind the scenes; therefore, black women were assigned to organize and teach citizenship schools. Clark and Robinson agreed with Williams's gendered interpretation of the ideal citizenship school teacher but disagreed with the hierarchy emerging within the SGCV. Citizenship school teachers were not intended to be a women's auxiliary for a male-led organization. Instead, they were recognized leaders, and teaching conferred further authority and expertise. Supervisors emerged from within the cadre of teachers, earning the role based on classroom skill and expertise.

Following the workshop, Robinson, Clark, and Anne Lockwood took steps to address these emerging problems. They revised workshop sessions and training materials to spell out teachers' and supervisors' duties and to add more "demonstration classes" where participants were "actually teaching."[34] Clark clarified the program's criteria for teachers: "Our experiment has proven that a housewife, a beautician, a seamstress, a businesswoman or woman with a high school education or less formal training can . . . teach or supervise the adult education program," she wrote. "In short, a degree-mind but not necessarily a person with a degree"; instead "some formal skill, a great dedication to the cause, and patience" were primary qualifications.[35] The revised description encapsulated Clark's gendered vision of the program, most clearly reflected in the concrete examples. Using this list, local people would connect citizenship schools with women's roles in local communities. The list would also ensure that newly recruited teachers shared characteristics with the cadre teaching classes on the Sea Islands and in Charleston. Local women did not need degrees to qualify because formal education was not as important as an ability to read, write, and organize. "Dedication to the cause" preserved Clark's adherence to earlier constructions of black womanhood that emphasized a life in service to community well-being and uplift, a model she had embodied in her early teaching days.[36]

Citizenship school teachers like Ethel Grimball and Allene Brewer arrived with impressive credentials and embodied the gendered role that Clark described. For teachers like Pearlie Ealey, citizenship school training and teaching served as orientation to the assigned role. Ealey did not make much of an impression on Robinson, who assessed her as simply "OK" at the end of the Highlander workshop. For Ealey, however, the experience was transformative. She later reflected, "Now I wasn't that brave . . . because . . . I remember Emmett Till . . . so it wasn't that I was that brave. But once I got to that school [and] when I left there, it took some of the fear out of me." Teaching citizenship schools instilled purpose and delivered a strategy suited to rural communities like Collins. This was not organizing a sit-in or a march through the town square; this was gathering with friends and neighbors in a familiar place. Citizenship schools were also well suited for young women like Ealey who excelled in school only to confront limited and frustrating prospects in places too far removed from urban Savannah. The structured citizenship school curriculum provided a model for community service, and teacher training instilled confidence. As Ealey taught local classes, "then more of [the fear] left. And courage kind of took its place," she recalled.[37]

Ealey displayed newfound courage when she and Norwood went to the courthouse to review the list of black registered voters. "It still was segregated," she emphasized, "but you know they let us see that list." With 17 percent of eligible black voters registered, Tattnall County was considered moderate compared to neighboring Toombs County, where only 3 percent were registered. Greta Rhynes recalled Toombs County black voters being taunted by white bystanders shouting, "Y'all go back home and go to work. You got no business up here." From Tattnall County, Ealey and her fellow CEP teachers chronicled the complex web working against black voters. The literacy test was the primary obstacle because many African Americans could not read or sign their names legibly. Greta Rhynes and Mary Lois Byrd added "lack of knowledge" and "they . . . make us wait" to the list. Rhynes remembered on that on election days, "People would just sit outside the polling place to watch and see who all went in." In a rural county where African Americans made up 32 percent of the population and 55 percent of black farm laborers worked on tenant contracts, white folks sitting at the polling place was enough to send black voters back home. Ealey recalled that white employers and politicians encouraged some African Americans to vote because "they wanted them to vote for them a lot of times." According to Rhynes, a pernicious cynicism set in: year after year without positive results and black voters believed that officials were "not going to do nothing but tear up [ballots] and throw them out." Ealey's father voted every Election Day but Rhynes's parents eventually stopped, telling their daughter, "Why go? They not going to count your vote no how." In nearby Bryan County, citizenship school teachers Eddie Gardner and E. D. Ritter documented the use of "unrequired tests," helping to ensure that only 29 percent of the county's eligible black voters successfully registered.[38]

At Norwood's request, Ealey organized citizenship schools at Saint Phillip Baptist Church in Reidsville and at Mount Olive Baptist Church closer to home in Collins. She held classes in local churches for pragmatic reasons. Churches had space, materials, and access to congregations. Often ensconced within black communities, these spaces offered some protection because as Rhynes recalled, "They kept it to themselves. . . . That was our business and our church." Ealey and her fellow citizenship school teachers also believed that meeting in churches could downplay affiliation with the SGCV and the "subversive" Highlander Folk School. Finally, citizenship schools in churches replicated a recognizable model of community work where women taught Sunday school and served on women's auxiliaries. Local teachers like Ealey could be viewed as, and present themselves as, respectable churchgoing women performing God's work for the collective good, disguising the political nature of their work. The protection only stretched so far, however. Ealey recalled friends and neighbors warning her before her first class. "They just went through Reidsville and they put up signs talking about Ku Klux Klan," they told her and asked, "You going over there?" Ealey boldly responded, "Yeah, I'm going over there, why not?" By "going," she enacted lessons from Highlander, demonstrating first-class citizenship through action and serving as a compelling example.[39]

Citizenship school teachers on the Sea Islands had confronted generational legacies of under-resourced segregated schools, and teachers in rural southeastern Georgia reported similar experiences. In Cobbtown, a seventy-year-old Mr. Johnson confided, "I never had [anybody] to teach me," but under Rhynes's instruction, he learned to sign his name "legible, where there'd be no excuse [for the clerk] to . . . throw it out." In Reidsville, Ealey helped William Bryant "form his letters for the first time because he could only make an X. And he learned to read." Like Robinson's first class at the Progressive Club, Tattnall County citizenship schools served as gathering places for more than basic reading and math instruction. Curiosity about the new meetings brought people through Ealey's door. Once inside, "we kind of sold them on the idea," she recalled. "Even those that didn't need to learn to read and write . . . were encouraged to vote. . . . [We] just covered everything."[40] Rhynes and Ealey demonstrated that the model developed and honed on the Sea Islands could be transferred to other rural communities with similar results.

As schools spread across southeastern Georgia, Clark tailored the citizenship school workbook for Georgia students so that it "fit the students they were designed to serve." She added a half-page description of the SGCV that strategically aligned the organization with the citizenship school's three main goals: increased voter registration, leadership development, and community improvement. Georgia's election law required correct answers to twenty out of thirty "rather difficult" questions. Clark reprinted all questions so that students practiced literacy skills while rehearsing for registration. The revised workbook included other "important innovations" that became standard features, including instructions on writing a friendly letter, introductory and advanced arithmetic problems, and lessons on good manners and being polite.[41] The revised workbook more explicitly articulated a construction of "first class citizenship" couched in bourgeois middle-class respectability. New etiquette lessons reflected beliefs that political rights should be conferred to those who were educated and demonstrated good moral judgment and civic responsibility. Citizenship school students qualified for first-class citizenship because they demonstrated these qualities. The schools challenged racist beliefs that African Americans could not learn, could not understand, and were uninterested in politics. While lessons did not challenge underlying assumptions about respectability and "first class" citizenship rights, in citizenship schools, students gained skills and knowledge in order to register to vote. This was not a promise of eventual acceptance by a white-dominated society. This was empowerment to erase markers of second-class citizenship.[42]

Managing the Expanding Program

The citizenship school program had firm footholds in southeastern Georgia by the spring of 1961; however, expansion increasingly ran counter to Horton's attempts to scale back Highlander's administrative responsibilities. Huntsville-area and Sea Islands schools were operating independent of Highlander, and Horton urged Hosea Williams to do the same.[43] Williams scrambled to find a solution. The CCCV remained financially dependent on the NAACP chapter, and an ongoing boycott was rapidly depleting reserves.[44] The chapter had scant resources to support city-based citizenship schools and was not inclined to fund schools organized outside of Savannah. The newly organized SGCV did not have the proper tax status to receive grants from foundations. When Williams asked for assistance, Horton threw him a lifeline, securing a grant from the Schwarzhaupt Foundation that worked in both Horton's and Williams's favor by paying for teacher training at the folk school and providing funds to support schools opening across the First Congressional District. Horton assured foundation officials that the arrangement was temporary until "the [SGCV] is in a position to sustain . . . on a fully self-supporting basis."[45]

Horton shored up the SGCV program amidst staffing changes at Highlander. Discussions about an assistant for Clark started after she suffered a second heart attack in four years. In March 1961, Robinson accepted the position where she and Clark would "take over full responsibilities of running this [citizenship school] program."[46] Hiring Robinson alongside the ongoing negotiations with the SCLC fit into Horton's plans to position Highlander for "what is likely to be a real social movement." While Clark convalesced in Charleston, Horton launched a "New Staff Member Crusade," identifying several promising candidates that included James Forman, John Lewis, and Andrew J. Young, all young African American men. The list sent a clear message. Clark and Robinson were well qualified to run teacher training sessions but were not suitable to be Highlander's face in the "real social movement." From Horton's perspective, black men were leading the movement, and he intended to hire a young man who could build bridges between Highlander and civil rights organizations like the SCLC. At the April staff meeting, in Clark's absence, Horton announced that Young had accepted the position as "executive for the Citizenship Committee," effective September 1.[47]

Originally from New Orleans, twenty-eight-year-old Young was at the National Council of the Churches of Christ (NCCC) in New York. A Congregationalist minister, he caught Horton's attention when he conducted a Bible study at Highlander in February 1961. Horton's offer came as Young "had about enough 'church work' and [was] anxious to do the work of the church." The Highlander position would bring him back south where he anticipated adding "a little theological perspective" and bridging what he saw as a gap between "the 'classes' and the masses." As he understood the position, Clark and Robinson would head efforts to teach "literacy, voting laws, community participation at its lowest level" to "illiterate, underprivileged Negroes" in the "grammar school approach for adults," and Young would complement this with a "high school and college level" program to engage "educated Negroes [who] are still at a very low level of citizenship and social responsibility."[48]

In late April, news from the Field Foundation reconfigured plans. Officials approved Horton's latest grant proposal but stipulated that "money could not be used for workshops at Highlander because of the present insecurity of the school's tax exemption status." The decision threatened to disrupt carefully made plans with the SCLC, which did not have the proper tax-exempt status to receive grant funds. Field's executive director suggested that Horton identify an organization to act as a fiscal agent, willing to manage the grant for the SCLC. Anticipating a need to relocate training workshops, Young negotiated use of the Congregational Church's Dorchester Academy in southeastern Georgia.[49] At Highlander, bad news kept coming. In early May, the Tennessee Supreme Court upheld the lower court's order to revoke the school's charter. In Clark's absence and through Young's connections, Horton and Wood forged an agreement with Herman Long, director of the Race Relations Division of the United Church Board of Homeland Missions (UCBHM). The UCBHM agreed to manage Field funds for the SCLC and to facilitate access to Dorchester. Wesley Hotchkiss, general secretary of the American Missionary Association

(AMA), would now oversee Field-financed portions of the citizenship school program.[50] Clark's salary would come from the Field grant, which put her on the UCBHM payroll assigned to the SCLC full time. Robinson's position was more precarious as Horton made plans to pay her through the SGCV's Schwarzhaupt grant, one of the few funding streams flowing into Highlander. The agreement threatened to dissolve Clark and Robinson's partnership as Clark headed to the SCLC office in Atlanta while Robinson remained in Monteagle to "develop the Citizenship classes not financed by the Field Foundation."[51]

The news arrived as Clark and Robinson prepared for a refresher workshop hastily relocated to Dorchester. They set aside anxieties about ongoing negotiations to run a "very successful workshop" with teachers from southeastern Georgia. Teachers reported that they adjusted the December-to-March time frame and opened classes in May. End-of-school-year activities had interfered with attendance, but teachers expected improvement into the summer months. Training session discussions revealed the teachers' sophisticated understanding of entangled economic and political dynamics in rural counties. They had expected resistance from white people who "don't want us to learn that a black child is worth just as much as a white child"; however, some of the strongest opposition came from within black communities as the new program threatened a delicate balance of power. In Candler County, the public school superintendent accused a local teacher of "bringing in outsiders [that] will cause people to get killed" and insisted that she close her citizenship school. When she refused, the superintendent organized competing classes where high school teachers would teach "only reading and writing." Other citizenship school teachers described interference from ministers and "educated Negroes" who, in the teachers' opinions, benefited from the status quo by "bowing and scraping, and living in fear." Clark again noted that rural Georgia counties did not have the network of "civic organizations where the adult students can belong," and as a result, the "civic leader," in this case the citizenship school teacher, "must get busy and form a group" to expand the school's influence beyond the makeshift classroom.[52]

Clark and Robinson likely discussed developments at Highlander while at Dorchester, and three days after their return to Charleston, they fired off a letter to Horton with copies to Wood, Long, and King. They insisted on "work[ing] together while training, regardless of who pays who," because "it was planned this way in the beginning." Clark flatly declared, "We refuse to be swapped around like horses." "We need each other," they implored. Daylong teacher training sessions "[put] a great bit of strain on one person." Incensed at being shut out of negotiations, they wrote, "We don't think anyone can plan *for* us, but *with* us." In late May, both Clark and Robinson had completed the exam to join the Peace Corps, and they reminded Horton that the door was still open.[53]

Unsettled negotiations tested relationships. Horton assured Robinson that he had "done everything" to keep the pair together and advised her to contact the SCLC if she did not want to remain at Highlander. "We are not concerned about the separation of salary," Robinson explained, "only the separation of services." She and Clark had built the program and forged a productive partnership.[54] Creating, managing, expanding, and refining the citizenship school program marked the culmination of years of professional development and community service. In addition, Clark and Robinson believed that the program was making a difference. Separation threatened to undermine all of this. Attempts to repair damage with Clark depended on the SCLC, and in the absence of a firm agreement, she directed anger at Horton. "I've been a working woman for years and accustomed to taking care of myself," she wrote. "I am not a clinging vine." However, despite repeated assurances that the SCLC welcomed her, Wood had not made contact, which she took as a sign of disrespect. Her sense of betrayal bled through as she confessed, "I think you did not want to tell me that you did not want me anymore but I'd rather have you say it to me than have others treat me so inhuman." She reminded Horton that if he did not want her, the Peace Corps did, and her move to the SCLC was far from certain.[55]

The other staff member caught in the storm had yet to arrive in Monteagle, and as negotiations reached a fever pitch, Young shared "feeble thoughts" from New York. He was anxious about Highlander's "court situation" but even more anxious about where he was going. Horton and Wood floated suggestions to locate Young at Highlander, close by in Nashville, at the SCLC's Atlanta office, or farther south at the Dorchester Center. Bewildered and with a wife and two young children to support, Young reminded Horton, "I have resigned as of September 1st. It would be helpful to know where I'm going." His fate was decided at the same time as Clark's and Robinson's. Young would join Clark on the UCBHM payroll with a full-time assignment with the SCLC, presumably as Clark's boss. For Clark, the UCBHM and the SCLC were unknowns. For Young, the UCBHM was home, and he wrote to "Wes" Hotchkiss "really enthusiastic about the possibilities." Housing the citizenship school program within the SCLC broke with the "avowed secularism of Highlander," and Young saw "no reason why S.C.L.C. and the A.M.A. should not cultivate the spiritual potential of this program."[56]

Throughout the summer, the SGCV's fate also hung in the balance as time ticked away on the six-month Schwarzhaupt grant. In early July, an anxious Williams wrote, "I trust an immediate decision will be reached. It certainly would help if we knew the destiny of our program." Adding urgency to his appeal, Williams reminded Horton, "Without additional funds it will be necessary to close out some of our schools." By mid-July, Williams had his answer. The SCLC would allocate Field funds to cover the SGCV's teacher training expenses, keeping Williams's program alive. The Schwarzhaupt grant expired in August, and Horton officially closed out Highlander's commitments.[57] With that, Williams turned his attention to the SCLC, a move that would take the SGCV farther away from the NAACP.

* * *

As the dust settled, Clark and Robinson could take pride in keeping the citizenship school program operating through six difficult months. By the fall of 1961, Highlander-trained teachers continued the program in the South Carolina Lowcountry and had opened schools in southeastern Georgia, western Tennessee, and Huntsville and Montgomery, Alabama. In all, the schools enrolled 1,500 people, resulting in over seven hundred newly registered voters.[58] The transfer to the SCLC left mixed emotions. They would work from different places, and new staff members meant that the citizenship schools were no longer "their program." However, the transfer resolved the administrative issues destabilizing the growing program. Citizenship schools were no longer affiliated with an organization under direct state and federal scrutiny; instead, the program found a new home in an organization grounded in the African American church and the nonviolent movement sweeping across the South. The Field Foundation and the UBCHM provided financial and administrative security while allowing for relative autonomy within a new and dynamic organization.

During this same six months, citizenship schools began as an experiment in Savannah-area neighborhoods and expanded into Georgia's First Congressional District. In Savannah, citizenship schools operated within a dynamic movement headed by the city's NAACP chapter. Under Hosea Williams's leadership, the Chatham County Crusade for Voters placed voter registration as a primary objective. For Williams, the CCCV opened an avenue to build an organization and engage a constituency independent of the city's NAACP branch. Through the connection to Highlander, Williams gained access to a program suited to the CCCV's goals and to resources that were not tied to the NAACP. Highlander staff members encouraged Williams and gave legitimacy to his efforts. The CCCV and NAACP fueled Savannah's movement as the rivalry between Williams and Law intensified.

Beginning with a few schools in Savannah, citizenship schools spread to surrounding rural counties. In the city, the schools served as an alternative to direct action protest and met needs for connection and community. Outside of Savannah, the Southeastern Georgia Crusade for Voters laid groundwork for new claims to first-class citizenship. Early efforts pointed to tangible results. Through their work, Tattnall County teachers created gathering spaces where local people replaced an X with a name and discussed the issues that directly affected their lives. In Canebrake-Burroughs, citizenship school classes provided the impetus for a self-help cooperative business that could break dependence on white employers. Students were not the only ones to benefit. With teaching seen as "women's work," citizenship schools drew women into the SGCV. Trained educators like Juanita Williams transferred skills and talents into makeshift classrooms while the program served as training ground for a new generation of leaders like Pearlie Ealey and Greta Rhynes, who honed skills as they taught. By July 1961, Bernice Robinson revised her assessment of Ealey, remarking that "with a little more grooming," the CEP teacher would be ready to train teachers.[59] In turn, rural Georgia teachers influenced the citizenship schools' evolution. Clark and Robinson adapted the student workbook for a new audience and refined teacher training workshops to allow for more rehearsal for local classes. Southeastern Georgia contingents also forced attention on gendered and class-based dynamics within communities, issues that foretold challenges ahead.

4

"Say It Is for Citizenship"

Citizenship Education in Southeastern Georgia, 1961–1964

Septima Clark and Bernice Robinson had grown accustomed to summers spent in and out of the Highlander Folk School, but in July and August 1961, they turned south for the shorter drive to McIntosh, Georgia, and the Dorchester Academy, where they made quick preparations for citizenship school teachers arriving from Georgia, Louisiana, and Virginia. Even in a new space, the workshop followed a now-familiar pattern. In interactive sessions, Clark and Robinson passed on lessons learned from experience. When recruiting students, they recommended, "Never say that the School is only for those who can't read and write, but say it is for citizenship," and connect all lessons to the voter registration process. They demonstrated how to teach handwriting skills by having students trace their own names, just as Robinson did in the back room of the Progressive Club. Use the registration laws as reading lessons, they encouraged. The five-day schedule allowed for open discussion, practice sessions, and interaction with experienced organizers, effectively transferring "the citizenship school method" to a new setting.[1]

Clark and Robinson worked to ensure continuity, but the citizenship school was changing. An invitation to affiliate with the Southern Christian Leadership Conference (SCLC) replaced Highlander-focused materials, signaling a transition to a new home. Relocating to the Dorchester Academy situated teacher training in a region rife with political activity, and Clark and Robinson capitalized on opportunities to include local people and their expertise. In July, Esau Jenkins was on hand to advise on voter registration strategies, and newly elected justices of the peace Earl M. Baggs and James Smith described how they had waited until "the last minute" before filing election paperwork in neighboring McIntosh and Riceboro. White candidates were unable to quickly respond, and both men ran unopposed and won. In August, workshop participants traveled to Collins where they got a firsthand look at a citizenship school in session. Teachers returning for a refresher workshop lent hands-on support to a struggling local teacher and stayed to teach a reading lesson from the Georgia election laws.²

Noticeable changes in the teacher training curriculum reflected broader program changes. Securing the renamed Citizenship Education Program (CEP) within the American Missionary Association (AMA) persuaded the Field Foundation to increase its investment. In the fall of 1961, funding from the Southern Regional Council's Voter Education Project (VEP) fueled further expansion. The move to the SCLC severed ties with the secular and increasingly troubled Highlander Folk School and situated the CEP within established church-based networks and within a growing non-violent movement where civil rights action was not disreputable rabble-rousing; instead, it was enacting Christian principles and duty.³ The move to the SCLC recast CEP classes in this mold, as service to a greater moral cause. Black women drawn into the movement by Dr. Martin Luther King Jr.'s oratory and charisma found a clearly defined role within the male-dominated SCLC. The call to service resonated through church-based networks, and local ministers and black women answered. Black churchgoing women's active participation conferred respectability to the CEP. For those not directly connected to a church, serving in an SCLC-sponsored program conferred status and respectability.

This chapter intertwines the CEP's programmatic changes with local action in southeastern Georgia where Hosea Williams leveraged the SCLC affiliation to expand reach across Georgia's First Congressional District. Supported by CEP and VEP funds, Williams broke with the NAACP, and by the fall of 1962, the Southeastern Georgia Crusade for Voters (SGCV) was an independent regional grassroots network built on a distinctly gendered hierarchy.⁴ In the CEP, this meant that "women's work" was largely unseen. Across the region, black women organized classes where they sparked discussions about the nature of citizenship and translated this abstract concept into individual achievement. These lessons sowed seeds for collective action through county-level voter registration and community improvement leagues. Their work sunk roots for local political organization across a rural district and in urban neighborhoods.

The Citizenship School Program Moves to the SCLC

Into the summer of 1961, the CEP moved to the SCLC, and it fell to Septima Clark and Bernice Robinson to navigate new relationships from different places. Robinson remained at Highlander, reasoning that this would reserve grant funds for teacher training and support.[5] Clark was officially assigned to the SCLC, and although she maintained her home in Charleston, she traveled frequently to Atlanta and to the Dorchester Academy, forging relationships and adapting to an organization of strong-minded ministers. A familiar face helped to ease the transition. Clark met Dorothy F. Cotton at Highlander's experimental workshop in January 1961, where Cotton received a crash course in the citizenship school program. Throughout the summer, Cotton carved out a niche in the training workshop, inviting participating organizations to affiliate with the SCLC and lending her voice to group singing that opened and closed each day.

Cotton came to the SCLC by way of Petersburg, Virginia, where she had joined local demonstrations organized by the Reverend Wyatt Tee Walker. Inspired by Walker's call to "take the gospel to the streets," Cotton picketed at the public library, and by early 1960, Walker asked her to train volunteers for picket lines at downtown department stores. At home, she was "restless," unsatisfied with a routine of work in the Virginia State University library and "keeping house" for husband George Cotton. When Walker agreed to be the SCLC's new executive director, he invited Cotton to come to Atlanta as his administrative assistant, and she accepted. In those early months, she was mired in Walker's letter-writing campaign to drum up support for the SCLC. A conversation with Martin Luther King Jr. offered a way out when King asked Cotton to represent the organization at Highlander.[6] By the summer, Cotton was the SCLC's liaison to the citizenship school program.

Clark and Cotton broke the ice at Dorchester workshops while Andrew Young was in and out as he closed out responsibilities in New York, officially arriving in Atlanta in early September. Clark was optimistic in the early days, remarking that the move "meant little more than a change in my base of operations" because the SCLC's "program . . . is almost identical to Highlander."[7] Young was hired as the CEP's executive secretary, and Clark served as educational director with Cotton named educational consultant. Although Young was Clark's and Cotton's supervisor, he quickly established a "non-hierarchical staff structure" to cultivate a collaborative working relationship. Young admired Cotton's experience with direct action campaigns and respected Clark's long teaching career and role in creating the citizenship school program.[8] Hoping to head off problems, he reached out to Clark in early summer for advice about "your Citizenship School program" and "my part of the program."[9]

Thirty years their senior, Clark assumed a mentoring role with Cotton and Young. Cotton's early recruiting efforts in Virginia fizzled when after letters, phone calls, and appeals at meetings, none of the recruits attended the training workshop. "I am impatient," she confessed to Clark. "I simply cannot see why many . . . have not caught the enthusiasm I feel." "Don't give up," Clark encouraged. "Keep trying. Recruiting is not an easy job." Young required a different kind of mentoring. Clark later recalled that he "had a hard time adjusting to working with people who were so poor," and at times, she bluntly pointed out blind spots. When Young arrived for a workshop by chartered plane and headed straight for the Dorchester kitchen, Clark reminded him that their road-weary volunteers were hungry too. When he snapped that there was no money for breakfast, Clark advised that he should not eat if there was not enough for all because participants saw everything and "what you are doing is not wise."[10]

Before integrating the CEP into the SCLC, they needed to clarify relationships with Horton and Highlander. The transfer had sidelined Horton, and the folk school's precarious situation heightened tensions. With the Monteagle property under threat of closure, the Hortons and the remaining staff moved operations to the renamed Highlander Research and Education Center in Knoxville.[11] For Horton, sustaining the folk school's role in training CEP teachers would secure one of their few remaining funding streams. In September, he reached out to Wesley Hotchkiss, proposing an arrangement similar to the SCLC where the AMA would serve as a conduit for Field Foundation funds to Highlander. The citizenship program stood to benefit, he argued, because Anne Lockwood and Bernice Robinson could consult with the SCLC, ensuring continuity in the program. His second wife, Aimee Isgrig Horton, was a well-qualified researcher, Horton added, and he humbly suggested that he "might be useful as an educational consultant." "We will probably otherwise be unemployed in a few months," he reminded Hotchkiss. Before Hotchkiss responded, Highlander's fate was sealed a month later when the U.S. Supreme Court rejected Horton's appeal. State officials rushed to auction off the Monteagle property, and the Hortons and the remaining staff scrambled to remove folk school records and personal belongings.[12]

Correspondence throughout the fall confirmed that the CEP was moving on without Highlander. "We miss Bernice," Young wrote to Horton, but

"Septima has me and Dorothy teaching" at Dorchester workshops. The CEP staff staked out space in the SCLC office, and "as soon as we learn to quit talking to each other, we'll be able to get a lot of work done," Young joked.[13] Horton fought to keep Highlander tied to the CEP, reminding Young about earlier agreements requiring a supervisory committee, but Young saw things differently. With the CEP folded into the SCLC, a committee of external supervisors would overcomplicate program management, he explained and begged off Horton's invitation to visit. "It is taking all of our efforts to . . . recruit, train and supervise 240 people and schools," Young wrote, and the meaning was clear: the CEP was steering away from Horton and Highlander.[14] Horton tried to revive the Citizenship School Committee again in January and April, but to no avail. In late 1961, the new Highlander Center opened to "difficulties and opposition from the local John Birchers," but Horton and the staff drew support from Knoxville's black community and faculty at the University of Tennessee. Robinson opened a new outpost for the citizenship school program through the Associated Council, the city's organization of black churches, fraternities, and sororities. She operated a citizenship school at Shiloh Presbyterian Church, and when word spread, community leaders in nearby Oak Ridge requested assistance to open their own class.[15]

Creating the Citizenship Education Program

Meeting the SCLC mandate to expand the CEP kept Young, Clark, and Cotton busy through the fall of 1961. Anxious to report progress in time for the SCLC's annual meeting, they loaded into "Dorothy's green two-toned Buick" for a recruiting tour that Young later described as "looking for those with Ph.D. minds, but third-grade educations." At each stop, they talked about issues and concerns with local leaders. When the summer trip yielded important contacts but few volunteers, Clark, Cotton, and Young cancelled training workshops and hit the road again. They split up to cover more ground, traveling from southern Virginia through the South Carolina up-country to northern Florida, from the Mississippi Delta to the Gulf Coast and into Alabama's Black Belt. In October, they presented a glowing report. "SCLC is quite enthused about the program," Young confirmed to Hotchkiss.[16]

The next month, the CEP staff regrouped at Dorchester with twenty-four recruits from seven states. The SGCV sent two new volunteers. Twelve prospective teachers arrived from the South Carolina up-country, and for the first time, five recruits made the journey from the Mississippi Delta.[17] Curriculum changes introduced that fall reflected the CEP's transformation into a multistate SCLC program. CEP classes remained spaces where local people taught literacy lessons for political empowerment, but classes also served as orientation to the SCLC, and this was infused throughout the revised student workbook. An introduction to the SCLC replaced descriptions of Highlander. Brief selections about African American history, and an overview of the principles of non-violence served as new reading comprehension exercises. A lesson titled "The Bible and the Ballot" fused political action and Christian duty, describing registration and voting as "Jesus's work." Armed with the ballot, teachers and students could select candidates who practiced Christian ideals of "justice, freedom, peace, and equal rights" and infuse these values throughout the political system. The process started with informed and empowered voters. Reflecting the CEP's broad reach, state-specific election laws and voter registration procedures were replaced with more generic instructions and worksheets for organizing a voter registration drive. Some elements carried over. CEP students continued to improve vocabulary by learning how individual letters formed words related to voting and government; for example, the letter *a* started words such as "attorney, amendments, and alderman." Like the first Johns Island students, CEP students practiced arithmetic and handwriting by filling out money orders and working math problems related to farming or counting out change. The workbook also retained the definition of first-class citizenship crafted at Highlander, a definition that included "an all-around education in community development which includes housing, recreation, health, and improved home life," "first rate handwriting," "good manners," and "be[ing] polite."[18]

Training workshops immersed prospective teachers in the SCLC's construction of "first-class citizenship." On loan from Highlander, Robinson demonstrated methods for teaching reading and writing, but there were noticeable changes to the workshop schedule. To ease the burden on local volunteers, Young, Cotton, and Clark shortened the weeklong workshops so that participants arrived by Monday evening and departed on Friday evening. Cotton and Young carved out niches in the new format. Workshops opened with Cotton leading group singing where strangers got acquainted by "praying, singing, and testifying" together. Cotton's session, "Being a Citizen," led off the first full day and set the tone for the week. Prospective teachers read and discussed parts of the U.S. Constitution and "began to realize . . . that each of us has the same rights as every other person in the

Figure 4. Citizenship Education Program teacher training group at the Dorchester Center, ca. 1961. Pictured: Andrew Young (*back row, far left*), Septima Clark (*back row, fourth from left*), Bernice Robinson (*back row, fourth from right*), and Dorothy Cotton (*front row, far left*). Courtesy of Wisconsin Historical Society, WHS-41219.

country," Cotton later recalled. "One could actually see confidence emerging." Young's workshop session reinforced "religious and ethical principles which relate to politics."[19]

Their efforts further standardized the CEP's structure, materials, and class discussions. Materials also reflected the program's internal tension. First-class citizenship reflected a bourgeois middle-class sensibility where citizens acted and expressed themselves in particular ways, measured "improvement" through education and refined mannerisms, and practiced Christianity and non-violence. However, in the segregated South, CEP workbook lessons were not simply lessons in etiquette and the three Rs. Lessons countered public school textbooks crafted to reinforce white supremacy. Teachers and students rewrote these narratives so that their claim to citizenship was rooted in a history of oppression, a connection reinforced in reading lessons emphasizing a "rugged determination to be free," forgotten African American "heroes of the past," and a fundamental faith in the "moral force" of nonviolence.[20] CEP teachers and students acquired literacy skills and talked openly about issues, gaining confidence to claim rights and privileges.

Newly trained teachers left Dorchester and got to work. Retired schoolteacher Susie Greene from Wadley, Georgia, was one example. After attending a November workshop, Clark observed that Greene "came with a purpose and linked it to learning . . . and left with a great determination to help the adults in [her] community to help themselves." Greene was spurred into action by a local election where she observed black voters using "cards with names crossed." She did not wait for CEP materials to arrive before recruiting for her class. When friends and neighbors explained that "because of their jobs, [they] were afraid to attend," Greene persisted and recruited eleven students for a class that met at Saint Mark African Methodist Episcopal Church.[21] For three months, they gathered in the poorly lit and ill-equipped room. Cold weather and illness "impeded progress," but they were "quietly and slowly moving on," Greene reported. In the absence of an official CEP workbook, she made creative use of publications from the National Conference of Christians and Jews and the American Jewish Committee. When workbooks arrived, she thanked the staff for the "life saver." At the end of the three-month term, the class had grown to twenty-five, and Greene observed that her students "have become more conscious of their personal and community problems." The CEP class served as a catalyst for a new civic organization focused on locally defined concerns and priorities. Students "[formed] a committee on drop-outs and absentees [and] one on petitions for street lights, sewerage, drainage and getting a by-pass cut in the Negro section and streets paved," Greene reported. They also registered to vote and influenced others to do the same.[22]

Fifty-five miles to the south, Pearlie Ealey and Greta Rhynes struggled to sustain classes in Tattnall County. Rhynes recruited in Cobbtown but the ten miles between her home in Collins and Cobbtown made her a stranger in town, and she "had to have meetings and participate in church affairs in order to meet the people." Both teachers expressed frustration when residents made promises and failed to attend. "Revivals and other special activities" competed for students' attention, Ealey wrote, and "some were somewhat afraid to participate in civic affairs because . . . they would lose friendship with the whites." As she acknowledged these realities, Ealey confided, "I know my people and they are lazy in the winter." "I am not tired and I do not plan to give up," she assured Clark. "I am going to teach the few that think enough of their race and themselves to want to do something about it."[23] For Ealey, teaching CEP classes was service to the community and by extension to the entire race, and this belief served as motivation for her to teach. In her estimation, this call to service should also serve as compelling motivation to attend CEP classes. She could appreciate that competing priorities and very real economic considerations influenced local people's decisions, but for Ealey, attending CEP classes reflected pride and self-respect. Being "lazy" was no excuse, she concluded.[24]

In her correspondence, Ealey raised a practical concern. Materials and transportation came with costs, and financially strapped rural churches often charged a fee to use the facility. Horton had reserved grant funds for teacher reimbursements, but current allocations were not enough to support the growing number of teachers. Ealey appealed for "enough finance" to fulfill her mission "to give the Negroes the education they want."[25] In early January, Young confirmed the need after meeting with the Elmore County Civic League in Wetumpka, Alabama. League members' enthusiasm for the CEP was tempered by concern about lost wages while away at Dorchester. Young made his case to Maxwell Hahn, executive director of the Field Foundation. "The economic plight . . . is such that volunteer work is almost impossible," he explained, and he requested funds for teacher stipends estimated at "one dollar per hour teaching time plus expenses." There were other advantages to this new policy, Young explained. Stipends would turn the volunteer workforce into quasi-paid employees, giving "the staff more control over the program and contribut[ing] a great deal to its effectiveness."[26]

Young foresaw other advantages to teacher stipends. With additional funds, local women could pay for "clothes and cleaning . . . and more frequent trips to the beauty parlor" in order to maintain "a position to demand the respect and admiration of their pupils," he wrote.[27] The addition revealed gendered and class-based assumptions about CEP teachers and reinforced the program's expectation that teachers would serve as model respectable "first-class" citizens. For Young, CEP classes were extensions of Sunday morning church services: part spiritual, part communal, and part performance. The respectability afforded churchgoing women on Sundays would carry over to CEP classes if teachers looked and acted the part.[28] CEP students were not the only eyes gazing on the teachers, however. In local communities, particularly in the rural South, these men and women were representatives of the SCLC and of the broader movement. Wearing proper clothes and keeping hair set countered racist claims of black female promiscuity and black male lasciviousness, claims wielded as reasons to deny first-class citizenship and as justification for racial violence.[29]

The CEP stipends extended a lifeline, providing financial support that was independent of white employers. As Young pointed out, stipends altered the program by anointing community work with a wage and elevating

CEP teachers' status to paid organizers. Teaching CEP classes was still Christian duty to community and race, but it was not solely altruistic mission work. Foundation-funded stipends and reimbursements added cumbersome reporting requirements and shifted supervisory responsibilities to the SCLC, away from local organizations. At Dorchester workshops, Clark painstakingly explained how to record student attendance, age, and registration status on standardized forms and expense vouchers. Under new rules, teachers were required to enroll at least fifteen adult students who attended classes that met twice weekly. Teachers recorded information on monthly attendance records and expense vouchers that they mailed to the SCLC for review and approval. Classes of fewer than fifteen adult students, with inconsistent enrollment from month to month, or that met beyond the three-month time frame, were not eligible for compensation. To comply, CEP teachers needed to be recognized leaders but were also expected to be detail-oriented. In Atlanta, stipends introduced new layers of program administration, and it fell to Cotton, Clark, or Young to approve payment for each CEP teacher. Inaccurate or incomplete forms touched off a flurry of correspondence to explain and correct the issue, ultimately delaying payments and often souring the relationship with a local teacher. Confusion about reporting requirements and delayed payments plagued the program for the duration of its existence.

Introducing the new policies got off to a rocky start. In late June, Young reached out to Susie Greene, who was teaching classes but had not submitted a request for reimbursement. "We can pay your expenses up to $30," he informed her, but they needed a "listing of your expenses." Stipends muddied relationships between the CEP staff and local teachers. For example, Pearlie Ealey dutifully completed paperwork for "two schools in good operation," believing this translated into thirty-dollar stipends for each school. When she received only sixty dollars for two months of classes, she fired off a response to Young. "I don't think that's right and I know that you know it isn't right," she admonished. "I guess I have lost confidence in S.C.L.C." In reply, Young attempted to explain that the SCLC did not "pay teachers." Stipends were for "teachers who would go back to their communities to work as *volunteers*."[30] Clarifying CEP teachers' roles and responsibilities and ensuring timely and accurate reporting would prove to be an ongoing source of tension between local teachers and CEP staff members.

Realigning Alliances in Southeastern Georgia

Stipends acknowledged that organizing, sustaining, and expanding a grassroots social movement required financial support. In Savannah, Hosea Williams grappled with the same issue. The SGCV affiliated with the SCLC in December, but SCLC support was limited to teacher training and stipends for local classes. Williams envisioned the SGCV as a vehicle for broader action, which required additional resources. Following W. W. Law's advice, Williams reached out to NAACP executive secretary Roy Wilkins. Anxious to impress, Williams described the CEP's "two-fold purpose: citizenship (voter registration) and academic (reading and writing)." The SCLC paid for teacher training, he explained, but SGCV affiliates needed operating funds, a cost Williams estimated at $250 per month. Despite the SCLC affiliation, Williams confided, "I would like to see the NAACP take over this program . . . because of my faith, confidence, and respect for the Association." In a separate letter, Law urged Wilkins to consider Williams's appeal, describing the SCLC as an "additional problem" and deriding "some great Messiah marching in and getting people to march down the streets." Wilkins was unconvinced, interpreting the CEP as a literacy program not in line with the NAACP's voter registration activities.[31] The failed negotiations pushed Williams closer to the SCLC.

As the NAACP door closed, the CEP door opened wider as new resources flowed in. In January 1961, civil rights leaders were cautiously optimistic about the new president, John F. Kennedy. Kennedy met with African American leaders on the campaign trail, and public statements, though vague, signaled that he might be more open to federal action than his predecessor. Early on, Kennedy expressed support for activities aimed at increasing black voter registration, support that intensified after Freedom Rides in the spring and summer of 1961 forced the president and his brother, Attorney General Robert F. Kennedy, into direct confrontation with local and state officials in Alabama and Mississippi. In early 1962, civil rights and philanthropic organizations joined forces for a southwide voter registration campaign and designated the Southern Regional Council to oversee the project. Initially designed as a two-year program, the VEP aimed to increase black voter registration and document continuing discrimination. The SCLC signed on with the Student Non-Violent Coordinating Committee (SNCC), the Congress of Racial Equality (CORE), the NAACP, and the National Urban League. Young directed the SCLC activities concentrated in areas where the CEP had planted roots: central South

Carolina to the Lowcountry, three counties in the Mississippi Delta, and "the crescent-shaped area . . . from Atlanta through Macon to Savannah" in Georgia. Young later recalled that the CEP was "not taken very seriously by the SCLC board and many of SCLC's most prominent ministers." The influx of grant money changed this. In January, Martin Luther King Jr. and Ralph D. Abernathy made their first visit to Dorchester, mingling with local CEP teachers at the workshop's closing banquet.[32]

As VEP funds flowed into the SCLC, Young hired new staff members to manage activities in Georgia, a decision that stoked tensions with Williams.[33] From the sidelines, Williams waited impatiently for recognition and support for the SGCV. By August, he sent a proposal directly to VEP director Wiley Branton. Williams described a sophisticated, multicounty, perpetually underfunded organization with citizenship schools as the cornerstone. The SCLC and the NAACP "realize the value of our structure but they have been unable to help," he explained. Neglecting to mention the SCLC affiliation and financial ties to the Savannah NAACP, Williams claimed "no allegiance or responsibility to any organization other than our own." The SGCV was seeking its own charter, a crucial step to receiving independent outside funding. Branton nudged Williams back to the SCLC and the NAACP, but Williams refused to budge, submitting more proposals until persistence paid off. In October, Young allocated VEP funding to the SGCV, and Branton approved a $4,000 grant specifically for the Chatham County voter registration project.[34]

Williams's correspondence with Branton forced Young's attention on the SGCV, and in December, he dispatched the CEP's newest staff member to Savannah. A Georgia native, thirty-year-old Annell Ponder had earned a master's degree in social work from Atlanta University and moved north. She returned home in the spring of 1962 and applied for work at the SCLC, accepting the only available job as a clerk-typist. Young learned of Ponder's background and hired her as the CEP's first field supervisor. Her first assignment took her to Albany, where she oversaw citizenship schools organizing in the wake of the direct action campaign earlier that spring. Southwestern Georgia was Ponder's training ground. She stayed for two months, building relationships with local leaders and civic groups, recruiting and training CEP teachers, and teaching her own classes.[35] She carried these lessons across the state to Savannah, where she served as Young's eyes and ears.

Ponder got a quick orientation at a "kick-off meeting" at Butler Street Presbyterian Church, where she observed the SGCV's gendered hierarchy

Figure 5. *Left to right*: Dorothy Cotton, Annell Ponder, and Septima Clark, ca. 1963. Courtesy of Avery Research Center for African-American History and Culture, College of Charleston, Charleston, South Carolina.

at work as each supervisor "introduced the teachers from *his* area with great pride and expectations." Ponder noted that local teachers had already organized schools, and seven Chatham County teachers planned a meeting at Hi-Hat Bowling Lanes to recruit students. Ponder was impressed with the SGCV's "very resourceful leader" and teachers who were "very dedicated workers for the most part."[36] Williams was equally impressed with Ponder. "She was a hell of a lot of help to me," he wrote to Young, and he asked if "Miss Ponder could deal directly with day-to-day problems." In case there was confusion about the ultimate aim, Williams closed with a wish for the SCLC to "take over all *THE RESPONSIBILITY OF THE SOUTHEASTERN GEORGIA CITIZENSHIP SCHOOLS*," punctuating the sentence with "(smile)." Young complied, and Ponder returned for a regional meeting where Williams announced VEP requirements. Interested SGCV affiliates needed to elect officers, "operate adult citizenship schools," and "refrain from partisan politics," he explained.[37] In the coming months,

CEP teachers organized in urban Chatham County while in rural Tattnall, Emanuel, and Wheeler Counties, the combination of the CEP and VEP revived dormant NAACP chapters and civic organizations driven underground by state-driven purges and Klan violence in the 1940s and 1950s. Working within the SGCV structure, prominent black men supervised and ran county organizations, and black women organized from the grassroots.

Citizenship Education in Rural Southeastern Georgia

In Tattnall County, Pearlie Ealey and David Norwood built on groundwork laid through CEP classes to organize the Tattnall County Christian Citizens League. They divided the county into five districts and recruited CEP teachers and students to serve as district workers who conducted house-to-house surveys, assisted with registration cards, administered the oath, and delivered registration cards to the courthouse.[38] Ealey balanced county-level responsibilities with teaching CEP classes in Reidsville and Collins. Many students had managed to register, so she adapted workbook lessons for discussions about non-violence and political education. Ealey documented individual achievements that extended beyond voter registration. "Miss Viola Willis, who previously refused to speak in public meetings, participated in a skit and speaks in public," she reported, while another student, "an unwed mother," was "taking courses through the mail to qualify for her high school diploma." One man, whom Ealey described as "a drunk," "stopped drinking, [joined] a church [and] was elected assistant superintendent."[39] Her examples emphasized the CEP's markers of first-class citizenship, including education, morality, temperance, and civic engagement, and reinforced her view of herself as the missionary lifting the race one person at a time.

Seeds took root more slowly in Emanuel County, where Thomas Allen had struggled to organize a movement. Three local women completed teacher training in the spring of 1962, but none managed to open schools. By the following spring, VEP funds helped to generate interest and organize a countywide voter registration effort with CEP classes meeting in Swainsboro, Garfield, and Twin City.[40] In Cross Green on the county's northern edge, the mother-daughter team of Lou Anna and Clara Nell Riggs initiated an intensive campaign in early 1963. Through "door to door calls, telephone calls, and lectures at public gatherings," they learned that "illiteracy is not too excessive [and] most of our people own their homes." The Riggses adjusted the CEP curriculum to emphasize handwriting and "thrash out any individual problems." When a bus driver in Lou Anna's class "wanted to know how many miles he drives per school term, driving 36.6 miles one way per day," Riggs taught students to solve the problem and "the entire class benefited." Individual lessons sparked discussions of community concerns and local solutions. Lou Anna's students' petition for better roads resulted in new construction, and after discussing "welfare problems," Clara Nell's students planned to "investigate the matter further." As they closed their schools, the Riggses concluded that they fulfilled the CEP's mission. "We have increased our voting power and organized our county," Lou Anna reported, while Clara Nell noted broader results. They could distinguish an "ordinary citizen" from a "*first class citizen*," she wrote, and through the CEP, "we have raised our standard of community development" in "recreation, health, and improved homelife."[41]

CEP classes spread into Wheeler County after the Reverend Adel Goram attended a Statewide Registration Committee conference and came home "inspired" by Williams and Young's presentation about the CEP.[42] In early November, four women organized schools during the laying-by time between fall harvest and spring planting. Goram kept a firm hand, dividing the county into districts and assigning each teacher to a specific area. Although cold weather kept some at home, approximately ninety-six people attended classes. In February 1963, teachers and students organized the Wheeler County Crusade for Voters, earning Williams's praise for "the first truly organized, non-partisan, voter education program established in [the] county." They elected Goram as chairman, and he reported that they were "on wheels, even if they were moving slowly." By April, the teachers' combined efforts resulted in 444 new registered voters, doubling the 1958 figure.[43]

At three hundred square miles, Wheeler County was nearly three times the size of Johns Island with a population of 5,342 residents spread across the entirely rural county. Similar to neighboring Tattnall County, African Americans made up 32 percent of the population. In makeshift classrooms, local teachers confronted the legacy of segregated schools and poverty that meant that African Americans completed, on average, four years of school. Elderly men and women attended CEP classes, though two teachers noted poor health and poor eyesight kept some students at home. Those who persisted showed marked improvement in reading and handwriting. Eighty-eight-year-old George Rountree went to school for the first time and "learned his ABCs," and seventy-year-old Lizzie Tillman was able to "write her friends and relatives."[44] CEP lessons broke bonds of dependence as one student learned to "read the newspaper and sign . . . without anyone's help." CEP student Lonnie James had always depended on a local merchant to endorse his paycheck. After two weeks of lessons, he "asked the man to give him a pencil" and signed his own name.[45]

CEP teacher Dollie Williams's reports revealed complex dynamics in this large rural county. When they opened schools, 12 percent of eligible black voters were registered, and Williams reported little resistance to increased registration. To the contrary, she wrote, "The white people thinks its [sic] wonderful to have these schools to help our people be better citizens and registered voters."[46] CEP lessons inspired the students' confidence to try to register; however, Williams's comment suggested that from "the white people's" perspective, CEP students were becoming "better citizens." This was respectability politics in rural Georgia where African Americans gained a measure of acceptance conditioned on literacy and proper behavior. In a county where African Americans were a distinct minority and remained dependent on white employers, more black voters were unlikely to threaten long-standing and deeply rooted political and economic structures. Williams's reports also documented resistance from different points in a community concerned about disruption to a status quo. Fear of violent reprisal kept "Mrs. J" out of class, afraid "those white folks [will] bomb me . . . in the church." Ethel Lona stayed home after receiving a threat that "they would burn up her house." She returned the following week and the other students "got the fear out of her."[47] CEP classes could disrupt white segregationist systems; however, an empowered black electorate might disrupt a delicate balance of power in black communities as well, and Williams ran headlong into this resistance as she canvassed for students. "The leading citizens among the colored" worried that CEP teachers would bring in "Dr. Martin Luther King and his gang" to initiate "a mess," she reported. Another teacher confided to Annell Ponder that the county supervisor, presumably Goram, insisted that classes meet outside of the Alamo city limits and instructed teachers to "keep 'controversial' subjects" out of discussion to "'maintain rapport' with local power structure."[48]

Citizenship Education in Savannah

Intracommunity dynamics were also impacting CEP teachers' work in Savannah where a rivalry between the NAACP and the SGCV intensified. In the fall of 1962, the NAACP branch office demanded an accounting of its $100 monthly allocation, but Williams refused to comply. When he secured the VEP grant, the NAACP cut off funds. The SGCV's executive board pushed forward with plans to obtain a business charter and apply for tax-exempt status.[49] As Williams and Law drew boundary lines, CEP teachers maintained flexible alliances with both organizations. In March 1963, Daisy Jones's students lent support for the NAACP's membership drive alongside a similar drive planned for the SGCV. Adell Black's students attended NAACP mass meetings while completing the three-month CEP course. Seeing no need to split loyalties, her students planned "to become members of the NAACP and the Crusade for Voters."[50]

From the fall of 1962 into the spring of 1963, CEP teachers organized classes in in-town neighborhoods and outlying communities where they too confronted the legacy of discrimination and segregation. Adell Black canvassed for students in the Yamacraw community on the city's west side where "people . . . slammed the door . . . and did many other things that were discouraging." Attending CEP classes required students to publicly admit that they could not read, and Adline Bradshaw "didn't get very much cooperation . . . because [they] thought it was embarrassing to let people know that they couldn't read and write." Cassie Pierce agreed. "The problem [is] getting the most illiterate to school," she wrote. "They seem ashamed or a fear [sic]."[51] CEP classes required an admission of perceived deficit as well as a public commitment to political action, and both presented risks.

Once class opened, Savannah CEP teachers incorporated religious rituals and traditions, reflecting the program's links to the SCLC and the city's church-based networks. Teachers opened classes by inviting a student to lead a devotional and scripture reading.[52] The reading exercise, "The Bible and the Ballot," drew direct connections between religion and political action. In her Fellwood neighborhood school, Ida Smalls-Mack made creative use of the lesson. She asked students to take turns reading the text, which positioned teachers and students as modern-day apostles, working to "release the captives of this segregated society, and bring liberty to those who are oppressed." "We must preach the good news of equality and brotherhood to the poor. . . . This was Jesus's work, and now it is ours," they read. Mack directly connected this religious calling to political action, drawing parallels between the "ten moral laws" in the Ten Commandments and the "first ten laws" in the Bill of Rights. She continued, pointing out that "we hear so much of freedom, but the word freedom is not a new word," using the Exodus story as an example of God's deliverance. As she hoped, the lesson stimulated dynamic discussion.[53]

CEP teachers described how similar dynamic discussions sparked individual enlightenment and collective action, descriptions that positioned the CEP teacher as the missionary guiding the conversion. Cassie Pierce introduced "round table discussions" where students shared opinions "with understanding and not harshness." Active debate about current issues "created interest in their everyday living locally and national issues," and discussions would "sometimes get so deep in the subject matter, we stay overtime," she enthused. Discussion and debate were fundamental to a democracy. As Pierce observed, "The project has . . . awakened the individuals that were asleep and caused interest and understanding." Daisy P. Jones reported similar results with residents "who were neglecting their duty" or were "blissfully ignorant of [their] duties as a citizen." CEP lessons "changed the students' points of view or attitude toward voting and helping his people and himself instead of always kowtowing to someone." Dorothy Boles's students translated talk into action. After discussing the city's neglect of their west side neighborhood, students wrote a letter to the mayor requesting paved roads in Carver Village. Before receiving a response, Boles noted a change, writing, "They walk, talk, and act like new people with determination and more courage to face the future."[54]

CEP teachers organized classes under the SGCV banner while maintaining ties to the NAACP, but this straddle became increasingly untenable as Hosea Williams organized public demonstrations in the summer of 1963. Williams had fumed as the city's restaurants, theaters, and hotels openly violated an earlier desegregation agreement. CEP students who managed to register were the exception, as prospective black voters faced lengthy wait times and a more difficult literacy test.[55] That spring, Williams had watched and learned from events in Birmingham, Alabama, where the SCLC joined with the Alabama Christian Movement for Human Rights (ACMHR) for sit-ins, boycotts, and marches. King's arrest attracted national attention, and images of city police and firefighters beating back nonviolent demonstrators with nightsticks, high-pressure firehoses, and police dogs prompted widespread outrage, resulting in a desegregation agreement between city officials, businessmen, and black civil rights leaders.[56] Independent of the NAACP, Williams launched a similar campaign, leading lunchtime marches through downtown and issuing fiery speeches outside of the courthouse. Business leaders complained and police responded, arresting more than two hundred under anti-trespassing laws. Williams turned up the heat with mass meetings and night marches. City leaders and the chamber of commerce attempted to negotiate, but Williams refused to budge.[57] The SCLC dispatched Cotton, Young, and James Bevel in a show of support. In late June, Young joined marchers and was arrested with Williams. Young negotiated their release only to have police re-arrest Williams, holding him on a $30,000 bond for sixty-six days.[58]

Williams's leadership in the direct action campaign raised questions, and in July, Branton declared that "the [SGCV's] voter registration program [was] bogged down as a result of the direct action program." "In light of the suspension of your program," Branton reasoned that Williams must return unused portions of the VEP grant. W. W. Law and other local NAACP leaders positioned themselves as the moderate force in Savannah. They publicly denounced the night marches and negotiated a sixty-day cooling-off agreement after which the city would desegregate theaters, restaurants, hotels, motels, and bowling alleys.[59] Williams was released to news that the NAACP chapter had ended segregation in Savannah. At the end of the bruising summer, Williams attempted to regroup. Young endorsed a request for resumed VEP funding, emphasizing the direct action campaign's outreach to "those districts of lower income." Branton approved a four-month grant to the SGCV, insisting on monthly reports and careful monitoring. By the spring of 1964, the SGCV boasted five thousand new voters on the Chatham County rolls.[60]

CEP activity declined after the Savannah demonstrations. In November, Williams accepted a full-time position with the SCLC and moved to Atlanta as the VEP grant expired. The SGCV network unraveled in his wake. Stalwarts sustained scattered CEP schools but failed to reach the levels achieved in the spring and summer of 1963 when there was an active county-level infrastructure to support and sustain their work. In Savannah, as the NAACP's Political Advisory Committee took over the city's voter registration drives, Carolyn Roberts held CEP classes in her home and in the Francis Bartow Homes community center. A promising program in Wheeler County dissipated to one CEP class outside of Glenwood. Tattnall County's Pearlie Ealey and Greta Rhynes joined a migration north, leveraging CEP skills to secure employment in social service agencies in Cincinnati and Boston, respectively. In their absence, three new teachers organized classes into early 1965. Emanuel County's program endured through classes at Swainsboro's Brown's Chapel, where the Reverend Cisero Brown blended CEP lessons with lessons in economic self-sufficiency, inviting "the social security man," his "insurance man," and "the vocational man from Augusta, GA" to address his students.[61]

* * *

Between 1961 and 1964, the Southeastern Georgia Crusade for Voters served as the infrastructure for CEP classes in Savannah and rural counties. The combination of CEP and VEP funds expanded the SGCV's reach across Georgia's First Congressional District with CEP classes at the center of voter registration and community development work. The SGCV replicated models of community and religious organizations where prominent race men served in the public eye and black women played what were seen as support roles. Teaching CEP classes was "women's work" and this assignment placed women in the center of the SGCV's strategy. Teachers adopted the assigned role, many seeing the work as an extension of church-based community service. Within the SGCV's gendered hierarchical structure, black women worked out of public view, blending community organizing skills with CEP lessons to draw people into churches and community centers where they confronted legacies of poverty, segregation, and discrimination, delivering services long denied or neglected by county systems. In three-month classes, they fulfilled the CEP's mission to improve literacy, generate discussion, and mobilize people to register to vote and demand equal treatment.

Infusion of resources realigned alliances in southeastern Georgia. In Tattnall, Emanuel, and Wheeler Counties, CEP and VEP funds fueled new county-level organizations that reinvigorated voter registration and launched community improvement projects. In each county, CEP teachers and students relied on respectability politics that proposed a conditional agreement. If African Americans became "first-class citizens," power systems within white and black communities would address injustice and inequality. CEP teachers' reports revealed both the possibilities and limitations of this agreement. In urban Savannah, infusion of CEP and VEP funds stoked interorganizational rivalries. CEP teachers deftly navigated increasingly fraught alliances to nurture practices fundamental to a democracy.

By 1963, CEP teachers in southeastern Georgia were part of a growing contingent. Andrew Young, Dorothy Cotton, and Septima Clark joined forces to establish the CEP as a region-wide SCLC program. The semi-annual report to the Field Foundation told the story. Between July 1962 and January 1963, 212 people from nine southern states completed teacher training and returned home to organize 150 classes that enrolled 2,091 students. CEP teachers reported 8,207 new registered voters from their classes and their students' broader influence. The program had turned a corner "after the difficult months... in our initial year," Young wrote. Beginning in February 1963, he built a case for a three-year grant that would allow CEP staff to develop long-range plans for materials, staffing, and local leadership. King endorsed the plan, declaring the CEP to be "one of the most important ventures underway in this nation." Field officials agreed on principle and approved a two-year $250,000 grant, beginning in July 1963. The grant stabilized the program and was a show of confidence in Young's ability. Field funding allowed the CEP to operate outside of contentious and competitive politics within King's inner circle.[62] This base buttressed program expansion in another place where the CEP had sunk roots. Local leaders from Mississippi arrived at Dorchester in late 1961. For the next three years, they organized classes across the Delta and into the state's southeastern corner as part of a collaborative movement taking direct aim at segregation in the "most southern place on earth."[63]

5

"We Shall Overcome Today"

Groundwork in the Mississippi Delta, 1961–1963

In late February 1963, Annell Ponder was planning a "more or less routine" visit to "a good citizenship training program" centered in Clarksdale, Mississippi, optimistic about "a new experience and a new challenge to face and overcome." Two days before her departure, news from the Delta altered her plans. James L. Bevel, the Southern Christian Leadership Conference's field secretary, reported that James "Jimmy" Travis, field secretary for the Student Non-Violent Coordinating Committee (SNCC), was in the Greenwood hospital, shot by night riders on his way out of town. In response, the Council of Federated Organizations (COFO) was planning a massive voter registration drive, and Bevel needed help to organize citizenship schools. He asked Ponder to extend her stay, and after "careful consideration," she agreed. Ponder's visit stretched into eighteen months in a place that Robert "Bob" Moses described as "the heart of the iceberg."[1]

Ponder followed the Citizenship Education Program's momentum west, transferring lessons from southeastern Georgia into a new outpost. Andrew Young, Septima Clark, and Dorothy Cotton had laid groundwork on a recruiting trip in late 1961. Over the next two years, a steady stream of community leaders followed the path to Dorchester, extending the program's reach well beyond coastal communities and deep into the rural South. In the Delta, the CEP fit into a constellation of activities coordinated through a multi-organization coalition. Field staff from the SCLC, SNCC, NAACP, and Congress of Racial Equality (CORE) set aside ideological differences to form COFO. CEP staff were partners in this alliance, facilitating access to resources and collaborating in support of grassroots community leadership development.[2] The CEP tapped into formal and informal networks,

Map 3. The Mississippi Delta. © Bruno Berry.

opening an access point for information, skills, and structure to ongoing community work. CEP teachers incorporated classes into voter registration and direct action strategies, expanding local initiatives and contributing to a foundation for broad challenges to state and national political systems.

In 1994, a veteran Delta organizer referred to the Mississippi movement as "a woman's war," and the CEP reflected this gendered division of labor.[3] Working closely with local women, Annell Ponder constructed and sustained a network that reached into six counties. Delta-area classes drew on CEP training and gendered traditions of resistance to replicate work under way in the South Carolina Lowcountry and in southeastern Georgia.[4] Place mattered and the Delta posed unique challenges. Urban Charleston and Savannah anchored CEP networks in South Carolina and Georgia. Connections to urban NAACP chapters and other civic organizations meant that teachers were not operating entirely in isolation. In contrast, the Delta was dotted with towns like Clarksdale, Greenwood, and Cleveland, but the closest urban communities were hundreds of miles away in Jackson or Memphis. Across the region, deeply rooted fear and imposed isolation posed daunting challenges. State and local officials on high alert for any signs of "agitation" meant that gendered notions about respectability would not protect CEP teachers from reprisal or violence.[5] If they could break through, CEP teachers and their students stood to transform the very way that black citizens saw themselves and envisioned their future.

The "Most Southern Place on Earth"

Implanting democratic citizenship in the Mississippi Delta would not be easy as Jim Crow maintained a tight grip on the region. Since the late nineteenth century, state lawmakers had perfected a complex web of political, economic, and educational restrictions for African Americans, with each strand entangling and reinforcing the others. Beginning with a state law passed in 1878 and codified in the 1890 state constitution, the Mississippi legislature ensured that black and white children would be educated in facilities that were "separate" and certainly not "equal." As late as 1950, the state spent $32.55 for each black student in the state's segregated schools while spending nearly three times more on each white student. Census figures recorded the legacy of these segregated schools. In Delta counties where the CEP would take root, black residents had completed, on average, five years of formal education.[6] As historian Neil McMillen has argued, "By limiting the quality and extent of black education, the white majority could hope to cramp black political aspirations, inhibit black ability to compete economically, and assure an adequate supply of low-wage menial black labor."[7] In the Delta, cotton was king, and towns and villages served as trading posts in the one-dimensional economy. Restricted educational opportunities locked generations of black laborers into an economic dependence reinforced through intimidation and physical violence.

By mid-century, mechanization was transforming southern agriculture with tractors and mechanical pickers humming across cotton fields, planting and harvesting the lifeblood of the region. In the machines' wake, sharecroppers received termination notices and lost both job and home. These same forces sweeping across the South Carolina Lowcountry had more force in Delta counties like Leflore and Sunflower, where just over 90 percent of black farmworkers were tenants. By 1964, those rates decreased by 10 and 20 percent, respectively.[8] For sharecropping families, machines added unwelcome uncertainty to a precarious and economically vulnerable existence while inadequate and incomplete education blunted options.

As in other southern states, education had political consequences due to the literacy test required for voter registration. At the height of Congressional Reconstruction in 1868, 96.7 percent of Mississippi's eligible black voters had registered. With the introduction of literacy tests and poll taxes in the 1890s, the percentage of registered black voters plummeted to 5.9 percent. As late as 1955, only 4.3 percent of the state's black voting population was registered. Results were even more dramatic in the Delta's majority-black rural counties where less than 1 percent of the eligible black population was registered.[9] Reinforced with extralegal harassment and violence, voter registration tests effectively ensured that Mississippi's black population had little political influence well into the twentieth century.

With Jim Crow under attack in the 1950s, state officials acted quickly. In South Carolina and Georgia, revised laws and gubernatorial committees obstructed or delayed enforcement of federal court decisions and civil rights organizing. Mississippi lawmakers went further, creating the Mississippi State Sovereignty Commission (MSSC) in the wake of the *Brown* decision. The MSSC was charged with "protecting the sovereignty of the State of Mississippi . . . and to resist the usurpation of the rights and powers reserved to this state and our sister states by the Federal Government or any branch, department or agency thereof." MSSC agents fanned out to investigate any and all perceived threats, their reports providing evidence to support a predetermined conclusion: that white supremacy was under siege and only swift and decisive state action would hold off the attack. In Indianola, city officials, bankers, landowners, and businessmen organized a Citizens Council in July 1954, pledging to pool political and economic power to root out and stop civil rights organizers. The idea spread and within three months, a state-level Citizens Council attracted twenty-five thousand members. Mississippi officials responded swiftly to any "outside agitators" who might inspire local black residents to action. When Young, Clark, and Cotton arrived in the Delta in the summer of 1961, Freedom Riders were serving out sixty-day sentences at Parchman Farm, the Mississippi State Penitentiary, for violating the state's segregation codes in their coordinated protests to desegregate interstate travel.[10]

Repression and discrimination had shaped African Americans' lives in the Delta for generations, but it was not the entire story. Within this environment, they nurtured seeds of resistance through NAACP chapters and locally organized groups. Earlier SCLC outreach forged connections with leaders like Clarksdale pharmacist Aaron Henry, who served as president of the Coahoma County NAACP branch and a member of the SCLC executive board.[11] Clark, Cotton, and Young hoped to strengthen ties, believing that NAACP chapters and grassroots endeavors could provide the catalyst for CEP classes in the Delta. In return, CEP classes could help sustain and expand local efforts, rocking foundations of economic and political power. Women like Clarksdale's Vera Mae Pigee would play a central role in these efforts.

Citizenship Education Arrives in the Delta

At the end of November 1961, thirty-six-year-old Pigee closed her beauty shop and headed east with four companions. Traveling 650 miles, they arrived at the Dorchester Center where they joined twenty fellow CEP volunteers from six states. Clark, Cotton, and Young were particularly glad to see Pigee, who had impressed them during their visit. Young later observed that in Clarksdale, Henry "provided intelligent and strong leadership," but it was Pigee who "really ran the operations."[12] Since the late 1950s, she had directed the state's NAACP Youth Council and served as the Coahoma County NAACP secretary. Pigee continued a trend within the CEP. Like Charleston's Bernice Robinson and Mary Lee Davis, Pigee was a beautician, and her shop in Clarksdale's black business district was a popular gathering place. For Pigee, the shop provided an income independent of white employers, conferring status in the community and offering some protection from economic reprisal as she engaged in political action.[13] Pigee made her mark at Dorchester when participants gathered for freedom songs. Cotton started singing "We shall overcome," inviting everyone to join in. "We shall overcome, someday," they sang. To everyone's surprise, Pigee stopped the singing to interject, "In Clarksdale, [we] have changed the words to 'We shall overcome *today*.'" At the end of the workshop, Cotton reflected, "Mrs. Pigee will make an excellent supervisor."[14]

CEP classes got under way in Clarksdale as money flowed in from the Southern Regional Council's Voter Education Project (VEP). In February, Henry invited Martin Luther King Jr. to Clarksdale to kick off the SCLC's "People to People" tour in what King called "the symbol of hard-core resistance to desegregation." News of King's visit triggered the state's "hard-core resistance" and drew the MSSC to Clarksdale. Among the commission's agents, Tom Scarbrough proved to be a dedicated and tenacious investigator, routinely filing detailed reports from the Delta. Scarbrough trailed King throughout his two-day visit, noting that Pigee, "a well-known agitator," coordinated a meeting between King and African American youths at Haven Methodist Church. He alerted superiors to a "pamphlet titled, 'Citizenship Education Program'" and warned of influence from "the same group of communist teachers . . . who were teaching at Mount Eagle, Tennessee." The pamphlet's presence in the Delta could only mean that "communist teachers" were close at hand.[15]

While the pamphlet got Scarbrough's attention, actual activity did not. By the time the inspector submitted his report, Pigee and the other CEP teachers had a foothold in Coahoma County. Scarbrough's oversight was due, in part, to teachers' efforts to hide activities from public view. Pigee's students arrived at her shop after closing time and met behind drawn shades. Scarbrough's omission also reflected gendered interpretations of political spaces and political actors. As CEP organizers confirmed with early classes in Charleston, beauty shops were viewed as women's spaces for gossip and self-care and did not draw suspicious gazes. In addition, as historians Tiyi Morris and Françoise Hamlin have argued, deeply rooted traditions of viewing black women's community activism as "ordinary activities" or "simply what black women did" rendered the political ramifications of their work "invisible" and opened space for "subversive" activities such as the CEP.[16] The teachers' efforts worked, as Young noted in an update to Horton. "Clarksdale [held] closing exercises for their 6 schools started in January," he wrote. He marveled, "I don't understand how, but folk are learning to read and write, and with persistent effort they are getting registered." The next month, Henry confirmed Young's assessment at the SCLC's annual board meeting. In the face of persistent scrutiny and harassment, CEP teachers had organized schools in the Clarksdale area, Henry reported. A veteran of voter education efforts, Henry acknowledged that CEP students had quickly learned to read and write and were actively involved in local voter registration efforts.[17]

The SCLC assigned field secretary James Bevel to build on foundations set by Pigee and the early CEP teachers. SNCC president John Lewis later reflected, "To say [Bevel] was loud would be an understatement. To say he was extreme would not say enough." Bevel hailed from Itta Bena in the heart of the Delta and came to the SCLC through SNCC, where he had been a leader in the Nashville sit-in movement. The Freedom Rides brought him back to Mississippi, and after his release from Parchman, Bevel stayed on to open a Freedom House in Jackson. In the spring, Bevel and his wife, Diane Nash, accompanied Bob Moses into the Delta. From NAACP leader Amzie Moore's home in Cleveland, Bevel spread word about the CEP.[18] Bevel's links to SNCC and local NAACP branches folded CEP classes into a broad coalition of collaborating organizations, temporarily diffusing the kind of interorganizational rivalry erupting in southeastern Georgia.

In Ruleville, Rebecca McDonald and Celeste Davis responded to Bevel's invitation. The pair reflected the program's reliance on recognized leaders as well as its ability to engage a new generation of activists. Teaching a CEP class was twenty-three-year-old Davis's first formal experience with civil rights action, and through the program, she received on-the-job training in literacy education and community organizing. Forty years her senior, McDonald served as role model and mentor for Davis, reflecting gendered traditions of community leadership in the rural South. Unlike the cadre of independent businesswomen, educators, and social service professionals in the CEP ranks, McDonald's expertise rested on being "one of the hard fighting old ladies who stuck it out and truly [did] believe," as SNCC organizer Charles McLaurin described her. McDonald could read and write, but more importantly, she served as a church deaconess, and her husband, Joe, was one of the few registered voters in Sunflower County. In the early 1960s, the McDonald kitchen was an important gathering place where organizational affiliations blurred.[19]

McDonald's and Davis's CEP classes provided a necessary educational component for a collaborative voter registration campaign orchestrated through a combination of indigenous leadership and outside organizations. Upon their return from Dorchester in late March, the women opened a citizenship school on Lafayette Street and attracted forty students. After three months, only one student successfully registered to vote. The trickle of black registrants roused suspicion, and in August, Ruleville mayor Charles Dorrough took steps to put out the smoldering fire, warning city sanitation worker Lenard Davis that he was prepared to run CEP students out of town and fire Davis if his daughter-in-law Celeste persisted.[20]

Disappointing voter registration results and Dorrough's intimidation failed to quell the movement as mass meetings and CEP classes attracted Ruleville residents. In August, forty-four-year-old Fannie Lou Hamer came to a mass meeting at Williams Chapel and was drawn in by Bevel's sermon that connected religious faith and political action. The daughter and wife of a sharecropper, Hamer imagined "votin' people outa office" that she knew "was wrong and didn't do nothin' to help the poor." She resolved to join the seventeen volunteers headed to the courthouse, an experience that became a defining moment in Hamer's narrative of activism. When it was her turn, the clerk turned to a section of the state constitution and asked her about "de facto laws." "I knowed as much about a facto law as a horse knows about Christmas Day," Hamer later reflected. She copied the required section but failed the interpretation part of the test. One by one, Hamer's companions were turned away. Highway patrolmen stopped them on the way back to Ruleville and charged with "driving a bus the wrong color." The passengers and driver pooled their cash, paid the fine, and returned to the bus.[21]

Voter registration attempts came with swift consequences in the Delta. Plantation owner W. D. Marlow met Hamer as she returned home and insisted that she withdraw her application or face dismissal and eviction. She replied, "Mr. Marlow, I didn't go to Indianola to register for you. I went to Indianola because I was trying to register for myself," and Marlow told her to leave. Hamer took refuge in a Ruleville under siege. In subsequent weeks, Mayor Dorrough exacted retribution on perceived agitators' families, following through on his earlier threat to terminate Lenard Davis's employment. Dorrough dismissed Fred Hicks from his job transporting day laborers after Hicks's mother went to the courthouse, and exploiting the city's regulatory powers, he closed the Surney family's dry cleaning business when Jeff Surney's name appeared on the list of volunteers. Finally, the mayor withdrew Williams Chapel's free water and tax exemptions, sufficiently intimidating church deacons into cancelling mass meetings and citizenship classes.[22]

Reprisals fueled the local movement, and by early September, twelve more African Americans had visited the courthouse, including Celeste Davis and Rebecca McDonald. MSSC investigator Scarbrough returned and dutifully recorded names and ages, attributing registration attempts to "James Bevels and his wife, Diane Nash Bevels," who were "busy insisting on Negroes going to the courthouse." After another voter registration attempt, night riders drove through Sunflower County, firing shots into forty-two homes, including the McDonalds' house and the home where Hamer stayed with friends. The latest round of violence and reprisals were "the breaking point in Ruleville," Bevel reported, forcing organizers "to turn our efforts from voter registration to re-locating families and finding funds to sustain people."[23] The combination of economic intimidation and physical violence threatened to end the nascent Delta movement.

"Flexible Associations" in Delta Soil

As reprisals swept through Ruleville, SCLC and SNCC organizers moved into surrounding towns. In early 1962, Amzie Moore introduced Bevel to his twenty-three-year-old neighbor Samuel T. "Sam" Block. Block had returned to the Delta after attending college in Saint Louis and serving briefly in the air force. Block's sister Margaret later recalled that Bevel and Moses met regularly in the Blocks' family kitchen, sharing news "that we didn't know because we couldn't get it on the local news or in the local newspaper." The movement veterans shared the growing folklore, describing student-led sit-ins in Greensboro and Nashville. The information sharing worked both ways as the Blocks described "how people were getting shorted sharecropping and what we could do for the sharecroppers."[24] These conversations chipped away at another pillar of Jim Crow by connecting local concerns to broader civil rights action and undermining the isolation that was so crucial to maintaining white supremacy in the Delta.

Sam Block accepted Bevel's invitation to teach CEP classes. On a practical level, the SCLC citizenship schools offered a way to gain direct experience in civil rights action. In addition, a monthly CEP stipend was income that was independent of white employers, leaving Block less vulnerable to the kind of economic reprisal that Hamer and other black families had faced. At thirty dollars a month, the stipend freed Block to devote more time to civil rights organizing and elevated the status of the work. He was not a volunteer; he was a paid organizer. Working with Lois L. Rodgers, Block enrolled forty-six students at the Cleveland Citizenship School. In May, the teachers led a voter registration "march" to the Bolivar County courthouse and managed to get "only two people registered." On their second attempt, "[nobody] would wait on the people there to be [registered]." In July, Rodgers reported that ten of forty-six students had registered to vote despite the clerk's continuing efforts to discourage or deny their applications.[25] At the end of the three-month CEP classes, the teachers' paths diverged. Block's CEP work caught the attention of SNCC organizers just as VEP funds flowed in, allowing the perpetually cash-strapped organization to hire additional field staff, including Block, who was assigned to direct a ninety-day voter registration campaign in Greenwood.[26]

VEP funds facilitated additional crossover between the citizenship school program and ongoing activities in Mississippi. Myles Horton agreed to host a workshop for SNCC field staff, and in June, Moses, Block, and fellow Mississippi organizers Curtis Hayes and Hollis Watkins traveled to Knoxville where they joined college students from across the South. During the weeklong workshop, Bernice Robinson, Hosea Williams, and Esau Jenkins passed on lessons, cross-fertilizing strategies and ideas from one area to another. Williams shared practical suggestions for voter registration campaigns that included canvassing and organizing citizenship schools. Jenkins picked up where Williams left off, describing tangible results from political action sparked by citizenship schools in the Lowcountry, where more than four thousand African Americans had registered. With political influence, they addressed local issues such as inadequate high school facilities and aggressive policing. In the final workshop session, Moses and Horton developed plans for "citizenship schools for functional illiterates, classes in registration procedures . . . as well as a series of eight workshops for [Mississippi] volunteers."[27]

At Moses's invitation, Robinson traveled to the Delta two weeks later for a workshop at the Mount Beulah Christian Center in Edwards. Robinson met Delta-area teachers at Dorchester training sessions, and the trip renewed those connections in Ruleville and Cleveland. In Clarksdale, she found "a coordinated group working on all fronts: conducting classes and voter registration campaigns, organizing boycotts, and fighting court cases." Robinson also confronted the Delta's grim reality. In Greenwood, she managed to recruit ten workshop participants, only to have eight "back out at the last minute." Civil rights organizing raised suspicion, and Robinson's affiliation with Highlander added further complications. Before the workshop, the local sheriff and Citizens Council members called in the Mount Beulah center director. During the four-hour interrogation, they demanded a list of workshop participants and warned the director "shouldn't be connected" with "Myles [Horton] . . . Director of 'That Communist Highlander Center.'" Moses went ahead with plans but advised Robinson to "soft-pedal" the Highlander association. The workshop opened under "threats . . . to blow up the meeting place." Robinson had experienced Jim Crow segregation and observed grinding poverty across the South Carolina Lowcountry, but the Delta was different. She later reflected, "This fear is real."[28]

The workshop was a crash course in political education and organizing where Robinson and Moses blended the citizenship school's roots in participatory democracy and SNCC's philosophy of mobilizing from the grass roots. They replicated the Highlander model where facilitators and participants relaxed together in the evening, and Robinson and Moore relayed practical advice and answered questions in the more informal setting.

At the end of the week, the group targeted Greenwood, Ruleville, and surrounding rural areas, places where the CEP had taken root. Over the coming months, Robinson made regular trips back to Mississippi. The crossover between SNCC and the citizenship school program continued when Charles McLaurin and Lafayette Surney attended the November teacher training session at Dorchester.[29]

Citizenship Education Takes Root in New Places

SNCC voter registration activities operated alongside CEP activity and intensifying opposition across the Delta. In Bolivar County, Lois Rodgers's Cleveland classes stalled when churches closed their doors. Moving operations out of Cleveland did not alleviate the problem as teachers faced similar obstacles in nearby Pace and Duncan. With Bevel's support, Rodgers concentrated on her hometown of Shaw, and after only one month, Bevel remarked, "I don't know whether we should call it a class, workshop, or mass meeting" when ninety-two turned out in cold January temperatures. Subsequent meetings attracted "about 150 to 200 students," and "a number of people have gone down to register and others [were] asking . . . about getting registered." The workshops fueled interest in CEP classes, and Bevel anticipated sending "two people from Shaw for [CEP] training." In April, Delta-area volunteers exceeded Bevel's modest estimate when twenty-two men and women from Shaw, Greenwood, Ruleville, and Itta Bena attended a CEP teacher training workshop.[30]

In Ruleville, Rebecca McDonald solved the problem that stopped other local efforts in their tracks. When church leaders closed Williams Chapel to civil rights activities, she moved citizenship classes into her home. In January 1963, she approached the deacon board and informed them "that she had put more money in the church than anyone else and therefore they were going to use the church whether the white people liked it or not," and Bevel confirmed, "We are now back in the church." McDonald practiced what she taught, returning again and again to the courthouse, determined to have her name added to the voter registration rolls. Fannie Lou Hamer also made repeated trips to the courthouse, and on January 10, her registration application was finally approved. To mark the milestone, W. D. Marlow evicted the entire Hamer family. One month later, four hundred of Hamer's neighbors marched to the courthouse in Indianola.[31]

In the wake of growing civil rights action, county officials discontinued federal food subsidies. Because landowners routinely shortchanged sharecroppers at harvests, low-income black families relied on subsidies for food during winter months. Officials reasoned that discontinuing the program would get the federal government out of the Delta and force desperately poor families to turn to local whites for assistance. As winter wore on, they realized that the plan had backfired. Rather than driving a wedge between black residents and civil rights activists, the groups galvanized around the very tangible need for food and clothing. In addition, donations poured in from across the country, shining a bright national spotlight on impoverished black residents. A Citizens Council member later lamented, "When we cut the food giveaway program, that was our biggest mistake—'cause that's when our nigras embraced the civil rights crusade."[32]

From the Delta, Bevel crafted a proposal to expand the SCLC's presence and role. He acknowledged the need for "clothing, food and medicine for people who have been affected by reprisals," but he reasoned that "sooner or later ... an effective voter registration campaign needs an economic-development program." A Delta center modeled on Highlander and Dorchester "where people can meet, study and work together" would "produce ... the kind of Negro people who will bring about a nonviolent revolution." By early January, Bevel identified a vacant school building in Greenville and outlined a series of summer conferences on "religious, economic, political, and educational problems ... [to] give people a clear picture of how segregation work [sic]." The proposal tested the SCLC's commitment to Mississippi, and CEP director Andrew Young responded with a strong dose of pragmatism and caution. Bevel's vision was unrealistic, he argued, because "you would be closed and the property confiscated in short order, that is if it wasn't bombed first." Instead of pursuing "an untried program," Young redirected Bevel to "our Citizenship Program which has a long history of effective work," and he wrote, "Perhaps if I was there with you, I'd see things differently.... Right now, I think we are all groping for a strategy in Mississippi."[33]

Perspective was everything. Where Bevel saw potential, Young saw a quagmire, and two months later, he set firm boundaries in a VEP proposal. According to Young, SNCC had accepted responsibility for voter registration in Mississippi. The SCLC "attempted to suppliment [sic] this work" through Bevel and the CEP, and the SCLC intended to maintain this "supplemental" role. The CEP had trained over one hundred teachers who, according to Young, were "the backbone of much of the work in the Delta," particularly in Ruleville, Shaw, Clarksdale, and "other whistle stop Delta communities." In 1963, the CEP would branch out further to "spread throughout the Delta, county by county." Young's pessimism about the Magnolia State showed through as he concluded, "The poll tax and economic situation is so serious that registration without a mass movement seems in vain" and only resulted in "a few more persecuted families."[34] The message was clear. If SNCC, through COFO, was willing to devote people and resources to the state, the SCLC would direct attention elsewhere. Through the CEP, the SCLC's presence remained out of public view in makeshift classrooms, rattling with tremors instead of an earthquake, and for Young, this was the pragmatic choice. By the time Bevel's proposal arrived, the SCLC was tilting toward Birmingham where their affiliate, the Alabama Christian Movement for Human Rights (ACMHR), prepared to ramp up a non-violent direct action campaign ahead of municipal elections in March.[35] Birmingham posed daunting challenges, but on the heels of disappointing results in Albany, Georgia, SCLC leaders were looking for a victory. Birmingham would be a time-limited urban campaign with clear objectives executed in coordination with local leaders who were integrated into the SCLC circle. This was not the Mississippi Delta.

The CEP and the Greenwood Movement

The SCLC would not remain in the background in Mississippi, however. Throughout the winter, Sam Block organized volunteers to distribute donated food and clothing from Greenwood's COFO office as CEP teacher Vera Mae Pigee and CORE field secretary Dave Dennis organized similar drives to the north in Clarksdale. In Greenwood, food and clothing drives coincided with an ongoing voter registration campaign, and increased attention brought escalating threats and harassment, including break-ins at the COFO office and reprisals directed against supporters. Much to the chagrin of white officials, threats and harassment only seemed to strengthen community support for civil rights action. When police arrested Block in February on charges of disturbing the peace, more than 150 black residents responded by attempting to register at the Leflore County courthouse.[36]

Events in Greenwood prompted a visit from Moses, accompanied by Jimmy Travis, a veteran of the Freedom Rides, and Robert Blackwell, the SRC's VEP field director. Bevel and Block gathered with the visitors and other Delta-based SNCC workers to outline plans to "mov[e] into other counties and ways of getting dug into Greenwood." At the end of the meeting, Bevel headed north while Moses, Blackwell, and Travis traveled east. Seven miles out of Greenwood, their trip was cut short as shots rang out from a passing car. Unable to shield himself from the blast, Travis was hit in the shoulder and the neck as the car swerved into a ditch.[37] With Travis in the hospital, the SCLC, SNCC, and CORE agreed to pool resources for a coordinated three-prong response: "canvassing, citizenship classes [and] mass meetings." Including the citizenship schools as a primary strategy reflected the SCLC's participation in Delta activities as well as the organization's access to valuable resources, such as staff, funding, and the networks of CEP teachers cultivated over the previous year in the Delta.[38]

Annell Ponder arrived the following week and was immediately swept up. That evening, she and Bevel met with the Reverend David Tucker and officers of Greenwood's Turner Chapel African Methodist Episcopal Church. Tucker made "a strong appeal in favor of [the SCLC's] request," and by the end of the meeting, the officers agreed to open the church for citizenship classes and "many of them signed up to attend." Staying true to the CEP's origins in community leadership development, Bevel agreed to teach the class only "until a local teacher could be recruited and trained." Within a week, eighteen-year-old Ida Mae Holland volunteered. Working with Bevel and Ponder, she received on-the-job training and quickly assumed responsibility for the class.[39]

Like Sam Block and Celeste Davis, the CEP was Holland's entry point to civil rights action. She had excelled in school, but she also realized that her professional and economic opportunities would always be restricted in the Delta. Faced with limited prospects, she had turned to prostitution. In early 1963, after an unsuccessful attempt to proposition Bob Moses, Holland visited SNCC's Greenwood office as activists planned the coordinated voter registration effort. Her literacy skills made her an asset, and she was immediately put to work. Black women like Ethel Grimball, Allene Brewer, and Rebecca McDonald leveraged a record of community service to gain their friends' and neighbors' trust as CEP teachers. For young women like Holland, teaching CEP classes became a way to redefine themselves as community workers. She later reflected, "Being around the SNCC people had turned my narrow space into a country bigger than I'd ever imagined. . . . There were always those . . . trying to beat my borders back, to make me small again. I swore I would not let that happen again."[40] Like a growing number of young CEP teachers, experience in the program encouraged Holland to gain self-confidence and assume a leadership role in the Greenwood movement.

Holland's characterization of all civil rights workers as "SNCC people" was testament to the close collaboration among civil rights organizations in Greenwood. Upon her arrival, Ponder was welcomed into the fold, forming working relationships amidst barely controlled chaos in the Greenwood office.[41] Ponder brought important skills and talents. On a practical level, she could teach CEP classes and train teachers. She was fresh from work in southeastern Georgia where she helped to strengthen a regional infrastructure to support local teachers. Finally, she was old enough to wield authority but still young enough to fit in with the cadre of COFO activists.

Ponder knew that the CEP's success depended on collaboration and her ability to mobilize community leaders. Early on, she met Atlean Smith, "an outspoken and dynamic leader in the Greenwood movement" and another of a growing number of beauticians involved with the CEP. Like Vera Mae Pigee and Bernice Robinson, Smith had cultivated extensive ties throughout the community and through her shop, she established economic independence from white employers. When Ponder described difficulties in securing meeting space, Smith agreed to host classes in her home. Smith learned quickly and "assumed responsibility for . . . the class."[42] For the COFO coalition, the CEP provided another vehicle to mobilize women with established reputations, economic resources, and considerable community contacts in support of local action.

With two classes under way, Ponder and Bevel confronted logistical challenges in expanding the program: they needed to organize more citizenship schools as soon as possible; they alone could not teach enough classes; and they could ill afford the time to send teachers to the Georgia coast for training. The pair decided to initiate onsite training in Greenwood. With SNCC workers' assistance, they recruited eight women, including Fannie Lou Hamer. On March 13, Bevel and Ponder opened the first session. As Young had predicted, holding training sessions in the Delta was dangerous work. Ponder and Bevel convened sessions during the day because "people were so afraid, it was impossible to find a place where we could hold training sessions in the evenings." The volunteers' reputations as respectable, churchgoing women did not shield them from "jeers and criticisms of their neighbors who would take no part in the 'mess' which [the SCLC] was stirring up." Despite these challenges, all recruits completed the training and organized classes. Based on this success, Bevel and Ponder immediately organized a second workshop, enrolling a dozen new recruits. They got additional support when Robinson returned for a ten-day visit, helping with workshop lessons and "giving historical interpretation of the program," Ponder reported. Robinson organized and trained canvassers in Greenwood during the day and taught citizenship classes in Shaw at night.[43]

In Greenwood, CEP classes offered an alternative to marches and demonstrations, and classes typically attracted older residents drawn by the promise of long-awaited literacy education. In Holland's class at Turner's Chapel, only five of her thirty-seven students were younger than thirty. Of Bettye Brown's eleven students at First Christian Church, only three were younger than fifty. After three months, Brown reported that the "beginning students are doing fine in their work and showing improvement [and] the advanced are doing very good." Alice Blackwell's classes at Wesley Chapel African Methodist Episcopal Church attracted an average of fifteen students whom Blackwell described as "elderly people [who] show intense interest in learning about citizenship, non-violence, and voter registration." In three months, "beginners . . . learned to read, write their name [and] write simple sentences."[44]

CEP teachers' attendance records and correspondence documented multigenerational involvement and leadership in the Delta movement. For black residents, local classes in familiar, relatively protected spaces offered an entry point to civil rights action. In addition, while "civil rights agitators" trained teachers and created an infrastructure to support local classes, CEP students gathered with teachers who were familiar friends and neighbors. Most importantly, classes continued Robinson's practice of starting where the students were, intentionally creating an environment where personal achievement built the foundation for more public demonstrations of citizenship. For CEP students, literacy education was the pathway to equal citizenship that had long been denied in Mississippi. As Bettye Brown explained, "I have one student who couldn't write his name (Mr. Grace). Now, he can write and spell his name." Following this accomplishment, Brown reported, "He has also been down to register."[45] Mississippi CEP teachers' reports documented numerous examples of "Mr. Graces," where literacy education resulted in political empowerment, one person and one class at a time.

Delta CEP teachers' reports echoed teacher and student testimonies from other rural areas where political empowerment was an important marker of citizenship, but on a more fundamental level, citizenship was rooted in the ability to exercise power and authority in a variety of contexts. For example, "advanced students" in Alice Blackwell's class completed CEP lessons and "learn[ed] how to deposit money in the bank [and write] friendly business letters." In the rural South in the early 1960s, and particularly in the Delta, these were not mundane daily activities. This knowledge and these skills served as the basis for safeguarding family resources and addressing concerns through legal and political channels. In addition, CEP classes served as information centers that broke the isolation imposed in the state's "closed society." Black residents learned about resources beyond the Delta, including federal programs such as Social Security. Following a class discussion, Ethel Shaw's students intended to "check with the office [to see] if we have put up enough time [to] have some benefits coming that will help comfort and protect our families."[46] Establishing economic independence to "comfort and protect families" was citizenship in the Delta.

The broader Greenwood campaign offered ready outlets for students to apply CEP lessons. Ponder reported on students and teachers participating in a wide range of activities, including "distributing information about the voter registration drive, canvassing, and accompanying people to the courthouse." Through their connections to community organizations and churches, teachers "held block parties, and made speeches." Teachers also "mothered the movement," working behind the scenes to "secure living quarters for workers . . . and prepare food for jailed workers."[47] These efforts demonstrated teachers and students enacting the CEP's construction of citizenship. Citizenship was a legal status conferred by the state, but more importantly, first-class citizens acted to ensure equal rights and protection under the law for all citizens, even those who did not directly participate in civil rights activities.

Although CEP teachers conducted classes in churches and homes within the relative safety of Greenwood's black neighborhoods, they did not escape physical harassment and economic intimidation, often meted out by state and local officials. In late March, Holland's participation in a protest march to city hall resulted in her arrest on charges of "disorderly conduct." When church leaders buckled under threats and harassment, teachers moved classes into their homes. While this strategy sustained classes, CEP teachers who rented their homes were subject to reprisals such as landlords' refusal to repair dilapidated homes or threats of eviction. One teacher "was shot at 16 times after attempting to register." As she continued to hold classes at her home, "policemen parked in front of her house, letting the police dog bark all night . . . and following her as she went about canvassing the neighborhood." Local officials also tried to stop this teacher's activities by ensuring that her husband "lost every job he got as soon as it became known that she was his wife."[48]

White officials' attention to CEP teachers' activities was due, in part, to the broader context of the Greenwood movement. With public demonstrations and the arrival of "outside agitators," officials were on edge for any sign of civil rights "agitation." The response to CEP teachers also demonstrated that officials were keenly aware of the threat posed by adult literacy education laced with political lessons. By teaching African Americans to read and write, the CEP threatened to crack a critical pillar of white supremacy in the rural South. If black sharecroppers could read contracts, they could not be manipulated into persistent debt and poverty as easily. If African Americans could read, they could pass literacy tests for voter registration and might obtain political power. In CEP classes, they learned about the structure of local, state, and federal government and pressure points to advocate for change in each. Local responses to CEP classes in Greenwood were part of a broader effort to stop civil rights action, but in specifically targeting CEP teachers, white officials clearly demonstrated that they understood the radical potential of this "less militant" activity. To white officials, these respectable churchgoing women were "agitators" just like the SNCC workers.

Amidst a wave of reprisals, CEP teachers sustained classes and broader community work. In March, newly trained CEP teacher Earnestine Foster joined Fannie Lou Hamer to organize a class at Williams Chapel, teaching fourteen faithful attendees. At the end of three months, six students registered to vote. Farther west, Lois L. Rodgers maintained a busy schedule in Shaw. She committed two days a week to canvassing neighborhoods and reserved three days to "take groups to register." On Thursdays and Fridays, she taught citizenship classes. When a white grocery store owner "shot a Negro woman for speaking about his discourteousness," Rodgers joined four others to "boycott [the store] in the Negro community." In April, she organized classes in Boyle and Cleveland and accompanied nineteen Shaw residents to the courthouse.[49]

Citizenship Education Spreads in the Delta

By mid-March, Bevel was increasingly dividing his time between the Delta and the SCLC's direct action campaign in Birmingham. In his absence, Ponder extended the CEP's reach. After attending a Dorchester workshop in April, forty-two-year-old Leonia Luckett opened a CEP class at Hopewell Church, the first school in Bevel's hometown of Itta Bena. Following guidance passed on during teacher training workshops, Luckett encouraged students to relate class lessons to their everyday activities. At the end of the first month, the class reached reading exercises about African American history in their CEP workbooks. In "One Hundred Years from Slavery," they sounded out words to learn about enslaved people who "were needed to clear the trees to make farm land and roads" and "planted and harvested the crops."[50] Although the passage emphasized "progress" and the "rugged determination to be free," Luckett's students had a "touching discussion" about "how conditions are much the same . . . because some [students were] treated almost the same way in . . . 1963 as in 1619."[51]

Ponder's outreach and Luckett's classes struck a chord with eighteen-year-old Willie Baxter. Like many young African Americans across the country, Baxter "knew something was wrong . . . when Emmett Till was killed." She later recalled, "Even though I didn't understand the full impact of it . . . things started bothering me." As news of sit-ins and protests filtered into the Delta, Baxter reasoned, "If they're doing stuff everywhere else, we need to do something." She canvassed with SNCC workers to encourage voter registration but soon realized "a lot of people couldn't read." She later recalled, "When [the] SCLC came out with their classes, that was the perfect situation." From Hopewell Church, Luckett and Baxter canvassed and distributed clothing and food during the day and convened citizenship classes and mass meetings at night. Baxter later recalled, "It was a full day, . . . going from early in the morning until two o'clock at night on some days." Baxter's classes attracted "mostly older" students, and using "little textbooks" and "letters . . . like in a primary tablet," they "mastered the material" and "went to register." Although some could read and write, the interpretation portion of the literacy test was a barrier. In response, Baxter and fellow Itta Bena teachers adapted "classes where all [they talked] about was the Constitution." The classes resulted in noticeable registration activity. By the end of the summer, Ponder reported, "Citizenship schools of Itta Bena . . . have disproportionately sent down more people to register than any other comparable place."[52]

The Greenwood movement also sparked action in nearby Holmes County. In 1960, Holmes looked like many Delta counties. African Americans made up a majority of the population, most worked in agriculture, and very few were registered voters.[53] Two factors distinguished Holmes County: black children completed a full year more formal education than peers in neighboring counties, and black people owned land through a combination of New Deal–era Farm Security Administration (FSA) programs and deeds dating back to post–Civil War emancipation. Holmes

County landowners valued the independence this brought, but they also knew that mechanization and outmigration was taking a toll. Between 1959 and 1964, their numbers had dropped by 20 percent.[54] For civil rights organizers, the county had the elements for an effective local movement: a base of independent landowners, established African American communities, and a relatively strong education system.

In the winter of 1962, landowner Hartman Turnbow and longtime NAACP members Ozell Mitchell and his sister Alma Mitchell Carnegie started attending mass meetings in Greenwood and invited SNCC workers to Mileston. Hollis Watkins and John Ball answered the call and organized "voter registration classes" at Mileston Sanctified Church. As they canvassed, they echoed ideas that had enlivened early citizenship schools, talking about "how citizenship was connected to their condition as it existed right now . . . and their condition as it might or should exist in the future."[55] The arguments resonated with landowners like Turnbow. "I hadn't never did it [voting] and hadn't heard anything 'bout it, so I just wasn't too interested in it," he remembered, but "the story about redishin' and votin', how [he] would be a first-class citizen and make [his] standard of living better," caused him to reconsider.[56] With "a made-up mind," he attended the Wednesday evening classes that quickly grew into community events with "a full house . . . something like a hundred peoples or more." Evening discussions pivoted on citizenship rights. Turnbow recalled discussing "that you got a right to vote for who you want to preside over you and . . . a right to not vote for the ones that you *don't* want over you. And then you paying tax like everybody else, and you's a taxpaying citizen and then deprived out of the biggest part of your right." "Redishin'" came with risks but, according to Turnbow, "we wouldn't be dying for a bunch of foolishness; we'd be dying for our God-given rights." In class, they studied and prepared to claim their rights.[57]

On April 9, fourteen volunteers, "the peoples [sic] that really meant business," made the trip to Lexington. Turnbow was in the group with Ozell Mitchell, Alma Carnegie and her husband, Charlie, the Reverend Jesse J. Russell, and landowner Ralthus H. Hayes. Watkins recalled that the group's arrival came as a "tremendous surprise" for officials. Turnbow and John Daniel Wesley were the only group members permitted to take the test.[58] MSSC investigator Virgil Downing dutifully recorded evidence of growing political activity, including the "voter registration school for Negroes" described in a pamphlet from "the Southern Christian Leadership Conference . . . under the leadership of Martin Luther King, Jr."[59] The CEP had arrived in Holmes County. One month later, night riders firebombed and shot into Turnbow's house. Turnbow returned fire and the men "vanished into the darkness." MSSC investigators and local law enforcement officials surveyed the scene and charged Turnbow with "set[ting] his home on fire" and doing "all the shooting," declaring that the registration drive "flopped" as African Americans steered clear of "agitators" who were "doing much harm." Turnbow contradicted the assessment, later reflecting that the attack "just made it worser, like putting more wood on a fire."[60]

Annell Ponder made her way to Holmes County in the wake of the Turnbow incident. The Greenwood-based collaboration ironed seams between the SCLC and SNCC, and Watkins and Ball "assist[ed] her in setting up citizenship classes wherever [they] were working." By June, five volunteers traveled to Dorchester, including two of the "First Fourteen." Similar to groups recruited from other Delta counties, the Holmes County contingent included experienced leaders and young people new to the movement. Sixty-six-year-old Alma Carnegie represented the former. In the 1920s, she had written to then Red Cross director Herbert Hoover, urging assistance for black sharecroppers. In the Depression years, her home served as safe haven for labor organizers working with tenant farmers in the Delta. Carnegie was an active member of the NAACP and an avid reader of the *Chicago Defender*. In 1963, she added citizenship school instruction to her impressive record. Likewise, landowner Ralthus H. Hayes had a long history of challenging systems. He was fired in 1954 after trying to register, and for thirteen consecutive years, county officials had refused to accept his poll tax payment. Hayes redirected energy into CEP classes and local organizing. Carnegie and Hayes were joined by new recruits including college student Eloise Davis, who spent part of her summer break teaching CEP classes, and Willie J. Burns, who had joined a second group attempting to register.[61]

Brief notes on CEP attendance records reveal details about their work. Davis opened a class with thirteen students at Tchula's Zion City Missionary Baptist Church. As in Greenwood, classes were multigenerational with Davis instructing students as old as sixty-five and seventy-two. Attendance was "irregular," and she assured CEP administrators that her students "learn very easy" and "really enjoy the classes." Into August, Davis discontinued the class when her students were "very busy working" and not able to attend. Burns's report reminded CEP administrators that groundwork had not erased a primary concern for local people. At the end of the summer, he wrote, "I am doing all I can to get the people to go and register, but this is the Delta and they are afraid." "Just will not go," he concluded.⁶² The CEP teachers' efforts were off to a slow start but would lay the foundation for a broader challenge by the following summer.

Winona

In early June 1963, Ponder accompanied Hamer and eight Delta-area teachers to an advanced training workshop on Johns Island. The trip was a welcome break from the near-constant physical and mental strain of working in the Delta. With SCLC staff and teachers from other areas, they learned new teaching strategies, discussed common concerns, and planned next steps. At the end of the week, Ponder and the teachers headed back. Riding through the night, the bus crossed into Mississippi in the early morning hours. Sixteen-year-old June Johnson grew increasingly concerned as she noticed that the bus driver placed a phone call at each stop. At 11:15 a.m., the bus pulled into Winona, one of the last stops before Greenwood.⁶³

Inspired by their experience on Johns Island and weary from the road, the travelers entered the bus terminal and attempted to order food at the restaurant, in violation of the local segregation ordinance. News traveled fast in the small town, and police responded quickly, transporting Ponder, Johnson, Hamer, and fellow travelers Rosemary Freeman, Euvester Simpson, and James West to the Montgomery County jail.⁶⁴ All were well aware of the danger. Friends and allies in Greenwood knew their travel plans but could attribute a delayed arrival to any number of factors and wait to sound the alarm. Staring into the angry faces of Winona police, the group members feared what could happen in that time. Their fears intensified when officers divided the group into available cells after a failed group interrogation. Over the next several hours, officers brought Johnson, Ponder, and Hamer separately into the booking room. Ponder later described how "three of them . . . gave us the runover with blackjacks, and a belt, fists, and open palms," demanding to know about each woman's involvement in civil rights action.⁶⁵ At the end of the ordeal, Johnson's clothes were badly torn and blood streamed down her face. Hamer recalled that Ponder was a "horrifyin'" sight, her "mouth was bleedin' and her hair was standin' up on her head." Hamer's back and legs were "hard as bone" and she was only able to lay facedown on a cot, unable to sit upright.⁶⁶

Three days later, SCLC staff in Birmingham received troubling news out of Mississippi. CEP workers were in the Winona jail, and farther south, NAACP state field secretary Medgar Evers had been murdered in his driveway. Young later recalled that the murder "brought home to us our own vulnerability" and remembered King's urgent instructions to arrange Ponder's group's release because "after the way Medgar was shot, there's no telling what might happen to them." Desperate for transportation, Young and Bevel asked to borrow Dorothy Cotton's new car. She insisted on going with them, but Young balked. "If you're gonna take my car," she snapped, "I'm going with you. . . . Those are women in jail in Winona. . . . If Mrs. Hamer's brave enough to challenge Mississippi, I'm brave enough to help get her out." With that, the three set out for the Delta.[67]

As Young, Cotton, and Bevel drove through the early morning hours, federal agents "got around to visiting" the Winona jail. Ponder later recounted the agents explaining "they were merely the 'guests of the police chief,' that they had to follow his regulations," so there would not be any pictures taken at the jail. After a nearly yearlong campaign in the Mississippi Delta, preceded by campaigns in other southern states, preceded by U.S. Supreme Court decisions, the federal government still seemed to be more concerned about white Mississippi law enforcement officials than black citizens. Later in the day, the bruised and beaten activists were released after Young posted bond.[68]

Three months after her ordeal, Ponder traveled with Delta CEP teachers to Richmond, Virginia, for the SCLC's annual convention. The Winona experience had changed her. In prepared remarks, she did not celebrate the spring campaign in Birmingham or the March on Washington that had drawn a quarter million people to the nation's capital that August. Instead, Ponder talked about Mississippi, "a study in extremes and contrasts," she reflected. In a place where she had "some of the most satisfying and rewarding experiences," Ponder had also witnessed "the most horrifying examples of man's separation from God and from his own truest self." She laid bare the daily injustices: the midnight curfew for black residents in Clarksdale, medical doctors snapping, "Let the movement help you" when black residents sought treatment, "unimaginably bad" living conditions, and children competing in school-sponsored "contests" to pick cotton for local landowners. "This is the only place I've heard of where a Negro can be fired from his job, evicted from his home, jailed and put in the state penitentiary, shot at, and starved for attempting to register to vote," she wrote. Amidst crushing hardship and injustice, she marveled at black Mississippians' ability to "maintain a 'business as usual' attitude in the face of experiences which would ordinarily be considered calamities of the highest order."[69]

In closing, Ponder invited the Delta teachers to stand and be recognized and encouraged attendees to seek them out. "They can tell the Mississippi story much better than I because they've lived there longer and have survived with spirits intact," Ponder explained. "Everyone talk with the delegates from Mississippi," she implored. "They need to talk—its [sic] good to know that someone shares the burden—and you need to know what they can tell you."⁷⁰ In her appeal, Ponder attempted to bridge a growing gap between SCLC's leaders planning more direct action campaigns and the CEP in Mississippi. Talking with CEP teachers and listening to their stories would funnel more SCLC resources to Mississippi, she believed. For CEP teachers, the conversations would validate their work, strengthen connections to the SCLC, and reignite commitment in the face of daunting challenges.

* * *

Ponder's remarks encapsulated two years of activity in the Delta. Beginning with Vera Mae Pigee's classes in Clarksdale, the CEP had spread across the region. Bevel and Ponder's experiments with local training connected the CEP with experienced grassroots leaders and opened access to extensive informal networks. The program served as training ground for a new generation. Armed with a structured program and supported with CEP stipends, local women played active roles in organizing and mobilizing communities. Meeting in living rooms and churches, CEP classes opened an entry point to the local movement that did not require public demonstration like a march to the courthouse. In these spaces, African Americans gained access to information and skills. In the Delta, literacy and knowledge of public services were the basis for political empowerment and economic security.

As Ponder's comments and experiences indicated, the Delta posed challenges for CEP teachers, students, and field staff members. In black-majority counties, the program directly threatened a central pillar of white supremacy within a state committed to resistance. Classes met in beauty shops, homes, and churches within black communities; however, in Mississippi, these were not entirely private spaces. As a result, enacting "first-class citizenship" drew swift economic and physical reprisal for teachers and students.

In the Mississippi Delta, CEP classes filled a niche in the growing movement. Early classes in Clarksdale and Ruleville connected the program with experienced local leaders in a mutually beneficial relationship. The

CEP added resources for community work while the leaders' participation served as endorsement. SCLC field staff's collaboration with SNCC and CORE fueled CEP expansion that, in turn, extended the Greenwood-based movement. Ponder confidently outlined plans to "expand the program throughout the state" and noted that the CEP had established a foothold beyond the Delta in the state's southeastern corner. Within two weeks, SCLC staff would lend their support to this nascent effort by holding a workshop in the area. Sitting in the audience, Hattiesburg-area teacher Victoria Jackson Gray was attending her first SCLC convention.[71] One year later, she would be among the Mississippi CEP teachers and students directly challenging national political structures.

6

Freedom Days

Citizenship Education in Mississippi, 1963–1965

In the fall of 1963, the Citizenship Education Program (CEP) had two centers of operation in Mississippi. In Greenwood, Annell Ponder opened a new Southern Christian Leadership Conference (SCLC) office down the street from the crowded Council of Federated Organizations (COFO) office, complete with telephone line and a lending library of "meaningful" books and pamphlets. From this base, Ponder recruited volunteers, visited area citizenship schools, and put final touches on "advanced classes" for CEP graduates. Ponder also coordinated field trips for area teachers to attend a meeting of the National Sharecroppers Fund and a second-step political education program on Johns Island, South Carolina. "All helped to make the program much better," she concluded.[1] To the southeast, thirty-six-year-old Victoria Jackson Gray established a new CEP outpost. Six months earlier, she had been "strictly business oriented," concentrating on her Beauty Queen cosmetics franchise in the heart of Hattiesburg's black business district. She changed course after a mass meeting where two organizers from the Student Non-Violent Coordinating Committee (SNCC) "made the altar call—the 'Invitation to Get on Board and Begin the Journey to First Class Citizenship.'" Gray raised her hand and volunteered to register to vote. At the courthouse, the clerk's belligerent rejection fueled her determination. Late in the summer, Gray attended CEP training at Dorchester, later recalling, "I guess that was really the beginning of the end of my business because . . . I came back and started organizing citizenship classes."[2]

From opposite ends of the state, CEP teachers mobilized within a rapidly changing context. By 1963, COFO had firmly established its presence in the

Magnolia State, and into the fall, Mississippi-based field staff organized a statewide Freedom Vote. The campaign set the stage for a broader challenge when hundreds of college students swelled the volunteer workforce the following summer, teaching Freedom Schools and registering voters for the Mississippi Freedom Democratic Party (MFDP). The massive program generated gravitational forces that consumed resources and eclipsed all other work. Mississippi CEP teachers, students, and staff supported the activities, and by the end of the summer, they joined in a movement that rattled political structures from local precincts all the way to the national stage at the Democratic National Convention. Freedom Summer rushed in like a wave, and as it receded, the COFO coalition splintered as CEP teachers and students applied lessons in a variety of new contexts.

At the same time, from Atlanta and from the Dorchester Academy, CEP administrators confronted mounting challenges. The CEP's rapid expansion "has also become a source of difficulty," they concluded. Part of the issue was financial. Participation at teacher training workshops swelled the numbers of CEP teachers, straining the budget for stipends and expense reimbursements. The other issue, from staff members' perspective, was programmatic. Young later reflected that the CEP sought "natural black leaders of the South," those "with Ph.D. minds but third-grade educations." This cast a wide net and opened the door to widely varied interpretations of criteria and tasks for local teachers.[3] Working within flexible alliances, Mississippi's teachers blurred lines between teaching classes, feeding and housing civil rights workers, organizing for the MFDP campaign, and gathering clothing and food for welfare and relief committees, equating all activities as service to the same cause. As the CEP expanded across the South, program administrators took steps to improve local supervision and to clarify structure and criteria for teachers. New policies rekindled tensions of enforcing structure and rules with the CEP's goals of mobilizing local leaders, meeting people where they are, and encouraging broad enactment of first-class citizenship.

CEP staff members shored up program infrastructure within an organization that was charting a different course. In the spring of 1963, a direct action campaign in Birmingham, Alabama, catapulted the SCLC onto the national stage. In August, Martin Luther King's "I Have a Dream" speech at the March on Washington solidified this position. Into the fall, the SCLC regrouped and reorganized. Changes reverberated through the CEP as Hosea Williams relocated from southeastern Georgia to head up voter registration efforts, James Bevel made a permanent break from Mississippi field work to oversee direct action campaigns, and Andrew Young succeeded executive director Wyatt T. Walker, who had tendered his resignation. Following the Birmingham campaign, Dorothy Cotton moved into King's inner circle of close advisors. Looking ahead, the organization committed to more Birmingham-style direct action campaigns, beginning with Saint Augustine, Florida.[4] These decisions further marginalized the CEP and its cadre of grassroots, mostly women, leaders.

Citizenship Education in Mississippi's Piney Woods

In late summer 1963, the CEP gained a new foothold as Victoria Gray got to work. She had deep roots in Forrest County, having grown up outside of Hattiesburg in Palmer's Crossing. After high school, she attended Wilberforce University in Ohio, coming home after only a year. She tried teaching school but gave it up when "the regimentation became a bother." Marriage to serviceman Anthony Gray took her to military bases out of state, and by 1962, they came back to Mississippi where Gray managed twenty-five sales representatives in her Beauty Queen franchise. She kept up a full schedule with the business, the parent-teacher association, and active involvement at Saint John Methodist Church.[5] In August 1963, Gray added CEP teaching and supervision to her list.

Hattiesburg was not the rural Delta. Nestled within Mississippi's Piney Woods region, Hattiesburg was the state's fifth largest city. In contrast to black-majority Delta counties, African Americans made up 28 percent of the Forrest County population. In the early twentieth century, lumber, not cotton, fueled the local economy. By 1960, two-thirds of Hattiesburg's black workers were operatives and laborers, many of them at Hercules Powder Works, a Delaware-based company that produced turpentine, pine oil, and insecticides. Although African American workers entered through a side door and funneled into low-wage, physically demanding, and dangerous positions, wage labor at Hercules and at area sawmills broke dependence on area landowners. Membership in an interracial affiliate of the AFL-CIO was another advantage. In the early 1960s, union representatives pressed for African American workers to advance into better-paying positions and assured workers that voter registration would not jeopardize their jobs, setting a foundation for later challenges to the county's discriminatory voter registration practices.[6]

By 1960, the majority of the county's black families lived within the city limits, clustered in the floodplain north of downtown. Within Hattiesburg's segregated neighborhoods and business district, black leaders sowed seeds of resistance. A television and radio repair shop enabled J. C. Fairley to sustain the city's NAACP branch, which moved underground as local officials took aim at branch members in the 1950s. Gray's operation was one of several beauty businesses along Mobile Street, providing steady income for the black women who operated the shops. Lenon E. Woods managed Woods Guesthouse, offering accommodations for black travelers and meeting space for political gatherings.[7] Black business owners, ministers, teachers, and doctors made up a distinct middle class, although as historian Alan Draper has argued, they were often "middle-class by Mississippi standards." In Forrest County, black schoolchildren completed, on average, two more years of formal education than their peers in the Delta. As post-*Brown* purges restricted black teachers' membership in civil rights organizations, the city's segregated schools remained important cornerstones of community pride and celebration.[8]

Outside of Hattiesburg, predominately black communities like Kelly Settlement and Palmer's Crossing ameliorated some of Jim Crow's effects. Victoria Gray and her cousins Dorie and Joyce Ladner later described Palmer's Crossing as a "tightly knit" and "pretty well contained African American community" where they were "part of this extended nuclear family and community."[9] In Mississippi's closed society, growing up in a place like Palmer's Crossing made a difference. African American porters routinely tossed black-press newspapers from trains that slowed as they passed through. The "Chitlin' Circuit" brought jazz and blues musicians to the Hi-Hat Club, where black soldiers stationed at nearby Camp Shelby sought respite from rigid military discipline and local racial segregation. News and regular visitors from outside of Mississippi broke the isolation so critical to maintaining the Delta's oppressive form of Jim Crow. Landownership also made a difference. Like many of their neighbors, Gray's grandfather owned his farm. As a result, Gray did not grow up with "a sense of . . . being watched over." Instead, her grandparents nurtured an "independence of spirit" and "personal freedom" that became "part of who [she] was."[10]

Hattiesburg's black community and Palmer's Crossing could not erase daily reminders of second-class citizenship, and within the city's segregated spaces, the Forrest County courthouse stood as an edifice to white supremacy. Two years before Gray completed CEP teacher training, a federal commission documented only twelve registered black voters in a county where 7,406 African Americans were eligible. Gray outlined the challenges in a report to the SCLC. "First one must fill out the application, then he must wait 30–33 days to find out whether or not he's filled the application correctly," she explained. If incorrect, the applicant was forced into a guessing game to correct mistakes, "not knowing what was wrong with the first." "This can go on for several months," she concluded.[11] The circuit clerk decided the outcome, and at 330 pounds, Theron Lynd cast an imposing figure. Thirty years after their first encounter, Gray vividly described the former football player as "tall, big, tall, [and] mean as a snake." By the time Gray arrived at the courthouse in 1963, Lynd had been on the job for four years, and through a well-practiced combination of belligerence, obfuscation, and delay, he had rejected all black registrants.[12]

Gray returned from CEP teacher training intent on challenging this process. Forrest County attracted federal attention in the spring of 1963 when the Fifth Circuit Court of Appeals followed up on an earlier court ruling and ordered Lynd to cease all discriminatory practices. Lynd defiantly vowed to appeal to the U.S. Supreme Court, and SNCC trained more attention on Hattiesburg, dispatching John O'Neal, Carl Arnold, and Lawrence Guyot, who set up shop at Woods Guesthouse.[13] In this emerging movement, Gray's CEP classes filled an important niche. In makeshift classrooms, local teachers helped build confidence, strengthened collective resolve, and most importantly, offered practical lessons in how to pass the literacy test.

By the time Gray arrived at the Dorchester Center, CEP administrators Andrew Young, Septima Clark, and Dorothy Cotton knew that classes thrived in places where a local person effectively tapped into and expanded existing networks. Like Vera Mae Pigee and Bernice Robinson before her, Gray stood out. She had local connections and well-honed organizational skills. In September, Young offered Gray a full-time salaried supervisory position, opening access to resources and defining a clear role and set of responsibilities within the local movement. The regular paycheck meant she could devote more time to civil rights activities. Gray maintained her cosmetics business, but later she recalled, "More and more time began to be spent this way [organizing] until finally, this is where most of my time was going." As she assumed the more public role, Gray faced harassment that included "your phone ringing at two o'clock in the morning and you're told what's going to happen to you. Get these ugly letters in the mail. Some people used to be your friends and associates, they kind of distance themselves." The SCLC salary and cosmetics business helped to shelter the

Grays from economic reprisal, but Anthony Gray's job with the city's Water Works Division left them vulnerable. Victoria Gray recruited for "literacy classes," reasoning that the neutral name might camouflage the CEP's broader purpose. The door-to-door cosmetics business also obscured her organizing work. During sales visits, Gray worked in news about COFO organizers and encouraged participation, extending the movement's reach into corners where COFO organizers would have attracted unwanted attention. Reinforcements arrived in October when Clark helped Gray to tailor lessons to emphasize "simple interpretations of the sections of the constitution." CEP students who struggled with "legal terms" could use the lessons to prepare for registration.[14]

In oral history interviews, Gray later reflected on the CEP's appeal. In Palmer's Crossing, "there was no separation between the spiritual and the secular," she told historian Vicki Crawford. Early lessons called on believers to "be ye doers of the word and not hearers only," and housed within the SCLC, the CEP reinforced this direct link between spiritual beliefs and civil rights action, a link Gray called her "faith connection." Gray also emphasized the CEP's "practical kinds of information that deal[t] with citizenship and community." She recognized that "when [people] get the information, ... when [they] really understand it, Mr. Lynd gets a lot less tall." In CEP classes, local people "began to understand the process, and the fact that they had every right to be participants." Echoing local teachers in the South Carolina Lowcountry and southeastern Georgia, Gray observed, "They began to lose the fear," and free from fear, CEP students became "the foot soldiers."[15]

The 1963 Freedom Vote

In October, Gray marshalled the "foot soldiers" in support of the Freedom Vote. The strategy followed the same pattern as South Carolina's Progressive Democratic Party freedom election of 1944. Mississippi organizers aimed to register voters for a statewide "mock election" alongside the state's gubernatorial race. Strong turnout would demonstrate black Mississippians' commitment to political participation and expose state-sponsored discriminatory practices, putting pressure on the federal government to act. Freedom delegates selected Clarksdale's Aaron Henry to run for governor and Tougaloo College chaplain Edwin King for lieutenant governor. The Freedom Vote platform foregrounded black Mississippians' political and economic concerns, calling for financial assistance for small farmers, fair hiring practices, an end to police brutality, and enforcement of federal wage and hours laws.[16]

In Hattiesburg, the campaign was a direct outlet for CEP students and teachers to enact the lessons from their makeshift classrooms. Registering voters and collecting ballots required coordination, and Gray called on "all available people [to be] used for this effort because we feel that it is [the] priority at this time." Outside of CEP classes, she worked to "find block captains, polling places, [and] campaign managers." In an early report to the SCLC, Gray enthused, "Participation of members of citizenship classes in mock election unbievably [sic] high after a short time of being exposed to things which here-to-fore most were never aware of." The Freedom Vote generated interest in CEP classes, which in turn fueled support for the campaign. Gray marveled, "It is truly wonderful to see people acquire courage as they acquire (however haltingly) an initial or better knowledge of reading and writing and other aspects of the Citizenship training Curriculum."[17] The groundwork paid off. Three days before polls opened, Aaron Henry campaigned at Hattiesburg's Masonic Temple. Two hundred black residents crowded into the hall while over one hundred overflowed into the street. That many black folks gathered for a political meeting virtually ensured the presence of local law enforcement, fire officials, and the Mississippi State Sovereignty Commission (MSSC). City firemen blared a siren at closely timed regular intervals throughout the meeting to disrupt the speeches. Inside, the crowd roared when Henry quipped, "There is a fire here alright, but water can never put it out." The candidate urged listeners to register and support the Freedom Vote campaign.[18]

Freedom Vote registration was open to all Mississippians of voting age, but organizers realistically expected black voters to register and cast ballots. As a result, they concentrated on black-majority Delta counties where CEP students and teachers proved to be important assets. Through local classes and registration activity, they had become savvy at exploiting obtuse political and legal processes. For example, during August primaries and runoff elections, CEP teachers and students joined a wave of "protest balloting," arriving at polls with affidavits and boldly charging local registrars with illegally disfranchising black voters. Teachers "manned booths, gave instructions, [and offered] . . . support at courthouses" to encourage more people to join the protest. Throughout the fall, they directed this experience into the Freedom Vote.[19]

Delta-area teachers seamlessly integrated the Freedom Vote into CEP classes, recording campaign activities alongside routine reports about class attendance and workbook lessons. In Greenville, the Reverend H. C. Robinson made a quick substitution when Henry and King came to town. He cancelled the scheduled lesson, went downtown with his class to hear the speeches, and marked all students "present in class." Annell Ponder noted CEP teachers and students "organiz[ing] local drives, . . . man[ning] ballot boxes, and canvass[ing]" across the Delta. In Bolivar County, CEP teacher Lois Lee Rodgers and Cleveland NAACP branch president Amzie Moore persuaded a minister to "set up [a] voting booth in the church [on] Sunday." Rodgers worked out similar arrangements with more ministers and "ran off leaflets" to help voters locate hastily established polling places. In the days before voting commenced, she "worked dispatching ballot boxes and material at eighteen voting booths [and assigning] citizenship school teachers and other volunteers to [work] the voting booths." At the end of the three-day voting period, Rodgers returned and "picked up all the ballot boxes to be taken to Jackson."[20]

Ponder estimated that "90,000 disfranchised Negroes . . . cast ballots at private homes, pool halls, cafes, churches, fraternal meeting halls, and stores." While the Freedom Vote fell short of the projected 200,000 ballots, COFO organizers claimed victory, arguing that the campaign "laid a groundwork for political organization around the state." To manage the Freedom Vote, COFO had established a central office in Jackson with communication links reaching north into the Mississippi Delta and hill country. The campaign brought in field staff from SNCC and the Congress of Racial Equality (CORE). Moving forward, COFO organizers made plans to expand the movement infrastructure and called for "more citizenship school teachers." Ponder observed that the Freedom Vote had achieved an important objective beyond numbers. Like local CEP classes, the statewide campaign "underscore[d] the urgency and the impatience of Mississippi Negroes for 'Freedom Now' . . . and reverse[d] the direction of the tide of fear." Five months after her ordeal at the Winona jail, Ponder believed that she saw "policemen shake and sheriffs tremble."[21]

Freedom Days in Hattiesburg

Into the New Year, COFO organized a series of Freedom Days to maintain attention on voter registration. In early January, the U.S. Supreme Court upheld a lower court's decision and ordered Forrest County clerk Theron Lynd to cease all practices blocking black voter registration. When Lynd remained defiant, COFO organized a march to the courthouse, reasoning county officials could not easily ignore or turn away a large group of prospective black voters while under intense federal and media scrutiny. A who's who of civil rights leaders converged on Hattiesburg including Ella Baker, Robert "Bob" Moses, Amzie Moore, Aaron Henry, John Lewis, Fannie Lou Hamer, and Annell Ponder. The United Presbyterian Church in the United States of America (UPCUSA) appealed for volunteers, and fifty-two ministers traveled south for the march. Behind the scenes, CEP supervisor Victoria Gray arranged food and lodging for the visitors.[22]

On January 22, the line formed in a cold rain, and news cameras captured marchers making their way through a quiet downtown. City police ordered the group to disperse, but no one left the line and the officers held their positions. At the end of the day, only twelve had taken the registration test while seventy-five waited in the rain. Organizers were disappointed but noted that this was the first time that a demonstration had lasted longer than fifteen minutes in Mississippi. Gray attributed the "minimum of interference" to "advance publicity and the presence of [federal] agents." Her analysis proved correct when reprisals came four days later. "There have been three arrests," Gray reported. "One of the men in my citizenship class lost his job, and two young men in my immediate community likewise." Arrests and dismissals did not have the desired effect as Gray observed that "local participation and involvement is moderately but steadily increasing."[23]

COFO volunteers kept up pressure, canvassing in new areas and organizing daily pickets at the courthouse. The UPCUSA created the Hattiesburg Ministers' Project, and over the next three months, approximately one hundred ministers came from as far away as Colorado, Illinois, and Kansas. Gray organized to open additional entry points, reasoning, "The idea . . . is to involve people at any level, their interest will eventually lead them to the Registrar's office. At the same time, we are meeting some pressing needs." Using "CE classes as the nucleus," she created a "Block Captains Club," and under Gray's leadership, they mobilized traditions of women's community work in service to the civil rights cause. They ensured that visiting clergymen had housing, food, and transportation. Block Captains also held "tea parties" that served as informal CEP classes where the host answered questions and encouraged voter registration. The activities drew in new volunteers, and by February, three made the trip to Dorchester. Gray would later remark that Peggy Jean Connor, Helen Anderson, and Ruth Ratliff Campbell formed "the heart of the Hattiesburg movement."[24]

Like a growing number of CEP teachers, thirty-year-old Peggy Jean Connor was in the beauty business. Through her shop window, she had watched Guyot, Arnold, and O'Neal organize the COFO office on Mobile Street. In time, Guyot made his way to Connor's shop, and she knew why. As CEP experience had confirmed, "Beauticians and midwives" had "some influence over . . . other people," and because they "own business[es] . . . there's no way of cutting [their] money off," Connor later acknowledged. At Guyot's invitation, she attended a mass meeting in Palmer's Crossing where guest speaker Fannie Lou Hamer's powerful testimony "set [the congregation] on fire." The mass meeting was not Connor's introduction to civil rights action, however. Her father, John Henry Gould, registered to vote in the 1940s and served as local secretary of the Committee of One Hundred, a precursor to Hattiesburg's NAACP chapter. Gould often enlisted his oldest daughter's assistance because her "big handwriting" proved useful in "writ[ing] out letters about the meetings and things." As she transcribed, Peggy Jean "learned some things." Connor's younger brother carried on the family tradition. Police arrested the younger Gould at the Freedom Day march and kept up harassment as he shined shoes on Mobile Street following his release.[25] For Connor, teaching CEP classes offered a clearly defined and distinctly gendered entry point into the local movement.

Connor traveled to Dorchester with two friends. Ruth Ratliff Campbell also came from a politically active family. Her father, the Reverend J. H. Ratliff, had served True Light Baptist Church for more than two decades and was one of Hattiesburg's first black registered voters, managing to get through following the 1944 *Smith v. Allwright* decision. Ratliff was also an active member of the Committee of One Hundred and had served as the first president of Hattiesburg's NAACP chapter. At forty, Helen V. Anderson was the oldest of the trio, and unlike Connor and Ratliff, she had not completed high school. Both Campbell and Anderson married Hercules men where union protection for political action extended to workers' families. Teaching CEP classes also helped Anderson to navigate gendered relationships at home. Connor remembered that Anderson's "husband kind of kept her—well, he didn't let her participate too much . . . where she would put herself in danger of going to jail or something like that." For Campbell's protective husband, teaching in a church hall was safe when compared to pickets, marches, and sit-ins.[26]

Upon their return from the Georgia coast, Gray called a meeting where they outlined plans to open more classes. "Everyone is rearing to be started," she wrote, and classes were up and running by the end of March.[27]

Hattiesburg-area teachers continued the CEP practice of connecting literacy skills to political action, often supplementing workbook lessons with practical assignments and active participation in ongoing civil rights action. Court challenges focused attention on judicial processes, and Connor's students gathered information about the state judicial system. In the tradition of "each one, teach one," students gave their reports in class. In February, Connor, Campbell, and five CEP students were arrested and charged with obstructing traffic after they joined the courthouse picket line.[28] CEP students kept up pressure on Lynd. In April, Connor reported, "Ten have applied for registration. Two have registered since classes began." As Connor's students filed into the registrar's office, Gray and CEP students testified in the federal case against Lynd, earning praise from U.S. attorney John Doar for an "excellent" performance.[29]

Laying-By Time in the Delta

While Hattiesburg teachers rode a wave of intensifying activity, Delta CEP teachers and field staff struggled through a lull. By the fall of 1963, COFO had waged battle against daunting forces, and fatigue was setting in. In the six months leading up to the Freedom Vote campaign, CEP teachers had organized forty-seven local schools across five Delta counties. Greenwood, a focal point for CEP work in the spring, accounted for thirty-four of the classes. Still, fewer than fifty of the fifteen hundred black citizens who attempted to register were successful.[30] Teachers and students pushed against persistent obstacles at courthouses where CEP lessons could not break through unfairly applied voter registration tests. From Itta Bena, McKinley Marcus attributed lack of success to the "injustice in the literacy test." In Holmes County, Ralthus H. Hayes's students met a "circuit clerk [who] will not let us pass the test but we are still going up," he assured the CEP administrators. The literacy test was not the only impediment. When the two-dollar poll tax proved insurmountable for cash-strapped sharecroppers, Mary Diggs's students organized "to raise money to pay tax." Following Diggs's lead, CEP supervisors urged area ministers to start similar clubs. Other obstacles came from within black communities. In the early fall, Ollie M. Hughes canvassed outside of Indianola where "the fear" pervaded cotton fields. "Every one that I talk to didn't want their name mention," she reported. Fear undermined efforts to secure space for local classes. Margaret Block discontinued her Cleveland class when the minister "put [them] out." The class remained in limbo for three weeks until "a broke down church" took them in.³¹ The Freedom Vote had lifted flagging spirits, but persistent harassment and intimidation and declining CEP attendance during fall harvest took its toll.

Ponder had other concerns in the fall of 1963. Successful recruiting was proving to be a double-edged sword. On the one hand, forty-one local people completed CEP teacher training between June and November, returning home to organize fifty-two schools in eight counties. These numbers added to an impressive total of 226 new CEP teachers who organized 277 schools that enrolled 3,692 students across eleven southern states. Their cumulative efforts resulted in 9,575 newly registered voters who either had attended a class or were influenced by local CEP activities. However, increased interest and more active classes strained the program budget, and administrators encouraged field staff like Ponder to tighten up.³² Criticism about "generally ... poorly equipped" teachers from the Delta put Ponder on the defensive, and she dug in to demonstrate improvements, starting with the new office that quickly became a multiservice center. A small lending library extended the CEP's influence by inviting residents to drop in to learn about services, programs, and ideas that transgressed the Delta's narrow boundaries. CEP teachers from across the region gathered for weekly meetings where they discussed common issues, heard about new teaching materials, and coordinated activities. From this base of operation, Ponder transferred program administration to local people. In the spring of 1963, she promoted high-performing teachers in Greenwood, Ruleville, and Cleveland into supervisor positions where they worked closely with area teachers and recruited for CEP teacher training. The experiment did not resolve concerns as Dorothy Cotton wrote in September to urge Ponder to be even more selective when recruiting for CEP training. In response, Ponder added supervisors in Itta Bena and Tchula and appointed two new area supervisors.³³

Ponder's efforts replicated Hosea Williams's structure in southeastern Georgia with one significant exception: the Delta CEP network was woman-led from Ponder through supervisors to local teachers. CEP supervisors embraced the role, adopting a "uniform" that established a distinct identity. A well-kept "white blouse with S.L.C. letters" reflected traditional ideas about respectable appearance and asserted organizational affiliation. On the other hand, "Blue Denims [sic] skirts" made of fabric typically associated with manual labor signified that CEP organizing was work and that supervisors were part of, not separate from, communities where this work took place. The combination of blouse, skirt, and SCLC lettering distinguished CEP teachers from SNCC workers who donned T-shirts, overalls, and blue jeans. The absence of a uniform for male supervisors underlined assumptions that the CEP was "women's work."[34]

A new office and supervision system focused attention squarely on the program rules. Area supervisor Pinkie Pilcher was charged with overseeing local classes, responsibility that she balanced with running a day care center. Under the new policies, teachers informed Pilcher when "a class starts officially and when it ends." While the class was in session, Pilcher "[kept] a running check on enrollment and attendance as well as help[ed] with subject matter." Policies empowered Pilcher to deny stipends if she determined that there was not a "bona fide class in operation."[35] Intended to democratize administration, the policies emphasized adherence to the rules. Varying compensation levels and authority established a hierarchy among local teachers and created a clique around Ponder. In a report to the SCLC, Ponder confided that "teachers and some supervisors have objected to [the] procedure."[36]

Supervisors visited local classes and molded their activities to local priorities. Throughout the summer of 1963, Bolivar County supervisor Lois L. Rodgers documented few class visits, and despite energetic canvassing and recruiting, classes were slow to organize during the fall's cotton harvest. Rodgers redirected energies into other activities. She collected clothing donations and distributed copies of the *Mississippi Free Press*. In late summer, she "[thought] beyond the ballot" and initiated "a Moral Education Program" aimed at reducing the incidence of teenage pregnancy. Rodgers traced the roots of the problem to poorly funded recreation and public health services, and by late August, she had collected reading materials and enlisted help from an African American public health nurse. In October, Rodgers met with local youth where she linked economic opportunity to education, urging participants "to stay in school" because "better job opportunities [call] for education." Rodgers's activities did not go unnoticed. In October, Annell Ponder hypothesized that Rodgers's sister's difficulties in renewing a restaurant license were likely linked to her sister's civil rights activities.[37]

Rodgers's report reinforced James Bevel's earlier assessments of Jim Crow's complex web of political, economic, and social restrictions and extralegal violence. When local people and civil rights activists tugged on political and social threads, white Mississippians tightened economic threads and poor Delta families felt this response most acutely. CEP lessons and voter registration only went so far. Teachers understood this and embraced a broad interpretation of "citizenship education," conflating CEP work with community work that laid claim to a wide variety of long-denied services, entitlements, and rights. This broad interpretation, however, tested the limits of CEP work. Upon receipt of Rodgers's report, Clark wrote back to ask, "Do you know that picking up clothing is not in the Citizenship Education Program?" Clark appreciated the need but insisted that "this project should be done by community people." As supervisors like Rodgers blurred the lines between the CEP and community work, Clark sought to engage more local people.[38]

Citizenship Education during Freedom Summer

CEP teachers were not the only organizers regrouping in the spring of 1964. After three years of constant activity in "the home of white supremacy," COFO organizers concluded that "much more comprehensive programs are needed to combat the terrible cultural and economic deprivation of Negro communities in Mississippi." In the spring of 1964, the Southern Regional Council dealt a blow, explaining, "A sizeable portion of the [Voter Education Project] budget had already been spent in Mississippi and the registration results were minimal." Without federal intervention, officials argued, "It does not appear to be wise for VEP to put any more of its already limited funds into Mississippi."[39] Weary civil rights workers responded with a strategy designed to shine a national spotlight into the Magnolia State's darkest corners, developing an ambitious plan for a massive summer project that would expand voter registration efforts in support of the MFDP and establish a network of "Freedom Schools" and multiservice community centers. Organizers believed that this comprehensive approach would spark the broad participation needed to generate sufficient groundswell for change. Most importantly, the strategy would make it more difficult for federal officials to ignore Mississippi. Throughout the spring of 1964, COFO recruited project volunteers. Intentionally echoing President John F. Kennedy's call to public service, brochures invited students from elite colleges and universities to participate in a "massive Peace Corps–type operation in Mississippi."[40]

Citizenship school veterans threw support behind the program. From the Delta, Ponder spearheaded efforts to open community centers and formalize emergency food and clothing distribution into a coordinated "statewide program of welfare and relief."[41] In late March, Myles Horton and Septima Clark lent expertise in designing the Freedom Schools curriculum.

COFO organizers envisioned a program of "remedial instruction" and "cultural influences which are not normally available" in Mississippi. Freedom School lessons would "implant habits of free thinking" and "lay the groundwork for a statewide youth movement." Clark chaired the subcommittee on remedial education, and the final curriculum reflected ideas and concepts that had enlivened CEP classes, including "flexible" materials and lessons drawn from "the students' every day [sic] lives." From this starting point, students "became active agents in bringing about social change."[42] As in CEP classrooms, education was the vehicle for this change.

Plans for Freedom Summer coalesced amidst reverberations from the nation's capital and from within Mississippi. In February, the U.S. House of Representatives passed a civil rights bill that promised to stamp out Jim Crow segregation, and powerful southern senators braced for what Georgia senator Richard B. Russell called "the war." When a four-month filibuster showed no signs of weakening, CEP teachers generated local support for the bill. Hattiesburg teacher Helen Anderson "built [a lesson] around the Civil Rights bill," with students "writing letters to Senators favorable to the bill," including "at least one good reason . . . that the Bill be passed." Peggy Jean Connor and Ruth Ratliff Campbell designed lessons about the legislation and urged MFDP voter registration. From the Delta, Margaret Block's students "had a very good discussion on the civil rights bill" and forty-four Cleveland residents registered "on the freedom registration book."[43]

In the spring and summer of 1964, women with ties to the CEP led direct challenges to Mississippi's political system. Victoria Gray and Fannie Lou Hamer ran against congressional incumbents in the state's primaries. They faced long odds with only 5 percent of the state's eligible African Americans registered to vote, and in the end, the MFDP candidates lost.[44] COFO sustained pressure on local political systems into the summer. According to Mississippi laws, state-level parties selected delegates to national conventions through a multistep process, beginning with precinct elections in early June, followed by county conventions and district caucuses, culminating in a state convention. COFO mobilized to test the process, enlisting support from CEP-trained local people. In late June, Pinkie Pilcher and Eddye Lane surprised officials at the Leflore County convention when they presented credentials as delegates from Greenwood's Southeast Precinct. After they arrived late for the official election, Pilcher and Lane explained, they enlisted help from fellow CEP teachers Alice Blackwell and the Reverend George Barber and held an impromptu vote at the COFO office. Faced with two sets of delegates, county officials disqualified Pilcher and Lane, arguing that they were chosen "at an unauthorized and unadvertised meeting held in an unauthorized place at an unauthorized time."[45] A similar scenario played out in neighboring Sunflower County. Unable to locate the official meeting, black residents held an election where they selected Fannie Lou Hamer and Rebecca McDonald as delegates to the county convention. On the appointed day, the women presented their credentials, and as in Leflore County, officials refused to recognize them as duly elected delegates to the district caucus. One week later, night riders hurled bottles at homes and cars and tossed a Molotov cocktail onto the steps of Williams Chapel, Hamer's and McDonald's home church and the site of mass meetings and CEP classes. As similar challenges played out across the state, the MFDP managed a parallel process, gathering support at precinct, county, and district meetings that were "open to all Democrats in Mississippi of voting age regardless of race, creed or color."[46]

Into early summer, COFO split its resources between MFDP registration and mobilization, Freedom Schools, and community centers. In two training sessions, students from elite colleges and universities gathered at the Western College for Women in Oxford, Ohio. Ponder led orientation sessions for community center volunteers while CEP teachers served as resource instructors, talking about their daily experiences and answering questions to prepare volunteers for "the challenges in working in the area." Ponder observed teachers delivering an important message. Student volunteers were welcome reinforcements, but CEP teachers reminded them that civil rights action was already under way, led by local people who possessed "strength and resourcefulness" and "militancy for freedom."[47]

Freedom Summer kicked off on July 1, and within two weeks, 450 volunteers arrived in Mississippi with another hundred close behind. COFO's numbers swelled to one hundred staff members, and 150 attorneys and law students stood by to address legal problems.[48] The summer project represented a departure for COFO organizers. In past efforts, COFO field staff members had cultivated relationships with local leaders and deployed resources in response to locally defined needs. This model was particularly important for the CEP because the program's growth and development depended on effective partnerships between SCLC staff and local teachers. Freedom Summer would test these partnerships as hundreds of volunteers arrived in the state for a relatively short-term project. In brochures to Mississippi's black residents, COFO organizers insisted, "This is your FREEDOM SUMMER. It will not work without your help." "Help" was not the same as "leadership." "Help" meant "providing housing," or "looking for buildings," or "getting names."⁴⁹ Across the state, African Americans who had supported earlier COFO efforts, including CEP teachers, mobilized for Freedom Summer.

A firm believer in collaboration and flexible alliances, Victoria Gray "welcomed support from wherever it came from." She later reflected, "I was not involved very much in the politics of the organizations, opinions, and that sort of thing. I was very much involved with getting the job done . . . and I worked with whosoever was willing to support that." Volunteers arrived in Hattiesburg over the Fourth of July weekend and opened five Freedom Schools, attracting more than six hundred young people and earning the Hub City the title "the Mecca of the Freedom School world." Area CEP classes had concluded in May, and local teachers suspended citizenship school activity for the duration of the summer. CEP teachers welcomed volunteers into their homes and "encouraged others to do likewise." On July 18, the Palmer's Crossing community center opened for business and became the center of activity. CEP teacher Ruth Ratliff Campbell organized a committee to coordinate food, clothing, and book drives. COFO organizer Staughton Lynd attributed the Hattiesburg program's success to "the intensive civil rights campaign in the community during the months of late winter and spring." In late June, Gray reported, "Citizenship teachers and classes . . . are not only providing help . . . but are being helped . . . to carry on after the summer."⁵⁰

With Ponder serving as statewide coordinator, COFO organizers envisioned that community centers like the one in Palmer's Crossing would be the summer home for the CEP. According to COFO plans, local teachers would continue their work in newly organized, multiservice centers, conducting classes alongside "job training programs; classes on child care; health programs; and music, drama, and arts and crafts workshops." Child care would be available free of charge for program participants.⁵¹ While this format situated CEP classes in centralized and more protected spaces, the characterization of the CEP as an "adult literacy program" narrowed the program's goals. Throughout the summer, the divide between Delta-area CEP teachers and COFO volunteers and staff widened as Ponder struggled to retain the CEP's focus and bridge the gap. In a memorandum to community center staff, Ponder praised the volunteers' efforts to open child care programs and Freedom Schools. However, she expressed disappointment with coordination between center staff and CEP teachers. She reminded volunteers that initial plans called for local CEP teachers to organize classes and register residents for the MFDP election. "This doesn't seem to be happening," Ponder wrote. She theorized, "This is due, we think, to a lack of communication between the SCLC citizenship teachers and the center spokesman." To correct the problem, she encouraged summer volunteers to contact CEP teachers directly. For Ponder, this "lack of communication" had implications beyond the summer project. In the same memorandum, she took the center staff to task, asking, "What happens when you leave? Are you getting local people drawn into the program management?" After three years of building a network of CEP teachers, Ponder reminded center volunteers that "citizenship school teachers are supposed to be your bridge in this direction."[52]

Ponder's questions and suggestions pointed to challenges in sustaining locally driven community organizing in the midst of a short-term, high-intensity strategy. In some places, the influx of volunteers pulled local students and teachers in new directions. From Greenwood, another center of activity during Freedom Summer, CEP supervisor Alice Blackwell reported, "Everyone has been busy canvassing and organizing block captains for voter registration meetings and attending mass meetings to hear the noted speakers. Also canvassing and picketing. Therefore, we have not been teaching citizenship classes the past weeks." Local teacher James G. Thompson confirmed Blackwell's assessment. "COFO workers made Block Captains of the peoples [sic] that would work and that stopped most schools," he wrote.[53]

Other CEP teachers seamlessly incorporated Freedom Summer activities into ongoing community service work. In Greenwood, beautician Atlean Smith provided practical comforts. Blending rural traditions of canning and freezing food and southern hospitality, Smith "made in [her] freezer all . . . summer for rights workers" and invited them in to use her bathroom. From Holmes County, CEP supervisor Willie Burns reported that local teachers and students expanded the curriculum to incorporate Freedom Schools, building a Holmes County Community Center, and voter registration. In Hattiesburg, teachers viewed the MFDP as the practical application of CEP lessons. Gray assumed a statewide leadership position and enlisted local teachers. Helen Anderson chaired the Palmer's Crossing precinct meeting where seventy-five residents "crowded into tiny St. John" and cast ballots. The local position opened new opportunities, and by the end of the summer, Anderson had served as county secretary and as a delegate to both county and state conventions alongside fellow CEP teacher

Peggy Jean Connor. By late summer, Gray acknowledged that both women "deserve[d] special mention," serving "in such a manner as to be especially proud."[54]

On August 6, a crowd of 2,500 gathered at Jackson's Masonic Temple for the MFDP state convention. Gray later reflected, "Here were the people who had and were risking it all, finally confronting Mississippi and planning to confront the United States and the world with their 'Moment of Truth.'" The group selected officers and delegates to carry the party's message to Atlantic City, and the CEP's influence was in evidence as Gray served as the MFDP's national committeewoman, Fannie Lou Hamer accepted the vice chairmanship of the delegation, and Peggy Jean Connor was selected secretary of the State Executive Committee. Former Holmes County student Hartman Turnbow and Hattiesburg teacher Helen Anderson traveled to Atlantic City as delegates to national convention.[55]

MFDP participation put CEP-trained local people on a collision course with the national Democratic Party. Before the convention got under way, governors of Alabama, Arkansas, Louisiana, Mississippi, and Florida pledged a boycott if MFDP delegates were seated. The governors' joint statement set the stage for a showdown. At the convention, MFDP delegates presented their accumulated evidence to the Credentials Committee. Speaking in a voice straight out of the Delta, Hamer presented her damning case against Mississippi's white-dominated power structures. In testimony replayed on nightly news programs, she recounted the trip to the Indianola courthouse and described the beating at the Winona jail in graphic detail. Hamer concluded her testimony with her own ultimatum. "If the Freedom Democratic Party is not seated now," she asserted, "I question America. Is this America, the land of the free and the home of the brave where we have to sleep with our phones off the hook because our lives be threatened daily, because we want to live as decent human beings?"[56] MFDP allies and delegates forced high-level negotiations with the national Democratic Party and Mississippi's all-white delegation, ultimately ending in an unsatisfactory compromise where Freedom Party delegates were offered two at-large seats on the convention floor. They rejected the compromise and returned to Mississippi, largely disenchanted and vowing to continue the fight. They would chart a course forward without Annell Ponder. After eighteen months in the Delta, she turned statewide supervisory duties over to Gray and returned to Atlanta.[57]

The CEP in Mississippi after the Challenge

As the Mississippi reassignment suggested, the CEP was in transition after a summer that pulled staff in different directions. While Ponder devoted time to COFO's Freedom Summer, Young and Cotton provided critical support for a direct action campaign in Saint Augustine, Florida. From within the CEP, Septima Clark's patience wore thin. In December, she had expressed dissatisfaction directly to King. From one side of a generation gap, she reflected, "Direct action is so glamourous and packed with emotion that most young people prefer demonstrations over genuine education." Day-to-day program management was mundane by comparison. At the SCLC office, one secretary struggled to stay atop an avalanche of attendance and expenditure reports. Confusion about rules and documentation often resulted in a back-and-forth between a teacher and staff member before payment was approved. When Young, Cotton, and Clark were out in the field, stipend payments and correspondence languished, and teachers routinely grew impatient. Clark reminded King that local teachers gave "eight hours a month of their time helping adults, and three times as much [time]" encouraging political and civic engagement and "all this for the maximum amount of $30.00 per month for expenses." The SCLC had struck a bargain. If local people committed time and talents to the CEP, they would receive compensation. Poor management threatened to erode teachers' trust in the CEP and in the SCLC more broadly. Exasperated, Clark offered to "search around" for an organizational home that "could serve the real purpose better."[58] Issues remained unresolved into the summer as Clark reminded Young about "vouchers from as far back as January waiting to be paid." "This kind of administration I greatly detest," she added. Young conceded that he "never pretended to be a great administrator," but he defended his time in Saint Augustine, arguing that "the slave system—segregation" would only end through the synergy of direct action and education programs like the CEP. The SCLC's reorganization brought Randolph Blackwell from the Southern Regional Council into the CEP, and Young anticipated improvements as the new fiscal year commenced.[59]

Into the next fiscal year, CEP staff adopted policies designed to improve budget management and program administration. They agreed to reduce the number of active schools to one hundred, deciding to "keep the best teachers and officially stop the other ones." Beginning in the fall of 1964, program staff conducted "more thorough recruiting" while trying to retain experienced teachers.[60] It fell to Victoria Gray to implement changes in Mississippi, starting in Hattiesburg. MFDP delegates Peggy Jean Connor and Helen Anderson settled back into the routine, organizing CEP classes due to start in the new community center in early October.[61] In November, Gray traveled into the Delta where structural weaknesses began to show. After Ponder's departure, and despite her efforts to transfer administration to local supervisors, the network frayed. New teacher stipend policies contributed to the decline, and Gray confronted "mixed and varied responses" to the news that the CEP would "continue paying . . . a few people." If Ponder's supervisor assignments implied favoritism among local teachers, limiting compensation to select teachers seemed to confirm it. From Greenwood, Alice Blackwell dismissed other teachers' practical financial concerns and viewed their response as betrayal to the cause. After Gray's visit, she wrote to Dorothy Cotton, "very much disturbed." "They don't want to work with out pay [sic]," she lamented, and "only three of them came to the meeting when Mrs. Gray was here."[62]

Throughout the fall, Gray divided her attention between the CEP and the MFDP. When Mississippi officials refused to place MFDP candidates on the state's general election ballot, the MFDP followed the Freedom Vote blueprint and collected ballots for its candidates, including Gray and Hamer, Canton's Annie Devine, Clarksdale's Aaron Henry, and MFDP delegate Harold Roby.[63] In November, state officials refused to certify the MFDP results, and Henry and Roby conceded. Hamer, Gray, and Devine stayed in. Declaring the election "void" because black voters were "systematically and almost totally excluded," the MFDP declared the three black women to be the "true representatives," chosen through the only election "open to all citizens."[64] The congressional challenge strained the COFO coalition, and in January, the NAACP board of directors withdrew support. Loyal NAACP members like Aaron Henry and Vera Mae Pigee followed. The SCLC remained, largely through its connection to Gray.[65]

Local people with CEP ties enacted lessons to increase black political representation, address economic inequality, and pressure local institutions to adhere to federal desegregation orders. With the MFDP taking aim at Congress, CEP veterans took on political systems closer to home. In Greenville, the Reverend H. C. Anderson launched a campaign to represent Ward Four in the "first contested general election in a long while." In Greenwood, Alice Blackwell, Pinkie Pilcher, and Mary Lane filed papers to run for city government.[66] News traveled fast about "the first time since reconstruction days that Negroes have sought elective office in Greenwood." The county Democratic executive committee announced that Pilcher was the only registered voter among the three, effectively ending Blackwell's and Lane's bids for office.[67] At the same time, Fannie Lou Hamer joined CEP veterans James G. Thompson and Ethel Lee Thompson in organizing the Mississippi Freedom Labor Union (MFLU), uniting sharecroppers, domestic workers, and tractor farmers to organize strikes on Mississippi plantations, economic boycotts and selective buying campaigns, and protests in front of businesses slow to desegregate after the Civil Rights Act of 1964. From Greenwood, Atlean Smith "organize[d] maids, field workers, [and] mothers of school children [to] help boycott places where negroes are denied their rights."[68] In Holmes County, after a successful push to integrate the public library, the Reverend Jesse J. Russell's students collected 160 signatures on a petition demanding school integration.[69] Also in Holmes County, CEP teachers added lessons about Farmers Home Administration (FHA) loans, and by the fall of 1965, CEP teacher Ralthus Hayes rallied black farmers and campaigned for the thirty-seven black candidates running in the Agricultural Stabilization and Conservation Service (ASCS) election and secured voting rights for farmers' wives whose names appeared on land deeds.[70]

* * *

The years 1963 and 1964 marked high points for the CEP in Mississippi. Under Victoria Gray's leadership, the program established a new outpost in the state's southeastern corner where CEP classes served as political education and organizing centers within an emerging movement. In the Delta, Annell Ponder built on foundations set with earlier classes to firmly implant the program, and the SCLC, in that corner of the state. In both places, the CEP tapped into deeply rooted networks, opening a new outlet for community service. Using the CEP workbook as a guide, local people demystified the voter registration process and encouraged active participation. From living rooms, church meeting halls, and community centers, they mobilized communities and claimed first-class citizenship on city streets and in courthouses.

CEP teachers contributed to and drew on political action organized through the Council of Federated Organizations. The 1963 Freedom Vote served as a direct outlet for CEP lessons, and subsequent Freedom Days sustained momentum into 1964. Flexible alliances and shared commitment to education as a vehicle for social change facilitated crossover between the citizenship school program and plans for Freedom Summer. As volunteers arrived in local communities, CEP teachers contributed to critical logistical support and helped to ensure success. CEP classrooms served as organizing centers for MFDP registration and related challenges to state political systems. By the end of the summer, CEP veterans were among the delegates challenging national political systems in Atlantic City.

CEP activity waned in the wake of the challenge. Collaboration during Freedom Summer came with costs as intense activity siphoned momentum away from local classes. After the summer, some CEP veterans funneled the program's lessons and broader organizing experience into activities designed to advance goals of economic security and to claim rights guaranteed by new federal legislation. Ponder's departure from the Delta further weakened ties holding the CEP network together. Program expansion in Mississippi contributed to internal discussions, resulting in revised criteria and requirements. As the COFO coalition splintered, organizational affiliation took on new importance, and Gray's connections to the MFDP narrowed the CEP's potential constituency as black Mississippians chose sides. All of these factors influenced a sharp decline in CEP classes. At the same time, a groundswell was building in Alabama's Black Belt. Mississippi teachers "made their witness," joining a march from Selma to Montgomery. Gray regretted missing the event but said she "was very much there in spirit." "When we sang 'We Shall Overcome' on that historical day," she wrote, "I knew that the Wallaces, Johnson's [sic] et al around this potentially great nation faced . . . this historical moment of truth because we had in fact, at that moment, 'Overcome' one more of the many obstacles."[71] Gray and the nation turned attention to southwestern Alabama.

7

"So Much Taking Place ... So Rapidly"

Citizenship Education in Mississippi and Alabama, 1965–1967

In April 1965, Victoria Gray submitted a progress report, admitting, "The past six months have been a struggle in many ways" as she and Mississippi's Citizenship Education Program (CEP) teachers were caught "in a maze of so much taking place around us so rapidly." After Annell Ponder's departure from Mississippi in the fall of 1964, Gray took the helm and worked to link Delta-based and Hattiesburg networks while expanding the program into "hitherto untouched counties." The ongoing congressional challenge by the Mississippi Freedom Democratic Party (MFDP) required much of her time.[1] Their work dovetailed federal reform measures. The Civil Rights Act and the Economic Opportunity Act, both passed the previous year, promised to dismantle Jim Crow segregation and address deeply rooted economic inequality. Into the spring of 1965, Gray was optimistic about a federal voting rights law that would remove "one more of the many obstacles" for black voters. In Mississippi, she and MFDP organizers focused on process, identifying pressure points and initiating legal and political challenges. At the same time, CEP momentum shifted into Alabama's Black Belt where the program organized after local demonstrations subsided.

This chapter entwines Mississippi and Alabama narrative threads to illustrate how CEP teachers adapted to a rapidly changing landscape. Passed in the summer of 1965, the Voting Rights Act was welcome reform but it also undermined the CEP's primary reason for existence. Septima Clark and Annell Ponder moved the program into a new phase with updated, revised, and refined lessons on political education and organization, federal entitlement and anti-poverty programs, and family economics. Mississippi and Alabama were among the first testing grounds where programmatic changes worked in concert with activities already under way in communities. As a result, lessons augmented local leaders' skills, tools, and expertise, and CEP teachers adapted the information to the local context. In these areas marked by systemic generational poverty and oppressive racial segregation, CEP teachers used every opportunity to mobilize people to lay claim to newly guaranteed rights and entitlements. In Mississippi, teachers and veterans supported MFDP candidates and helped to funnel anti-poverty resources into the state, transferring CEP principles into local programs. In Alabama, the CEP offered an outlet to extend community work beyond the springtime Selma campaign. Through structured three-month classes and informal application of CEP lessons, local women enacted first-class citizenship and empowered others to do the same.[2]

Moving the CEP into the next phase would not be easy as white segregationists and moderate conservatives were also adapting. Civil rights and anti-poverty legislation opened doors for federal intervention, and in response, conservative forces gathered into a counteroffensive against what they saw as excessive liberalism that undermined individual initiative and violated states' rights. By early 1965, elected officials took aim at President Lyndon B. Johnson's War on Poverty, arguing that the federal programs represented a dangerous and wasteful expansion of the social welfare state. From the federal, state, and local levels, white southern Democrats blocked funding and blunted implementation. Officials scrutinized new programs, keeping a sharp eye out for accounting and administrative errors and instances where public funds could be characterized as promoting a civil rights agenda.[3] Sustaining reform or turning back the tide depended on political power. In this context, voter registration took on new importance, and by the spring of 1965, Alabama's Black Belt and Mississippi were ground zero.

Citizenship Education in Mississippi after Freedom Summer

On January 4, 1965, the congressional session opened with Victoria Gray and more than five hundred MFDP supporters holding vigil outside the House chamber. When the Speaker called Thomas Abernethy of Mississippi to be sworn in, Congressman William Fitts Ryan objected. Debate ensued, and in the end, House members agreed to conditionally seat Mississippi's delegation pending investigation into voter discrimination charges. The MFDP had forty days to collect evidence.[4] Before returning to Mississippi, MFDP supporters picketed at the White House, registered formal complaints about "unfair cotton allotments" at the U.S. Department of Agriculture (USDA), and met with federal anti-poverty officials to report cases of black voters who were "cut off the county welfare list" after they registered with the MFDP. "CEP people were very much in action," Gray emphasized in her report.[5] Gray's insistence on this point illustrated her pragmatic approach. As the COFO alliance fractured, she seamlessly blended SCLC and MFDP strategies because in her view, they were two sides of the same coin. According to Gray, "the ills" affecting black citizens were "all caused basically from . . . non-representation and consequently, no kind of power." Addressing "the ills" depended on alliances where organizations played complementary roles. In a 1965 interview, she explained that the SCLC "deal[t] with the results of what the system has produced," and the MFDP worked "to remove the cause of these kind of things." In Mississippi, this translated into a collaboration where CEP teachers laid groundwork and the MFDP served as an important outlet to enact CEP lessons.[6]

Into the spring, Gray attempted to channel CEP activity into "the political arena generally and the Congressional Challenge in particular," but she acknowledged that federal reform had redefined the "struggle," shifting from "a common enemy to more diverse directions and objectives."[7] By the fall of 1964, the federal Economic Opportunity Act created a dizzying array of job training, public assistance, community development, and education programs. The new services expanded supports for poor families and had the potential to upend local power structures through federal "maximum feasible participation" requirements that empowered "poor people" to plan, implement, and evaluate alongside service professionals and political officials accustomed to making decisions for, not with, poor families. As War on Poverty task force member Norbert Schlei explained, "Maximum feasible participation" had practical consequences because employment and leadership in federal anti-poverty initiatives gave "a sense of responsibility, being in control of their own destiny."[8] The CEP's training in leadership development and community empowerment strategies ideally suited teachers and students for these programs. CEP veterans across the South leveraged the CEP's lessons and skills to gain positions on local governing councils and employment in federally funded anti-poverty programs. With federal funds and assistance, teachers addressed unresolved civil rights concerns, such as continuing disparities between white and black Americans in terms of earning, education, housing, and health care. Through their work, they transplanted principles of participatory democracy and local decision-making into new federal programs. For CEP teachers, this was the next phase of political action.[9]

A cornerstone of the federal War on Poverty was "Project Head Start." Initially proposed as an early education summer program for "underprivileged children," the program was expanded to operate year-round by the fall of 1965.[10] The Child Development Group of Mississippi (CDGM) assisted local organizers in securing funds and opening comprehensive early childhood education centers. As the effort rolled out, Gray observed, "The People who are the most militant in trying to . . . maintain the projected objectives of the Federal Programs, are for the most part, people who have been exposed to CE[P] at some point."[11] In Itta Bena, CEP veteran Willie Baxter helped to establish a center, and fellow teachers Ellis Jackson and Mary Strong served on the policy council and taught classes. In nearby Sidon, Ethel Gray held Head Start classes in the same home where night riders had fired shots and deposited rattlesnakes on the doorstep when she taught for the CEP. CEP supervisor and preschool teacher Pinkie Pilcher collaborated with Mary Lane to open four centers in Leflore County and hired Alice Blackwell as a resource teacher for Greenwood's Community Center Head Start School. In Hattiesburg, Helen Anderson and Peggy Jean Connor leveraged CEP and MFDP experience to teach in the new Head Start program.[12] After 1965, Head Start became a primary strategy that sustained the CEP's roots in the Delta and in Hattiesburg.

CEP veterans serving in anti-poverty programs and supporting political action fulfilled the founders' vision of the program as a training ground for broader community involvement and leadership development; however, migration into these areas thinned the cadre of experienced teachers and siphoned off potential teachers. Gray insisted that the CEP was needed "like never before" to "enable people to relate . . . movement jargon with and to their daily lives and expectations," equipping them to "withstand . . . pressures . . . rather than trading their hard-earned freedom for a mess of pottage."[13] After a bumpy introduction the previous fall, she returned to the Delta in February, securing a commitment from area supervisors and teachers to "enlarge the scope of our Citizenship Classes far beyond our former efforts." By late April, Gray documented twenty-one classes across the state, including new classes in Lauderdale and Carroll Counties; however, the overall number of CEP recruits declined. In August 1964, eleven volunteers had traveled to Dorchester. In the first three workshops of 1965, fifteen Mississippi volunteers made the trip, but only four of these teachers organized classes upon their return.[14] In contrast, during the same period, thirty-two residents representing three of Alabama's Black Belt counties completed the Dorchester teacher training workshop in February. Recruiting was particularly successful in Wilcox County, where twenty volunteers from Coy made up nearly half of all participants in the March workshop.[15]

Citizenship Education and the Selma Campaign

The CEP groundswell was the direct result of a civil rights campaign in southwestern Alabama. The Selma campaign followed James Bevel's blueprint that called for a statewide election modeled on the MFDP, active citizenship schools, and a frontal assault on obstacles to black voter registration in "one hard-core city," all designed to build pressure for federal action.[16] Located fifty miles west of Montgomery on the Alabama River, Selma was the county seat of Dallas County. The city's heyday was tied to a time and place where personal wealth rested on land and labor, a combination that gave rise to the region's name. Cotton plantations had flourished in the Black Belt's dark rich soil, and antebellum planters fueled an interstate slave trade so that before the Civil War, enslaved black laborers outnumbered white residents. A century after emancipation, African Americans remained a majority in many Black Belt counties, but political and economic power still rested firmly in white hands. In Dallas County, where African Americans made up 58 percent of the population, fewer than 3 percent were registered in 1960. In neighboring Wilcox County, no African Americans managed to register while creative record keeping ensured that more than 100 percent of eligible white voters' names were on the books.[17] Bevel emphasized these points and highlighted the area's potential. With open registration, black candidates could win elections for the first time since Reconstruction, he argued, and the SCLC would not start from scratch. Two years earlier, the Dallas County Voters League (DCVL) had organized voter registration drives and the Student Non-Violent Coordinating Committee (SNCC) dispatched organizers to southwestern Alabama. The movement was still active, drawing violent response from Selma sheriff Jim Clark, his deputies, and a quickly assembled posse of untrained and well-armed men during a round of sit-ins and registration marches in the fall of 1964. DCVL leader Amelia Boynton echoed Bevel's points and personally appealed for assistance.[18]

On Sunday, January 2, seven hundred people crowded into Selma's Browns Chapel African Methodist Episcopal Church to launch the cam-

Map 4. Alabama's Black Belt counties. © Bruno Berry.

paign. From the pulpit, Martin Luther King Jr. assured the crowd, "We are not asking, we are demanding the ballot." If turned away at courthouses, King promised an appeal to Alabama governor George Wallace and the state legislature. If that failed, they would "arouse the Federal Government by marching by the thousands by the places of registration." Armed with voting rights, King envisioned African Americans ushering in a new brand of politics, replacing "men who . . . stand in the doorway of universities to keep Negroes out" with "men who will uphold the cause of justice." The address launched the campaign, and within days, Septima Clark and Dorothy Cotton arrived to recruit CEP teachers.[19] Earlier attempts to implant the CEP into the Black Belt had withered, but a localized direct action campaign focused on voter registration and political empowerment might generate renewed interest.

Cotton and Clark retraced roads that Andrew Young had traveled during the early years of CEP implementation. In 1962, Perry County emerged as a promising site for local classes after a federal court injunction against county clerks in Montgomery had inspired the Reverend S. L. Johnson and his wife, Virginia, to attend CEP teacher training. They organized classes early the next year as Governor Wallace's inaugural pledge of "segregation now ... segregation tomorrow ... segregation forever" hung in the air. Virginia Johnson reported, "Only 3 persons registered out of 450 Negroes who have gone up," and CEP teacher James Carter offered a blunter assessment, writing, "They don't register no negroes in Perry County." The Johnsons and their students sent "173 letters to the Federal Judge" and organized the Perry County Voters League (PCVL), holding countywide mass meetings to discuss "the value of the citizenship school to registration and voting."[20] In the absence of federal support, the window closed; however, as the SCLC moved into Selma in 1965, the Fifth Circuit federal court dispatched officials to oversee registration in Perry County. Local bricklayer Albert Turner reignited the PCVL, and in February, three residents attended CEP teacher training.[21]

Clark and Cotton built on similar foundations in Wilcox County, where the Reverend Lonnie Brown and his wife, Nancy, ministered to the flock at Pleasant Grove Baptist Church. Like the Johnsons, the Browns were seasoned organizers. Four years earlier, they created the Wilcox County Civic and Progressive League (WCCPL), advocating for voting rights, equal economic opportunity, and an end to police violence. In late March 1963, SNCC organizers accompanied the Browns and WCCPL members to the courthouse, where county officials sent them away. Public action drew quick response. Like many rural African American ministers, Lonnie Brown worked to make ends meet with a second job, in this case, selling insurance policies to local sharecroppers. Following the courthouse visit, white landowners banned Brown from their property, so he was unable to collect payments. When Brown persisted in his voter registration efforts, "persons unknown" shot into his home. Two years later, Nancy Brown and five Wilcox County women joined the Perry County contingent at CEP teacher training.[22]

Newly trained CEP teachers joined a groundswell sweeping across the Black Belt. Mass meetings in Selma and surrounding counties drew hundreds, and marchers lined up at courthouses daily. Six weeks into the campaign, the tenor and direction shifted. During a night march in Perry County, a state trooper shot Jimmy Lee Jackson as he rushed to his mother's defense. Jackson died eight days later. Incensed, Bevel called for a fifty-mile march from Selma to Montgomery to confront Governor Wallace.[23] On Sunday, March 7, SCLC's Hosea Williams and SNCC president John Lewis led marchers to Selma's Edmund Pettus Bridge. That evening, television networks interrupted regular programming with a special report. Viewers saw marchers solemnly making their way down the arc of the bridge. A phalanx of state troopers, city police, and Sheriff Jim Clark's posse stood shoulder to shoulder across the highway. Spectators and journalists lined the highway. Troopers and police put on gas masks as marchers approached. A trooper's warning broke the silence. Marchers stood their ground. Tension built until the order, "Troopers advance!" Tear gas canisters streaked through the air as the phalanx crashed into the marchers. Television cameras recorded troopers with nightsticks, mounted troopers giving chase, marchers' shrieks and gasps, and cheering white spectators. This was Bloody Sunday.[24]

National outrage about the confrontation intensified pressure on the federal government and on King. Two days later, King led another group across the bridge. This time, troopers and local police stepped aside, tempting him to violate a federal injunction. King knelt in prayer and turned back. On March 10, the Reverend James Reeb, a white minister from Boston, died from injuries sustained during an attack by local white men. The aborted march and Reeb's murder sparked demonstrations from California to the White House. From Mississippi, Alice Blackwell reported that Greenwood-area CEP veterans prayed and "demonstrated at the court house."[25] Eight days after the first confrontation, President Johnson addressed a national audience. "There is no Negro problem," he began. "There is no Southern problem. There is no Northern problem. There is only an American problem." Johnson's speech laid bare the practices that CEP teachers and students knew all too well: unfairly administered literacy tests, flexible criteria for determining good character, unpredictable hours at local courthouses—all now described by a chief executive with a distinct southern accent. Johnson vowed to introduce legislation to "strike down restrictions to voting" and to deploy registrars to enforce federal law. "It is wrong—deadly wrong—to deny any of your fellow Americans the right to vote in this country," he admonished, and he appealed to "all of us" to "overcome this crippling legacy of bigotry and injustice." Speaking directly into the television camera, the president pledged, "And we shall overcome."[26] A week later, King led three thousand marchers across the Pettus Bridge bound for Montgomery, and the CEP mobilized in their wake.

Citizenship Education in Alabama's Black Belt

Before Congress opened deliberations on the voting rights bill, federal court decisions coupled with a glaring national spotlight prompted action to "speed the . . . process and protect Negroes trying to register." To ease long lines at the courthouse, Dallas County officials instituted an "Appearance Book" where applicants recorded contact information and received an appointment for the next registration day.[27] This strategy solved one problem and created another because many black applicants could not sign their names. SNCC organizers in the area charged that the book was "another cumbersome, unnecessary device [to keep] down demonstrations while not dealing in good faith toward allowing all the people to become registered voters." Septima Clark chose a different approach, adapting the three-month CEP curriculum to "get writing clinics in full force." The response was consistent with the CEP's approach, which did not question the existence of a literacy test but instead sought to equip people with skills to overcome this challenge with the understanding that literacy could serve a broader purpose. Annell Ponder articulated a similar rationale for the handwriting clinics. Handwriting had wide applicability for "everyday needs," including "sign[ing] checks, sign[ing] applications, apply[ing] for jobs, [and] writ[ing] letters," she explained.[28] This basic skill was thus a foundation for political rights and economic security.

Based on the CEP model, Clark and Ponder issued a call for "local people who could read well aloud and write legibly" to lead clinics that met for two hours at a time, five days a week, with sessions operating in the mornings, afternoons, and evenings.[29] The abbreviated curriculum allowed students to learn skills faster than traditional CEP classes. Local tutors carried the abbreviated program into rural areas like Orville, where Sallie Petties's students "sign[ed] their application sheets" and received "a number card." Clinic graduates successfully registered, and in southwestern Alabama, registration was more than adding a name to the county rolls. Clark observed African American applicants claiming first-class citizenship when they "confront[ed] the white man . . . on a legitimate equal basis." Clinics built a foundation for a new way of viewing themselves, their community, and their nation. Forty-five clinics operated for two months, during which time "7002 had signed the book," Clark reported.[30]

Women who served as clinic tutors had established reputations as community leaders through their occupations, church and community club memberships, and informal support and advice for friends and neighbors.

The SCLC and SNCC had depended on their active support during the Selma campaign. For example, Alice West's home had served as an informal organizing hub where she "fix[ed] cups of instant coffee" as Bevel and others crowded in.[31] The campaign required public participation that risked economic reprisal and physical injury to which local women were not immune. Sallie Petties had marched to Montgomery and returned with injuries incurred on the journey. Fifty-five-year-old beautician Addie Lily was "wounded—standing for dignity and fighting for freedom" at the courthouse in 1964 and "wounded and gassed" on the Pettus Bridge.[32] Like Alice West, fifty-five-year-old Annie Lee Cooper fed and housed civil rights workers, and like Addie Lily, she had marched. In 1963, Cooper lost her job when her employer spotted her in line at the courthouse and fired her the next day.[33] In February 1965, her altercation with Sheriff Jim Clark gained national attention as newspaper reporters captured Cooper answering the sheriff's rough shove with a well-placed punch to the jaw. Three deputies wrestled and handcuffed her, leading her into an alley where "they pushed . . . and jugged me with those clubs," Cooper told reporters. By May 1965, battle scars served as tangible symbols of commitment to a non-violent movement. Respectability and community leadership were demonstrated through economic and physical sacrifice and, in Cooper's case, refusal to accept police brutality.[34] The CEP opened a new outlet for community leadership.

Organizing handwriting clinics foreshadowed "hard spots" for CEP teachers in the Black Belt. Federal legislation promised a new day, but black residents remained wary and cautious. Getting people to the registrar's office was only part of the problem. The spring campaign shook the foundations of white supremacy and rattled long-standing class-based relationships within black communities. Bernice Robinson spent little time in the area before concluding, "People in Selma think they have to elect a doctor or some minister as president of their organization." The campaign drew in new people, but "they haven't grown to see themselves as leaders," she reflected.[35] Frustrated with "foolishness from those preachers," she packed up and left. Clark stayed on, dogged by ministers who demanded to know "Who's going to pay for this? Who's going to do so-and-so?" She "toughed it out" through a convoluted series of meetings, making sure to give credit to all "the names they wanted" in printed materials.[36]

Handwriting clinics accomplished important goals after spring demonstrations. Tutors earned $1.25 per hour, allowing "unemployed workers to earn and teach at the same time." In a region marked by generational systemic poverty, clinics put cash in hands and validated community work with a wage. On a practical level, foundation-funded stipends provided income independent of white employers, a resource that became more critical as economic reprisals swept across the region. For Clark, the clinics served as a trial run for CEP classes. In the wake of the previous fall's discussions about a more selective criterion for CEP teachers, Clark used the clinics to assess the volunteers and recommended training for those deemed most qualified, a group that included Cooper, West, and two additional Selma recruits along with ten prospective teachers from Perry County, including Jimmie Lee Jackson's sister Emma.[37]

In the summer of 1965, fourteen teachers opened CEP classes where they did the post-campaign work of educating and organizing local people. In July, Alice West proudly announced that she was "now a registar [sic] voter," a credential that helped to bring in prospective students. West advertised her "free Adult Citizenship Classes" in the *Southern Courier* and visited the courthouse to record names of those turned away. When she determined that many lived outside of Selma, she organized classes to serve the rural population. Other CEP teachers and students extended influence beyond makeshift classrooms. Sallie Petties turned Sunday school classes into informal CEP gatherings, instructing parishioners to "never sign or ans[wer] any question on the Application form unless it had a number on the left hand side." On voter registration days, she held impromptu lessons on the courthouse steps, instructing "'my people' what to do and what not to do." Women attending Petties's Orville class "went home and taught their husband [sic]," and in August, Petties confirmed that "all are registered voters." Petties and fellow teacher Leonia Jackson attended ward meetings while Mary Lee Strong's students organized into committees to pressure the mayor and city council for long-overdue infrastructure improvements including "Street light, paved Street, and Sewers [sic] lines." "We are not going to waite [sic] any longer," she assured CEP administrators. Federal reform sparked optimism about new opportunities, and CEP teacher Ralph Henry prepared fifty local people "to take the Post Office test to work for the government."[38] All of these activities reinforced core CEP principles of claiming what was long denied, with local teachers creatively adapting to a new landscape.

The CEP expanded into Wilcox County with Nancy Brown's class at Pleasant Grove Baptist Church in Gee's Bend. A century after the Civil War, many black residents traced direct lineage to enslaved workers who had labored on the Gee plantation. In the 1930s, Gee's Bend white landowners looked to recover financial losses from falling cotton prices. Federal officials purchased the property and extended low-interest loans to black farmers. Thirty years later, Gee's Bend farmers continued to struggle economically, but the population of independent landowners proved to be fertile soil for the CEP. In April, Brown's class drew fourteen students with "more . . . ready for the class on the next round."[39] Domestic worker Sarah Westbrook held CEP class at night. Twenty-eight students learned "how to fill in blanks." "We took lots of people down . . . and most of them got registra [sic]," she reported. Into the summer, Westbrook continued "teaching and helping people who can not write plain and who cannot read at all."[40]

CEP classes contributed to a surge of African Americans claiming rights across the Black Belt. Within six months of the march to Montgomery, black voter registration in Dallas County quadrupled to 1,100 with an additional 1,500 processed and awaiting registration. After eleven years of delay, the Dallas County School Board passed a freedom-of-choice plan for school integration. In August, black residents in Wilcox County filed a complaint with the U.S. Justice Department, prompting Attorney General Nicholas Katzenbach to dispatch federal officials. SNCC field workers moved into neighboring Lowndes County, where they collaborated with the Lowndes County Christian Movement for Human Rights (LCCMHR) on bold plans to desegregate schools and organize a new political party. Black candidates prepared for fall 1966 elections with newly registered voters primed to flex political power.[41]

The SCLC sent more resources into Alabama. In the spring, Hosea Williams announced the Summer Community Organization and Political Education (SCOPE) project modeled on COFO's Freedom Summer. Williams proposed to recruit five hundred college students for a ten-week "all out effort" to increase black voter registration in forty-six black-majority counties across the South. In early June, volunteers gathered in Atlanta for training, and CEP staff members actively supported the project.[42] SCOPE volunteers fanned out across the Black Belt where they joined newly hired SCLC field staff. Perry County's Albert Turner was appointed Alabama field secretary in the fall of 1965. The Reverend Harold Middlebrook and CORE veteran Shirley Mesher managed the Selma office. Daniel Harrell Jr., a veteran of Louisiana's sit-in movement, was named Wilcox County project director and moved from Mobile with his wife, Juanita, who served as CEP supervisor.[43] Like Mississippi's Freedom Summer, the proliferation of volunteers, staff, and programs funneled much-needed resources into the

Black Belt. On the ground, each group struggled to turn local efforts into a coordinated approach.

The CEP after the Voting Rights Act

In Atlanta, the combination of federal legislation, grassroots organizing in Mississippi and Alabama, and the impending end of the Field Foundation's two-year grant prompted a reexamination of the CEP curriculum and goals. Field's grants had sustained the CEP since 1960, and program staff decided to press for a five-year commitment. In early 1965, Clark reminded foundation officials of the return on investment, summarizing the program's record of training over one thousand local leaders from eleven states who organized 947 classes, taught 23,829 students, and influenced 95,000 newly registered voters. She touted increased voter registration in Georgia and South Carolina, identified Alabama and Louisiana as "priority projects" where "there is much to be done," and acknowledged that Mississippi "still needs more support than the rest of the southern states." Local classes had "paid off in big numbers" when black voters lined up for the 1964 presidential election, but the need for literacy education remained acute. Federal reform and anti-poverty resources presented opportunities, and the CEP was branching out from "basic reading and writing" to address "new problems as they appear." A refashioned program required more staff, and a multiyear grant would help "to keep efficient staff," Clark argued.[44]

Clark included sample lesson plans to demonstrate alignment with federal reform measures and lessons from grassroots organizing. Collectively, the revised curriculum equipped local teachers to operate as sophisticated information brokers and political organizers. For example, in a lesson about the 1964 Civil Rights Act, students honed reading skills by reciting, "This new law was passed to help the Negro citizens live with more freedom and respect as Americans" by banning discrimination based on "race, color, religion, sex, or national origin." The lesson included a survey that students could use to assess "various [local] companies and industries . . . which must obey this law" and a form letter to report discrimination to federal officials.[45] In another lesson, students practiced math skills by analyzing income gaps between black and white workers. Students connected their calculations to information about the fair employment section of the Civil Rights Act.[46] A comprehensive resource guide described an array of federally funded education, health, and financial assistance programs. By March

1966, Annell Ponder rushed out a "simplified memorandum" so teachers could assist "elderly persons" in signing up for the new Medicare program.[47]

The revised curriculum shifted emphasis from voter registration to political education with refined materials about the layers and levers of political and economic power. A lesson about the convention process walked students step by step from precinct conventions to county conventions through district, state, and national levels. "Any political party may hold a precinct convention," they read, and county-level committees exercised significant influence, from appointing election managers to approving poll watchers and "spend[ing] the party's money in whatever manner they see fit to secure the election of their candidates." Teachers received detailed instructions for mapping precincts, cataloging registered and unregistered voters, and organizing block captains.[48] Another lesson focused on Agricultural Stabilization and Conservation Service (ASCS) committees, managed through the U.S. Department of Agriculture (USDA). Using a reprinted article from the *New Republic*, students read about Joe Lee, "a Negro tobacco and all-around farmer" in Florida's Panhandle. The article explained that Lee was unaware of available assistance because of the USDA's "pervasive and senseless discrimination," but Title VI of the Civil Rights Act empowered federal officials to "cutoff US funds when non-compliance is established." The lesson ended with a set of questions to guide students' surveys of their local ASCS committees.[49]

Banking and consumer economics lessons blended tools for economic security with an emphasis on personal responsibility. In a revised banking exercise, students read and discussed stories from bank customers and practiced filling out deposit slips and checks. A consumer economics lesson encouraged students to "develop attitudes and habits . . . [to] spend their money in the most beneficial and economical manner." The lesson provided materials to help teachers explain "advertising tricks" and to advise students in "enlightened shopping methods," such as avoiding the "corner grocery" and "loan sharks." The lesson concluded with an exercise to prepare a family budget.[50] These lessons added to existing workbook exercises about Social Security and calculating prices, teaching students advanced skills to secure family finances and to avoid exploitive schemes.

Supplemental materials simultaneously updated and expanded the program's construction of first-class citizenship. Inherent in the materials was an understanding that first-class citizens knew about resources and "economical" practices and applied this knowledge to secure political rights and ensure their families' economic well-being. New materials consistently reinforced rights and privileges of citizenship. First-class citizens had rights to accurate information; federal protection of individual and property rights, registration and voting; and access to federal resources. After 1965, the CEP armed southern African Americans to claim these entitlements. Lessons also retained the CEP's emphasis on behavior and comportment as central components of first-class citizenship. First-class citizens behaved in particular ways and made what the CEP defined as responsible choices, reflecting the program's long-standing internal tension between middle-class standards of respectability and practical information that could secure political rights and economic resources. Implied in the lessons was the cumulative effect of these practices. According to CEP materials, if more African Americans understood political and economic systems and enacted first-class citizenship, entire communities would be empowered and more economically secure, ultimately improving conditions for the entire race.

"Backlash" in Alabama's Black Belt

Into the summer of 1965, CEP teachers' experiences in Alabama's Black Belt were beginning to show the limitations of this approach as reprisals kept pace with political action. For white officials and residents, lines outside courthouses, black children in classrooms, white college students in black neighborhoods, and the arrival of federal "carpetbaggers breathing down neck[s]" were irrefutable signs that they were under siege. A white Selma resident explained, "The problem up until now is that the whites have been too complacent. We still are, but not as much as before." As the Voting Rights Act made its way through Congress, the Selma chapter of the Women for Constitutional Government (WCG) braced for a "Negro bloc vote" and canvassed for white voter registration. The Private School Foundation warned of "floods of Negro children" into public schools and organized privately funded alternatives.[51] In Lowndes County, Klan members threatened black parents who enrolled children in Lowndesboro High School while merchants cut off credit and called in loans. African Americans were not the only targets. On August 20, a part-time deputy sheriff shot and killed Jonathan Daniels, a twenty-four-year-old white Episcopal seminarian working with SNCC in Lowndes County.[52]

Rural CEP students were not immune as white landowners and employers manipulated economic ties to undermine civil rights action. Minter teacher Rosie Mae Davis had marched and been to jail, so she sought to serve by example. "I am register [sic] now, I finally got through in May," she wrote. She was enthusiastic about the CEP, but "by living in the country, it is hard to get the people to cooperate," she admitted. "I have two more to take up there the first Monday," she reported. "I will still try to get people to go to the Court house."[53] Three miles south of Selma, Ceola Miller did not fare much better. "My [students are] very much afraid of losing their farm," she wrote. She was hopeful "when the Voting Bill past" but confirmed that "some are still afraid to vote, because of their landowner might kick them off."[54] Davis and Miller's students had good reason to be concerned. As Mississippi CEP teachers knew all too well, evictions, homelessness, and firings reinforced tightly intertwined politics and economics. Ten weeks after the march to Montgomery, *Jet* magazine reported on "hard cases" who refused help because accepting assistance could be interpreted as support for a civil rights organization. As a result, families who had little made do with less. Civil rights organizations scrambled as landowners abruptly terminated contracts and evicted entire families. In Lowndes County, SNCC workers constructed a tent city to shelter families. CEP teacher Martha Saulsberry reported on local efforts to "build homes for people who are being put out" in neighboring Wilcox County. Under Daniel Harrell's direction, the newly formed Wilcox County SCLC, Inc. bought thirty acres and applied for a Federal Housing Administration loan for one hundred new modern homes.[55]

Reprisals swept into Selma. Sallie Petties lost her job after attending the weeklong CEP training in February 1965, and into the fall, her reputation preceded her as employers caustically sneered, "Let Martin Luther get you a job." The CEP stipend kept her afloat and out of "domestic work for that $3 a day."[56] Ella Mae Moton lost her job when her employer charged that she "slowed down with all that marchin!" She completed CEP teacher training, but unemployed with four children to support, she delayed plans to organize local classes. Undeterred and armed with lessons from Dorchester, she "'influenced' some seventy-five to one hundred persons to vote."[57] Annie Lee Cooper volunteered with the Selma Emergency Relief Fund (SERF), a local organization that distributed food, clothing, and financial support "for those having lost their means of support because of civil rights activities." By late May, SERF extended services to families denied public welfare or medical assistance. Reprisals hit home for Cooper when she submitted an application for SERF support.[58] The backlash took its toll in a number of ways as Bernice Robinson observed during her spring visit. Although she acknowledged a very real need, Robinson perceived that local leaders "waste a lot of time with surplus food and second-hand clothing." This activity siphoned "energy [that] could be used on education of the people and getting them the kind of help their taxes are paying for."[59]

Reprisals impacted CEP teachers' work amidst fraying alliances undermining the fragile unity forged during the Selma campaign. With the Voting Rights Act in place by the end of the summer, local leaders and SCLC field staff turned attention to anti-poverty programs where stiff competition erupted for control. In March, Selma mayor Joe Smitherman organized an all-white governing board and submitted an application for community action funds from the federal Office of Economic Opportunity (OEO). When officials rejected the application, the SCLC's Harold Middlebrook and the Reverend Ernest M. Bradford organized the Dallas County Economic Employment Opportunity Committee (DCEEOC) to "take over the white people's program, . . . add our own proposals to it, and submit the whole thing to the OEO."[60] As the DCEEOC gathered support from Atlanta-based OEO officials and local white businessmen, Smitherman formed a new committee "almost overnight." The Reverend Frederick D. Reese's endorsement split the black community as residents took sides. Confusion prompted a visit from an OEO investigator who detected "a great deal of interest in the anti-poverty program," but "a power struggle" had created a "rather chaotic" situation. By the end of the year, the *Southern Courier* reported, "Selma still [had] two anti-poverty committees—and no anti-poverty program."[61]

Rifts over OEO programs opened as organizers strategized for primary elections in May 1966. Collaboration between the SCLC and SNCC dissolved at a January meeting where SNCC president Stokely Carmichael urged participants to seize "pure unadulterated political power" through independent county-level parties like the recently organized Lowndes County Freedom Organization (LCFO). Arriving late, Hosea Williams missed Carmichael but was anxious to neutralize the perceived threat. Describing third parties as "a bed for the Black nationalist or the Black Muslim," Williams denounced Carmichael's plan as "suicide" in state and national elections.[62] The next month, Williams unveiled plans for the Confederation of Alabama's Political Organizations (COAPO), a COFO-style collaboration to channel political support for vetted candidates. COAPO got off to a slow start when only "SCLC people" attended the first meeting. Two months later, twice as many attended; however, the meeting was hardly a demonstration of broad-based unity as "SNCC people" sat silently and the NAACP and Alabama Democratic Conference, Inc. were noticeably absent.[63]

CEP experience in southeastern Georgia and in Mississippi showed that the program thrived when civil rights organizations collaborated, and conversely, the program was acutely affected by corrosive divisions. Similar dynamics now played out in Alabama. When Selma's DCVL supported white candidates in the upcoming election, rural leaders organized the Dallas County Independent Free Voters Organization (DCIFVO) along the same class-based cleavages splitting anti-poverty efforts.[64] In Selma and "the rurals," CEP teachers chose sides. Perry County CEP teacher Patt J. Davis remained loyal to the SCLC in his campaign to unseat longtime sheriff William U. "Bill" Loftis and exceeded expectations when he forced a runoff. At the same time, CEP teacher Addie Lily entered the race for tax assessor on the DCIFVO ticket.[65]

In May, CEP supervisor Louise Shelton visited four active classes, down from fourteen a year earlier. Teachers and students focused on runoff elections in Perry and Wilcox Counties, and election enthusiasm spread into Dallas County as CEP teachers used class time to build support for candidates. Leonia Jackson's "very young" adult students were "preparing for the runoff election and talking it up." Annie Lee Cooper's students had a "full discussion on the election," and Shelton believed that "the adult student will go to the polls."[66] Enthusiasm did not translate into positive results with African American candidates falling short in a surge of white voter registration.[67] As results rolled in, Williams announced that the SCLC was "moving out," redeploying fifty of Alabama's seventy staff members to Chicago and southwestern Georgia. A "strong skeleton staff" would stay behind in Selma, a city Williams described as "the most divided city in the country."[68]

Amidst splintering factions, CEP teachers made pragmatic choices. Addie Lily followed through with her DCIFVO candidacy and sought support at a DCVL gathering at Browns Chapel. As she began her appeal, the Reverend P. H. Lewis, DCVL vice president, interjected, "We don't have any candidates running," and he refused to let Lily continue. Lily publicized the rejection in a letter to the *Southern Courier* editor. Marching in 1964 and on Bloody Sunday served as her credentials, she argued, as did the "seven classes" she organized after the march to Montgomery. "Through my teaching, I was able to help my people see a better life for themselves," she asserted. Now, she was being shushed and the public dismissal "hurt me deeply," she wrote.[69]

Clark returned to Selma after the runoff elections to find the city "divided into three factions." Louise Shelton was "thoroughly disgusted" with anti-poverty meetings "publicized for one thing and . . . end in name calling or blasting of one organization against another." Alice and Alonzo West joined the chorus of disappointment, with Alonzo blaming "the middle class Negroes [that] hate to see the lower income group come to the forefront," and given the situation, he saw "no hope for a sound poverty program." While the Wests remained "sold to S.C.L.C.," Annie Lee Cooper noted growing resentment from local black businessmen who insisted that "they could handle everything" if the SCLC pulled out of town. Exasperated, Clark agreed with Alonzo West. "It is pitiful . . . to listen to the middle class in Selma and note how little they think of the people in lower socioeconomic circumstances," she wrote. Class differences were a matter of resources and opportunity, she argued, because poverty kept "the grass roots" on "the farm, plantation, small town, or East side of Selma," and as a result, they did not receive the same "education." In the end, she found the situation "maddening."[70]

External divisive forces undermined CEP activity as perpetual internal administrative problems soured relationships. In July 1965, Wilcox County CEP teacher Bessie King detailed ongoing frustrations. After submitting paperwork and waiting for stipend payments, she expressed exasperation, writing, "I am not going to write my June report over No More. . . . I would like to have my money." At the end of 1965, fellow teacher Julia McKnight requested class materials, adding, "You are sending $60.00 checks to people who aren't teaching." The letter roused suspicion, and the following spring, Annell Ponder wrote to Caroline Saulsberry. Ponder acknowledged receipt of Saulsberry's paperwork but advised that the CEP would approve payment only after the local supervisor visited the class. Saulsberry interpreted Ponder's letter as accusation, insisting, "I've taught class for three months." "I wouldn't have told a lie for nothing like that," she assured Ponder, and she accused the local CEP supervisor of visiting local classes only once and "getting her money." Saulsberry invited Ponder to contact her students and requested "another supervisor because the one we have is a big liar."[71] Without a presence in the Black Belt, resolving these issues proved difficult for the Atlanta-based CEP staff.

Citizenship Education in Mississippi after the Voting Rights Act

In Mississippi, Victoria Gray kept close watch on Alabama, hoping to apply lessons learned in her state's upcoming primary elections. She had struggled to sustain momentum after the House voted against the MFDP motion in September 1965. Gray later reflected that "white Mississippians knew that business as usual was not going to continue," but this was not apparent at the time as Mississippi governor Paul Johnson dismissed the challenge as "nothing at all to start with."[72] One month later, the MFDP filed suit in U.S. district court to contest the state's "present apportionment scheme," which "establishes irrational, invidious, discriminatory and unequal districts." CEP veterans Peggy Jean Connor, Ralthus Hayes, and Alma Carnegie served as plaintiffs in the case.[73] In December 1965, Gray attempted to revive the CEP with a series of in-state workshops. Efforts got off to a slow start at a "rather disappointing" session that drew fourteen prospective teachers to Waveland on the coast. Attendance improved the next week when twenty-seven attended a workshop in the Delta.[74]

Ahead of May primaries, she invited Cotton, Clark, and CEP director Robert L. "Bob" Green to Sunflower County where Delta-area MFDP representatives and CEP veterans gathered under the watchful eye of the police chief and two companions "riding by the church . . . a machine gun (most conspicuous) resting on the front seat of the vehicle." Fresh from the disappointing Alabama elections, Clark and Green reflected that registration did not automatically translate into votes for black candidates because black voters accepted white elected officials as "the way it's supposed to be" or "are afraid after being threatened by a white plantation owner." As a remedy, they recommended "strong poll watchers," workshops to introduce MFDP candidates, and "election committees" consisting of street captains, poll workers, and watchers. Green advised participants to seek federal intervention, "but don't expect them to do much."[75]

As in the Black Belt, discussions about politics quickly pivoted to economic issues. When Annie Devine asked about federal anti-poverty programs, Ralthus Hayes expressed frustration with a process where although "whites are getting most of the top jobs," federal officials still approved funding. "If these government programs are disigned [sic] to help the poor," he asked, "why aren't poor people in charge of them?"[76] One workshop participant made the discussion personal, describing a recent decision that cut off the family's access to the federal food subsidy (commodities) program. The issue was not new. CEP veterans and MFDP supporters raised the alarm with officials in their visit to the capital in January 1965. Six months before the Sunflower workshop, CEP veteran Atlean Smith wrote to Annell Ponder about "get[ting] Food Stamps for people who are [also] receiving comodities [sic]." Smith had appealed directly to Governor Paul Johnson to address assistance levels "cut so low . . . until it's no way for us to feed the children balanced meals."⁷⁷ At the workshop, Devine took action, leading the group to confront "the welfare woman" at the courthouse, who quickly reinstated the participant. Back at the workshop, Gray emphasized the need to "get the right information" so that local people understood that these were federal programs, not "money . . . coming in from local whites." The workshop "culminated with a mock election day."⁷⁸

Across the state, CEP teachers organized similar mock election days and reported "harassment and attempted intimidation." Gray poured energy into "last minute assignments" as national attention turned to Memphis, where James Meredith set out from the Peabody Hotel on a self-described "March Against Fear," intending to walk alone along Mississippi highways to the state capital. Just across the state line, Meredith lay on the side of the highway, hit by three shotgun blasts. News of the attack "momentarily paralyzed" statewide organizing activities, and when word came that Meredith would survive, Gray was relieved but also worried that voters would stay home in the wake of the shooting. She urged supporters to "meet that night and help people realize that this challenge could best be met by a strong turnout." Gray scrambled to keep attention on the primary election as Martin Luther King, Stokely Carmichael, and CORE's Floyd McKissick locked arms and walked south from the spot where Meredith's blood stained the asphalt, intent on finishing a march they had initially discouraged. The next day, Mississippi voters went to the polls. News reporters anxious to capture a confrontation between King and Carmichael missed what Gray described as a "tremendous" surge in black voter participation.⁷⁹

For the next three weeks, marchers finished what Meredith started with CEP teachers and veterans feeding and housing them along the way. When it was over, Gray acknowledged that the march "culminated in a terrific impact" but also "took up most of June and July." Into the fall, she struggled to "reactivate" activities that "suffered during the summer of excitement." "A few new classes got underway," she reported.⁸⁰ As the general election approached, Gray focused attention on state officials intent on keeping MFDP candidates off the ballot. After votes were tallied, she expressed "much disappointment and unbelief in spite of the warnings" as MFDP candidates lost across the state. She remained optimistic that the CEP could overcome persistent problems and appealed for more resources for recruitment, statewide workshops, and county supervisors and program staff.⁸¹

* * *

January 1965 to the end of 1966 was a period of testing. CEP teachers in Mississippi and Alabama tested political systems long used to deny first-class citizenship. In Selma, teachers contributed to a groundswell that swept away voter registration tests. They tested claims to first-class citizenship, even as economic reprisals kept pace with voter registration. Reprisals and fracturing alliances tested the strength of newly planted CEP seeds in the Black Belt, and by the end of 1966, these forces threatened to uproot the program's foothold in the area. To the west, Mississippi CEP teachers joined efforts to test political systems right into the halls of Congress. In the end, their test demonstrated the limits of federal reform, and momentum gathered during Freedom Summer dissipated further as the challenge shifted into the federal courts with CEP veterans lending their names to this next test. In local communities, CEP teachers organized to test education and public welfare systems, and through their efforts, they opened Head Start centers and other federal anti-poverty programs where they would have a direct say in their children's, families,' and communities' futures. They demonstrated first-class citizenship.

Passage of the Voting Rights Act was welcome reform but would test the CEP and the SCLC in fundamental ways. In Selma, CEP administrators tested the program's flexibility, adapting the curriculum to empower African Americans to claim newly secured voting rights. Federal reform tested the program's reason for being, and with the removal of the literacy test, the CEP retooled. The resulting curriculum retained the program's central premise that education was the path to first-class citizenship. New lessons drew on grassroots organizing in CEP communities and federal reform to define the next phase priorities, including economic security and political organization. The SCLC had also faced tests in 1965 and 1966. The Selma campaign and the March to Montgomery significantly influenced passage of federal voting rights legislation; however, subsequent organizing efforts in Alabama failed to fulfill the promise of black elected officials in local and state offices. Fractured alliances were signs of a splintering movement with factions moving in divergent directions. Into 1967, Martin Luther King Jr. would call for a "revolution of values" aimed at a fundamental redistribution of the nation's political and economic systems. As King's inner circle organized a new national campaign, CEP staff, teachers, and veterans navigated into the CEP's next phase.

8

The Citizenship Education Program's "Second Phase," 1966–1969

In September 1966, Dorothy Cotton took the helm of the Citizenship Education Program (CEP) amidst questions about the program's stability and relevance. Since its arrival at the Southern Christian Leadership Conference (SCLC), the Field Foundation sustained the CEP through successive grants. That summer, newly appointed director Leslie W. Dunbar signaled a change. Viewing foundation commitments through fresh eyes, Dunbar questioned CEP staff involvement in direct action campaigns. While the campaigns were not "of second rate importance," he acknowledged in a letter to Martin Luther King Jr., "the more basic issue is the integrity of the C.E.P. program." As lines of responsibility and accountability blurred, Dunbar suggested that the CEP "seek its own tax exemption, so grants could be made directly." Either way, it was "unwise for one foundation to be the sole support of the project," he concluded. Dunbar's assessment prompted a response from the program's fiscal agent at the United Church Board of Homeland Missions (UCBHM). Wesley Hotchkiss agreed that participation in direct action campaigns "confused" program administration and could ultimately "inhibit the progress of the CEP." Hotchkiss urged a transition to "the second phase" where CEP teachers formed "the nucleus of a movement for community improvement." Without this adaptation, they would "waste investments in teacher training." Field approved an annual grant, warning the SCLC that "if the Foundation supports CEP in future years," they should expect "declining amounts."[1]

The correspondence highlighted challenges ahead for the CEP. Faced with "declining amounts" from Field, CEP staff needed to secure new sources of funding, requiring grant proposals that presented a compelling case for investment. The Voting Rights Act of 1965 swept away literacy tests for voter registration, effectively erasing the CEP's main reason for existence. Adaptation was imperative, and Hotchkiss pointed to a broader issue. As the CEP approached its ten-year anniversary, program staff boasted of training over 2,500 local people. As Hotchkiss urged, now was the time to activate this region-wide network in service to new goals.

This chapter draws on scant remaining records to reconstruct the CEP's transition to "a second phase." Teacher training rosters document robust participation in workshops; however, attendance records and correspondence fall off sharply, severing the communication link between Atlanta and local communities. As a result, this chapter tells the story largely through staff members' reports and correspondence. The incomplete record reveals CEP staff, local teachers, and CEP-trained veterans pivoting away from basic literacy lessons to focus on "second phase" goals of community health and safety, economic security, and political empowerment.[2] In some cases, they blended community organizing skills with CEP principles as they moved into federal anti-poverty programs like Head Start or other initiatives funded through the Office of Economic Opportunity (OEO). In other examples, CEP staff, teachers, and veterans enacted program principles through locally organized groups and one-time issue-specific initiatives. As a result, these records collectively shed light on local people moving the movement forward by refashioning program lessons, tools, and skills to lay claim to a broad range of rights and entitlements.[3]

Finally, the records provide a glimpse into Dorothy Cotton's tenure as program director. As she took the helm, Cotton sought to shore up financial foundations while steering the program into the "second phase." Dunbar and Hotchkiss recommended independence, but Cotton navigated a course to more fully integrate the CEP into the SCLC. Since 1961, separate grant funding and salaries funneled through the UCBHM meant that the CEP was simultaneously a part of and apart from the SCLC. As Martin Luther King Jr. called for "a true revolution of values that will look uneasily on the glaring contrast of poverty and wealth," Cotton sensed opportunity. King's appeal would coalesce into a national Poor People's Campaign.[4] From within the SCLC's inner circle, Cotton envisioned the CEP's blend of grassroots education and political empowerment as an essential component to this expansive vision.

This chapter assembles pieces and situates this "second phase" within a broader context. Beginning in the summer of 1964, cities burned with alarming frequency, the flames highlighting the limits of liberal reform to root out de facto segregation and racial discrimination. Fragile unity of major civil rights organizations frayed as leaders proposed different strategies to address unresolved issues. This movement fractured as another gained strength. "White backlash" dominated coverage of the 1966 midterm elections when the Democratic Party, long the party of the Solid South and the party of the sitting president, suffered stinging losses.[5] Congressional committees scrutinized anti-poverty programs and private foundations, effectively slowing funding streams as escalating costs associated with the Vietnam War choked more of the lifeline for a movement now aimed at increasing voter registration and ensuring economic justice. All of these forces tugged at the threads holding the CEP together.

Dorothy Cotton Takes the Helm

In the fall of 1966, Dorothy Cotton hoped to restore stability to the CEP after two directors came and went in rapid succession. Two years earlier, the program was placed under Randolph Blackwell's purview. Kept busy supervising the SCLC's rapidly expanded field staff, Blackwell left few fingerprints on the CEP, and Cotton and Septima Clark assumed administrative duties. When Annell Ponder returned from Mississippi, she joined forces to keep up with letters and reports, answering phones, and mailing stipend checks. This changed in September 1965 when the SCLC board appointed Robert L. "Bob" Green as CEP director. One of Andrew Young's "closest friends," Green secured a yearlong leave of absence from Michigan State University and moved south to demonstrate "a deeper commitment" to the movement.[6] Green left two legacies when he returned to Michigan. Under his leadership, CEP staff helped to establish "Learning Centers" in Wilcox County, Alabama, a project that remained a priority for Clark and Cotton. Green also participated in Mississippi's Meredith March. Young later described his friend as "caught up in 'freedom high,'" most visibly in Grenada, where Green scaled a statue of Jefferson Davis, draped an American flag over the concrete head, and yelled, "The South he represented will never rise again!"[7] This got Hotchkiss's and Dunbar's attention and prompted their questions about CEP administration.

With Dunbar and Hotchkiss pressing for signs of internal stability, Cotton was the logical choice for the director position. Septima Clark was the senior member of the CEP staff, but at sixty-nine years old and after two heart attacks, she did not want a full-time position that would keep her away from Charleston. In contrast, thirty-six-year-old Cotton lived in

Atlanta and had maneuvered into King's inner circle, the only woman to successfully break into the "team of wild horses."[8] Unlike Blackwell and Green, Cotton had been an integral part of the CEP since its arrival at the SCLC, and she knew all parts of the program, from managing the Atlanta office to preparing teachers at the Dorchester Center to building and maintaining relationships with local teachers. Cotton was the logical choice, but in choosing her, the SCLC board selected someone who had always viewed the CEP from within the SCLC. Early in her tenure as director, she took steps to strengthen this connection.

In the spring of 1967, Cotton prepared a round of grant proposals, requesting a three-year commitment from Field while assuring Dunbar that she had feelers out to the Ford Foundation and "some private funds are also in the offing," so they were not pinning all hopes on Field. Cotton used the proposals to articulate her vision for the CEP. The program's strong track record in teaching basic literacy skills meant that it was ideally suited to address entwined issues of widespread illiteracy and poverty, she asserted. According to Cotton, the CEP went beyond traditional adult education that failed to address "a legacy of slavery and segregation" that cut deep scars, leaving African Americans with "no confidence, full of fear and stripped of the drive required to exert themselves." Federal legislation had removed legal barriers; now it was time for "persistent effort" to "effectuate gains." CEP teachers were critical change agents in this process. Cotton likened the teachers to missionaries who "reach the uninvolved" through classes that acted as a form of religious conversion. Cotton replaced references to "first-class citizenship" with "full personhood" and "courage-to-be," emphasizing her belief that social change began with individual transformation. Revised CEP lessons in literacy skills, consumer education, family planning, and politics and government started an "awakening" process that raised expectations and inspired broader action.[9] The formulation emphasized benefits to students while ensuring that the CEP teacher remained the essential change agent.

Cotton's analysis rested on two assumptions: that CEP students were "anxious for guidance" and that "awakened" students would encounter systems open to their "involvement." The argument was consistent with the CEP's practice of encouraging students to define priorities and to enact lessons through voter registration and everyday acts that established economic and social independence.[10] In her proposal, Cotton deemphasized voter registration as the CEP's primary goal and instead linked the CEP to federally funded anti-poverty programs that opened new avenues for "awakened" students. She described changes to CEP teacher training workshops that more explicitly prepared teachers for "innumerable programs designed to . . . solve community problems and how to implement them." Armed with this information, teachers outlined a tangible path for students to "effectuate the gains" of federal reform. The proposal secured an annual grant from the Field Foundation, enough to keep the CEP afloat but two years short of the requested long-term commitment.[11]

According to Cotton, personal transformation started with local teachers, and their conversion began at Dorchester. Beginning in 1965, training workshops were overhauled alongside curriculum revisions. Bernice Robinson and Dorothy Cotton continued to demonstrate CEP methods for teaching reading and handwriting, preserving the program's focus on basic literacy. Cotton's session about the U.S. Constitution and Robinson's tried-and-tested recruiting tips also remained in a workshop that had become a crash course in community organizing, broadly defined. Opening sessions drew direct attention to rural poverty, setting the stage for a series of sessions where guest speakers spoke on a variety of topics, including federal anti-poverty programs, political trends, organizing local credit unions, African American history, family planning, and SCLC initiatives such as Operation Breadbasket.[12] In 1965, Victoria Gray had observed that federal reform redefined the "struggle," shifting from "a common enemy to more diverse directions and objectives." The revised CEP teacher training schedule was the program's response; they would equip local people for all "diverse directions and objectives." It was a lot for participants to take in, and as Aimee Isgrig Horton observed on a visit, prospective teachers spent less time in "small group and individual teaching-learning activities" in a weeklong workshop that was "more content, less participation."[13]

Enacting the "Second Phase"

CEP staff tracked program success by intentionally documenting activities with direct connection to CEP workshop sessions. Beginning in February 1967, Alabama organizer Lewis Black guided prospective teachers through the process to establish a local credit union. The strategy fit with a new emphasis on community-based self-help strategies for economic security. Through credit unions, residents pooled resources that remained within the African American community. In addition, borrowers were less likely to encounter discriminatory policies and practices in a community-based institution. Clark and Robinson demonstrated commitment to the strategy by encouraging Dorchester participants, and through their participation in the Citizens Committee of Charleston, an outgrowth of Esau Jenkins's early work on Johns Island. In September 1966, the committee opened a credit union, and within six months, 174 residents purchased more than $3,000 in shares, allowing the agency to extend seven hundred loans. Robinson boasted, "Officers and members . . . have either been Citizenship School teachers or students and many of them have attended our community leadership training workshop."[14] Into 1968, Robinson leveraged this experience to spark interest among community groups organized from CEP classes in the South Carolina up-country and along the coast.[15]

CEP teachers and veterans threw support behind additional community-based self-help initiatives that invested back into African American communities while shielding consumers from exploitive practices. Ten years after the first citizenship school gathered in the Johns Island Progressive Club store, CEP teachers helped to organize similar "cooperative supermarket[s]" in Selma, Alabama, and Grenada, Mississippi, and in October 1966, Clark reported that Selma's market "is doing business at the rate of fifteen to twenty thousand dollars a week." In January 1967, Clark traveled to Louisiana and Mississippi where she sat in on planning discussions for a community supermarket in Plaquemine and shopped in a newly opened "community store" in Natchez. In Grenada, she heard about a different kind of self-help program as local leaders laid groundwork for a tutorial program during the school's spring break.[16]

Clark's correspondence also noted, "Many of our teachers . . . [are] now working in O.E.O. programs in the rural communities."[17] As local teachers in Mississippi had demonstrated, Head Start programs served as a primary vehicle for advancing goals of improved education and economic security. Across the South, CEP veterans successfully navigated federal requirements and application procedures to open local centers. From Burke County, Georgia, Reba Maria Belle shared news that her community "started a poverty program, the Head Start program [and was] planning on starting some more programs." In Gadsden, Alabama, Bennie J. Luchion and CEP veterans partnered with the local Catholic school to open Operation Head Start, where 820 black and white children ate two meals a day and received regular medical and dental care. In the South Carolina up-country, students from Hope Williams's CEP class organized the Calhoun County Improvement League and opened Operation Head Start serving 150 preschool children, while on the coast, the Reverend Lewis H. Simmons's students opened "5 centers in Dorchester County and [were] working on other anti-[poverty]

programs."[18] The reports showed CEP-trained teachers charting their own paths into the "second phase," transferring program principles into new areas. Including these examples in their reports indicated that local teachers viewed anti-poverty work as an extension of their CEP activities.

CEP veterans' correspondence and staff reports also highlighted challenges. From Saluda, Minnie L. Butler reached out to the CEP for help. Federal guidelines required integrated planning groups and classrooms, but in her corner of the South Carolina up-country, "we haven't been able to get the white children to attend," she wrote, and "white teachers" stayed away.[19] Successful implementation depended on a willingness to transgress local dividing lines and, on a broader scale, public support and political will for federally funded War on Poverty programs. Erosion came quickly with CEP veterans working in Head Start centers being some of the first to feel the effects, as Victoria Gray's reports showed. The Child Development Group of Mississippi (CDGM) attracted scrutiny when it accepted grant funds directly from the OEO, bypassing the state's elected officials. In response, Mississippi State Sovereignty Commission (MSSC) agents catalogued Head Start center locations and the names and home addresses of staff and board members. From his seat on the U.S. Senate Appropriations Committee, Senator John C. Stennis scrutinized CDGM records for accounting errors or evidence of federal funds being used to support political, in this case civil rights, causes.[20] According to Gray, constant scrutiny resulted in "six months of struggle" and "extreme measures" to secure continued funding, attributing the eventual success to "SCLC and MFDP initiated people who carried the ball in the final determination." By the fall, the CDGM "was in trouble again" when Governor Paul Johnson granted a state charter to Mississippi Action for Progress (MAP). From Hattiesburg, Gray mobilized "people of common thinking" who "once again engaged in a crisis situation which caused us to neglect other programs."[21]

In Alabama, the SCLC and local CEP teachers continued work started in the wake of the Selma campaign, and into 1966, the SCLC's project director, Daniel Harrell, implemented plans for a comprehensive community project in Wilcox County. The project would blend self-help and OEO-funded projects, including a credit union, year-round Head Start, a farming cooperative, and federal loans for new home construction. Clark and Cotton returned to design a "literacy education" program where "the three r's are just the beginning." The CEP's imprint was clear in topics such as "consumer education, . . . citizenship responsibility and rights, political organization, . . . and community development." In June 1966, the education

Figure 6. Dorothy Cotton leading literacy education session in Wilcox County, ca. 1966. Courtesy of Bob Fitch Photography Archive, Department of Special Collections, Stanford University Libraries.

program slipped through the labyrinth of state-level reviews and approvals, and by the start of the next year, ten centers operated across the county, providing child care during the day and adult education for "seasonal workers" in the evenings. Within five months, the program "burst over its banks." Initially designed for two hundred, "the project [ran] triple sessions . . . for over 500 families."[22]

The SCLC dispatched newly hired Mew Soong Li to oversee the project while Clark conducted abbreviated training workshops for local "nonprofessionals" hired to teach the basic education classes.[23] Similar to Clark's work with Mississippi's Freedom Schools, the seasonal migrant program offered an outlet to infuse CEP principles into a new education program. In spring 1967, Clark observed local teachers at work, noting their use of CEP methods. Gee's Bend students showed "Much improvement" in "Oral Expression and Writing skills," Clark observed. "They are asking questions and all have learned to write their names." In Camden, local teacher Ethel Brooks creatively drew on her students' experiences to blend lessons in oral expression and the program's emphasis on job preparation. Each student took turns describing "their first job for a salary," and at the end of each presentation, students offered constructive feedback about grammar and oral expression. Clark documented the local residents' commitment to learning and improving basic skills in the most challenging circumstances. In Camden, an "exceptionally large class" crowded into two rooms and spilled out into the hallway. At Annemanie, students swatted flies and mosquitos in rooms without screens, and in Pine Apple, the teacher's husband hauled water from three miles away. In Camden and Coy, students squinted to read in dim overhead lighting.[24]

Annell Ponder also lent direct support for the project and attributed its success to the SCLC's groundwork in "voter registration, citizenship education, [and] school desegregation." Adult education classrooms inspired the same kind of conversion that happened in CEP classrooms, she argued, observing, "Many people stand taller, walk more briskly, and look with eager anticipation of things to come in." She painted with a broad brush as she connected individual transformation with two self-help cooperative projects: Southwest Alabama Self-Help Housing (SWASH) and the Southwest Alabama Farmers Cooperative Association (SWAFCA), initiatives that resulted from complex local partnerships. According to Ponder, earlier CEP classes set the foundation for a farm machinery cooperative

Figure 7. Septima Clark guiding student's hand in a Wilcox County literacy education class, ca. 1966–1967. Courtesy of Bob Fitch Photography Archive, Department of Special Collections, Stanford University Libraries.

in Boling Springs and "credit committees" that expected to evolve into "a credit union."[25]

In Mississippi and in South Carolina, state CEP field coordinators Victoria Gray and Bernice Robinson tuned their work to "next phase" political action, seizing on elections as opportunities to flex power and influence. In a state where many CEP-trained teachers had moved on, Gray carried on, classifying political organizing and education work as part of her CEP responsibilities. In 1966, Holmes County CEP veteran Ralthus Hayes had run an unsuccessful campaign for the U.S. House of Representatives, but anticipation ran high for elections the next year. "All county and state offices were at stake," Gray wrote, and "for the first time in this Century, Negroes were registered in sufficient numbers." Throughout the summer and fall, she organized workshops that acted as abbreviated CEP classes where "illiterate voters" learned candidates' names and received a crash course on voting rights and the "duties and limitations of various polling officials and federal registrars." Civil rights organizations collaborated under the banner Mississippians United to Elect Negro Candidates and "probably made the difference . . . at every level," Gray reflected. Twenty-four black candidates won, and "of prime importance," according to Gray, African Americans "held off efforts and threats" aimed at preventing newly elected officials from taking office.[26]

Likewise, in South Carolina, Bernice Robinson devoted time to "next phase" political organizing. After ten years, she was no longer the unsure citizenship school teacher standing in front of equally unsure students in a makeshift classroom. Her work with the Highlander Folk School and the CEP took her to communities across the South and broadened her perspective.[27] Her organizing acumen was on display in early 1966 when all of South Carolina's local precincts would hold biannual conventions to define precinct boundaries and select representatives. For two months, she crisscrossed the state, visiting remaining CEP outposts and adapting lessons into urgent appeals for engagement at all levels. In Newberry County, local classes served as ready-made forums for discussions about precinct organization and newly available federal jobs. The next month, she reminded "well over 200" at the James Island Improvement League that "the Rod Is in Your Hand" and then returned to Newberry County for "a very good session" with the Whitmire Leadership Club. Robinson practiced what she preached through the Political Action Committee of Charleston County. When city officials announced precinct reorganization plans, the committee demanded seats in planning sessions. As a result, African

Americans secured precinct positions and elected delegates to county and state conventions "for the first time in the history of Charleston," Robinson remarked. Later in the month, she joined a group of sixty-five residents who arrived en masse to watch for "any slip up" and ensure that officials "followed through letter to letter on promises."[28]

Citizenship Education and the SCLC's Next Phase

Both the CEP and the SCLC marked ten-year anniversaries in 1967. In August, the SCLC faithful gathered at Atlanta's Ebenezer Baptist Church to commemorate the significant milestone. It was late in a summer marked by images of armed Black Panther Party members on the steps of the California state capitol, hippies "invading" San Francisco's Haight-Ashbury district, and National Guard troops patrolling the streets of Detroit and Newark as riots tore each city apart.[29] "Where do we go from here?" The question served as the title for Martin Luther King's book published that summer and as the annual convention theme. CEP staff, teachers, and veterans answered the question through organizing, nurturing, and sustaining local initiatives designed to lay claim to a broad range of "first-class citizenship" rights. King was at home in Ebenezer's pulpit as he outlined his answer.

King opened with a review of the SCLC's ten-year history. In a section likely drafted by Cotton, he acknowledged CEP teachers who "lay the solid foundation of adult education and community organization upon which all social change must ultimately rest." Local leaders completed training in "literacy, consumer education, planned parenthood, and many other things," and according to King, "establishing O.E.O. projects" was an important "auxiliary feature" of the CEP's work. The CEP was one of several ongoing SCLC initiatives used as a backdrop for a bold call to "restructur[e] the whole of American society." Slavery and Jim Crow segregation cast a long shadow and "left the Negro far behind," King argued in words that echoed Cotton's grant proposals suggesting that they had discussed their ideas. However, where Cotton had emphasized individual "awakening" as the critical foundation for collective action, King attacked the entangled forces of capitalism and racial discrimination that perpetuated substandard housing, high unemployment and infant mortality rates, poor educational outcomes, and depressed incomes, culminating in "dislocating" black families from economic and political power. King called for a federally guaranteed annual income, thundering, "If our nation can spend thirty-five billion dollars to fight an unjust, evil war in Vietnam, and twenty billion dollars to put a man on the moon, it can spend billions of dollars to put God's children on their own two feet right here on earth."[30]

Into the fall, King gravitated toward an idea presented by a young attorney fresh from Mississippi's civil rights battles. At an SCLC executive board retreat, Marian Wright suggested that poor people could make their own case if given the chance. Modeled on the Bonus Army of World War I veterans, she envisioned caravans converging to establish an encampment on the National Mall and demand federal action on the issue of poverty. By December, King announced a plan to mobilize "3,000 solid people" and appointed Bernard Lafayette to coordinate the SCLC's "Poor People's Campaign for Jobs or Income."[31] The CEP used its newsletter to reach its constituents, reprinting King's invitation to "channelize the smoldering rage and frustration of Negro people into an effective militant and nonviolent movement of massive proportions." Their voices would join a chorus of "millions of non-Negro poor" in this inclusive movement.[32]

Planning bogged down in February as turf battles erupted. King urged his staff to reach "the people we are talking about . . . the hard-core poor people." "If we can not do it, I would rather pull out now," he confessed, concerned about "embarrassment and criticism" if they failed to reach their goals.[33] Six months before, King had extolled the CEP's ability to "lay the solid foundation . . . upon which all social change must ultimately rest." Now, the SCLC's inner circle and field staff searched for local contacts and argued about whether they were the "hard-core poor." The weak link between the campaign and a far-reaching grassroots program highlighted the CEP's marginal position, a position predetermined by the organization's gendered dynamics. When SCLC leaders communicated with local representatives, they relied on SCLC affiliates, an approach that privileged relationships among ministers and marginalized the largely woman-led CEP. Likewise, although Cotton and Clark served on the SCLC's executive council, both later commented on gendered treatment. Clark remembered the common practice of placing the CEP last on meeting agendas while Cotton recalled requests to fetch coffee or to take minutes, setting her apart from the men sitting around the table. Young later confirmed, "Septima and Dorothy would grumble privately about how women were treated in the SCLC."[34] While all rushed to deny that the treatment reflected disrespect toward female staff members, the examples pointed to an environment where the CEP was customarily seen as secondary to more important priorities. A final factor eroding potential links between the Poor People's Campaign and the CEP likely stemmed from within the program itself. By early 1968, the CEP had an extensive mailing list of Dorchester participants, but, as Wesley Hotchkiss had alluded, this did not translate into an organized network. Instead, the CEP was on shaky ground as the Field Foundation carried through on earlier promises, decreasing its support to only $150,000 for 1968. The CEP needed matching funds of $75,000 or Field was pulling out in 1969.[35]

As the SCLC organized for a national campaign, CEP staff remained focused on local initiatives. In January, South Carolina CEP teachers and veterans gathered for a specialized workshop ahead of spring elections scheduled to coincide with the state's requirements for all voters to re-register every ten years. Longtime CEP organizer Benjamin Mack worried, "It will be just as hard to get people to re-register as it was to get them registered initially." Some of the program's most experienced teachers joined Esau Jenkins and the CEP staff to outline "methods of organizing . . . [and] get-out-the-vote campaigns," hoping to stem erosion of hard-fought gains.[36] After the workshop, Bernice Robinson visited CEP classes to lead lessons in "government from precinct level upward and in parliamentary procedures." The work paid off, she reported, as groups attended meetings "in full force and took over all important positions, in their individual precincts." Political action took center stage in Savannah where a small group of stalwart CEP teachers partnered with the city's NAACP chapter to register eight hundred new voters. In Mississippi, Victoria Gray helped independent candidates to meet filing deadlines and organized to "find the unregistered."[37]

Gray's report also described a surge of local activism in Palmer's Crossing. In the summer of 1964, Hattiesburg had been the "Mecca" for Freedom Schools and an important MFDP hub. In the four years since, people drifted away, leaving Gray and CEP veteran Helen Anderson as two of only "a handful of people" willing to "tak[e] on the entire responsibility" for organizing. They rekindled interest with a door-to-door survey and within a month, residents turned out for weekly meetings, registered to vote, and defined local priorities that translated the gains of the civil rights movement into tangible improvements. They wanted the county government to pave the roads and improve drainage systems. With an eye on community health and safety, these priorities represented continuity with earlier initiatives when CEP teachers "mothered the movement" and took steps to remove visible markers of segregation. The Palmer's Crossing group organized a petition drive, and three representatives presented their complaints to city officials. "It's a marvelous thing just to see people beginning to believe that they have the right to do these things," Gray enthused.[38]

The turn of phrase was telling. After nearly five years of intense organizing, Gray marveled at "people beginning to believe." One victory, or even a series of victories, was not permanent social change. A once-sown field needed constant attention. The movement went on and organizers like Gray confronted a challenge. Before 1965, unjust segregation laws and discriminatory voting tests were clear targets. As Cotton had argued, CEP teachers contributed to the groundswell for change by creating spaces for personal transformation that fueled collective action. When federal legislation banned discriminatory laws and practices, civil rights battles had moved into communities where claiming rights often translated into micro-local issues. In a broad sense, safe and healthy communities mattered to African Americans across the country, and the SCLC's Poor People's Campaign was designed to address these issues; however, Palmer's Crossing residents did not want to wait for a national campaign. Instead, they were fighting on their own against city- and county-level power systems that moved at a frustratingly slow pace. Registering to vote, signing petitions, presenting evidence, and negotiating all took time. Gray reported that in Forrest County, the county supervisor fell back on a tried-and-true strategy of "finding all the excuses possible." Negotiations dragged and momentum waned.[39]

In Savannah, local women in the Chatham County Crusade for Voters (CCCV) reported similar challenges. For this small group, CEP teacher training workshops and refresher sessions were lifelines to resources and information. Between 1967 and 1968, they focused on community improvements, starting in predominately black west side neighborhoods where the city's neglect showed in dimly lit, poorly paved streets and the absence of safe play areas. As in Forrest County, requests were met with a string of excuses, with city officials agreeing to the improvements only after persistent agitation organized by the CEP veterans.[40] In the spring of 1968, they extended their reach beyond the city limits to Ogeecheeton, where seventy-five black families drew water from "a lone hand pump." CEP veteran and CCCV member Alberta Williams joined a three-woman delegation at a county commission meeting. "We need to improve our homes," one of the women acknowledged, "but right now the worst thing is, we don't have water." The women also requested school bus service. It was a matter of equity, they explained, but also a matter of safeguarding the community's "small school girls." Already, there were reports of "men in cars" and "lurking in bushes" ready to "entice" the girls as they walked to school. The women's appeals raised awareness but backfired when county officials slated Ogeecheeton for demolition as part of a "slum clearance" program. "We realize that urban renewal is a new name to take people's lots," Rebecca Jenkins had lamented in 1967.[41]

Reports from Palmer's Crossing and Savannah documented a slow pace of change in places where federal legislation was not enough to erase Jim Crow's dividing lines. A week before the Savannah group approached Chatham County officials, Martin Luther King Jr. was in another southern city, raising awareness about similar long-standing neglect and injustice. He had agreed to lend support to striking garbage workers in Memphis, seeing the strike as part of the movement's next phase to ensure economic equality and dignity for all American workers. On Thursday, April 4, news from Memphis shattered routines. King was dead, shot by an assassin. Bernice Robinson dropped everything and rushed to Atlanta. Already there, Dorothy Cotton hurried to the King home where she joined mourners in collective shock and grief. In the hours and days after the assassination, violence engulfed 110 cities across the country. Robinson planned to attend a memorial service in Columbia on her way home but cancelled her trip when organizers called off the service after "disturbances" prompted a citywide curfew.[42] In Savannah, Mayor Curtis Lewis announced a voluntary curfew in the wake of "sporadic rock throwing and arson attempts," a decision "fortified" by the Savannah NAACP chapter and the women of the CCCV. Savannah and Hattiesburg officials moved to head off further unrest. At citywide memorial services, Savannah's white and black clergy urged "practical" action on specific improvements in King's memory. The list included many of the issues CEP teachers consistently raised including employment, education, and "sub-standard living conditions." In Mississippi, Victoria Gray channeled "grief and concern" into non-violent direct action, organizing weeklong school and business boycotts and three-day work stoppages. She later surmised that the assassination and subsequent "non-violent demonstration and protest" broke the logjam with the roads supervisor and optimistically predicted that the "sense of awareness" would reignite CEP classes.[43]

In Atlanta, the SCLC's new president, Ralph D. Abernathy, pledged to follow through with the Poor People's Campaign "stronger and more determined than ever before."[44] Caravans departing from Mississippi, Chicago, Boston, Denver, and Los Angeles would meet in Washington, D.C., by

May 18. From Georgia, CEP teacher Rosa Robinson and the Augusta SCLC chapter sent four representatives to Washington "with suit cases of food" and shipped clothes and shoes directly to the encampment. In Charleston, Bernice Robinson spent three days checking on buses, raising funds, organizing food committees, cooking meals, and lining up volunteers. When the caravan arrived, she joined the march and ensured that visitors were housed and fed. The next day, she gathered clothing and food. Two days later, Robinson resumed a routine of meetings and visits to CEP teachers across the state.[45]

As planned, caravans pulled in and set up "Resurrection City" in King's memory. Resurrection City tested the SCLC in ways that earlier campaigns had not. In Selma and Birmingham, local people organized food and housing for as many as three hundred out-of-town volunteers for a short-term stay. At its peak, Resurrection City was home to seven thousand people, planning to live in tents for several weeks. For a month, staff members struggled to obtain adequate supplies, enforce law and order, and adhere to a schedule of meetings with Congress and federal agencies. Then in late May, the rain started and the tent city turned into a river of mud. Andrew Young later reflected, "We simply weren't functioning well," and tempers flared between exhausted staff members. By mid-June, supporters filtered away and the encampment shrunk to seven hundred. Crowds returned for "Solidarity Day" on June 19, a long afternoon of speeches that, in the end, failed to recapture the magic of the March on Washington held five years earlier. When the site's six-week permit expired four days later, police moved in and arrested over three hundred tent city residents, sparking unrest in surrounding neighborhoods. Defeated, SCLC leaders returned to Atlanta to regroup.[46]

Citizenship Education at the End of the 1960s

CEP teachers and veterans continued their work at the grass roots. In Savannah, the CCCV stalwarts paid close attention to plans for the city's Model Cities program. Following federal guidelines, city officials designated a downtown neighborhood for targeted intervention and organized a collaborative body of service organizations and civic groups. The Savannah NAACP branch secured a seat at the table as project boundary lines effectively shut out CCCV members living outside of the designated neighborhood.[47] More than representation was at stake as Model Cities funneled federal benefits employment into the city. CCCV secretary Rebecca Jenkins refused to be shut out. In January, she attended a meeting of the city's interracial council, "didn't like what they were saying," and called the city manager's office to tell him so. By the next month, "many of our people" were hired to canvass in targeted communities, she reported. Savannah-area teachers also worked to ensure local representation, organizing CEP students to go "door to door asking [residents] to attend meetings." CEP classes served as forums where invited speakers could "explain the plan" because as one teacher reported, "so many people just don't understand and it's hard to get them to understand."[48]

CEP teachers in the South Carolina up-country also worked to ensure representation, earning seats at the table of the Community Action Agency (CAA) serving Newberry and Saluda Counties. CEP teacher Marie Epps and her former student Essie Eichelberger served as community representatives on the CAA board while fellow CEP teacher Vennie Reed secured a salaried "non-professional" position at Whitmire's Neighborhood Service Center.[49] Their participation did not result in noticeable changes, as Reed reported to Cotton in December 1968. "We have an OEO Board, but it is not helping the poor very much," she wrote, adding, "They fight each other too much" and community needs went unaddressed. Reed had attended a recent teacher training workshop and reached out for assistance with practical issues like "a day care center because a lot of poor women work but don't have anyone to keep their children." Visiting OEO evaluators confirmed Reed's assessment the following spring. "Administrative overhead is rather high and actual benefits to the poor minimal," they observed, pointing to an "established sector" that was "unwilling or unable to grasp and deal with . . . the growing consciousness of the poor." Noting that CAA program staff observed "three rather curious" holidays commemorating the Confederacy and board members "frequently used . . . [the] appellation 'nigger,'" evaluators concluded, "Possibly, there is an inherent residue of bitterness and deeply ingrained biases in too many board members."[50]

Local CEP teachers filled in the CAA gaps. Marie Epps organized classes and served as secretary of the Whitmire Community Club, where she applied organization skills learned through the CEP. She also "[ran her] car all of the time," her list of activities simultaneously demonstrating compassion for neighbors and signifying her commitment to first-class citizenship grounded in political empowerment and access to federal support. Epps transported neighbors to doctors' appointments, took "one or two people to be registered," and "help[ed] . . . older people get on welfare . . . and food stamp . . . and get their Social Security." She assured the staff, "The hardest the task get, the harder I work."⁵¹ Reed was also hard at work, blending lessons in home economics with information about federal programs. She encouraged her students to "spend their food stamps wisely" and "plant [a] garden because food is so high." Reed continued Bernice Robinson's early sewing lessons and "the ladies like this very much," she reported.⁵²

In Augusta, Georgia, the mother-daughter team of Rosa Robinson and Blondell Conley wrote in with news of their "sewing factory." They recruited six "ladys [sic] who can sew," enrolled students in sewing classes, and made plans to secure a small business loan.⁵³ The city's OEO office offered space and equipment, a textile mill donated cloth, and local families brought in unused sewing machines, scissors, and a steam iron. In April 1969, the Southland Sewing Center opened in the city's Turpin Hill neighborhood. The "factory" served multiple purposes. Fourteen students enrolled in the first month and mastered sewing skills alongside experienced seamstresses. The volunteers made hats, children's clothing, pillows, and aprons that were sold in the factory store. "Since it's a poor people's project," Robinson explained, "we let the people come and buy at their own price." Center organizers funneled profits back into the business, buying "buttons, zippers, and thread and needles for the machine." From this promising start, Robinson hoped to "grow into a factory and business that will work 350 peoples [sic]."⁵⁴

Local initiatives served as evidence of the CEP's impact. The program continued to train teachers and attendance at Dorchester sessions held steady throughout 1968, but teachers organized fewer classes upon their return to home. In January 1969, financial challenges came to a head as Field Foundation officials made good on promises to withhold grant funds until the CEP secured matching funds from another source. Dunbar rejected Abernathy's offer to use SCLC funds as the required match, despite assurances that the SCLC viewed the CEP as "one of the most vital and productive of all of our activities among the poor and deprived."⁵⁵ The foundation's "hard line" touched off a scramble. Wesley Hotchkiss assembled a list of foundations with track records of supporting voter registration and education programs, and Cotton got to work. Her appeals positioned the "largely unpublicized" CEP as "the base upon which much ... social change has been built in the last decade." An eleven-year track record in basic education and community organizing uniquely qualified the CEP to realize King's dream, she asserted, because the CEP did the "unfinished business of a democratic society," sparking the "self-discovery" that inspired "basic political education, voter registration, ... organization of community groups, ... credit union and co-op organization . . . [and] petitioning for services." With additional funds, they could reach "ten million functionally illiterate adults" who had been "historically shut out of the mainstream of American life" and expand the CEP into an integrated program where participants would "build a new South with black and white working together."[56]

Cotton emphasized the urgent need for $75,000 in matching funds, but she encouraged investment in an ambitious $326,900 budget for program expansion. Responses trickled in. "Regretfully, I must report," most letters began, and Cotton did not need to read further. The answer was no.[57] In February, she sent "little expense money" to local teachers and advised that "until we get our grant renewed, we must cut down on expenses." From southeastern Georgia, Bernice Green assured Cotton that "if it wasn't one penny, I'll work just as hard, for this is part of me." Ruth Mallard expressed similar conviction, writing, "The importance [of the work], *not the money*, keeps me trying to go on."[58] Good news came in early March when SCLC friends threw a lifeline. Stanley Levison, King's attorney and now the director of the Frieda Foundation, pledged the matching funds, and Dunbar authorized release of the remaining Field funds. In May, the CEP received another boost with a "one time gift" from Governor Nelson A. Rockefeller "in view of the importance of this effort to reach functionally illiterate adults."[59] The combination of Field and Frieda grants along with the Rockefeller gift resolved the immediate financial crisis, but it was not a long-term solution and fell well short of the CEP's projected budget.

* * *

The CEP had ended 1966 amidst questions about the program's financial foundation and urgent appeals to move into the "second phase." Following passage of the Voting Rights Act, director Dorothy Cotton navigated a course that retained the CEP's focus on basic literacy education as the avenue to individual transformation and collective action. Cotton's proposals replaced references to "first-class citizenship" and voter registration with direct links to self-help and federal anti-poverty programs as avenues to enact newfound "courage-to-be." Under Cotton's direction, local teachers experienced their own conversion in informational sessions at Dorchester, and like missionaries, they would lift the poor and downtrodden. The formulation emphasized individual transformation with local women as essential change agents.

The SCLC was also defining a next phase after 1965. In contrast to Cotton's emphasis on individual enlightenment, Martin Luther King Jr. took aim at the systems sustaining racial discrimination and economic inequality, calling for a national Poor People's Campaign. Planning for the campaign revealed the CEP's marginal position within the organization, a position highlighted by CEP-trained veterans' and staff members' emphasis on locally defined priorities. Their actions collectively defined the program's "next phase," capturing the optimism in the post-1965 South as CEP staff members lent direct support for a variety of initiatives to improve basic literacy and more explicitly address economic inequities. CEP teachers and staff mobilized to funnel federal anti-poverty resources into local communities and organize self-help community projects. Federal law lifted restrictions on voter registration, igniting interest in politics from the local to the federal level. CEP teachers and staff retuned their work to emphasize political education and organization. In Savannah, Hattiesburg, and the South Carolina up-country, CEP-trained veterans organized to realize the promise of federal reform, turning attention to local projects that would finally erase remaining markers of segregation.

They did this work as the foundation eroded under their feet. The backlash experienced in Alabama's Black Belt spread across the South as elected officials took aim at federal anti-poverty programs, just when CEP veterans and staff looked to these programs as vehicles for community empowerment and economic security. In Savannah, Hattiesburg, and the South Carolina up-country, CEP veterans ran up against local officials intent on delaying and obstructing to maintain the status quo. King's assassination dramatically altered the landscape of the civil rights movement. The SCLC saw King's vision through with Resurrection City but left the nation's capital exhausted with little to show from their efforts. As the 1960s came to a close, the CEP's sole source of financial support set limits, forcing Cotton to seek new sources of funding as the program and the movement struggled for traction.

Epilogue

In August 1969, the Southern Christian Leadership Conference (SCLC) held its annual convention in Charleston. Staff members had been to the city several times that spring in support of a strike by the city's black hospital workers. Now in late summer, executive director Andrew Young met in closed session with SCLC board members and President Ralph D. Abernathy. Young began with "ominous signs" from the federal government. Preoccupied with foreign affairs, newly elected Richard M. Nixon opted for "total avoidance of any domestic issue," permitting "obvious hedging" on renewal of the Voting Rights Act. Foreseeing "dangerous days ahead," Young concluded, "There are no more 'cheap victories.' We have no friends in power." Amidst mounting criticism that the SCLC had "left no visible evidence" in local communities, Young called for bold action away from "massive dramatic actions or . . . utopian schemes" to the "hard detailed job of organizing and building local power units which can sustain themselves." For this task, he pointed to the CEP, highlighting the five thousand "generally politicized" teachers trained in the "SCLC philosophy and methods." To meet the challenge, the program needed to change by cutting back on monthly teacher training workshops and opening "Citizenship Education Centers in as many counties as possible." Modeled on the Wilcox County experiment, Young envisioned the centers as economic development hubs, including tutoring, family planning, consumer education, and political action.[1]

Young's proposal would push the marginalized CEP into the center of the SCLC's operation. It was a vision that would not be realized. Under Abernathy's leadership, the SCLC was unable, or unwilling, to embrace this vision of grassroots organizing. Into the 1970s, Abernathy remained wedded to King's vision of ending poverty through a broad national movement. As historian Thomas Peake has argued, poverty was rooted in a complex set of social, economic, and political factors, which left the SCLC without a clearly defined nemesis.[2] Momentum waned as short-term, high-intensity direct action campaigns gave way to the grinding work of sustaining a movement where action shifted from city streets to legislative hearings, conference rooms, and polling places.

Critics who charged that the SCLC did not leave footprints in communities overlooked the people trained through the CEP. Across the South, these people were gaining footholds as the federal government was in retreat. Elected officials attempted to gut the Voting Rights Act, as if a century of disfranchisement could be permanently reversed in four short years. Young characterized Nixon as distracted by foreign affairs; however, his administration was actively dismantling the Office of Economic Opportunity (OEO) and neutralizing the federal Civil Rights Division. In Congress, a resurgent conservative majority used the tax code to impose new regulations for philanthropic support of voter registration projects, setting limits on contributions from a single foundation and requiring multistate projects to operate in five or more states. The regulations had a chilling effect on private financing of civil rights activities and effectively slowed the flow of money to a trickle.[3] Erosion of federal commitment opened the door for "obvious hedging" in statehouses, city and county council meetings, and in bureaucratic systems where decisions about resource allocations and priorities were made.

In this context, the CEP came to an end, its final years recorded in silences as the paper trail tapers off. Dorothy Cotton secured financial support in the spring of 1969, but the absence of grant proposals and financial records suggests that she was unable to repeat the feat. In April 1970, Abernathy included citizenship education as an SCLC priority, but the slow trickle of CEP teachers' attendance records, correspondence, and workshop attendance rosters suggested otherwise.[4] The last teacher training roster is from late April when thirty-two volunteers from four states arrived at Dorchester. The last attendance records filtered in at the same time.[5] The program appears in a 1971 grant proposal to the Field Foundation where Abernathy and his successor, Stoney Cooks, described the CEP as "the basis for local community development and an inspiration to movement building" and CEP-trained teachers as "the main stay of a movement that is concentrated throughout the South."[6] By the time of the proposal, many CEP staff members had moved on. Victoria Gray resigned in May 1968 after remarrying and relocating for her husband's job. Annell Ponder accepted a position at the Atlanta University School of Social Work in March 1967, briefly returned to the CEP by 1969, then quietly left again.[7] Andrew Young and Septima Clark arrived together in 1961, and nine years later, they departed at the same time. Bernice Robinson also left in 1970. Three years later, Dorothy Cotton resigned, the last of the original CEP staff to do so.[8]

After more than a decade, the CEP could boast impressive numbers. Between 1961 and 1970, the CEP reached into all southern states, preparing 2,349 local leaders in teacher training and refresher workshops. By January 1968, program administrators estimated that teachers organized 7,280 classes, enrolling 26,686 people. In February 1965, Septima Clark estimated that CEP teachers and students influenced 95,000 newly registered voters, and the work continued through the end of the decade.[9] Across the South, local people, mostly women, completed CEP training and organized classes. The program's criteria cast a wide net so that some people arriving at the Dorchester Academy were experienced organizers, while for others, the CEP served as an entry point and valuable training ground. They adopted a familiar role grounded in a gendered political culture and created intimate gathering spaces where individual transformation sowed the seeds for collective action.

Assessing the program's impact is more than adding up numbers. As demonstrated throughout *The Citizenship Education Program and Black Women's Political Culture*, teachers' anecdotal accounts documented the variety of ways that local people laid claim to rights and entitlements. This work was under way before the CEP and continued as the program came to a close. In 1969, Savannah CEP teacher Alma Middleton and her students were "get[ting] some place for the children to play during the summer months," and when the program ended, they were working on a permanent recreation center. In the South Carolina up-country, Eddie Lou Holloway and Grace Salley held "parties" and asked "churches for donations" for a new community center while Vennie Reed organized a boycott of all "but food and medicine until the people get their right," including "some job in the bank and stores."[10] In Akron, Alabama, Ceola Hollis used her CEP training to help "quite a few people" obtain birth certificates and secure pension payments, and by the spring of 1970, Hollis launched "a money profit organization to help ourselves," starting a sewing club that made quilts, aprons, and pot holders for sale. In one of the last areas reached by the program, Miami CEP teachers in the Hialeah Heights Civic Club advocated for tenants' rights, arranged "more frequent and on schedule" trash pickup, collected food for needy families, and started a "Buying Club" to pass on consumer education lessons. In Model Cities meetings, their opposition blocked low-income housing projects planned for their "already over-crowded" neighborhood.[11] This was enacting first-class citizenship.

The program's influence showed in other ways. In June 1969, CEP teacher Eddie Lou Holloway graduated from high school, forty years after she had dropped out. Community work had inspired her to "want to know more and be more qualified," she told a reporter. A year later, CEP and MFDP veteran Helen Anderson earned a high school equivalency certificate through the federal Systematic Training and Redevelopment (STAR) Program.[12] Across the South, CEP teachers moved into public service, elected office, and education programs. Johns Island teacher Ethel Grimball supervised the island's first Head Start program and eventually managed social service programs in Charleston County. In 1977, she joined Septima Clark, Bernice Robinson, and Alleen Brewer on the Charleston Committee for Day Care. Southeastern Georgia CEP veterans Pearlie Ealey and Greta Rhynes had long careers in public welfare programs in Cincinnati and Boston, respectively. Peggy Jean Connor was instrumental in establishing Hattiesburg's Freedom Trail to commemorate the movement she helped to lead.[13] For each former teacher, the CEP was a chapter in a life of service. Through the CEP, they added to a community-organizing toolkit, found new avenues of influence, and established new networks.

CEP staff members' service also extended beyond the program's time frame. Victoria Gray Adams moved to Petersburg, Virginia, and worked in campus ministry at Virginia State University, Dorothy Cotton's alma mater. In 1976, Septima Clark won election to Charleston's school board, the first black woman elected to the post, and she was a steady and consistent advocate for city schoolteachers during her two terms on the board.[14] Bernice Robinson returned to the Sea Islands where she supervised VISTA volunteers for the South Carolina Commission for Farm Workers. In 1972, she ran an unsuccessful campaign for a seat in the South Carolina House of Representatives, the first black woman candidate in the state's history.[15] In 1972, Andrew Young won election to the U.S. House of Representatives, becoming the first African American from a southern state elected to Congress since Reconstruction. In 1973, at Young's encouragement, Dorothy Cotton relocated to Birmingham, where she supervised the city's Head Start program.[16]

Establishing community institutions, initiating self-help organizations, mentoring the next generation, and organizing collective action to ensure individual rights fulfilled the CEP's construction of first-class citizenship, but ten years after her resignation, the program's first teacher offered a nuanced assessment. "Of course, there's still a lot of illiteracy on the islands," Bernice Robinson began. "We didn't scratch the surface, so it would seem that there is no point." She quickly changed tone. "We have had an influence," she insisted, pointing to the 876 black officials elected in the decade after the Voting Rights Act and adult education programs that "meet an adult in an adult world." Then she shifted back. In the years following President Ronald Reagan's election, "We are sitting on a time bomb," she said. "We have to protect that progress and hold it."[17] Robinson's reflections encapsulated the CEP's complicated legacy. The need for improved literacy education, community organizing, and political empowerment remained acute in an era of restricted foundation funding and reduced budgets for anti-poverty programs. Even with its extensive reach, the CEP had "scratched the surface." Its influence endured in elected offices, public service, and adult education, but as Robinson observed, those gains were not fixed and needed to be "protected."

Foregrounding the CEP retells the story of the civil rights movement, shifting perspective to lesser-studied areas and reframing familiar narratives. This study adds to scholarship that restores black women's extensive community-based activism to the story, producing a clearer and more complete picture of how, when, and where the movement happened. Examining the CEP's full history highlights the forces that initiated and sustained the program, the forces that pulled it apart, and the high cost of erosion. Indeed, historically black neighborhoods in Charleston and Savannah, parts of the Sea Islands untouched by tourism, and rural areas of southeastern Georgia, the Mississippi Delta, and Alabama's Black Belt remain some of the poorest areas in the South and the entire nation. Retelling the CEP story informs our understanding of what it takes for lasting and meaningful redistribution of political, economic, and social power. The CEP operated for more than a decade with full-time staff members who trained and supported nearly three thousand volunteers. Local classes reached almost 24,000 people and influenced even more. Foundations invested nearly $1 million in the program. Still, as Robinson observed, the CEP "didn't scratch the surface" of systemic racial inequality.

The CEP is a story about what is possible when people gain "a new awareness of their own power" and how quickly this can erode. The program's history also offers insight into what it takes to do more than "scratch the surface." The CEP tapped into black women's community networks that existed before and endured beyond the program's existence. The CEP armed local people with new tools, information, materials, and financial support; with these resources, local women "met people where they are," translating citizenship into everyday activities like participating in community organizations, writing letters and signing petitions to address concerns, and being informed about current events and issues. Through their work, they demonstrated a keen understanding of the interconnections between politics and economics, the relationship between local action and a national movement, and their fundamental rights as U.S. citizens. Learning to read and write and registering to vote were the tools for first-class citizenship. Citizenship was something they did, not something they had. This kind of effort takes money, time, talent, and political will. Engaged citizens are only part of the equation. Sustaining this form of active democratic citizenship requires institutions that are ready and able to respond to the needs of engaged citizens. The CEP narrative shows that for a brief time in a variety of places, it was done and could be done again.

Notes

Introduction

1. Mrs. Septima Clark to Mr. Leslie Dunbar, November 7, 1966, box 8, folder 2, Septima Poinsette Clark Papers, Avery Research Center, College of Charleston (hereafter cited as SPCP-ARC); Young, *Easy Burden*, 149; Branch, *Parting the Waters*, 576.

2. Cotton, *If Your Back's Not Bent*, 131–132; Boyte, "Dorchester Center."

3. Moye, "Discovering What's Already There," in Payne et al., *Mississippi Women*, 2: 249.

4. For Highlander's role in early citizenship schools, see Frank Adams, *Unearthing Seeds*, 110–120; Aimee Isgrig Horton, *Highlander Folk School*, 207–225; Aldon D. Morris, *Origins of the Civil Rights Movement*, 139–155; Oldendorf, "The South Carolina Sea Island Citizenship Schools," in Crawford et al., *Women in the Civil Rights Movement*, 169–182. For SCLC administration, see Branch, *Parting the Waters*, 381–382, 575–578, 717–718, 819–821; Fairclough, *To Redeem the Soul*, 51–52, 68–70.

5. Clark, *Echo in My Soul*, chapters 12, 13, and 18; Lewis, *Walking with the Wind*, 89, 307–312; Young, *Easy Burden*, 138–157.

6. For gendered leadership, see Payne, *I've Got the Light*, 266–283. Payne later revised this argument in "'Sexism Is a Helluva Thing,'" in Crosby, *Civil Rights History*, 147–171. For studies that expand on this definition, see, for example, Greene, *Our Separate Ways*; Ransby, *Ella Baker*; Robnett, *How Long?*; Spencer, *Revolution Has Come*; Hamlin, *Crossroads at Clarksdale*; Tiyi M. Morris, *Womanpower Unlimited*; Charron, *Freedom's Teacher*; Orleck, *Storming Caesar's Palace*.

7. Charron, *Freedom's Teacher*, chapters 7 and 8. For earlier analyses, see McFadden, "Septima P. Clark and the Struggle," in Crawford et al., *Women in the Civil Rights Movement*, 85–97; Robnett, *How Long?*, 88–97; Rouse, "'We Speak to Know,'" in Collier-Thomas and Franklin, *Sisters in the Struggle*, 95–120.

8. Theoharis and Woodard, introduction to *Groundwork*, 1–16, quotation on 3. Crosby proposed an "interactive synthesis" to "engage the collective insights of local studies" and "the full range of movement-related scholarship." Crosby, "Politics of Writing and Teaching," in Crosby, *Civil Rights History*, 1–39, quotation on 13. For examples of local studies, see Dittmer, *Local People*; Green, *Battling the Plantation Mentality*; Ashmore, *Carry It On*; Moye, *Let the People Decide*; Jeffries, *Bloody Lowndes*; Eskew, *But for Birmingham*; Crosby, *Little Taste of Freedom*; Tuck, *Beyond Atlanta*. For edited collections, see Crosby,

Civil Rights History; Theoharis and Woodard, *Groundwork*; Theoharis and Woodard, *Freedom North*; Orleck and Hazirjian, *War on Poverty*. For local studies including CEP teachers, see Fleming, *In the Shadow*, 154–156, 166; Hamlin, *Crossroads at Clarksdale*, 64–70; Payne, *I've Got the Light*, 73–77, 153–154, 166–169.

9. See Levine, "Citizenship Schools"; Levine, "Birth of the Citizenship Schools"; Levine, "Learning for Liberation."

10. Tiyi M. Morris, *Womanpower Unlimited*, 13. For scholarship foregrounding black women's community work during the 1950s and 1960s, see, for example, Jones-Branch, *Crossing the Line*; Greene, *Our Separate Ways*; Hamlin, *Crossroads at Clarksdale*; Sanders, *Chance for Change*; Tuuri, *Strategic Sisterhood*; Naples, *Grassroots Warriors*; Orleck, *Storming Caesar's Palace*; Orleck and Hazirjian, introduction to *War on Poverty*.

11. Civil rights scholarship has challenged, complicated, and disrupted a standard narrative presented in works like the *Eyes on the Prize* PBS series. See Hall, "Long Civil Rights Movement." For sample works examining early roots in the South, see Gilmore, *Defying Dixie*; Tuuri, *Strategic Sisterhood*; Green, *Battling the Plantation Mentality*; Lau, *Democracy Rising*. For sample works extending beyond 1968, see Ashmore, *Carry It On*; de Jong, *You Can't Eat Freedom*; Sanders, *Chance for Change*; Moye, *Let the People Decide*; Estes, *Charleston in Black and White*; Germany, *New Orleans after the Promises*; Rhonda W. Williams, *Politics of Public Housing*.

12. Clark, *Ready from Within*, 63. For black women teachers in the segregated South, see, for example, Charron, *Freedom's Teacher*; Fairclough, *Class of Their Own*; Shaw, *What a Woman Ought to Be*; Chirhart, *Torches of Light*.

13. DeMuth, "Tired of Being Sick and Tired." DeMuth documented Fannie Lou Hamer's reflection in this article. Hamer attended a CEP teacher training workshop in March 1963.

14. Perman, *Struggle for Mastery*, 313–318; Brown, "Negotiating and Transforming," 125.

15. Southern Christian Leadership Conference, "Citizenship Workbook," n.d., box 153, folder 23, series III/2/ii, part 4, Southern Christian Leadership Conference Collection, Martin Luther King Jr. Center for Non-Violent Social Change, Atlanta (hereafter cited as SCLC–MLK).

16. For racial uplift, see Gaines, *Uplifting the Race*. For black women's centrality in this ideology, see Higginbotham, *Righteous Discontent*; White, *Too Heavy a Load*; Wolcott, *Remaking Respectability*. For moderate black women's organizations in the civil rights movement, see Tuuri, *Strategic Sisterhood*; Tiyi M. Morris, *Womanpower Unlimited*. For interracial activities by middle-class black and white women, see Jones-Branch, *Crossing the Line*; Harwell, *Wednesdays in Mississippi*.

17. Jeffries and Green reexamine goals and strategies in the black freedom struggle. Jeffries posits a framework of "freedom rights—the assortment of civil and human rights that emancipated African Americans." Likewise, Green examines a "culture of resistance," urging examination of "specific, complex meanings of freedom" that encompassed more than "juridical and legislative achievements." Jeffries, *Bloody Lowndes*, 4; Green, *Battling the Plantation Mentality*, 4.

18. For interpretation of improvement projects, see Green, *Battling the Plantation Mentality*, 200; Greene, *Our Separate Ways*, chapter 4.

19. Shaw, *What a Woman Ought to Be*, 176. Charron argues that limited supervision opened space for black schoolteachers to teach African American history that "[drove] a wedge into the walls of segregation." See Charron, *Freedom's Teacher*, 69–80, quotation on 79. See also Chirhart, *Torches of Light*; Fairclough, *Class of Their Own*; Littlefield, "'I Am Only One'"; Shaw, *What a Woman Ought to Be*.

20. For southern black women's leadership in racial uplift strategies, see Gilmore, *Gender and Jim Crow*; Higginbotham, *Righteous Discontent*; Shaw, *What a Woman Ought to Be*. For intersection of race and class, see Wolcott, *Remaking Respectability*; Green, *Battling the Plantation Mentality*; Lee, *For Freedom's Sake*.

21. Morris described citizenship schools as "less militant" and "'quiet structures' behind what appeared to be spontaneous uprisings." See Aldon D. Morris, *Origins of the Civil Rights Movement*, 239.

22. This analysis draws on extensive historiography of African American education from slavery through the late nineteenth century. See, for example, Anderson, *Education of Blacks*; Jones, *Labor of Love*; Heather Andrea Williams, *Self-Taught*.

23. Boyte, "Dorchester Center"; Robnett, *How Long?*, 88.

24. For organizational studies, see Fairclough, *To Redeem the Soul*; Garrow, *Bearing the Cross*; Branch, *Parting the Waters*; Branch, *Pillar of Fire*; Branch, *At Canaan's Edge*; for SCLC campaigns, see Eskew, *But for Birmingham*; Honey, *Going Down Jericho Road*; Honey, *To the Promised Land*; for women's religious organizations as auxiliaries, see Higginbotham, *Righteous Discontent*, 3, 8, 120–121. For sexism within the SCLC, see Charron, *Freedom's Teacher*, 342–343; Cotton, *If Your Back's Not Bent*, 193–194; Ransby, *Ella Baker*, 175–176, 183–185; Robnett, *How Long?*, 93–97; Young, *Easy Burden*, 138–139. Peter J. Ling offers a nuanced interpretation, arguing that SCLC male leaders embodied diverse constructions of masculinity. Ling, "Gender and Generation," in Ling and Monteith, *Gender and the Civil Rights Movement*. For interpretations of Cotton and Clark, see Fairclough, *Redeem the Soul*, 69–70, 169; Garrow, *Bearing the Cross*, 161–168, 375–376, 416, 534.

25. Between 1957 and 1970, the CEP trained local people from all southern states. In addition to locations discussed in this study, CEP teachers were active in Louisiana, Tennessee, North Carolina, Virginia, and southern Florida. Charron and Levine organize teachers' activities into categories, producing an overview across the spectrum of the program. This study embeds CEP implementation in specific places to examine factors contributing to expansion and decline. See Charron, *Freedom's Teacher*, chapters 8 and 9; Levine, "Citizenship Schools"; Levine, "Learning for Liberation."

26. Citizenship schools scholarship emphasizes the period before the Voting Rights Act of 1965 when the program expanded rapidly with relatively stable leadership and secure funding. See Charron, *Freedom's Teacher*, chapters 8 and 9 and epilogue; Levine, "Citizenship Schools"; Levine, "Learning for Liberation."

Chapter 1. "We're Going to Learn Together": Groundwork on Johns Island, South Carolina, 1948–1957

1. Robinson, quoted in Wigginton, *Refuse to Stand*, 250.

2. Tjerandsen, *Education for Citizenship*, chapter 4; Charron, *Freedom's Teacher*, 247–301; Levine, "Citizenship Schools," chapter 2; Levine, "Birth of the Citizenship Schools"; Ling, "Local Leadership."

3. Myles Horton, quoted in Tjerandsen, *Education for Citizenship*, 160; Clark, *Echo in My Soul*; Clark, *Ready from Within*; "Dedication Ceremony Program, Septima P. Clark Day Care Center," May 19, 1978, box 14, folder 5, SPCP-ARC; "The South Carolina Department of Highways and Public Transportation and The Charleston Legislative Delegation cordially invite you to attend a dedicatory ceremony," October 7, 1978, AMN 1000a, SPCP-ARC.

4. Barnett, "Invisible Southern Black Women Leaders." For studies of Clark, see Charron, *Freedom's Teacher*; McFadden, "Septima P. Clark and the Struggle," in Crawford et al., *Women in the Civil Rights Movement*, 85–97; Rouse, "'We Speak to Know,'" in Collier-Thomas and Franklin, *Sisters in the Struggle*, 95–120; Robnett, *How Long?*, 86–97.

5. Myles Horton, *Long Haul*, 105.

6. Bernice Robinson to [Carl Tjerandsen], [1974], box 3, folder 8, Bernice Violanthe Robinson Papers, Avery Research Center, College of Charleston (hereafter cited as BVRP-ARC), quoted in Tjerandsen, *Education for Citizenship*, 161–162. For dissertations, see Franson, "Citizenship Education"; Oldendorf, "Highlander Folk School." For oral history interview, see Wigginton, *Refuse to Stand*, 171–190, 236–254, 299–301.

7. For postwar constructions of black masculinity, see Estes, *I Am a Man!*, 11–38. For black veterans' leadership in local movements, see Dittmer, *Local People*; Hamlin, *Crossroads at Clarksdale*, 9–41.

8. In 1980, Carl Tjerandsen, executive secretary of the Schwarzhaupt Foundation, documented the foundation's citizenship education demonstration projects that included the citizenship schools. See Tjerandsen, *Education for Citizenship*, chapter 4. In citizenship schools historiography, South Carolina Sea Islands roots have received the most scholarly attention. See Charron, *Freedom's Teacher*, 247–301; Levine, "Citizenship Schools," chapter 2; Levine, "Birth of the Citizenship Schools"; Ling, "Local Leadership"; Franson, "Citizenship Education"; Oldendorf, "Highlander Folk School."

9. Charron, *Freedom's Teacher*, 28.

10. Clark, quoted in Wigginton, *Refuse to Stand*, 6, 8, 10; Clark, *Echo in My Soul*, 18–19; Charron, *Freedom's Teacher*, 31, 42–46. For Avery, see Drago, *Initiative, Paternalism*.

11. Fields, *Lemon Swamp*, 110; Clark, *Echo in My Soul*, 27. For school policy, see Charron, *Freedom's Teacher*, 58; Drago, *Initiative, Paternalism*, 124–126; Lau, *Democracy Rising*, 41–45. For black women and teaching, see Charron, *Freedom's Teacher*, 43–47; Fairclough, *Class of Their Own*, 234–245; Shaw, *What a Woman Ought to Be*, 175–185.

12. Charron, *Freedom's Teacher*, 50–54; Clark, *Echo in My Soul*, 33; Clark, *Ready from Within*, 108–109.

13. Clark, *Echo in My Soul*, 38, 36; Clark, quoted in Wigginton, *Refuse to Stand*, 16. For evolution of South Carolina segregated schools, see Charron, *Freedom's Teacher*, 54–64.

14. Clark, *Echo in My Soul*, 28, 45; Clark, *Ready from Within*, 106. See also Charron, *Freedom's Teacher*, 65–72.

15. Clark, *Echo in My Soul*, 40–41, 49.

16. Ibid., 51–56, quote on 54; Clark, *Echo in My Soul*, 49, 48. See also Charron, *Freedom's Teacher*, 64–77. For contemporaries' views on racial uplift, see Gaines, *Uplifting the Race*; White, *Too Heavy a Load*, chapters 1 and 2; Giddings, *When and Where I Enter*, chapters 6 and 10; Shaw, *What a Woman Ought to Be*.

17. Clark, *Echo in My Soul*, 60–61; Sullivan, *Lift Every Voice*, 78; Charron, *Freedom's Teacher*, 91–95; Clark, *Echo in My Soul*, 109–111.

18. Clark, *Ready from Within*, 111; Clark, *Echo in My Soul*, 73–75, quotations on 73 and 74.

19. Robinson, quoted in Wigginton, *Refuse to Stand*, 172–180, quotation on 175. For class analysis, see Collier-Thomas, *Jesus, Jobs, and Justice*, xxiv; Theoharis, *Rebellious Life*, 72–73.

20. Robinson, quoted in Wigginton, *Refuse to Stand*, 182–186, quotations on 183, 184, 185, and 186.

21. Fraser, *Charleston!*, 387–393; Schulman, *From Cotton Belt to Sunbelt*, 146–147.

22. Charron, *Freedom's Teacher*, 182; Robinson, quoted in Wigginton, *Refuse to Stand*, 185–189, quotations on 189, 185, 186–187.

23. Frederickson, *Dixiecrat Revolt*, 42–46; Lau, *Democracy Rising*, 135–144. South Carolina's 1892 election law broadened registrars' discretion and allowed multiple ballot boxes to confuse voters and facilitate disqualification. In 1895, the state assembly added a poll tax, literacy test, and understanding clause. Powers, *Black Charlestonians*, 264; Perman, *Struggle for Mastery*, 91–115.

24. Waring, quoted in Frederickson, *Dixiecrat Revolt*, 109. In 1944, the U.S. Supreme Court ruled in *Smith v. Allwright* that the Texas all-white Democratic primary was unconstitutional. Frederickson, *Dixiecrat Revolt*, 39.

25. Charron, *Freedom's Teacher*, 189–192; Lau, *Democracy Rising*, 176–179; Levine, "Birth of the Citizenship Schools," 395. The 35,000 new black voters "represented a 700 percent increase" but was still "only a fraction of the eligible black vote." Lau, *Democracy Rising*, 179–180.

26. Clark, quoted in Charron, *Freedom's Teacher*, 205–209, 214; Robinson, quoted in Wigginton, *Refuse to Stand*, 245; Levine, "Birth of the Citizenship Schools," 395–396, 404.

27. Robinson, quoted in Wigginton, *Refuse to Stand*, 245, 246. For black-owned beauty shops as gendered community organizing centers, see Gill, *Beauty Shop Politics*; Greene, *Our Separate Ways*, 26–31; Hamlin, *Crossroads at Clarksdale*, 64–70.

28. Clark, *Echo in My Soul*, 109–111; [Septima Clark], "Report on March 7, 1955 Meeting of the Citizens Club, Johns Island, South Carolina," n.d., box 3, folder 7, Highlander Folk School Collection, Tennessee State Library and Archives, Nashville (hereafter cited as HFSP-TSLA). See also Charron, *Freedom's Teacher*, 225–226; Ling, "Local Leadership," 406; Tjerandsen, *Education for Citizenship*, 150.

29. For the Talented Tenth, see Gaines, *Uplifting the Race*.

30. Charron, *Freedom's Teacher*, 225; Jenkins interview, Guy and Candie Carawan Collection #20008, Southern Folklife Collection, Wilson Library, University of North

Carolina at Chapel Hill (hereafter cited as GCCC–UNC). For his father's farm, see Charron, *Freedom's Teacher*, 223.

31. Jenkins, quoted in Carawan and Carawan, *Ain't You Got a Right*, 145–146, quotations on 144, 145, 143–144.

32. For Jenkins, see "Esau Jenkins, Civil Rights Leader Dies," *Charleston Evening Post*, October 30, 1972; Charron, *Freedom's Teacher*, 223; Ling, "Local Leadership," 405; Tjerandsen, *Education for Citizenship*, 151. Particularly in rural communities, rejection of imposed deference and open opposition to blatant injustice set "race men" apart. As in Jenkins's case, economic independence was a critical component and offered some protection from direct reprisal. Scholarship on postwar race men focuses on World War II veterans and leaders who embraced armed self-defense. Jenkins was neither, exemplifying black male leaders who sought redress through formal organization and working within existing systems. Jenkins, and others like him, would later be characterized as moderate or conservative. For veterans and armed self-defense, see Umoja, *We Will Shoot Back*; Tyson, *Radio Free Dixie*; Hamlin, *Crossroads at Clarksdale*.

33. Jenkins, quoted in Carawan and Carawan, *Ain't You Got a Right*, 154; Jenkins interview, GCCC–UNC.

34. Pinckney and Brown, quoted in Carawan and Carawan, *Ain't You Got a Right*, 4; Jones-Jackson, *When Roots Die*, 132–135; Joyner, *Down by the Riverside*, 203–222.

35. Smalls, Hunter, and Wine, quoted in Carawan and Carawan, *Ain't You Got a Right*, 67, 79, 75. For "black spaces" as "unmonitored, unauthorized social sites," see Kelley, "'We Are Not What We Seem,'" 79. See also Levine, "Birth of the Citizenship Schools," 407–408.

36. Jenkins, quoted in Charron, "Teaching Citizenship," 443.

37. Ling, "Local Leadership," 408.

38. Jenkins interview, GCCC–UNC; Highlander Folk School, "Transcription of a meeting at the home of Mrs. Septima P. Clark in Charleston, SC," February 17, 1959, box 3, folder 4, HFSC–TSLA. See also Levine, "Birth of the Citizenship Schools," 394–395.

39. Bureau of the Census, *Census of the Population: 1950*, vol. 2: *Characteristics of the Population*, part 40, *South Carolina* (Washington, D.C.: Government Printing Office, 1953), 40–10 (table 6); U.S. Department of Commerce, *U.S. Census of Agriculture: 1959*, vol. 1, part 27 (Washington, D.C.: Government Printing Office, 1961), 164–165; Fraser, *Charleston!*, 387–393; Schulman, *From Cotton Belt to Sunbelt*, 146–147; Brown, quoted in Carawan and Carawan, *Ain't You Got a Right*, 10–11.

40. Wine, quoted in Carawan and Carawan, *Ain't You Got a Right*, 45; Jenkins, quoted in ibid., 38.

41. Danielson and Danielson, *Profits and Politics in Paradise*, 12–16; Graves, "Between 'Preservation' and 'Progress,'" 75. For black farmers, see *U.S. Census of Agriculture: 1959*, 164–165. Statistics only include black and white farmers listed as full owners.

42. Brown, quoted in Carawan and Carawan, *Ain't You Got a Right*, 162–163. For heirs' property rights, see Cooper, *Making Gullah*, 182–188; Graves, "Between 'Preservation' and 'Progress,'" 75; Kahrl, *The Land Was Ours*, 250–258.

43. Wine and Simmons interview, GCCC–UNC; portions published in Carawan and Carawan, *Ain't You Got a Right*, 45. Wine's death certificate listed "cachexia [wasting dis-

ease] and inanition [exhaustion from lack of nutrition] and starvation due to carcinoma esophagus with distant metastases, far advanced" as cause of death. "Standard Certificate of Death for Lee Grant Wine," November 26, 1948, State File No. 014227, South Carolina Death Records, Year Range: 1925–1949, County: Charleston, South Carolina Department of Archives and History, Columbia, South Carolina. The death certificate lists his birth date as 1904, making him forty-three or forty-four years old when he died.

44. Wine, quoted in Charron, *Freedom's Teacher*, 258; Wine, quoted in Carawan and Carawan, *Ain't You Got a Right*, 149, 156. In Jenkins's version, Wine approached him. Jenkins, quoted in Carawan and Carawan, *Ain't You Got a Right*, 149. This version was repeated in Clark's narratives, Tjerandsen's report, and subsequent published studies. See Clark, *Echo in My Soul*, 136–137; Clark, *Ready from Within*, 46; Tjerandsen, *Education for Citizenship*, 151; Levine, "Birth of the Citizenship Schools," 397–398.

45. Wine, quoted in Carawan and Carawan, *Ain't You Got a Right*, 149, 156.

46. Tjerandsen, *Education for Citizenship*, 152; Charron, *Freedom's Teacher*, 224; Ling, "Local Leadership," 408; Jenkins interview, GCCC-UNC.

47. [Myles Horton], "Notes on Johns Island," October 15, 1955, box 3, folder 2, HFSC-TSLA. See Charron, *Freedom's Teacher*, 255; Levine, "Birth of the Citizenship Schools," 399; Oldendorf, "Highlander Folk School," 61–62.

48. Lau, *Democracy Rising*, 208, 210. For Citizens Councils, see Moye, *Let the People Decide*, 64–67.

49. Clark, *Echo in My Soul*, 111; Robinson, quoted in Wigginton, *Refuse to Stand*, 245; Clark, quoted in Wigginton, *Refuse to Stand*, 242; Clark, *Echo in My Soul*, 117–118, quotation on 117. See also Charron, *Freedom's Teacher*, 243–244.

50. Clark, *Echo in My Soul*, 120–121; Highlander Folk School, "A Guide to Community Action for Public School Integration," October 1, 1955, box 84, folder 6, Highlander Research and Education Center Papers, Wisconsin Historical Society, Madison (hereafter cited as HRECP-WHS). See also Charron, *Freedom's Teacher*, 221–223.

51. Myles Horton, *Long Haul*, 96–98; Highlander Folk School, "Proposed Follow-Up on the Supreme Court Decisions and the Public Schools Workshops," August–September 1953, box 49, folder 8, HFSC-TSLA.

52. Myles Horton to Mr. Maxwell Hahn, January 1, 1954, box 49, folder 8, HRECP-WHS; Leo Gerngross to Myles Horton, June 4, 1953, box 51, folder 1, HRECP-WHS; Myles Horton, quoted in Tjerandsen, *Education for Citizenship*, 144. See Ling, "Local Leadership," 410–411.

53. Frank Adams, *Unearthing Seeds*, 89–109; Aimee Isgrig Horton, *Highlander Folk School*, 198; Myles Horton, *Long Haul*, 86–87; Horton and Freire, *We Make the Road*, quotations on 46–47, 164, 168, 177; Highlander Folk School, *The Highlander Fling*, vol. 6, no. 6, June 1948, box 84, folder 7, HRECP-WHS. See also Levine, "Citizenship Schools," 49–56.

54. Horton and Freire, *We Make the Road*, 27. See also Levine, "Citizenship Schools," 49–56.

55. Clark, *Echo in My Soul*, 121; Esau Jenkins, "Transcript from Workshop," n.d., box 1, folder 5, HFSC-TSLA; Z. Horton, quoted in Tjerandsen, *Education for Citizenship*,

152; Clark, *Ready from Within*, 45. See also Charron, *Freedom's Teacher*, 225–227; Levine, "Birth of the Citizenship Schools," 393–394; Ling, "Local Leadership," 408.

56. Myles Horton, "Report on Feb. 28–Mar. 4 trip to Charleston and John's Island," box 2, folder 4, HFSC-TSLA; for Clark, see Wigginton, *Refuse to Stand*, 240; Tjerandsen, *Education for Citizenship*, 153; Aimee Isgrig Horton, *Highlander Folk School*, 217. See also Charron, *Freedom's Teacher*, 228–230.

57. Jenkins, "Transcript from Workshop"; Myles Horton, "Report on Feb. 28–Mar. 4 trip"; Septima Clark, quoted in [Myles Horton], "Report on March 7, 1955 Meeting of Citizen's Club, Johns Island, South Carolina," [March 1955], box 3, folder 7, HFSC-TSLA. For Jenkins's school board campaign, see Clark, *Ready from Within*, 42–45; Clark, *Echo in My Soul*, 139–140; Tjerandsen, *Education for Citizenship*, 152–153; Levine, "Birth of the Citizenship Schools," 394; Ling, "Local Leadership," 409–410.

58. [Myles Horton], "Report on trip to Johns Island, October 17th–20th, 1955," [October 1955], box 3, folder 2, HFSC-TSLA; Myles Horton, "Report on Feb. 28–Mar. 4 trip." See also Ling, "Local Leadership," 412–413; Tjerandsen, *Education for Citizenship*, 153–155.

59. For Horton's use of these phrases, see Tjerandsen, *Education for Citizenship*, 154.

60. Myles Horton, quoted in ibid., 156.

61. Esau Jenkins to Mr. [Myles] Horton, April 28, 1955, box 5, folder 5, HFSC-TSLA; [Septima Clark], "Saturday Night," [May 1955], box 5, folder 5, HFSC-TSLA; [Septima Clark], "Report by Mrs. Septima Clark on a Special Meeting held May 29, 1955, at the Methodist Center," [May 1955], box 3, folder 2, HFSC-TSLA; Septima Clark, "Report of Civic Club, Johns Island, South Carolina," September 6, 1955, box 3, folder 7, HFSC-TSLA. See also Charron, *Freedom's Teacher*, 228–230; Levine, "Birth of the Citizenship Schools," 399; Ling, "Local Leadership," 414; Tjerandsen, *Education for Citizenship*, 157–158.

62. Bernice [Robinson] to Myles [Horton] & Zilphia [Horton], July 19, 1955, box 5, folder 5, HFSC-TSLA; Clark, *Echo in My Soul*, 144; Myles Horton, *Long Haul*, 98–99.

63. Robinson, quoted in Wigginton, *Refuse to Stand*, 248–249. See also Charron, *Freedom's Teacher*, 233–234.

64. Clark, *Ready from Within*, 47; Jenkins, quoted in Carawan and Carawan, *Ain't You Got a Right*, 156. See also Charron, *Freedom's Teacher*, 248–249; Levine, "Birth of the Citizenship Schools," 398; Oldendorf, "Highlander Folk School," 62; Tjerandsen, *Education for Citizenship*, 160.

65. Clark, *Ready from Within*, 48–49; Myles Horton, *Long Haul*, 102; Robinson, quoted in Wigginton, *Refuse to Stand*, 249. See also Charron, *Freedom's Teacher*, 249–250; Levine, "Birth of the Citizenship Schools," 391; Oldendorf, "Highlander Folk School," 65; Tjerandsen, *Education for Citizenship*, 160–161.

66. Oldendorf, "Highlander Folk School," 71; Robinson, quoted in Wigginton, *Refuse to Stand*, 250–251; Robinson to [Tjerandsen], [1974]. See also Charron, *Freedom's Teacher*, 250–251; Ling, "Local Leadership," 417; Tjerandsen, *Education for Citizenship*, 161–162.

67. Clark, *Ready from Within*, 50; Myles Horton, quoted in Oldendorf, "Highlander Folk School," 72.

68. Robinson to [Tjerandsen], [1974]; Robinson, quoted in Wigginton, *Refuse to Stand*, 251. See also Oldendorf, "Highlander Folk School," 65–66.

69. Robinson, quoted in Carawan and Carawan, *Ain't You Got a Right*, 203. See also Oldendorf, "Highlander Folk School," 70–73; Levine, "Citizenship Schools," 5–8.

70. Clark, quoted in Wigginton, *Refuse to Stand*, 244; Robinson, quoted in ibid., 251; Bernice Robinson to Septima Clark, January 20, 1957, quoted in Myles Horton to Carl Tjerandsen, February 16, 1957, box 51, folder 2, HRECP-WHS. See also Levine, "Birth of the Citizenship Schools," 399–400.

71. Bernice V. Robinson, "Speech at Literacy Conference, Santa Cruz, CA," September 11, 1986, BVRP-ARC; Robinson to Clark, January 20, 1957. See also Levine, "Birth of the Citizenship Schools," 399–401.

72. Robinson to [Tjerandsen], [1974]; Robinson to Clark, January 20, 1957. See also Charron, *Freedom's Teacher*, 251–252; Ling, "Local Leadership," 417–418; Oldendorf, "Highlander Folk School," 71–73.

73. Robinson, quoted in Wigginton, *Refuse to Stand*, 250, 252–253; Clark, *Echo in My Soul*, 151. For Vastine, see Oldendorf, "Highlander Folk School," 72. See also Charron, *Freedom's Teacher*, 252; Levine, "Birth of the Citizenship Schools," 400–401.

74. Robinson, quoted in Wigginton, *Refuse to Stand*, 252; Robinson to Clark, January 20, 1957; Myles Horton to Carl Tjerandsen, February 16, 1957, box 51, folder 2, HRECP-WHS; Robinson, quoted in Wigginton, *Refuse to Stand*, 251. See also Charron, *Freedom's Teacher*, 252–254; Tjerandsen, *Education for Citizenship*, 162–163.

75. Clark, *Ready from Within*, 50; Robinson to [Tjerandsen], [1974].

76. Clark, *Echo in My Soul*, 150; Highlander Folk School, "My Reading Booklet," 1958–1959, box 2, folder 14, HFSC-TSLA. See also Charron, *Freedom's Teacher*, 252; Oldendorf, "Highlander Folk School," 73–74.

77. Myles Horton to Tjerandsen, February 16, 1957; Robinson, quoted in Wigginton, *Refuse to Stand*, 253; Clark, *Echo in My Soul*, 153.

78. Clark, *Echo in My Soul*, 205.

79. Frank Adams, *Unearthing Seeds*, 194, 197–200; Aimee Isgrig Horton, *Highlander Folk School*, 213–214; Levine, "Citizenship Schools," 153–154.

Chapter 2. "New Outposts in the Growing Movement": Citizenship Schools in South Carolina and Alabama, 1958–1961

1. Myles Horton to Mr. Maxwell Hahn, October 29, 1958, box 49, folder 8, HRECP-WHS; Clark, *Echo in My Soul*, 156–157; Charron, *Freedom's Teacher*, 255. The 1950 Census recorded 2,189 residents on Wadmalaw Island, increasing to 2,326 in 1960, with 1,980 residents identified as "Negro." Bureau of the Census, *Census of the Population: 1950*, vol. 2: *Characteristics of the Population*, part 40, *South Carolina* (Washington, D.C.: Government Printing Office, 1953), 40-10 (table 6); Bureau of the Census, *Census of the Population: 1960*, vol. 2: *Characteristics of the Population*, part 42, *South Carolina* (Washington, D.C.: Government Printing Office, 1963), 42-48 (table 25).

2. Ethel Jenkins Grimball married Gilbert St. Julian Grimball. Juanita Grimball married James Grimball, Gilbert Grimball's father's brother. "Ethel Grimball Obituary," *Charleston Post and Courier*, December 28, 2006; U.S. Bureau of the Census, *Fourteenth*

Census of the United States: 1920, State: South Carolina, County: Charleston, Township or other division of county: Wadmalaw Township, Population Schedule, S.D. 1, E.D. No. 99, Sheet No. 5, Enumerated on January 9 and 10, 1920; U.S. Bureau of the Census, *Fifteenth Census of the United States: 1930*, State: South Carolina, County: Charleston, Township or other division of county: Wadmalaw Township, Population Schedule, S.D. 11, E.D. No. 10–72, Sheet No. 7B, Enumerated on April 8, 1930.

3. [Septima Clark], "Trip to Charleston, Wadmalaw, St. Helena's and Hilton Head," April 20–27, 1958, box 3, folder 3, HFSC–TSLA.

4. Citizenship school scholarship uses expansion to neighboring Sea Islands as evidence of the program's success, measured in voter registration, improved literacy, civic and political organization, and employment for teachers and students. Program expansion is also seen as an influencing factor in Horton's decision to transfer the program to the SCLC. Studies that focus on the Sea Islands conclude that the program influenced significant transformation on the Sea Islands and in Charleston. See Levine, "Birth of the Citizenship Schools"; Ling, "Local Leadership"; Oldendorf, "South Carolina Sea Islands Citizenship Schools," in Crawford et al., *Women in the Civil Rights Movement*, 169–182. Charron examines a longer narrative of Clark's activism and traces variable results in different communities. See Charron, *Freedom's Teacher*, 255–261. Levine's dissertation examines the program's entire history, emphasizing the evolution of pedagogical approaches at Highlander and the SCLC and an overview of local teachers' activities in a variety of places. Levine, "Citizenship Schools."

5. Select Committee to Investigate Highlander Folk School, "Joint Committee Report to the Members of the 81st Session of the General Assembly of the State of Tennessee at Nashville, Tennessee," March 6, 1959, box 154, folder 11, series III/3/ii, part 3, SCLC–MLK.

6. Myles Horton, Henry Shipherd, and Richard Borden, "Field Trip Report," December 11, 12, 13, 1954, box 3, folder 2, HFSC–TSLA; Myles Horton to Mr. Maxwell Hahn, October 29, 1958, box 49, folder 8, HRECP–WHS; [Myles Horton], "Notes on Trip to Charleston and Johns Island, Charleston, S.C.," May 24, 1955, box 3, folder 2, HFSC–TSLA.

7. [Myles Horton], "Index of Developments on Johns Island," July 22, 1955, box 3, folder 1, HFSC–TSLA; Septima Clark, "Report from Johns Island," July 1955, box 3, folder 2, HFSC–TSLA; Septima Clark, "Notes on Johns Island," October 15, 1955, box 3, folder 2, HFSC–TSLA; Charron, *Freedom's Teacher*, 230–231.

8. [Myles Horton], "Report on trip to Johns Island, October 17th–20th, 1955," [October 1955], box 3, folder 2, HFSC–TSLA; Myles Horton, "Report on Planning Meeting for Series of Workshops in Charleston County," October 19, 1955, box 3, folder 2, HFSC–TSLA; Horton, quoted in Tjerandsen, *Education for Citizenship*, 158.

9. Tjerandsen, *Education for Citizenship*, 167; Jenkins, quoted in Myles Horton to Mr. Carl Tjerandsen, August 2, 1958, box 51, folder 2, HRECP–WHS; Myles Horton to Mr. Maxwell Hahn, October 29, 1958, box 49, folder 8, HRECP–WHS; Clark, *Echo in My Soul*, 156–157; Charron, *Freedom's Teacher*, 255.

10. [Myles Horton], "Notes on Johns Island," October 15, 1955, box 3, folder 2, HFSC–TSLA. Horton's notes include text from a letter written by Esau Jenkins. For Grimball's

residence, see [Myles Horton], "Report on Trip to Johns Island, October 17th–20th, 1955," [October 1955], box 3, folder 2, HFSC-TSLA. See also Clark, *Echo in My Soul*, 157; Charron, *Freedom's Teacher*, 255; Levine, "Birth of the Citizenship Schools," 401; Oldendorf, "Highlander Folk School," 76–77.

11. For black women's club work, see White, *Too Heavy a Load*; Giddings, *When and Where I Enter*. For expectations of black schoolteachers, see Shaw, *What a Woman Ought to Be*; Fairclough, *Class of Their Own*; Charron, *Freedom's Teacher*.

12. Clark, *Echo in My Soul*, 157; (Mrs.) Ethel I. Grimball, "Adult Citizenship School, Wadmalaw Island, South Carolina," n.d., box 3, folder 18, BVRP-ARC; [Septima Clark], "Factual Report of Adult Schools, Dec. 1, 1958–Feb. 26, 1959," [February 1959], box 3, folder 8, HFSC-TSLA; Charron, *Freedom's Teacher*, 255; Oldendorf, "Highlander Folk School," 76.

13. Grimball, "Adult Citizenship School, Wadmalaw Island"; Charron, *Freedom's Teacher*, 258; Clark, *Echo in My Soul*, 157–158. See also Levine, "Birth of the Citizenship Schools," 402; Oldendorf, "Highlander Folk School," 76.

14. Charron, *Freedom's Teacher*, 258–259; Levine, "Birth of the Citizenship Schools," 403; Clark, *Echo in My Soul*, 158; [Clark], "Factual Report of Adult Schools, Dec. 1, 1958–Feb. 26, 1959"; Tjerandsen, *Education for Citizenship*, 167. See also Oldendorf, "Highlander Folk School," 76.

15. According to the 1960 U.S. Census, African Americans were an 82 percent majority on Edisto Island (1,306 of the total 1,589 population). Bureau of the Census, *Census of the Population: 1960*, vol. 2: *Characteristics of the Population*, part 42, *South Carolina* (Washington, D.C.: Government Printing Office, 1963), 42–48 (table 25); Clark, *Echo in My Soul*, 158.

16. Jenkins, quoted in Carawan and Carawan, *Ain't You Got a Right*, 186; Minutes of Edisto Island Voters Association, October 5, 1958, box 3, folder 6, HFSC-TSLA; Clark, *Echo in My Soul*, 159; [Clark], "Factual Report of Adult Schools, Dec. 1, 1958–Feb. 26, 1959." See also Charron, *Freedom's Teacher*, 256–257; Levine, "Birth of the Citizenship Schools," 401; Oldendorf, "Highlander Folk School," 77. Jenkins's comment reinforces analysis of black women's community work as "invisible." See Tiyi M. Morris, *Womanpower Unlimited*; Hamlin, *Crossroads at Clarksdale*.

17. Tjerandsen, *Education for Citizenship*, 169–170; [Judith Gregory], "Report of Septima Clark, mostly on trip to Charleston, October 13–20, 1958, as told to JPG," October 29, [1958], box 3, folder 3, HFSC-TSLA; quotations from Clark, *Echo in My Soul*, 161–162. Gregory was a staff person at Highlander.

18. Charron, *Freedom's Teacher*, 257; B[ernice] V. Robinson, "North Area Adult School, Charleston Heights, South Carolina, December 15th thru March 15th, 1959," [March 1959], box 3, folder 4, HFSC-TSLA. See also Levine, "Birth of the Citizenship Schools," 401; Oldendorf, "Highlander Folk School," 78; Tjerandsen, *Education for Citizenship*, 170.

19. In a 1967 oral history interview, Bryan stated that she was born on Daufuskie Island in 1906. She married and had five children. She recalled Clark's visit and Clark's emphasis on voter registration. See Bryan interview with Blake, J. Herman Blake and

Emily L. Moore Papers, Emory University Library, Atlanta (hereafter Blake and Moore Papers–Emory). Hersh and Robinson described Bryan as a community leader and a host for VISTA volunteers in the late 1960s. See Hersh and Robinson, *Daufuskie Island*, 62.

20. [Septima Clark], "Trip to Charleston, Wadmalaw, St. Helena's and Hilton Head," April 20–27, 1958, box 3, folder 3, HFSC-TSLA; [Judith Gregory], "Trip to Daufuskie Island by JPG," [January 1959], box 3, folder 4, HFSC-TSLA; [Judith Gregory], "Miscellaneous Notes on Daufuskie," January 30, 1959, box 3, folder 4, HFSC-TSLA; Septima [Clark] to Myles [Horton], January 27, 1959, box 543, folder 2, Series 10/10.2, Southern Christian Leadership Conference Collection, Emory University, Atlanta (hereafter cited as SCLC-Emory).

21. [Clark], "Factual Report of Adult Schools, Dec. 1, 1958–Feb. 26, 1959"; Septima P. Clark, "Sea Island Program from January 1 to July, 1959," [July 1959], box 49, folder 9, HFSP-WSHS. See Tjerandsen, *Education for Citizenship*, 167; Charron, *Freedom's Teacher*, 257–258.

22. Viola Bryan to Mrs. Septima P. Clark, March 11, 1959, box 543, folder 2, series 10/10.2, SCLC-Emory; Clark, "Sea Island Program from January 1 to July, 1959"; Clark, *Echo in My Soul*, 166.

23. Myles Horton to Mr. Maxwell Hahn, October 29, 1958, box 544, folder 7, series 10/10.2, SCLC-Emory; Myles Horton to Maxwell Hahn, October 29, 1958, box 49, folder 8, HRECP-WHS; Maxwell Hahn to Myles Horton, January 26, 1959, box 49, folder 8, HRECP-WHS.

24. Horton, quoted in Aldon D. Morris, *Origins of the Civil Rights Movement*, 153; [Highlander Folk School], "Selection of Teachers for Citizenship Schools," n.d., box 155, folder 15, series III/3/ii, part 4, SCLC-MLK; Myles Horton to Mrs. Septima P. Clark, October 6, 1960, box 3, folder 1, HRECP-WHS. Horton's letter reminded Clark of the amount and rules for teacher stipends.

25. [Highlander Folk School], "Schedule-Training Leaders for Citizenship Schools," n.d., box 155, folder 15, series III/3/ii, part 4, SCLC-MLK. See Charron, *Freedom's Teacher*, 255. For expectations of black women schoolteachers in the early twentieth century, see Fairclough, *Class of Their Own*, 234–245; Shaw, *What a Woman Ought to Be*, 175–185.

26. Highlander Folk School, "My Reading Booklet," 1958–1959, box 2, folder 14, HFSC-TSLA.

27. Clark, *Echo in My Soul*, 196, 200, 201.

28. Highlander Folk School, "My Reading Booklet."

29. Clark, *Ready from Within*, 52–53; Highlander Folk School, "My Reading Booklet."

30. Clark, *Echo in My Soul*, 194–195; Highlander Folk School, "My Reading Booklet."

31. [Highlander Folk School], "A Brief History of the Present Litigation Involving Highlander Folk School," n.d., box 8, folder 1, HFSC-TSLA. See Charron, *Freedom's Teacher*, 267–268; Frank Adams, *Unearthing Seeds*, 127–131.

32. Select Committee, "Joint Committee Report to the Members of the 81st Session of the General Assembly."

33. Charron, *Freedom's Teacher*, 268–270; [Highlander Folk School], "A Brief History of the Present Litigation"; Clark, *Ready from Within*, 57–58. See also Tjerandsen, *Educa-*

tion for Citizenship, 175; Frank Adams, *Unearthing Seeds*, 131–133; Charron, *Freedom's Teacher*, 267–272.

34. Highlander Folk School, "'The Citizenship School Idea,'" September 4th–7th, [1959], box 4, folder 1, HFSC-TSLA; Highlander Folk School, "The Citizenship School—an Idea and a Reality," September 1959, box 4, folder 1, HFSC-TSLA.

35. Bernice [Robinson] to Myles [Horton], April 8, 1959, box 24, folder 13, HRECP-WHS; Clark, "Sea Island Program from January 1 to July, 1959."

36. Mrs. Septima P. Clark, "Highlander Folk School Educational Program for Fiscal Year Ending Sept. 30, 1960," box 2, folder 1, HRECP-WHS; Allene Brewer, "Final Report of the Edisto Adult School for 1959–60," March 1960, box 2, folder 1, HFSC-TSLA; [Allene Brewer], "Edisto Island Adult School, Held at Larimer Community Center, Nov. 3rd thru March 4," [1960], box 3, folder 18, BVRP-ARC. See also Levine, "Birth of the Citizenship Schools," 401–402; Tjerandsen, *Education for Citizenship*, 167–169; Oldendorf, "Highlander Folk School," 77–78.

37. Quoted in Oldendorf, "Highlander Folk School," 110, 96.

38. Finney and Vanderhorst, quoted in ibid., 100; Charron, *Freedom's Teacher*, 259; Lula Bligen, "[Minutes of the Edisto Island Voters Association]," September 4, 1960, box 3, folder 6, HFSC-TSLA; Levine, "Birth of the Citizenship Schools," 403. Bligen served as secretary beginning in September 1960 and continuing through April 1961.

39. Septima Clark, "Recent Developments in 'The Citizenship School Idea,'" September 25, 1960, box 545, folder 3, series 10/10.2, SCLC-Emory; Clark, *Ready from Within*, 66–67; Charron, *Freedom's Teacher*, 276–277; Clark, quoted in Tjerandsen, *Education for Citizenship*, 174; [Highlander Folk School], Minutes from Staff Meetings, November 18, 1960, and December 5, 1960, box 3, folder 1, HRECP-WHS.

40. Highlander Folk School, "Progress Report on the Citizenship School Program," January 27, 1961, box 38, folder 2, HRECP-WHS; [Septima Clark to Myles Horton], [1960], box 38, folder 2, HRECP-WHS; Clark, *Ready from Within*, 66–67; Charron, *Freedom's Teacher*, 276–277.

41. [Clark to Horton], [1960]; Myles Horton to Mrs. Septima P. Clark, October 6, 1960, box 3, folder 1, HRECP-WHS.

42. Septima [Clark] to Anne [Lockwood], Myles [Horton], and Alice [Cobb], November 18–20, 1960, box 2, folder 1, HFSC-TSLA; Clark, "Recent Developments in 'The Citizenship School Idea,'" September 25, 1960. For Huntsville outreach and citizenship schools, see Charron, *Freedom's Teacher*, 276–277; Levine, "Citizenship Schools," 143; Tjerandsen, *Education for Citizenship*, 173–175.

43. [Clark to Horton], [1960]; Clark, *Ready from Within*, 66–67; Charron, *Freedom's Teacher*, 276–277; Bureau of the Census, *Census of the Population: 1960*, vol. 2: *Characteristics of the Population*, part 2, *Alabama* (Washington, D.C.: Government Printing Office, 1963), 2–95 (table 28), 2–228 (table 88); Clark, "Recent Developments in 'The Citizenship School Idea'"; Clark, *Ready from Within*, 66–67.

44. Clark, "Recent Developments in 'The Citizenship School Idea'"; [Highlander Folk School], "Summary of Highlander Folk School Programs and Enrollments: 1953–1961," [1961], box 38, folder 4, HRECP-WHS. Summary report documented citizenship schools

through June 1961. For Montgomery bus boycott, see Theoharis, *Rebellious Life*; Thornton, *Dividing Lines*, 61–96; Branch, *Parting the Waters*, 143–205.

45. [Highlander Folk School], Staff Meeting, April 9 and 10, 1961, box 3, folder 2, HRECP-WHS; Horton, quoted in Aldon D. Morris, *Origins of the Civil Rights Movement*, 154–155; Myles Horton, *Long Haul*, 107; [Highlander], Minutes from Staff Meeting, December 5, 1960.

46. Highlander Folk School, "Progress Report on the Citizenship School Program," January 27, 1961, box 38, folder 2, HRECP-WHS.

47. Theoharis, *Rebellious Life*, 35–42, 146; Frank Adams, *Unearthing Seeds*, 121–122, 148–151. Highlander Folk School, "A Calendar of Events," [1961], box 2, folder 1, HRECP-WHS; Charron, *Freedom's Teacher*, 281.

48. Branch, *Parting the Waters*, 228–229; Fairclough, *To Redeem the Soul*, 47–49, 51; Ella Baker to Committee on Administration, October 23, 1959, box 32, folder 43, series II/3, part 2, SCLC-MLK; Charron, *Freedom's Teacher*, 291–293; Aldon D. Morris, *Origins of the Civil Rights Movement*, 108–116; Ransby, *Ella Baker*, 182–189. According to Fairclough, King endorsed Baker's recommendation. In 1959, the SCLC struggled to establish an effective administrative structure to work with independent affiliates and was not prepared to move forward with the recommendation. See Fairclough, *To Redeem the Soul*, 52–54.

49. Baker was instrumental in organizing SNCC. Branch, *Parting the Waters*, 291–293; Fairclough, *To Redeem the Soul*, 58–64; Garrow, *Bearing the Cross*, 131–134; Ransby, *Ella Baker*, 241–260.

50. Branch, *Parting the Waters*, 381–383.

51. Highlander Folk School, Memorandum on SCLC-Highlander Financial Arrangements, December 1, 1960, box 38, folder 2, HRECP-WHS; James Wood, "Public Relations Report: Leadership Training Program," November 11–13, 1960, box 136, folder 8, series I/2/i, part 4, SCLC-MLK; Charron, *Freedom's Teacher*, 293–294.

52. James Wood, "Public Relations Report: Leadership Training Program."

53. Lockwood Romasco interview, in author's possession; Horton, quoted in Aldon D. Morris, *Origins of the Civil Rights Movement*, 237; Highlander, Minutes from Staff Meeting, December 5, 1960.

54. [Highlander], Minutes from Staff Meeting, November 18, 1960; Highlander Folk School, "Workshop on Training Leaders for Citizenship Schools," January 19–21, 1961, box 4, folder 15, HFSC-TSLA.

55. [Highlander Folk School], "Summary of Highlander Folk School Programs and Enrollments: 1953–1961," box 38, folder 4, HRECP-WHS; Highlander, "Workshop on Training Leaders for Citizenship Schools"; Highlander Folk School, "Progress Report," March 15, 1961, box 38, folder 2, HRECP-WHS.

56. For workshops, see James L. Macanic to Mrs. Septima Clark, March 4, 1961, box 2, folder 11, HFSC-TSLA; Septima P. Clark to Highlander Folk School Staff, March 13–18 [1961], box 2, folder 11, HFSC-TSLA; Septima P. Clark and Bernice V. Robinson to the Highlander Staff, "Report of Training Leaders for Citizenship Schools," April 10–15, 1961, box 2, folder 11, HFSC-TSLA.

57. [Highlander Folk School], "Highlander Center Summary of Activities," April 15,

1964–May 15, 1965, box 2, folder 3, HRECP-WHS; [Highlander Folk School], "Tape 1," [1963], box 2, folder 3, HRECP-WHS; Robinson, quoted in Carawan and Carawan, *Ain't You Got a Right*, 203. The undated document is a transcript of a discussion held at the Highlander Folk School.

Chapter 3. "Bring This Community Leadership Program to Your Town and County": Groundwork in Southeastern Georgia, 1960–1961

1. Tjerandsen, *Education for Citizenship*, 178; Bernice V. Robinson, "Report on Field Trips for May-June-July and August, 1960," August 1960, box 38, folder 2, HRECP-WHS; "Crusade for Voters States Four Objectives," *Savannah Tribune*, May 12, 1960.

2. Scholarship on civil rights action in Georgia focuses on Albany and the southwestern corner of the state and on Atlanta. For Albany, see, for example, Fairclough, *To Redeem the Soul*, chapter 4; Branch, *Parting the Waters*, chapters 14 and 16; for recent examination, see Wall, "'Settling Down.'" For Atlanta, see, for example, Brown-Nagin, *Courage to Dissent*; Grady-Wills, *Challenging U.S. Apartheid*. For local movements across the state, see Tuck, *Beyond Atlanta*.

3. Donaldson, "'The Fighting Has Not Been in Vain,'" in Harris and Berry, *Slavery and Freedom*, 199–207; Dittmer, *Black Georgia*, 16–18; Fraser, *Savannah in the New South*, 118–120; Samuel J. Brown to Gloster Current, December 27, 1957, part 27, series A, reel 6, National Association for the Advancement of Colored People (NAACP) Papers [microfilm] (hereafter cited as NAACP Papers); Tuck, *Beyond Atlanta*, 20–23.

4. Tuck, *Beyond Atlanta*, 44–49; Law interview, Georgia Government Documentation Project, Georgia State University Library (hereafter cited as GGDP-GSU).

5. Law interview, GGDP-GSU; Williams, quoted in Raines, *My Soul Is Rested*, 436, 439; "'Sitdown' Strategy Resumed after Lull," *Savannah Morning News*, March 1, 1960, 1; "Citizens Council Is Formed Here," *Savannah Morning News*, March 3, 1960, 2A; "Three Negro Students Arrested for 'Sitdown,'" *Savannah Morning News*, March 17, 1960, 10D; "Vandiver Welcomes Calm Here," *Savannah Morning News*, March 1, 1960, 1; Tuck, *Beyond Atlanta*, 109.

6. "Three Negro Students Arrested for 'Sitdown'"; "Three Local Sit-Downers Arrested," *Savannah Tribune*, March 19, 1960. See also Bolster, "Civil Rights Movements," 226–227.

7. Johnson interview with author. Johnson served two terms as Savannah mayor from 2004 through 2012.

8. The three students were Ernest Robinson, a Savannah State student, and Joan Tyson and Carolyn Quilloin, seniors at Beach High School. "Court Hearings for 3 in 'Sitdown' Postponed," *Savannah Morning News*, March 19, 1960; "Local Lunch Counter 'Sit Downs' Continue," *Savannah Tribune*, March 26, 1960; "Committee Plans Laid as 11 Jailed," *Savannah Morning News*, March 22, 1960; "Threat of Boycott Made by NAACP," *Savannah Morning News*, March 21, 1960. See also Bolster, "Civil Rights Movements," 226–227; Fraser, *Savannah in the New South*, 218–220.

9. Dr. Henry M. Collier and funeral director Sidney A. Jones posted bail. Telfair Academy of Arts and Sciences, "... *We Ain't What We Used to Be*," 51; Johnson interview; Law interview, GGDP-GSU. See Fraser, *Savannah in the New South*, 220–225.

10. Law interview, GGDP-GSU; Johnson interview; Fraser, *Savannah in the New South*, 281–303; Bolster, "Civil Rights Movements," 230.

11. For Bennette, see Telfair Academy of Arts and Sciences, "... *We Ain't What We Used to Be*," 49–50. For analysis of similar gendered dynamics in local movements, see Greene, *Our Separate Ways*, chapter 3; Robnett, *How Long?*, 55–68; McGuire, *At the Dark End of the Street*, 96–114; Tiyi M. Morris, *Womanpower Unlimited*, 40–45; Theoharis, *Rebellious Life*, 89–105. Green examines the role of female black radio personalities in the Memphis movement in *Battling the Plantation Mentality*, 163–181.

12. Hosea Williams, "Text of Hosea Williams Remarks at Student Non-Violent Registration Workshop," 1962, box 15, folder 8, Myles Horton Papers, Wisconsin Historical Society (hereafter cited as MHP-WHS); Bolster, "Civil Rights Movements," 233.

13. Letter from W. W. Law to Roy Wilkins, February 8, 1962, part 27, series A, reel 6, NAACP Papers; Bolster, "Civil Rights Movements," 233; Tuck, "'City Too Dignified to Hate,'" 547–549; Tuck, *Beyond Atlanta*, 128–129; "$500 Check Answers Prayer of CV," *Savannah Tribune*, June 18, 1960.

14. For Williams's autobiography, see Raines, *My Soul Is Rested*, 435–445, quotations on 437 and 438; Whitfield, quoted in Telfair Academy of Arts and Sciences, "... *We Ain't What We Used to Be*," 14. For radio addresses, see "$500 Check Answers Prayer of CV." For Juanita Terry Williams, see "Three, Including Negro, Enter Clerk Race," *Savannah Morning News*, July 15, 1961. See also Bolster, "Civil Rights Movements," 241; Young, *Easy Burden*, 258–259.

15. "Crusade for Voters Organizing Precincts," *Savannah Tribune*, July 2, 1960; "Crusade Gets Free Shelter from Mr. Jones," *Savannah Tribune*, June 11, 1960; "Secretary Hired by Crusade for Voters," *Savannah Tribune*, June 4, 1960; Johnson interview; "Voter Registration Increased," *Savannah Tribune*, June 25, 1960.

16. Robinson, "Report on Field Trips."

17. Highlander Folk School, "Minutes of Executive Council Meeting," July 21–22, 1960, box 2, folder 1, HRECP-WHS; Myles Horton to Bernice Robinson, August 4, 1960, box 24, folder 13, HRECP-WHS.

18. Robinson, "Report on Field Trips"; Highlander Folk School, "Highlander Folk School Educational Program for Fiscal Year Ending Sept. 30, 1960," box 2, folder 1, HRECP-WHS; Septima P. Clark, "Field Trip to Savannah," October 7–9, 1960, box 38, folder 12, HRECP-WHS; Septima Clark to Hosea Williams, December 6, 1960, box 38, folder 12, HRECP-WHS.

19. Septima Clark to Anne [Lockwood], Myles [Horton] and Alice [Cobb], November 18–20, [1960], box 2, folder 1, HFSC-TSLA.

20. Clark to Williams, December 6, 1960.

21. Hosea Williams to Septima Clark, December 29, 1960, box 38, folder 12, HRECP-WHS; Highlander Folk School, "Summary of Highlander Folk School Programs and Enrollments, 1953–1961," box 38, folder 4, HRECP-WHS; Miss Emogene G. Stroman, "Factual Report of Adult School," four reports dated December 19, 1960, January 31, 1961, February 28, 1961, and March 30, 1961, box 3, folder 8, HFSC-TSLA; East and West Savannah Adult School to Mrs. [Septima] Clark, April 20, 1961, box 5, folder 5, HFSC-TSLA.

22. Hosea Williams to Septima Clark, February 9, 1961, box 38, folder 12, HRECP–WHS; Highlander, "Summary of Highlander Folk School Programs and Enrollments"; Mrs. Juanita Williams, "Factual Report of Adult School," four reports dated December 30, 1960, January 19, 1961, February 27, 1961, and March 29, 1961, box 3, folder 8, HFSC–TSLA.

23. Tjerandsen, *Education for Citizenship*, 30; Hosea Williams to Septima Clark, November 5, 1960, box 38, folder 12, HRECP–WHS.

24. For Georgia's First Congressional District in 1960, see U.S. Department of Commerce, Bureau of the Census, *Congressional District Atlas of the United States* (Washington, D.C.: Government Printing Office, 1960), 15.

25. Cooper interview with author. The administrator was Evans B. Cooper, and the teachers included Cooper's wife, Neloweze. In 1958, the Liberty County population was 9,700, with 4,000 whites and 5,700 African Americans. The county included 4,600 registered voters, 2,128 white and 2,472 African Americans. See Price, *Negro and the Ballot*, 68.

26. "Negro Qualifies for County Commissioner in Special Election," *Liberty County Herald*, April 7, 1960; Bailey interview with author; "J. E. Hook Named New Commissioner," *Liberty County Herald*, May 26, 1960.

27. Tuck, *Beyond Atlanta*, 74–80; "Statement of Leslie Perry, Representing the NAACP, New York, NY," Antilynching and Protection of Civil Rights, Hearings before Subcommittee of the Committee on the Judiciary, House of Representatives, 81st Congress, 1st and 2nd Session, June 1949; Rhynes Morrison interview with author.

28. John H. Calhoun to Roy Wilkins, February 17, 1957, supplement to part 4, reel 5, NAACP Papers; Statewide Registration Committee, "Suggested Procedure for County Organization–Voter Registration Campaign," supplement to part 4, reel 5, NAACP Papers; Memorandum: John H. Calhoun to Statewide Registration Committee of Georgia, October 26, 1957, supplement to part 4, reel 5, NAACP Papers. Calhoun reported 160,000 registered voters in 1956 and 165,000 voters in 1957. In oral history interviews, Green's narrators describe similar dynamics as "plantation mentality." See Green, *Battling the Plantation Mentality*.

29. Hosea Williams to [unnamed recipients], "New and better community leadership, through literacy schools, Leadership Training Programs, and Voter Registration," December 28, 1960, box 38, folder 12, HRECP–WHS. Emphasis in original.

30. Myles Horton, "Savannah, Georgia Trip," January 7, 1961, box 38, folder 12, HRECP–WHS.

31. Ealey Forrest interview with author; McDonald, *Voting Rights Odyssey*, 74. In 1958, 1,680 (17 percent) African Americans were registered in Tattnall County. Price, *Negro and the Ballot*, 69.

32. Ealey Forrest interview; Highlander Folk School, "Training Leaders for Citizenship Schools," February 13–18, 1961, box 10, folder 9, MHP–WHS.

33. James L. Macanic to Mrs. Septima Clark, March 4, 1961, box 2, folder 11, HFSC–TSLA; A[nne] L[ockwood] to Septima [Clark], [1961], box 9, folder 12, HRECP–WHS. Lockwood sent "notes that Bernice made on the way down to the airport" describing participants at the February 1961 workshop.

34. A[nne] L[ockwood], "Recommendations concerning Training Leaders for Citizenship Schools—Test Run on the Week Workshop Program," February 20, 1961, box 3, folder 2, HRECP-WHS.

35. Septima [Clark] to Anne [Lockwood], [1961], box 9, folder 12, HRECP-WHS.

36. See Charron, *Freedom's Teacher*, 69–80. For teachers and racial uplift, see Fairclough, *Class of Their Own*, 234–239; White, *Too Heavy a Load*, 52, 88–89; Shaw, *What a Woman Ought to Be*, 174–185.

37. Ealey Forrest interview.

38. Ibid.; Price, *Negro and the Ballot*, 69 (Tattnall and Toombs Counties); Greta Rhynes and Mary Lois Byrd, "Questionnaire on Community Background of Students," n.d., box 2, folder 13, HFSC-TSLA; Mary Lois Byrd, "Questionnaire on Community Background of Students," n.d., box 2, folder 13, HFSC-TSLA; Rhynes Morrison interview; Bureau of the Census, *Census of the Population: 1960*, vol. 1: *Characteristics of the Population*, part 12, *Georgia* (Washington, D.C.: Government Printing Office, 1963), 12–148 (table 28); U.S. Bureau of the Census, *U.S. Census of Agriculture: 1959*, vol. 1, part 28, *Georgia* (Washington, D.C.: Government Printing Office, 1961), 192 (County Table 3); Eddie Gardner and E. D. Ritter, "Questionnaires on Community Background of Students," n.d., box 2, folder 13, HFSC-TSLA; Price, *Negro and the Ballot*, 66 (Bryan County).

39. Ealey Forrest interview; Rhynes Morrison interview.

40. Rhynes Morrison interview; Ealey Forrest interview.

41. Clark, *Echo in My Soul*, 202–205, quotations on 205, 201, 204.

42. For respectability politics, see Gaines, *Uplifting the Race*; Higginbotham, *Righteous Discontent*; White, *Too Heavy a Load*.

43. Myles Horton to Jane Lee J. Eddy, [1961], box 28, folder 12, HRECP-WHS.

44. At the sit-ins' first anniversary, Law wrote Gloster Current at the national office, "We need a big meeting—one that is highly successful—at this time. The lawyers have taken everything." W. W. Law to Gloster Current, February 24, 1961, part 27, series A, reel 6, NAACP Papers. See also Savannah NAACP Branch, "Savannah NAACP Marks Year-Long Withholding of Patronage Campaign," March 19, 1961, part 27, series A, reel 6, NAACP Papers.

45. Myles Horton to Jane Lee J. Eddy.

46. Clark, *Ready from Within*, 60–61; [Highlander Folk School], Staff Meeting Minutes, March 23, 1961, box 3, folder 2, HRECP-WHS.

47. Highlander Folk School, Staff Meeting Notes, January 17, 1961, box 3, folder 2, HRECP-WHS; Clark, *Ready from Within*, 60–61; [Highlander Folk School], Staff Meeting, April 9 and 10, 1961, box 3, folder 2, HRECP-WHS; Charron, *Freedom's Teacher*, 283–286, 293–294.

48. Andrew Young to Robert Spike, April 25, 1961, box 30, folder 5, HRECP-WHS; Young, *Easy Burden*, 129–132; Charron, *Freedom's Teacher*, 294.

49. [Highlander Folk School], Staff Meeting, May 8, 1961, box 3, folder 2, HRECP-WHS; Myles Horton, "Report to Executive Council Members," [1961], box 2, folder 2, HRECP-WHS; [Highlander Folk School], Staff Minutes, April 24, 1961, box 3, folder 2, HRECP-WHS; Young, *Easy Burden*, 133.

50. Clark, *Echo in My Soul*, 212; Myles Horton to Citizenship School Program Committee and staff, June 21, 1961, box 154, folder 1, series III/3/i, part 4, SCLC-MLK.

51. Myles Horton, quoted in Septima P. Clark and Bernice V. Robinson to Mr. Myles Horton, June 19, 1961, box 7, folder 2, SPCP-ARC; Highlander Folk School, "Citizenship School Committee Meeting," June 8, 1961, box 38, folder 2, HRECP-WHS; Myles Horton to Mrs. Septima P. Clark, June 12, 1961, box 154, folder 3, series III/3/I, part 4, SCLC-MLK; Charron, *Freedom's Teacher*, 294–295.

52. [Citizenship School Program], "I. Participants," n.d., box 545, folder 2, series 10/10.2, SCLC-Emory; Septima [Clark] to Myles Horton, July 3, 1961, box 7, folder 2, SPCP-ARC. The Candler County citizenship school teacher was Mollie Grace Mincy.

53. Septima Clark and Bernice Robinson to Myles Horton, June 19, 1961, box 7, folder 2, SPCP-ARC, emphasis in original; Charron, *Freedom's Teacher*, 295–297.

54. Bernice [Robinson] to Myles [Horton], June 25, 1961, box 7, folder 3, SPCP-ARC.

55. Septima [Clark] to Myles [Horton], June 29, 1961, box 7, folder 2, SPCP-ARC.

56. Andrew Young to Myles Horton, June 20, 1961, box 38, folder 3, HRECP-WHS; Andrew J. Young to Dr. Wesley Hotchkiss, June 26, 1961, box 136, folder 2, series I/2/ii, part 4, SCLC-MLK.

57. Hosea Williams to Highlander Folk School, July 4, 1961, box 38, folder 12, HRECP-WHS; Anne Lockwood to Hosea Williams, July 13, 1961, box 38, folder 12, HRECP-WHS; Myles Horton to Mr. Hosea Williams, August 2, 1961, box 38, folder 3, HRECP-WHS.

58. Highlander Folk School, *Highlander Reports*, October 1960–September 1961, box 14, folder 12, HFSC-TSLA.

59. Bernice V. Robinson, "Report on the Training Leaders for Citizenship Schools, July 17–23, 1961," box 2, folder 11, HFSC-TSLA.

Chapter 4. "Say It Is for Citizenship": Citizenship Education in Southeastern Georgia, 1961–1964

1. Mrs. Septima P. Clark and Miss Bernice V. Robinson, "Report on Training Workshop, Dorchester Community Center; McIntosh, Georgia," July 17–21, 1961, box 155, folder 21, series III/3/ii, part 4, SCLC-MLK; [Citizenship Education Program], "Refresher Workshop," July 21–23, 1961, box 155, folder 21, series III/3/ii, part 4, SCLC-MLK.

2. Clark and Robinson, "Report on Training Workshop"; [Citizenship Education Program], "Refresher Workshop"; Dorothy F. Cotton, "Southern Christian Leadership Conference, AMA–Field Foundation Project in Citizenship Education, Report for July and August 1961," [August 1961], box 155, folder 21, series III/3/ii, part 4, SCLC-MLK.

3. Aldon D. Morris, *Origins of the Civil Rights Movement*, 86–98. For gendered dynamics within black churches, see Gilkes, *If It Wasn't for the Women*, 43–60, 142–157; Higginbotham, *Righteous Discontent*; Collier-Thomas, *Jesus, Jobs, and Justice*.

4. Scholarship on the Savannah movement focuses on disagreements between Williams and Law, arguing that the CCCV's day and night marches positioned the NAACP as the more moderate organization, opening the door for an agreement with city leaders. This chapter foregrounds CEP teachers, revealing the extent of grassroots organizing across the congressional district and highlighting a lesser-known part of this movement.

See Tuck, *Beyond Atlanta*, 127–137; Bolster, "Civil Rights Movements," 242–254; Russell, "Upheaval in Savannah."

5. Bernice Robinson to Dorothy [Cotton], August 1, 1961, box 38, folder 3, HRECP-WHS.

6. Cotton, quoted in Wigginton, *Refuse to Stand*, 285–286; Cotton, *If Your Back's Not Bent*, background on 84–103, quotations on 68–69.

7. Young, *Easy Burden*, 135–136; Clark, *Echo in My Soul*, 215.

8. Program titles in [Citizenship Education Program], "Citizenship Education Program in the South—Field Foundation, Statement of Expenditures—July 1, 1961–June 22, 1962," June 22, 1962, box 136, folder 3, series I/2/i, part 4, SCLC-MLK; Young, *Easy Burden*, 137–141, quotation on 139. For Young's leadership, see Ling, "Gender and Generation," in Ling and Monteith, *Gender and the Civil Rights Movement*, 120–126.

9. [Andrew Young] to Mrs. Septima Clark, [June 1961], box 136, folder 10, series I/2/ii, part 4, SCLC-MLK.

10. Dorothy Cotton to Septima Clark, April 18, 1961, box 38, folder 3, HRECP-WHS; Septima Clark to Dorothy Cotton, April 20, 1961, box 38, folder 3, HRECP-WHS; Clark, quoted in Wigginton, *Refuse to Stand*, 311; Clark, quoted in Branch, *Parting the Waters*, 577. See also Charron, *Freedom's Teacher*, 310–311.

11. Highlander Research and Education Center, Inc., "Minutes of the Meeting of the Board of Directors," August 30, 1961, box 2, folder 2, HRECP-WHS; Frank Adams, *Unearthing Seeds*, 140–141.

12. Myles Horton to Dr. Wesley Hotchkiss, September 7, 1961, box 30, folder 5, HRECP-WHS; Myles [Horton] to Rev. Andrew J. Young, October 12, 1961, box 30, folder 5, HRECP-WHS. See also Frank Adams, *Unearthing Seeds*, 140–141.

13. Andy [Young] to Mr. and Mrs. Myles Horton, November 29, 1961, box 30, folder 5, HRECP-WHS.

14. Myles [Horton] to Mr. Andrew J. Young, December 19, 1961, box 30, folder 5, HRECP-WHS; Andy [Young] to Mr. Myles Horton, December 13, 1961, box 30, folder 5, HRECP-WHS.

15. Myles [Horton] to Rev. Andrew J. Young, January 13, 1962, box 30, folder 5, HRECP-WHS; Myles Horton to Rev. Andrew Young, April 10, 1962, box 30, folder 5, HRECP-WHS; Myles [Horton] to Mr. Andrew J. Young, December 8, 1961, box 30, folder 5, HRECP-WHS; Myles Horton to Friends in the Knoxville Area, January 26, 1962, box 2, folder 2, HRECP-WHS.

16. Young, *Easy Burden*, 141; Clark, *Echo in My Soul*, 220–222; Clark, *Ready from Within*, 63; (Mrs.) Septima P. Clark to Mr. Maxwell Hahn, November 14, 1961, box 544, folder 7, series 10/10.2, SCLC-Emory; Andrew J. Young to Doctor W. A. Hotchkiss, October 3, 1961, box 136, folder 2, series I/2/i, part 4, SCLC-MLK. For annual meeting in Birmingham, see Branch, *Parting the Waters*, 647.

17. [Citizenship Education Program], "Report of Citizenship School—Workshop and Other Activities," December 11, 1961, box 136, folder 28, series I/2, part 4, SCLC-MLK.

18. Southern Christian Leadership Conference, "Citizenship Workbook," n.d., box 153, folder 23, series III/2/ii, part 4, SCLC-MLK. For comparison, see Highlander Folk School, "My Reading Booklet," 1958–1959, box 2, folder 4, HFSC-TSLA.

19. Young, *Easy Burden*, 149; Cotton, *If Your Back's Not Bent*, 132–135, quotation on 134; Citizenship Education Project, "Semi-Annual Report to the Field Foundation, July 1, 1962–January 31, 1963," [1963], box 136, folder 29, series I/2/iii, part 4, SCLC-MLK; Highlander Folk School, "Training Leaders for Citizenship Schools: Outline of Training Workshops," [1961], box 155, folder 17, series III/3/ii, part 4, SCLC-MLK. This is an outline of the original training workshop format with Clark's handwritten revisions indicating schedule changes. See Charron, *Freedom's Teacher*, 305–308; Levine, "Citizenship Schools," chapter 5.

20. Southern Christian Leadership Conference, "Citizenship Workbook."

21. Septima Clark to Susie Greene, December 11, 1961, box 160, folder 55, series III/5, part 4, SCLC-MLK; Susie Greene to Mrs. [Septima] Clark, December 13, 1961, box 543, folder 2, series 10/10.2, SCLC-Emory; Susie Greene, "Questionnaire for Workshop on Training Leaders for Citizenship Schools," [1962], box 160, folder 55, series III/5, part 4, SCLC-MLK; Susie Greene to Septima Clark, January 12, 1962, box 160, folder 55, series III/5, part 4, SCLC-MLK.

22. Susie Greene to Septima Clark, February 19, 1962, box 160, folder 55, series III/5, part 4, SCLC-MLK; Susie Greene, "Citizenship School Semi-Annual Report," [1962], box 160, folder 56, series III/5, part 4, SCLC-MLK.

23. Greta Rhynes, "Questionnaire for Workshop on Training Leaders for Citizenship Schools," n.d., box 158, folder 45, series III/5, part 4, SCLC-MLK; Greta Rhynes, "Citizenship School Semi-Annual Report," n.d., box 158, folder 45, series III/5, part 4, SCLC-MLK; Pearlie Ealey to Septima Clark, February 18, 1962, box 158, folder 49, series III/5, part 4, SCLC-MLK; Pearlie Ealey, "Questionnaire for Workshop on Teaching Leaders for Citizenship Schools," n.d., box 158, folder 49, series III/5, part 4, SCLC-MLK.

24. See "plantation mentality" in Green, *Battling the Plantation Mentality*.

25. Ealey, "Questionnaire for Workshop."

26. Andrew J. Young to Mr. Maxwell Hahn, January 5, 1962, box 136, folder 2, series I/2/i, part 4, SCLC-MLK.

27. Southern Christian Leadership Conference, "SCLC Newsletter," February 1962, box 122, folder 20, series IX/2, part 3, SCLC-MLK; Citizenship Education Program, "Participants of the Citizenship School Workshop," February 19–23, 1962, box 155, folder 21, series III/3/ii, part 4, SCLC-MLK; [Citizenship Education Program], "Request for Supplementary Budget," n.d., box 136, folder 15, series I/2/iii, part 4, SCLC-MLK; Maxwell Hahn to Dr. Wesley A. Hotchkiss, February 8, 1962, box 136, folder 5, series I/2/i, part 4, SCLC-MLK.

28. For analysis of dress for Sunday church services and respectability, see Wolcott, *Remaking Respectability*, 157–165; Higginbotham, *Righteous Discontent*, 188–211.

29. For presentation and respectability, see Chappell, Hutchinson, and Ward, "'Dress Modestly, Neatly,'" in Ling and Monteith, *Gender and the Civil Rights Movement*, 69–100; McGuire, *At the Dark End of the Street*; Theoharis, *Rebellious Life*. For working-class attire in the movement, see Ford, *Liberated Threads*, chapter 3.

30. Reverend Andrew J. Young to Miss Susie Greene, June 28, 1962, box 160, folder 56, series III/5, part 4, SCLC-MLK; Miss Pearlie Inez Ealey to Mr. Andrew Young, May 31, 1962, box 158, folder 50, series III/5, SCLC-MLK; Reverend Andrew J. Young to Miss

Pearlie Inez Ealey, June 6, 1962, box 158, folder 50, series III/5, SCLC–MLK, emphasis in original.

31. For affiliation, see Hosea L. Williams to Mrs. Dorothy Cotton, December 14, 1961, box 160, folder 26, series III/5, SCLC–MLK. For NAACP, see Hosea Williams to Roy Wilkins, February 7, 1962, supplement to part 4, reel 5, NAACP Papers; W. W. Law to Roy Wilkins, February 8, 1962, part 27, series A, reel 6, NAACP Papers; Hosea Williams to Roy Wilkins, February 27, 1962, supplement to part 4, reel 5, NAACP Papers; Roy Wilkins to Hosea Williams, March 7, 1962, supplement to part 4, reel 5, NAACP Papers. See also Bolster, "Civil Rights Movements," 239–240; Tuck, *Beyond Atlanta*, 132–133.

32. Faulkenberry, *Poll Power*, 37–41; Southern Regional Council, "First Annual Report of the Voter Education Project of the Southern Regional Council for the Fiscal Year April 1, 1962–March 31, 1963," box 138, folder 9, series I/3/ii, part 4, SCLC–MLK; Southern Christian Leadership Conference, "SCLC Voter Registration Prospectus for 1962," [1961], box 138, folder 17, series I/3/ii, part 4, SCLC–MLK; Young, *Easy Burden*, 144; [Southern Christian Leadership Conference], "Citizenship Training at Dorchester, Georgia," *SCLC Newsletter*, February 1962, box 122, folder 20, series IX/2, part 3, SCLC–MLK. For the VEP organization, see Faulkenberry, *Poll Power*, 47–56.

33. Young hired John H. Calhoun, veteran of the Georgia Voters League and Atlanta's NAACP branch, and Fred C. Bennette, who organized Atlanta sit-ins in the spring and summer of 1960. Between March and May, Calhoun and Bennette convened one-day clinics across the state ahead of Georgia's registration deadline. Fairclough, *To Redeem the Soul*, 94.

34. Hosea Williams to Wiley Branton, August 14, 1962, series VI, reel 179, Voter Education Project Papers, Southern Regional Council Collection [microfilm] (hereafter cited as VEPP-SRC); Wiley Branton to Hosea Williams, September 12, 1962, series VI, reel 179, VEPP-SRC; Andrew Young to Hosea Williams, October 19, 1962, box 160, folder 28, series III/5, part 4, SCLC–MLK; Wiley Branton to Hosea Williams, November 29, 1962, series VI, reel 179, VEPP-SRC.

35. Southern Christian Leadership Conference, "Citizenship Education Project: Semi-Annual Report to the Field Foundation, July 1, 1962–January 31, 1962," box 136, folder 29, series I/2/iii, part 4, SCLC–MLK; Annell Ponder, "Citizenship Education Program, Albany, Georgia," Summer and Fall 1962, box 158, folder 11, series III/5, part 4, SCLC–MLK.

36. [Citizenship Education Program], "Dorchester November 5th–9th, 1962," [November 1962], box 565, folder 1, series 10/10.2, SCLC–Emory; Annell Ponder, "Report of Field Trip to Savannah, Georgia," November 17–18, 1962, box 545, folder 3, SCLC–Emory, emphasis added; Crusade for Voters, "Announces the Opening of This Year's 'Citizenship School Program,'" [November 1962], box 139, folder 22, series I/3/iii, part 4, SCLC–MLK.

37. Hosea Williams to Andrew Young, December 9, 1962, box 139, folder 22, series I/3/iii, part 4, SCLC–MLK, emphasis in original; Hosea Williams to Wiley Branton, May 1, 1963, series VI, reel 179, VEPP-SRC. See also Faulkenberry, *Poll Power*, 80–81.

38. Pearlie Ealey to Southeastern Georgia Crusade for Voters, n.d., series VI, reel 179, VEPP-SRC. CEP students W. C. Ealey and Fred Mingo served as registration workers

in Reidsville, and Collins and CEP teacher Anna Laura Stephens was "deputized" to administer the oath and certify voters in Glennville.

39. Pearlie Ealey to Southeastern Georgia Crusade for Voters, April 1963, box 158, folder 51, series III/5, part 4, SCLC-MLK. See also Levine, "Citizenship Schools," 240–241.

40. Melvina Pughsley taught in Swainsboro, Walter Sanford in Garfield, and Daisy Pearl Redding in Twin City. See Melvina Pughsley, "My Narrative," [1963], box 160, folder 47, series III/5, part 4, SCLC-MLK; Walter Sanford, "Narrative," March 16, 1963, box 158, folder 59, series III/5, part 4, SCLC-MLK; Daisy Pearl Redding, "Narrative," March 16, 1963, box 160, folder 50, series III/5, part 4, SCLC-MLK.

41. Lou Anna Riggs, "Narrative," [1963], box 159, folder 39, series III/5, part 4, SCLC-MLK (door to door, "thrash out," petition); Clara Nell Riggs, "A Brief Narrative of the Cross Green Community Citizenship Classes," February 14, 1963, box 159, folder 36, series III/5, part 4, SCLC-MLK (illiteracy); Clara Nell Riggs, "Narrative," [1962], box 159, folder 35, series III/5, part 4, SCLC-MLK (welfare); Lou Anna Riggs, "The Effect of the School in the Community," June 14, 1963, box 159, folder 39, series III/5, part 4, SCLC-MLK (voting); Clara Nell Riggs, "The Effect of the School in the Community," June 14, 1963, box 156, folder 37, series III/5, part 4, SCLC-MLK, emphasis in original.

42. Rev. A. Goram, "The Real Fact about the Adult Citizenship Schools in Wheeler," April 9, 1963, box 158, folder 1, series III/5, part 4, SCLC-MLK.

43. The four women were Dollie Mae Williams, Mamie Hall, Mary Troupe, and Merdis Walker. [Citizenship Education Program], "Dorchester November 5th-9th, 1962," [November 1962], box 565, folder 1, series 10/10.2, SCLC-Emory; Hosea Williams to Wiley Branton, May 1, 1963, series VI, reel 179, SRC Papers. For Goram, see John H. Calhoun, "Report on Voter Registration Activities, 1st Congressional District Clinic," March 16, 1963, box 140, folder 7, series I/3/iii, part 4, SCLC-MLK. In 1958, 435 African Americans were registered to vote in Wheeler County. See Price, *Negro and the Ballot*, 69.

44. Bureau of the Census, *Census of the Population: 1960*, vol. 1: *Characteristics of the Population*, part 12, *Georgia* (Washington, D.C.: Government Printing Office, 1963), 12–150 (table 28). For poor health and eyesight, see Dollie Mae Williams, "Research Paper," n.d., box 158, folder 6, series III/5, part 4, SCLC-MLK; Mary Troupe, "The Value of the Adult Citizenship School," n.d., box 158, folder 4, series III/5, part 4, SCLC-MLK. For Rountree and Tillman, see Dollie Mae Williams, "Citizenship School Semi-Annual Report," n.d., box 158, folder 7, series III/5, part 4, SCLC-MLK.

45. Troupe, "Value of the Adult Citizenship School"; Dollie Mae Williams, "Research Paper."

46. Dollie Mae Williams, "Research Paper."

47. Ibid.; Mamie Hall, "Pleasant Hill Citizenship School, Hornsmission District," June 14, 1963, box 158, folder 2, series III/5, part 4, SCLC-MLK.

48. Dollie Mae Williams, "Research Paper"; Annell Ponder, "Report of Field Visit to Savannah, GA," December 12-20, [1962], box 545, folder 2, series 10/10.2, SCLC-Emory.

49. Hosea Williams, "A Report on the VEP Activities of the Southeastern Georgia Crusade for Voters," May 1, 1963, series IV, reel 179, VEPP-SRC. For accounting of expenses, see Cooper, quoted in Telfair Academy, ". . . We Ain't What We Used to Be," 4.

50. Daisy Jones, "Adult Citizenship School," March 4, 1963, box 160, folder 11, series III/5, part 4, SCLC-MLK; Adell Black, "Narrative," April 9, 1963, box 158, folder 35, series III/5, part 4, SCLC-MLK.

51. Black, "Narrative"; Adline Bradshaw, "A Narrative of My Citizenship School," n.d., box 160, folder 2, series III/5, part 4, SCLC-MLK; Cassie Pierce, "A Narrative on Citizenship School," February 26, 1963, box 160, folder 16, series III/5, part 4, SCLC-MLK.

52. For religious rituals in CEP classes, see Florence Jenkins, "The Effect of the School in the Community," June 14, 1963, box 160, folder 9, series III/5, part 4, SCLC-MLK; Pierce, "My Narrative on Citizenship School."

53. Ida Mack, "Fellwood Adult Citizenship School," February 15, 1963, box 160, folder 14, series III/5, part 4, SCLC-MLK; Southern Christian Leadership Conference, "Citizenship Workbook."

54. Cassie Pierce, "Citizenship School," March 16, 1963, box 160, folder 17, series III/5, part 4, SCLC-MLK; Daisy P. Jones, "The Effect of the School in the Community," [1963], box 160, folder 11, series III/5, part 4, SCLC-MLK; Dorothy Boles, "Narrative from the West Gwinnett Citizenship School," [1963], box 160, folder 1, series III/5, part 4, SCLC-MLK.

55. Hosea Williams to Wiley Branton, "A Report on VEP Activities of the Southeastern Georgia Crusade for Voters," series VI, reel 179, VEPP-SRC.

56. For Birmingham campaign, see, for example, Eskew, *But for Birmingham*; Branch, *Parting the Waters*.

57. Telfair Academy, "... We Ain't What We Used to Be," 29–30; "Total of Arrests Here Reaches 119," *Savannah Morning News*, June 9, 1963; Raines, *My Soul Is Rested*, 439–440; "Thousands Join 'Freedom' March," *Savannah Morning News*, June 12, 1963; "Demonstrations Resumed as Negotiations Break Down," *Savannah Morning News*, June 18, 1963. See also Bolster, "Civil Rights Movements," 248; Fraser, *Savannah in the New South*, 229–236; Tuck, *Beyond Atlanta*, 134–137.

58. Fairclough, *To Redeem the Soul*, 143–144; "Clark Out, Williams In: Charge Marches Cause 'Lost Sleep,'" *Crusader*, July 12, 1963; Young, *Easy Burden*, 260–263.

59. Wiley Branton to Juanita Williams, July 30, 1963, series VI, reel 179, VEPP-SRC; Paid advertisement from NAACP, *Savannah Morning News*, June 23, 1963; Bolster, "Civil Rights Movements," 252–254; Fraser, *Savannah in the New South*, 229–236; Tuck, *Beyond Atlanta*, 134–137. Former student activist Otis Johnson described perceptions of Williams and Law: "In the '50s, Law was seen as a militant and a radical. And he was treated that way.... Along comes a Hosea Williams and all of the sudden, in the eyes of white folks, now W. W. Law ... becomes a moderate, a reasonable person that we can talk with." Johnson interview with author.

60. "Adult Citizenship Schools Open," *Crusader*, December 5, 1963, series VI, reel 175, VEPP-SRC; Andrew Young to Wiley Branton, October 16, 1963, box 138, folder 3, series I/3/i, part 4, SCLC-MLK; Wiley Branton to Andrew Young, November 1, 1963, box 138, folder 3, series I/3/i, part 4, SCLC-MLK; Voter Education Project, "Second Annual Report of the Voter Education Project of the Southern Regional Council for the Fiscal Year April 1, 1963–March 31, 1964," box 21, folder 6, Student Non-Violent Coordinating

Committee Collection, Martin Luther King Jr. Center for Non-Violent Social Change (hereafter cited as SNCC–MLK).

61. Young, *Easy Burden*, 279. For Savannah, see Law interview, GGDP–GSU; Carolyn Roberts, "Citizenship School Monthly Attendance and Record Sheet," records for November and December 1963, January and February 1964, and April–June 1964, box 160, folder 20, series III/5, part 4, SCLC–MLK. For Wheeler County, see Morlene King, "Citizenship School Monthly Attendance and Record Sheet," records for November and December 1963 and January 1964, box 158, folder 67, series III/5, part 4, SCLC–MLK. For Ealey and Rhynes, see Ealey Forrest interview with author; Rhynes Morrison interview with author. For Tattnall County, see Marlene Battle, "Citizenship School Monthly Attendance and Record Sheet," records for August, October–December 1963 and January–March 1964, box 158, folders 46 and 47, series III/5, part 4, SCLC–MLK; Mary Lois Byrd, "Citizenship School Monthly Attendance and Record Sheet," records for December 1963 and January and February 1964, box 158, folder 43, series III/5, part 4, SCLC–MLK; Marjorie Byrd, "Citizenship School Monthly Attendance and Record Sheet," records for December 1963 and January–March 1964, box 159, folder 45, series III/5, part 4, SCLC–MLK. For Emanuel County, see Reverend Cisero Brown, "Citizenship School Monthly Attendance and Record Sheet," records for July–September 1963, December 1963, January and March 1964, and April and June 1964, box 160, folders 38, 39, and 40, series III/5, part 4, SCLC–MLK.

62. Citizenship Education Project, "Semi-Annual Report to the Field Foundation, July 1, 1962–January 31, 1963," [January 31, 1963], box 136, folder 29, series I/2/iii, part 4, SCLC–MLK; Martin Luther King Jr. to Mr. Maxwell Hahn, box 136, folder 6, series I/2/ii, part 4, SCLC–MLK; Maxwell Hahn to Dr. Wesley A. Hotchkiss, April 9, 1963, box 136, folder 6, series I/2/ii, part 4, SCLC–MLK; Young, *Easy Burden*, 152–153.

63. James Cobb coined this description in his 1992 study of the Mississippi Delta. See Cobb, *Most Southern Place*.

Chapter 5. "We Shall Overcome Today": Groundwork in the Mississippi Delta, 1961–1963

1. Annell Ponder, "Mississippi Report to Annual Convention of the Southern Christian Leadership Conference," [September] 1963, box 155, folder 26, series III/4/i, part 4, SCLC–MLK; Robert Moses, quoted in Annell Ponder, "Citizenship Education in the 'Heart of the Iceberg,'" box 155, folder 34, series III/4/i, part 4, SCLC–MLK.

2. Hamlin describes "flexible associations," arguing that the national NAACP's intransigence influenced local leaders' decisions to collaborate with organizations like the SCLC and SNCC and Mississippi-based organizations such as the Regional Council of Negro Leadership (RCNL) and Delta Ministry. See Hamlin, *Crossroads at Clarksdale*, chapters 1 and 2.

3. Payne, *I've Got the Light*, 266.

4. Payne and Estes documented links between black women's civil rights activism and church- and community-based networks. Payne argued that SNCC's collaboration with local leaders led field staff to local black women. Estes focused on obstacles to

black men's participation, emphasizing a long history of violence directed primarily at black men. See Payne, *I've Got the Light*, chapter 9; Estes, *I Am a Man!*, 79–81. Recent scholarship examines continuities in civil rights organizing and leadership and gendered traditions of community work. See, for example, Sanders, *Chance for Change*; Hamlin, *Crossroads at Clarksdale*; Tiyi M. Morris, *Womanpower Unlimited*; Tuuri, *Strategic Sisterhood*, chapters 5 and 6.

5. Green examines a "plantation mentality." See Green, *Battling the Plantation Mentality*.

6. For school expenditures, see McMillen, *Dark Journey*, 73–89. For education laws in Mississippi, see Bolton, *Hardest Deal*, 24–25. See also Hale, *Freedom Schools*, 27–33. By 1964, CEP teachers organized classes in Bolivar, Coahoma, Holmes, Leflore, and Sunflower Counties. Median school years completed for non-white residents over twenty-five in each county in 1960: Bolivar: 4.7, Coahoma: 4.9, Holmes: 5.8, Leflore: 5.1, and Sunflower: 4.7. Median school years completed for all residents over twenty-five years in each county in 1960: Bolivar: 6.7, Coahoma: 7.3, Holmes: 7.7, Leflore: 7.9, and Sunflower: 7.0. See U.S. Bureau of the Census, *U.S. Census of the Population: 1960*, vol. 1, *Characteristics of the Population*, part 26, *Mississippi* (Washington, D.C.: U.S. Government Printing Office, 1963), 26–201, 26–202, 26–203, 26–204, and 26–206.

7. McMillen, *Dark Journey*, 73.

8. McMillen, *Dark Journey*, 73; U.S. Department of Commerce, *U.S. Census of Agriculture*, 1964, vol. 1, part 33 (Washington, D.C.: Government Printing Office, 1967), 264, 266. For mechanization and displacement, see Daniel, *Dispossession*, 9–17.

9. McMillen, *Dark Journey*, 36; Price, *Negro and the Ballot*, 11.

10. Katagiri, *Mississippi State Sovereignty Commission*, chapter 1, quotation on 6; Dittmer, *Local People*, 45–46; Moye, *Let the People Decide*, 64–66. For Freedom Rides and Riders' experiences in Mississippi, see Arsenault, *Freedom Riders*, 315–317, 325–330, 343–365; Moye, *Let the People Decide*, 88–90. For a firsthand account, see Lewis, *Walking with the Wind*, 169–174.

11. Hamlin, *Crossroads at Clarksdale*, 53–54.

12. Citizenship Education Program, "Report of the Citizenship School—Workshop and Other Activities," December 11, 1961, box 136, folder 28, series I/2/iii, part 4, SCLC-MLK; Young, *Easy Burden*, 141–143, quote on 142. For Henry, see Payne, *I've Got the Light*, 56–66; Hamlin, *Crossroads at Clarksdale*, 10–11, 24–29.

13. For Pigee, see Gill, *Beauty Shop Politics*, 118–119; Hamlin, *Crossroads at Clarksdale*, 59–70.

14. Citizenship Education Program, "Report of the Citizenship School—Workshop and Other Activities," December 11, 1961, emphasis in original.

15. Branch, *Parting the Waters*, 577–578; Southern Christian Leadership Conference, "Press Release: Dr. King and Staff Head for Delta Country in Mississippi," February 6, 1962, series IV, reel 173, VEPP-SRC; Tom Scarbrough, "Martin Luther King and Others," February 13, 1962, SCR ID# 1-16-1-61-7-1-1, Mississippi State Sovereignty Commission Papers, Mississippi Department of Archives and History (hereafter cited as MSSCP-MDAH). For VEP in Mississippi, see Faulkenberry, *Poll Power*, 65–66.

16. Hamlin, *Crossroads at Clarksdale*, 65–70; Tiyi M. Morris, *Womanpower Unlimited*, quotation on 13. Hamlin includes description of Pigee's CEP classes. For black

women's beauty salons as centers for political activism, see also Gill, *Beauty Shop Politics*, chapter 5.

17. Andrew Young to Myles Horton, April 24, 1962, box 30, folder 5, HRECP-WHS; Branch, *Parting the Waters*, 588.

18. Andrew Young to Myles Horton, April 24, 1962, box 30, folder 5, HRECP-WHS; Lewis, *Walking with the Wind*, 70–71; Fairclough, *To Redeem the Soul*, 34–35; Dittmer, *Local People*, 99, 116–120. For Moore, see Payne, *I've Got the Light*, 29–47.

19. McLaurin, quoted in Mills, *This Little Light*, 50. For Davis's age, see Tom Scarbrough, "Sunflower County–Negro Voter Agitators—Robert Moses, Samuel Block, John O. Hodges, Albert Garner, Charles R. McLauren, Lafayette Burney (a 17-year-old Negro boy)," September 7, 1962, SCR ID# 2-38-1-45-3-1-1 and SCR ID# 2-38-1-45-4-1-1, MSSCP-MDAH. For McDonald's age and education, see U.S. Bureau of the Census, *Fourteenth Census of the United States: 1940*, State: Mississippi, County: Sunflower, Township: Ruleville, Population Schedule, S.D. 3, E.D. 67–37, Sheet 12A, Enumerated April 13, 1940. See also Dittmer, *Local People*, 136; Lee, *For Freedom's Sake*, 34; Moye, *Let the People Decide*, 108; Payne, *I've Got the Light*, 154. Tuuri and Sanders documented examples where black women leveraged experience in segregated poor rural communities as credentials for community organizing work. See Tuuri, *Strategic Sisterhood*, chapter 5; Sanders, *Chance for Change*, chapter 3.

20. [Citizenship Education Program], "March 26–30 Citizenship School Class," [1962], box 565, folder 1, series 10/10.2, SCLC-Emory; Rebecca McDonald and Celeste Davis to Septima Clark, May 1962, box 163, folder 25, series III/5, part 4, SCLC-MLK; Payne, *I've Got the Light*, 154.

21. Hamer, quoted in Raines, *My Soul Is Rested*, 249–250, quotation on 250; Hamer, quoted in Mills, *This Little Light*, 37; Hamer interview, KZSU Project South, Stanford University Library (hereafter cited as KZSU-Stanford). For Hamer narrative, see Payne, *I've Got the Light*, 154–55; Lee, *For Freedom's Sake*, 24–31; Moye, *Let the People Decide*, 97–100; Mills, *This Little Light*, 36–37.

22. Hamer interview, KZSU-Stanford; Moye, *Let the People Decide*, 101; Lee, *For Freedom's Sake*, 24–31; Mills, *This Little Light*, 36–37.

23. Scarbrough, "Sunflower County–Negro Voter Agitators." For night riders, see Moye, *Let the People Decide*, 102; for Hamer, see Hamer interview, KZSU-Stanford; [James Bevel], "Voter Registration in the Mississippi Delta," [1962], box 141, folder 8, series I/3, SCLC-MLK.

24. For Sam Block, see Payne, *I've Got the Light*, 142; quotations in Margaret Block interview with author.

25. Payne, *I've Got the Light*, 142; Young, *Easy Burden*, 152; Sam Block to Andrew Young, May 31, 1962, box 161, folder 53, series III/5, part 4, SCLC-MLK; Lois Lee Rodgers, "Citizenship School Report," July 1962, box 161, folder 56, series III/5, part 4, SCLC-MLK.

26. Wiley Branton to James Foreman, May 4, 1962, box 23, folder 5, SNCC-MLK; Payne, *I've Got the Light*, 144. In a letter to Young, Block mentioned the SNCC offer and asked about summer employment with the SCLC. Block was not added to the SCLC staff. Sam Block to Andrew Young, May 31, 1962, box 161, folder 53, series III/5, part 4, SCLC-MLK.

27. Myles Horton, "Memorandum to Friends in East Tennessee re: Report on Activities," May 29, 1962, box 2, folder 2, HRECP-WHS; Highlander Research and Education Center, "Text of Hosea Williams's remarks at SNCC Voter Registration Workshop," June 1962, box 15, folder 8, MHP-WHS; Jenkins remarks in Payne, *I've Got the Light*, 143; Bernice Robinson, "Mississippi Voter-Education Report by Bernice Robinson of Highlander Center," July 19, 1962, box 38, folder 6, HRECP-WHS. For links between Highlander and SNCC in Mississippi, see Hale, "Early Pedagogical Influences."

28. Robinson, "Mississippi Voter-Education Report."

29. Bob Moses to Members of the Governing Board of the Mississippi Adult Education Program and Interested Persons, "Results of the first workshops held by the Mississippi Adult Education Program at Mt. Beulah," July 1-6, 1962, box 38, folder 6, HRECP-WHS; [Citizenship Education Program], "Dorchester November 5th-9th, 1962," [November 1962], box 565, folder 1, series 10/10.2, SCLC-Emory.

30. James Bevel, "Mississippi Report, SCLC Field Secretary," January 1963, box 141, folder 5, series I/3/iii, part 4, SCLC-MLK; [Citizenship Education Program], "Dorchester Participants," June 17-21, 1963, box 565, folder 1, series 10/10.2, SCLC-Emory.

31. Bevel, "Mississippi Report, SCLC Field Secretary," January 1963; Mills, *This Little Light*, 49-50; Lee, *For Freedom's Sake*, 36-39; Moye, *Let the People Decide*, 108.

32. Daniel, *Dispossession*, 20-21, 60-61; Dittmer, *Local People*, 144-145; Moye, *Let the People Decide*, 110-114; Council member quoted in Holland, *From the Mississippi Delta*, 210.

33. [James Bevel], "Field Secretary Report," [January 5, 1963], box 141, folder 4, series I/3/iii, part 4, SCLC-MLK; Andrew Young to Reverend and Mrs. James Bevel, February 21, 1963, box 141, folder 5, series I/3/iii, part 4, SCLC-MLK.

34. Andrew Young, "Southern Christian Leadership Conference, Prospectus for Voter Registration, April-September 1963," [1963], series VI, reel 178, VEPP-SRC.

35. For the SCLC in Birmingham, see Branch, *Parting the Waters*, 688-692; Eskew, *But for Birmingham*, 209-211; Fairclough, *To Redeem the Soul*, 114-115; Young, *Easy Burden*, 188-193.

36. Payne, *I've Got the Light*, 146-148; Dittmer, *Local People*, 146-147; Hamlin, *Crossroads at Clarksdale*, 105-109.

37. Southern Regional Council, "First Annual Report of the Voter Education Project of the Southern Regional Council for the Fiscal Year April 1, 1962-March 31, 1963," box 138, folder 9, series I/3/ii, part 4, SCLC-MLK; Branch, *Parting the Waters*, 478-482; Faulkenberry, *Poll Power*, 68-71; James Bevel, "Field Secretary Report," February 28-March 8, 1963, box 141, folder 6, series I/3/iii, part 4, SCLC-MLK; Payne, *I've Got the Light*, 162-163.

38. Southern Christian Leadership Conference, "Citizenship Education Project: Semi-Annual Report to the Field Foundation, July 1, 1962-January 31, 1963," box 136, folder 29, series I/2/iii, part 4, SCLC-MLK; Annell Ponder, "Citizenship School Report, Greenwood, Miss.," March 1963, box 141, folder 7, series I/3/iii, part 4, SCLC-MLK.

39. Ponder, "Citizenship School Report: Greenwood, Mississippi"; Holland, *From the Mississippi Delta*, 214-215.

40. Holland, *From the Mississippi Delta*, 214-219, quotation on 219. Holland refers to

literacy education efforts as SNCC-sponsored "Freedom Schools" and describes events in the spring of 1963. Holland attended CEP teacher training in March 1963 and attendance records show that Holland taught classes during this period. See Ponder, "Citizenship School Report: Greenwood, Mississippi"; Ida Mae Holland, "Citizenship School Monthly Attendance and Record Sheet," May 1963, box 162, folder 24, series III/5, part 4, SCLC–MLK.

41. Ponder, "Citizenship School Report: Greenwood, Mississippi."

42. Ibid. For class, see Atlean Smith, "Citizenship School Monthly Attendance and Record Sheet," April and May 1963, box 162, folder 37, series III/5, part 4, SCLC–MLK.

43. Training description in Ponder, "Citizenship Education in the 'Heart of the Iceberg'"; Robinson in Ponder, "Citizenship School Report: Greenwood, Mississippi"; Bernice Robinson to Myles Horton, March 25, 1963, box 2, folder 3, HRECP-WHS.

44. Ida Mae Holland, "Citizenship School Monthly Attendance and Record Sheet," May 1963, box 162, folder 24, series III/5, part 4, SCLC–MLK; Bettye Brown, "Citizenship School Monthly Attendance and Record Sheet," May 1963, box 162, folder 20, series III/5, part 4, SCLC–MLK; Alice Blackwell, "Citizenship School Monthly Attendance and Record Sheet," June 1963, box 162, folder 15, series III/5, part 4, SCLC–MLK.

45. Bettye Brown, "Citizenship School Monthly Attendance and Record Sheet," June 1963, box 162, folder 20, series III/5, part 4, SCLC–MLK.

46. Blackwell, "Citizenship School Monthly Attendance and Record Sheet," June 1963; Pinkie Pilcher, "Supervisor Report for Ethel Shaw," January 1964, box 162, folder 35, series III/5, part 4, SCLC–MLK.

47. Ponder, "Citizenship School Report: Greenwood, Mississippi." For "mothering the movement," see Hamlin, *Crossroads at Clarksdale*, 59–63, 84–88; Tiyi M. Morris, *Womanpower Unlimited*, 4–8, 70–76. For factors influencing black women's leadership in community activities, see Estes, *I Am a Man*, 79–81; Payne, *I've Got the Light*, 266–283; Robnett, *How Long?*, 66.

48. Ida Mae Holland, "Report: Greenwood Mississippi," March 31, 1963, box 141, folder 7, series I/3/iii, part 4, SCLC–MLK; Holland, *From the Mississippi Delta*, 227–229; Ponder, "Citizenship Education in the 'Heart of the Iceberg.'"

49. Earnestine Foster, "Citizenship School Report," May 1963, box 163, folder 24, series III/5, part 4, SCLC–MLK; Earnestine Foster to the SCLC, May 3, 1963, box 163, folder 24, series III/5, part 4, SCLC–MLK; Lois Lee Rodgers, "Report for the Month of March," April 9, 1963, box 161, folder 57, series III/5, part 4, SCLC–MLK; Lois Lee Rodgers, "Report for April," May 6, 1963, box 161, folder 57, series III/5, part 4, SCLC–MLK.

50. For Bevel in Birmingham, see Branch, *Parting the Waters*, 756–802; Eskew, *But for Birmingham*, 259–269; [Citizenship Education Program], "Dorchester April 22–26, 1963," [April 1963], box 565, folder 1, series 10/10.2, SCLC–Emory; Leonia Luckett, "Citizenship School Monthly Attendance and Record Sheet," April 1963, box 162, folder 53, series III/5, part 4, SCLC–MLK. Luckett attended Delta-based teacher training in March 1963. Ponder, "Citizenship School Report: Greenwood, Mississippi."

51. Southern Christian Leadership Conference, "Citizenship Workbook," box 153, folder 23, series III/2/ii, part 4, SCLC–MLK; Leonia Luckett, "Report for January," January 1963, box 162, folder 53, series III/5, part 4, SCLC–MLK.

52. Baxter McGee interview with author; Ponder, "Mississippi Report to Annual Convention."

53. In 1960, the population of Holmes County was 27,906; non-white population was 19,481. Of non-white workers, 2,561 of 4,575 (56 percent) were classified in "Agriculture, Forestry, and Fisheries." See U.S. Bureau of the Census, *U.S. Census of the Population: 1960*, vol. 1, *Characteristics of the Population*, part 26, *Mississippi* (Washington, D.C.: U.S. Government Printing Office, 1963), 26–24 and 26–203.

54. In 1960, the median completed school for the Holmes County non-white population was 5.8 years. In Bolivar and Sunflower Counties, the figure was 4.7 years. See U.S. Bureau of the Census, *U.S. Census of the Population: 1960*, vol. 1, *Characteristics of the Population*, part 26, *Mississippi*, 26–201, 26–203, 26–206. For Holmes County school year, see Payne, *I've Got the Light*, 278. In 1959, 593 black farmers owned land in Holmes County, more than Coahoma, Leflore, and Sunflower Counties, where fewer than two hundred black farmers owned land. See U.S. Department of Commerce, *U.S. Census of Agriculture*, 1964, vol. 1, part 33 (Washington, D.C.: Government Printing Office, 1967), 260–266; Daniel, *Dispossession*, 76; Dittmer, *Local People*, 191; Payne, *I've Got the Light*, 278.

55. Quotations in Watkins interview, Oral History Digital Collections, University of Southern Mississippi Libraries (hereafter cited as OHDC–USM). Watkins listed the Holmes County contingent: "Hartman Turnbow, Ozelle Mitchell, and Mr. Mitchell's sister, Ms. Conechie." Lorenzi Sojourner confirmed these participants. Dittmer identified Ozelle Mitchell's sister as Alma Mitchell Carnegie. "Mrs. Alma C. Carnegie" from Tchula, Mississippi, completed CEP training in June 1963. All of these references likely refer to the same woman: Alma Mitchell Carnegie. See Watkins interview, OHDC–USM; Sojourner, *Thunder of Freedom*, 24; Dittmer, *Local People*, 191; [Citizenship Education Program],"Dorchester Participants, June 17–21, 1963," [June 1963], box 565, folder 1, series 10/10.2, SCLC–Emory. See also Payne, *I've Got the Light*, 278.

56. Turnbow, quoted in Raines, *My Soul Is Rested*, 260–261.

57. Turnbow interview, OHDC–USM, emphasis in original. For Russell's church, see Payne, *I've Got the Light*, 278.

58. Turnbow interview, OHDC–USM; Virgil Downing, "NAACP Sponsoring Voters Registration of Colored People in Holmes County," April 10, 1963, SCR ID# 2-54-1-77-2-1-1 and 2-54-1-77-3-1-1, MSSCP–MDAH; Watkins interview, OHDC–USM; Turnbow, quoted in Raines, *My Soul Is Rested*, 261–262. For accounts of the First Fourteen, see Dittmer, *Local People*, 192; Sojourner, *Thunder of Freedom*, 23–36, 40–43.

59. Downing, "NAACP Sponsoring Voters Registration." For Turnbow, see Sojourner, *Thunder of Freedom*, 31–33; Umoja, *We Will Shoot Back*, 73–76.

60. Tom Scarbrough, "Holmes County," May 14, 1963, SCR ID# 2-54-2-5-2-1-1 and 2-54-2-5-3-1-1, MSSCP–MDAH; Turnbow interview, OHDC–USM. For attack on Turnbow's home, see Sojourner, *Thunder of Freedom*, 31–33; Estes, *I Am a Man*, 66–67; Payne, *I've Got the Light*, 279; Umoja, *We Will Shoot Back*, 74–75; Dittmer, *Local People*, 191–193.

61. Watkins interview, OHDC–USM; [Citizenship Education Program], "Dorchester Participants, June 17–21, 1963," [June 1963], box 565, folder 1, series 10/10.2, SCLC–Emory. For Carnegie, see Dittmer, *Local People*, 191; Sojourner, *Thunder of Freedom*, 98. For

Hayes, see Mississippi Freedom Democratic Party, "Biographies of the Candidates," April 4, 1966, reel 2, segment 2, Mississippi Freedom Democratic Party Collection, Digital Collections, Wisconsin Historical Society (hereafter cited as MFDP-WHS). For Davis, see Eloise Davis, "Citizenship School Report," July 15, 1964, box 163, folder 37, series III/5, part 4, SCLC-MLK. For Burns registration, see Tom Scarbrough, "Holmes County," May 14, 1963, SCR ID# 2-54-2-5-3-1-1, MSSCP-MDAH.

62. Eloise Davis, "Citizenship School Monthly Attendance and Record Sheet Attendance Sheet," July 1963, box 163, folder 37, series III/5, part 4, SCLC-MLK; Eloise Davis, "Citizenship School Monthly Attendance and Record Sheet Attendance Sheet," August 1963, box 163, folder 37, series III/5, part 4, SCLC-MLK; Willie Burns, "Citizenship School Monthly Attendance and Record Sheet Attendance Sheet," August 1963, box 163, folder 34, series III/5, part 4, SCLC-MLK.

63. Accounts vary on the number in the group. I use Ponder and Hamer's testimonies. Annell Ponder, untitled testimony, [1963], box 24, folder 8, Mississippi Freedom Democratic Party Collection, Martin Luther King Jr. Center for Non-Violent Social Change (hereafter cited as MFDP-MLK); Fannie Lou Hamer, "Fannie Lou Hamer Interview—Winona, Mississippi," box 98, folder 20, SNCC-MLK. For arrested travelers, see Dittmer, *Local People*, 170. See also Lee, *For Freedom's Sake*, 45–46; Branch, *Parting the Waters*, 819.

64. Hamer, quoted in Raines, *My Soul Is Rested*, 253.

65. Ponder, quoted in Watters and Cleghorn, *Climbing Jacob's Ladder*, 364; Branch, *Parting the Waters*, 819.

66. Hamer, quoted in Raines, *My Soul Is Rested*, 253; Hamer, "Fannie Lou Hamer Interview—Winona, Mississippi."

67. Payne, *I've Got the Light*, 288; Young, *Easy Burden*, 253–254. Cotton confirmed the exchange but disagreed with Young's characterization that she behaved recklessly and did not appreciate the gravity of the situation. See Cotton, *If Your Back's Not Bent*, 216–218.

68. Ponder, "Citizenship Education in the 'Heart of the Iceberg'"; Young, *Easy Burden*, 256–258.

69. Ponder, "Mississippi Report to Annual Convention."

70. Ibid.

71. Ponder, "Citizenship Education in the 'Heart of the Iceberg'"; Ponder, "Mississippi Report to Annual Convention"; (Mrs.) Victoria J. Gray, "Citizenship Education Project, Hattiesburg, Miss. (Forrest County), Sept. 27, 1963 to Oct. 27, 1963," [October 1963], box 567, folder 15, series 10/10.2, SCLC-Emory. Gray noted that she was "enroute home from Richmond" on September 27–29, 1963.

Chapter 6. Freedom Days: Citizenship Education in Mississippi, 1963–1965

1. Annell Ponder, "Summary Report of Citizenship Education Program (Mississippi) for August, September, October 1963," October 26, 1963, box 559, folder 12, series 10/10.2, SCLC-Emory.

2. Gray Adams interview, OHDC-USM; Gray Adams, "Mississippi," in Erenrich, *Freedom Is a Constant Struggle*, 75, capitalization in original. For Gray Adams, see also Levine, "Learning for Liberation," 75–76; Charron, *Freedom's Teacher*, 326–327; Craw-

ford, "'Be Ye Doers'"; Crawford, "African American Women," 127–130; Dittmer, *Local People*, 181–184; Sturkey, *Hattiesburg*, 281–283. Victoria Jackson Gray changed her name to Victoria Gray Adams after remarrying in 1964.

3. Andrew J. Young et al., "Annual Report, Citizenship Education Program sponsored by Southern Christian Leadership Conference, American Missionary Association," 1963–1964, box 137, folder 3, series I/2/iii, part 4, SCLC-MLK; Young, *Easy Burden*, 141.

4. Fairclough, *To Redeem the Soul*, 164–168, 178–191.

5. Crawford, "'Be Ye Doers,'" 172; Branch, *Pillar of Fire*, 61; Dittmer, *Local People*, 181–183; Charron, *Freedom's Teacher*, 326; Sturkey, *Hattiesburg*, 282–284.

6. In 1960, 14,754 non-white residents lived in Forrest County. See U.S. Bureau of the Census, *U.S. Census of the Population: 1960*, vol. 1, *Characteristics of the Population*, part 26, *Mississippi* (Washington, D.C.: U.S. Government Printing Office, 1963), Forrest County population: 26–10, total non-white population for Forrest County: 26–202. See also Newman, *Divine Agitators*, 47; for labor statistics, see U.S. Bureau of the Census, *U.S. Census of the Population: 1960*, vol. 1, *Characteristics of the Population*, part 26, Mississippi, 26–160. For Hercules, see Sturkey, *Hattiesburg*, 246–247, 266–267, 248–250, 272–274; Martin, *Count Them*, chapter 12.

7. Sturkey, *Hattiesburg*, 289–290. Lenon E. Woods's husband, John Bradley (J. B.) Woods, opened Woods Guesthouse. From 1921 into the 1930s, Mr. Woods hosted meetings for black Republicans. Sturkey, *Hattiesburg*, 137–139; Dittmer, *Local People*, 181.

8. Draper, "Class and Politics," 277. In 1960 census, non-white residents in Bolivar and Coahoma Counties completed, on average, 4.7 and 4.9 years of formal education, respectively. Non-white residents in Forrest County completed, on average, seven years of formal education. See U.S. Bureau of the Census, *U.S. Census of the Population: 1960*, vol. 1, *Characteristics of the Population*, part 26, *Mississippi*, 26–201, 26–202. For schools, see Sturkey, *Hattiesburg*, 269–270.

9. Ladner and Ladner interview, Civil Rights Oral History Project Collection, Library of Congress Archive of Folk Culture, American Folklife Center (hereafter cited as CROHPC-LOC); Gray Adams interview, OHDC-USM. Dorie and Joyce Ladner joined the Hattiesburg NAACP Youth Council as teenagers, later serving as SNCC field secretaries in Mississippi. Dittmer, *Local People*, 85, 225.

10. Ladner and Ladner interview, CROHP-LOC; Gray Adams interview, OHDC-USM. See also Crawford, "African American Women," 127–130; Sturkey, *Hattiesburg*, 282–283.

11. Newman, *Divine Agitators*, 47, 247n3; Victoria Gray, "Citizenship School Monthly Attendance and Record Sheet," October 16, 1963, box 567, folder 15, series 10/10.2, SCLC-Emory.

12. Dittmer, *Local People*, 179–180; Sturkey, *Hattiesburg*, 275–281. For Gray's description, see Gray Adams interview, OHDC-USM. "Tall" repeated in original.

13. Watkins interview, OHDC-USM; Dittmer, *Local People*, 184; Sturkey, *Hattiesburg*, 275–281.

14. Andrew Young to Wiley Branton, [1963], box 138, folder 1, series I/3/i, part 4, SCLC-MLK; Gray Adams interview, KZSU-Stanford; Gray Adams interview, OHDC-USM; Sturkey, *Hattiesburg*, 283; Victoria Gray, "Citizenship Education Project, Hat-

tiesburg, Miss. (Forrest County)," [October 1963], box 567, folder 15, series 10/10.2, SCLC-Emory. For Anthony Gray employment, see Carson, *Student Voice*, 149; Charron, *Freedom's Teacher*, 327.

15. Gray Adams, quoted in Crawford, "African American Women," 129–130; Gray Adams interview, OHDC-USM; Victoria Gray, "Citizenship Education Project, Hattiesburg, Miss. (Forrest County)." For reflections on the CEP, see also Charron, *Freedom's Teacher*, 326–328.

16. Annell Ponder, "90,000 Negroes Vote in Mississippi Mock Election," *SCLC Newsletter*, November–December 1963, box 122, folder 23, series IX/2, SCLC-MLK. Historians have examined the Freedom Vote from a variety of perspectives, each arguing that this statewide campaign in 1963 set the stage for Freedom Summer in 1964. For the statewide campaign, see Dittmer, *Local People*, 201–203; Payne, *I've Got the Light*, 294–298. For local studies, see Hamlin, *Crossroads at Clarksdale*, 128–132; Moye, *Let the People Decide*, 114–116.

17. Gray, "Citizenship Education Project, Hattiesburg, Miss. (Forrest County)."

18. L. E. Cole Jr. and Louie Risk, "Special Report—Mississippi State Sovereignty Commission," October 30, 1963, SCR ID# 1-16-1-70-1-1-1 and SCR ID# 1-16-1-70-4-1-1, MSSCP-MDAH.

19. Ponder, "Summary Report of Citizenship Education Program (Mississippi) for August, September, October, 1963." See also Dittmer, *Local People*, 200; Payne, *I've Got the Light*, 291–293.

20. Reverend H. C. Anderson, "Citizenship School Monthly Attendance and Record Sheet," October 1963, box 162, folder 10, series III/5, part 4, SCLC-MLK; Ponder, "90,000 Negroes Vote in Mississippi Mock Election"; Lois Lee Rodgers, "Report for October 1963," November 26, 1963, box 162, folder 2, series III/5, part 4, SCLC-MLK (all Rodgers quotes). For Rodgers, see also Charron, *Freedom's Teacher*, 327.

21. Ponder, "90,000 Negroes Vote in Mississippi Mock Election" (all Ponder quotes); Council of Federated Organizations, "What Is COFO? Mississippi: Structure of the Movement and Present Operations," COFO Publication #6, [1964], box 141, folder 11, series I/3/iii, part 4, SCLC-MLK. COFO publication summarizes the Freedom Vote and outlines plans for summer 1964.

22. Dittmer, *Local People*, 219–220; Newman, *Divine Agitators*, 48–49; Sturkey, *Hattiesburg*, 286–290; Mrs. Victoria J. Gray, "Citizenship Ed. Project—Hattiesburg, Mississippi," [January 1963], box 567, folder 15, series 10/10.2, SCLC-Emory.

23. Dittmer, *Local People*, 219–221; Newman, *Divine Agitators*, 49–50; Sturkey, *Hattiesburg*, 286–290; Gray, "Citizenship Ed. Project-Hattiesburg, Mississippi," [January 1963].

24. Newman, *Divine Agitators*, 49–50; Sturkey, *Hattiesburg*, 286–290. For ministers' home locations, see Branch, *Pillar of Fire*, 219; Mrs. Victoria J. Gray, "Citizenship Education Project-Hattiesburg, Miss.," [February 1964], box 567, folder 15, series 10/10.2, SCLC-Emory; Gray, quoted in Adickes, *Legacy of a Freedom School*, 16. For Dorchester participation, see [Citizenship Education Program], "Participants for Five-Day Training at Dorchester," February 17–21, 1964, box 545, folder 2, series 10/10.2, SCLC-Emory. List

includes two names from Hattiesburg but does not include Ruth Ratliff Campbell. For Campbell, see Connor interview, OHDC–USM.

25. Connor interview, OHDC–USM (Connor quotes); Sturkey, *Hattiesburg*, 285. For Connor's age, see U.S. Bureau of the Census, *Sixteenth Census of the United States: 1940*, State: Mississippi, County: Forrest, Incorporated Place: Hattiesburg City, Population Schedule, S.D. 5, E.D. no 18–13, sheet no. 10B, enumerated on April 9, 1940. For Committee of One Hundred, see McMillen, *Dark Journey*, 309–312; Sturkey, *Hattiesburg*, 135–136. For Gould arrest, see Branch, *Pillar of Fire*, 649n220.

26. For the Reverend J. H. Ratliff, see Sturkey, *Hattiesburg*, 227; for Campbell's age and relationship to J. H. Ratliff, see U.S. Bureau of the Census, *Sixteenth Census of the United States: 1940*, State: Mississippi, County: Forrest, Incorporated Place: Hattiesburg City, Population Schedule, S.D. 6, E.D. no. 18–11, sheet no. 13B, enumerated on April 10, 1940; Connor interview, OHDC–USM (all Connor quotes and Campbell and Anderson employer); for Anderson's education, see Adickes, *Legacy of a Freedom School*, 151.

27. Gray, "Citizenship Education Project–Hattiesburg, Miss.," [February 1964]; Mrs. Victoria Gray, "Summary of Activities for Period March 27 through April 27, 1964," [April 1964], box 567, folder 15, series 10/10.2, SCLC–Emory.

28. Victoria J. Gray, "Supervisor's Evaluation Report," March 26, 1964, box 567, folder 15, series 10/10.2, SCLC–Emory; Connor interview, COHCH–USM. For student participation, see Mrs. Victoria J. Gray, "Report on Activities in Forrest County, Mississippi, February 27 through March 26, 1964," April 15, 1964, box 567, folder 15, series 10/10.2, SCLC–Emory. Gray documented "two teachers and at least five members of our classes in jail, now." Dates corroborate information about arrests in Connor's interview.

29. Mrs. Peggy Jean Connor, "Citizenship School Monthly Attendance and Record Sheet," April 1964, box 162, folder 41, series III/5, part 4, SCLC–MLK; Gray, "Summary of Activities for Period March 27 through April 27, 1964."

30. [Citizenship Education Program], "Semi-Annual Statistical Report," June 1963–November 1963, box 137, folder 1, series I/2/iii, part 4, SCLC–MLK; Annell Ponder, "Mississippi Report to Annual Convention of the Southern Christian Leadership Conference," September 1963, box 155, folder 26, series III/4/i, part 4, SCLC–MLK.

31. Ollie Hughes, "September 4, 1963," report covering period from September 4, 1963, to October 13, 1963, box 162, folder 26, series III/5, part 4, SCLC–MLK; Block interview with author; Lois Lee Rodgers, "Supervisors Evaluation Report," May 13, 1964, box 162, folder 3, series III/5, part 4, SCLC–MLK; McKinley Marcus, "Citizenship School Monthly Attendance and Record Sheet," June 1964, box 162, folder 55, series III/5, part 4, SCLC–MLK; R[althus] H. Hayes, "Citizenship School Monthly Attendance and Record Sheet," March 1964, box 163, folder 39, series III/5, part 4, SCLC–MLK; Mrs. Mary Diggs, "Citizenship School Monthly Attendance and Record Sheet," September 1963, box 163, folder 31, series III/5, part 4, SCLC–MLK; [Ollie Hughes], "September 4, 1963," October 17, 1963, box 162, folder 26, series III/5, part 4, SCLC–MLK.

32. [Citizenship Education Program], "Semi-Annual Statistical Report, June 1963–November 1963"; Young et al., "Annual Report, Citizenship Education Program."

33. Ponder, "Summary Report of Citizenship Education Program (Mississippi) for August, September, October, 1963"; Annell Ponder to Citizenship workers in Leflore,

Sunflower, and Bolivar Counties, September 14, 1963, box 543, folder 5, series 10/10.2, SCLC-Emory; Annell Ponder, "Report of Citizenship School Program in Greenwood-Leflore Area, Mississippi, Month of April, 1963," May 7, 1963, box 559, series 10/10.2, SCLC-Emory.

34. [Hughes], "September 4, 1963." For SNCC organizers' adoption of natural hairstyles, jeans, denim skirts, and overalls, see Ford, *Liberated Threads*, 68.

35. Annell Ponder to Citizenship Staff, "Supervisors' Pay Scale in Mississippi (as of September, 1963)," September 14, 1963, box 556, folder 3, series 10/10.2, SCLC-Emory; Ponder, "Citizenship Education in the 'Heart of the Iceberg'"; Annell Ponder to Citizenship workers in Leflore, Sunflower and Bolivar Counties. See also "Miss Pinkie Pilcher," n.d., box 162, folder 34, series III/5, part 4, SCLC-MLK; Sanders, *Chance for Change*, 82.

36. Ponder, "Summary Report of Citizenship Education Program (Mississippi) for August, September, October, 1963."

37. Lois Lee Rodgers, "Report for August," September 6, 1963, box 162, folder 2, series III/5, part 4, SCLC-MLK; Ponder, "Summary Report of Citizenship Education Program (Mississippi) for August, September, October, 1963." For Rodgers, see also Charron, *Freedom's Teacher*, 324–325.

38. (Mrs.) Septima P. Clark to Mrs. Lois L. Rogers [sic], October 17, 1963, box 162, folder 2, series III/5, part 4, SCLC-MLK.

39. Student Non-Violent Coordinating Committee, "Mississippi Summer Project," [1964], box 141, folder 14, series I/3/iii, part 4, SCLC-MLK; Southern Regional Council, "Second Annual Report of the Voter Education Project of the Southern Regional Council for the Fiscal Year April 1, 1963–March 31, 1964," March 1964, box 21, folder 6, SNCC-MLK; Faulkenberry, *Poll Power*, 70–71.

40. SNCC, "Mississippi Summer Project."

41. Ponder, "SCLC Helps Mississippians Move Toward Freedom."

42. Hale, *Freedom Schools*, 92–97; COFO, "What Is COFO?" (COFO quotes); Lois Chaffee to Mrs. Septima Clark, March 24, 1964, box 544, folder 23, series 10/10.2, SCLC-Emory (Clark's committee assignment); [COFO], "Summary of Freedom School Curriculum," [1964], box 101, folder 4, SNCC-MLK. See Hale, *Freedom Schools*, 72–79, 92–99.

43. Branch, *Pillar of Fire*, 231–234, 267, 282, 356–357, Russell quote on 267; Mrs. Victoria J. Gray, "Supervisor's Evaluation Report," May 25, 1964, box 567, folder 15, series 10/10.2, SCLC-Emory; Margaret Block, "Citizenship School Monthly Attendance and Record Sheet," March 25, 1964, box 161, folder 54, series III/5, part 4, SCLC-MLK; Margaret Block, "Citizenship School Monthly Attendance and Record Sheet," April 29, 1964, box 161, folder 54, series III/5, part 4, SCLC-MLK.

44. For voter registration and MFDP primary challenges, see Carson, *Student Voice*, 155, 158–159, 161, quotations on 159.

45. Mississippi Freedom Democratic Party, "Brief Submitted by the Mississippi Freedom Democratic Party," [1964], box 1, folder 10, Mississippi Freedom Democratic Party Records, MFDP-WSHS; Members of the Credentials Committee, "Report of the Credentials Committee of Leflore County Democratic Convention Held June 23, 1964, with Reference to Claim by Carrie Davis, Pinkie Pilcher, and Eddye Lane to Be Delegates to

the Convention," SCR ID# 2-165-3-5-6-1-1 through 2-165-3-5-10-1-1, quote on 2-165-3-5-9-1-1, MSSCP–MDAH; "Negroes Come Too Late at Leflore Convention," *Clarion-Ledger* (Jackson, MS), June 24, 1964, 7.

46. "Affidavit," August 18, 1964, SCR ID# 2-165-3-3-2-1-1 and 2-165-3-3-3-1-1, MSSCP–MDAH; Mississippi Freedom Democratic Party, "Brief Submitted by the Mississippi Freedom Democratic Party" (precinct meeting in Sunflower County and final quote). See also Dittmer, *Local People*, 273; Lee, *For Freedom's Sake*, 74 (night riders in Ruleville).

47. Young et al., "Annual Report, Citizenship Education Program." Hale described how training sessions confronted volunteers' assumptions that they were going to Mississippi to "save" black children. Ponder's comment suggests that CEP teachers participated in sessions and likely engaged in informal chats to correct this view before volunteers arrived in Mississippi. See Hale, *Freedom Schools*, 90–91.

48. Carson, *Student Voice*, 169–170. Estimates vary on Freedom Summer volunteers. Dittmer estimated the number at "no more than 650" while Hale documented "nearly 280" volunteers." Dittmer, *Local People*, 244; Hale, *Freedom Schools*, 80.

49. COFO, "Mississippi Freedom Summer," [1964], box 141, folder 14, series I/3/iii, part 4, SCLC–MLK. Capitalization in original.

50. Gray Adams interview, OHDC–USM (first two quotes); Adickes, *Legacy of a Freedom School*, 55–56 (volunteers in Hattiesburg); Victoria J. Gray, "Report of the Activities of the Forrest County Project, Hattiesburg, Mississippi, June 27–August 27, 1964," September 14, 1964, box 567, folder 15, series 10/10.2, SCLC–Emory; Staughton Lynd, "Mississippi Freedom Schools: Retrospect and Prospect," July 26, 1964, box 98, folder 6, SNCC–MLK; Mrs. Victoria J. Gray, "Citizenship School Report," June 23, 1964, box 567, folder 15, series 10/10.2, SCLC–Emory; Adickes, *Legacy of a Freedom School*, 73 (community center opening); COFO, "Information Report for Food, Clothing, and Books: Storage Facilities and Distribution Procedures," August 25, 1964, SCR ID# 2-166-3-33-10-1-1, MSSCP–MDAH.

51. COFO, "Mississippi Freedom Summer."

52. Annell Ponder, "Memorandum to Community Center Staff," [1964], box 155, folder 35, series III/4/ii, part 4, SCLC–MLK.

53. Alice Blackwell, "Supervisor's Evaluation Report," June 28, 1964, box 162, folder 18, series III/5, part 4, SCLC–MLK; James G. Thompson, "Citizenship School Report," July 30, 1965, box 155, folder 2, series III/5, part 4, SCLC–MLK.

54. Atlean Smith, "Citizenship School Report," [Summer 1965], box 155, folder 2, series III/5, part 4, SCLC–MLK; Willie James Burns, "Supervisor's Evaluation Report," July 31, 1964, box 163, folder 35, series III/5, part 4, SCLC–MLK; Victoria J. Gray, "Report of the Activities of the Forrest County Project, Hattiesburg, Mississippi, June 27–August 27, 1964." For St. John, see Adickes, *Legacy of a Freedom School*, 75; "Temporary State Executive Committee Mississippi Freedom Democratic Party," *Hattiesburg (MS) American*, July 18, 1964, 11. COFO volunteer Sue [Lorenzi] Sojourner noted that CEP classes were some of the first activities to move into the Holmes County community center. See Sojourner, *Thunder of Freedom*, 67–77.

55. Gray, "Report of the Activities of the Forrest County Project, Hattiesburg, Mis-

sissippi, June 27–August 27, 1964"; MFDP, "Brief Submitted by the Mississippi Freedom Democratic Party." See also Dittmer, *Local People*, 285; Draper, "Class and Politics," 299–304.

56. Carson, *Student Voice*, 187, 190; Lee, *For Freedom's Sake*, 89.

57. Annell Ponder to Dear, October 8, 1964, box 543, folder 7, series 10/10.2, SCLC-Emory.

58. Septima P. Clark to Dr. M[artin] L[uther] King, December 16, 1963, box 543, folder 5, series 10/10.2, SCLC-Emory.

59. Septima [Clark] to Andy [Young], July 12, 1964, box 154, folder 6, series III/3/i, part 4, SCLC-MLK; Andy [Young] to Mrs. Septima Clark, July 20, 1964, box 154, folder 6, series III/3/i, part 4, SCLC-MLK.

60. Young et al., "Annual Report, Citizenship Education Program"; Citizenship Education Program, "Staff Meeting," September 16, 1964, box 137, folder 4, series I/2/iii, part 4, SCLC-MLK; Young, *Easy Burden*, 141.

61. Victoria J. Gray, "Report of Activities Forrest County Project, Hattiesburg, Miss. for Aug. 27–Sept. 26, 1964."

62. Victoria Jackson Gray, "Mississippi Report of Citizenship Education Project for November 1, 1964–April 28, 1965," May 13, 1965, box 567, folder 15, series 10/10.2, SCLC-Emory; Alice Blackwell to Mrs. Dorothy Cotton, November 17, 1964, box 162, folder 17, series III/5, part 4, SCLC-MLK.

63. "Mississippi Freedom Democrats Launching Major Campaign," *Delta Democrat-Times* (Greenville, MS), October 30, 1964. Advertisement approved by the MFDP.

64. Carson, *Student Voice*, 191, 203–204, quotation on 203. For Roby, see MFDP, "Brief Submitted by the Mississippi Freedom Democratic Party." For Hamer's role in the 1964 election, see Lee, *For Freedom's Sake*, 107–114.

65. "NAACP to Decide Today on Pulling Out of COFO," *Clarion-Ledger* (Jackson, MS), January 4, 1965, 1; Dittmer, *Local People*, 339–342; Young et al., "Annual Report, Citizenship Education Program."

66. "Voters Pick Councilmen Here Monday," *Delta Democrat-Times* (Greenville, MS), December 12, 1965; Alice Blackwell, "Supervisor—Mrs. A. Blackwell, Teacher—Mrs. Annie Thomas," April 7, 1965, box 162, folder 19, series III/5, part 4, SCLC-MLK.

67. "G'wood Negro Women File Seat Applications," *Clarion-Ledger* (Jackson, MS), April 12, 1965, 6; "One Negro Woman Is Qualified," *Clarion-Ledger* (Jackson, MS), April 15, 1965.

68. James G. Thompson, "Citizenship School Report," July 30, 1965, box 155, folder 2, series III/5, part 4, SCLC-MLK; Ethel Lee Thompson, "Citizenship School Report," July 29, 1965, box 155, folder 3, series III/5, part 4, SCLC-MLK; for Hamer and MFLU, see Dittmer, *Local People*, 364–365, and Lee, *For Freedom's Sake*, 121–135; Atlean F. Smith, "Citizenship School Report," n.d., box 155, folder 2, series III/5, part 4, SCLC-MLK.

69. Mrs. Victoria J. Gray, "Citizenship School Report, July 1964–June 1965," August 2, 1965, box 155, folder 2, series III/3/ii, part 4, SCLC-MLK; Rev. Jesse J. Russell, "Citizenship School Monthly Attendance and Record Sheet," June 1965, box 163, folder 49, series III/3/ii, part 4, SCLC-MLK.

70. Willie James Burns, "Supervisor's Evaluation Report," reports dated 6-28-64

and 7-31-64, box 163, folder 35, series III/5, part 4, SCLC-MLK; "FDP County Reports," November 6-November 19, 1965, SCR ID# 2-165-5-10-1-1-1 and 2-165-5-10-2-1-1, MSSCP-MDAH.

71. Dittmer, *Local People*, 341; Gray, "Mississippi Report of the Citizenship Education Project for November 1, 1964-April 28, 1965."

Chapter 7. "So Much Taking Place ... So Rapidly": Citizenship Education in Mississippi and Alabama, 1965-1967

1. Victoria Jackson Gray, "Mississippi Report of the Citizenship Education Project for November 1, 1964-April 28, 1965," May 13, 1965, box 567, folder 15, series 10/10.2, SCLC-Emory.

2. This analysis adds to scholarship on 1960s War on Poverty programs. For local studies in southern states, see, for example, Ashmore, *Carry It On*; de Jong, *You Can't Eat Freedom*; Sanders, *Chance for Change*; Germany, *New Orleans after the Promises*; Greene, *Our Separate Ways*, 109-137; Rhonda W. Williams, *Politics of Public Housing*, chapter 5. For communities outside of the South, see, for example, Naples, *Grassroots Warriors*; Orleck, *Storming Caesar's Palace*. For view of the variety of programs and responses, see Orleck and Hazirjian, *War on Poverty*.

3. For recent studies examining scrutiny of and interference in local anti-poverty initiatives, see Ashmore, *Carry It On*, chapters 5, 6, and 7; de Jong, *You Can't Eat Freedom*, chapters 3 and 4; Sanders, *Chance for Change*, 107-144. Germany develops a case study where federal, state, and local officials collaborated more effectively. Germany, *New Orleans after the Promises*.

4. Gray, "Mississippi Report of the Citizenship Education Project for November 1, 1964-April 28, 1965"; Branch, *Pillar of Fire*, 555; Dittmer, *Local People*, 339-340; Crawford, "African American Women," 132-133. For Ryan, see Carson, *Student Voice*, 203.

5. Gray, "Mississippi Report of the Citizenship Education Project for November 1, 1964-April 28, 1965." For federal officials, see "Freedom Party Makes Calls on Agencies in Washington," *Greenwood (MS) Commonwealth*, January 6, 1965, 1. For Hamer, see Lee, *For Freedom's Sake*, 107-114.

6. Gray interview, KZSU-Stanford.

7. Mrs. Victoria Gray, "Mississippi CEP Report," [1966], box 545, folder 4, series 10/10.2, SCLC-Emory.

8. Schlei, quoted in Gillette, *Launching the War on Poverty*, 98-99. Norbert A. Schlei was assistant attorney general and a member of the president's task force in the War on Poverty, instrumental in drafting the Economic Opportunity Act.

9. Charron, *Freedom's Teacher*, 339.

10. Vinovskis, *Birth of Head Start*, 73-74, quotation on 74.

11. Sanders, *Chance for Change*, 44; Gray, "Mississippi CEP Report," [1966].

12. Baxter McGee interview with author; Ethel Gray, "Citizenship School Report," July 28, 1965, box 155, folder 3, series III/3/ii, part 4, SCLC-MLK; Sanders, *Chance for Change*, 82 (Pilcher and Lane); Alice Blackwell, "Citizenship School Report, July 1964-June 1965," July 22, 1965, box 155, folder 2, series III/3/ii, part 4, SCLC-MLK; "Two New Members Approved for Anti-Poverty Board," *Hattiesburg (MS) American*, September 28,

1966, 11. For links between civil rights organizing and CDGM employment, see Sanders, *Chance for Change*, 54.

13. Gray, "Mississippi CEP Report," [1966].

14. Gray, "Mississippi Report of the Citizenship Education Project for November 1, 1964–April 28, 1965"; [Citizenship Education Program], "August 10–14, 1964," [August 1964], box 565, folder 4, series 10/10.2, SCLC-Emory; [Citizenship Education Program], "January 11–15 Workshop," January 11–15, 1965, box 565, folder 2, series 10/10.2, SCLC-Emory; [Citizenship Education Program], "Workshop Participants," February 22–26, 1965, box 565, folder 2, series 10/10.2, SCLC-Emory; [Citizenship Education Program], "Participants in Workshop Dorchester," March 22–26, 1965, box 565, folder 2, series 10/10.2, SCLC-Emory; active classes compiled from teacher training participant lists and Citizenship School Attendance Records for Julia M. Small, box 161, folder 43; Birdia Keglar, box 161, folder 45; Colton Ginn, box 162, folder 50; Henry Lee Jenkins, box 162, folder 52, all in series III/5, part 4, SCLC-MLK.

15. [Citizenship Education Program], "Workshop Participants—Dorchester, February 22–26, 1965"; [Citizenship Education Program], "Participants in Workshop Dorchester," March 22–26, 1965.

16. Southern Christian Leadership Conference, "Executive Staff Retreat," November 10–12, 1964, box 143, folder 4, series II/1/i, part 4, SCLC-MLK.

17. For county demographics, see Thornton, *Dividing Lines*, 414. For voting statistics, see Fairclough, *To Redeem the Soul*, 209–210; Young, *Easy Burden*, 336–337.

18. Southern Christian Leadership Conference, "Executive Staff Retreat"; Branch, *At Canaan's Edge*, 524; Thornton, *Dividing Lines*, 475–476.

19. John Herbers, "Alabama Vote Drive Opened by Dr. King," *New York Times*, January 3, 1965; Young, *Easy Burden*, 342–343.

20. Andrew J. Young, "Report on Alabama Meetings, Oct. & Nov.," [1962], box 559, folder 12, series 10/10.2, SCLC-Emory; Thornton, *Dividing Lines*, 130; [Citizenship Education Program], "Dorchester," November 5th–9th, 1962, box 565, folder 1, series 10/10.2, SCLC-Emory; Virginia Johnson, "Citizenship School Semi-Annual Report," [1963], box 157, folder 4, series III/5, part 4, SCLC-MLK; George Wallace, "Inaugural Address, that was delivered at the Capitol in Montgomery, Alabama," Box SG030847, Administrative Files, Alabama Textual Materials Collection, Alabama Department of Archives & History, Montgomery, Alabama, accessed on March 4, 2017, http://digital.archives.alabama.gov/cdm/ref/collection/voices/id/2952; James Carter, "Citizenship School Semi-Annual Report," [1963], box 157, folder 27, series III/5, part 4, SCLC-MLK; "Look!!! Listen!!! You are invited to a County-Wide Mass Meeting," April 1963, box 157, folder 3, series III/5, part 4, SCLC-MLK.

21. Thornton, *Dividing Lines*, 486; "A Fighter for the Vote," *New York Times*, March 26, 1965, 23; [Citizenship Education Program], "Workshop Participants—Dorchester, February 22–26, 1965"; [Citizenship Education Program], "January, Refresher Workshop," 1966, box 565, folder 4, series 10/10.2, SCLC-Emory.

22. Student Non-Violent Coordinating Committee, "Survey: Current Field Work," Spring 1963, and "SNCC Work in Central Alabama," series VI, folder 33, VEPP-SRC; McCarty, *Reins of Power*, 140; Fleming, *In the Shadow of Selma*, 137, 156; Student Non-

Violent Coordinating Committee, "Special Report: Selma, Alabama," September 26, 1963, series VI, folder 33, VEPP-SRC; [Citizenship Education Program], "Workshop Participants—Dorchester, February 22-26, 1965."

23. Fairclough, *To Redeem the Soul*, 238-241; Branch, *At Canaan's Edge*, 8-9, 25; Pratt, *Selma's Bloody Sunday*, 47-51.

24. Branch, *At Canaan's Edge*, 49-51; Lewis, *Walking with the Wind*, 327-330; Pratt, *Selma's Bloody Sunday*, 58-65.

25. Branch, *At Canaan's Edge*, 75-100; Pratt, *Selma's Bloody Sunday*, 72-78; Alice Blackwell, "Supervisor—Mrs. A. Blackwell, Teacher—Mrs. Annie Thomas," box 162, folder 19, series III/5, part 4, SCLC-MLK.

26. Lyndon B. Johnson, "Speech before Congress on Voting Rights," March 15, 1965, transcript accessed at the Miller Center website, http://millercenter.org/president/speeches/speech-3386 on October 19, 2016.

27. For judicial decisions, see Thornton, *Dividing Lines*, 489-490. For registration in Selma, see [Citizenship Education Program], "CEP Conducts Clinics," *CEP News*, September 1965, box 153, folder 17, series III/2/ii, part 4, SCLC-MLK.

28. [Student Non-Violent Coordinating Committee], "We are protesting the right to freely register and vote," [1965], frame 0032, reel 37, Student Non-Violent Coordinating Committee [microfilm], Auburn Avenue Research Library, Atlanta (hereafter cited as SNCC-AARL); Septima Clark to Mr. Maxwell Hahn, April 6, 1965, box 544, folder 7, series 10/10.2, SCLC-Emory; [Annell Ponder], "Attention! Free Handwriting Clinics Being Offered," [1965], box 155, folder 26, series III/4/ii, part 4, SCLC-MLK.

29. Annell Ponder, "CEP Work in Selma, Alabama, May 10-25, 1965," box 155, folder 26, series III/4/ii, part 4, SCLC-MLK; [CEP], "CEP Conducts Clinics"; Clark, *Ready from Within*, 68.

30. Sallie Petties, "Citizenship School Monthly Attendance and Record Sheet," April 1965, box 157, folder 35, series III/5, part 4, SCLC-MLK; Mrs. Septima P. Clark to Dr. Robert Green, "Citizenship Education Projects—Yearly Report, July 1, 1965-June 30, 1966," October 5, 1966, box 545, folder 4, series 10/10.2, SCLC-Emory. For statistic, see Clark interview with Walker, Southern Oral History Program, University of North Carolina, Chapel Hill (hereafter abbreviated SOHP-UNC). See Charron, *Freedom's Teacher*, 331-332; Levine, "Citizenship Schools," 203-207.

31. [Citizenship Education Program], "Report: Selma Handwriting Clinic, Selma, Alabama," [1965], box 146, folder 12, series II/2, part 4, SCLC-MLK. For West, see Webb and Nelson, *Selma, Lord, Selma*, 21-22, 51-53.

32. Sallie Petties to Delores Hall, June 21, 1965, box 157, folder 35, series III/5, part 4, SCLC-MLK; Tommie Lucile Johnson, "Selma News," *Montgomery Advertiser*, November 29, 1964; Mrs. Addie Lily, letter to the editor, *Southern Courier*, November 12-13, 1966.

33. Bruce Gordon, "Field Report from Bruce Gordon—Selma, Alabama," November 9, 1963, frames 60-63, reel 37, SNCC-AARL; Chr. Dallas County Voters League to Mr. Willard Wertz, January 9, 1964, frames 0066-0067, reel 37, SNCC-AARL.

34. Cooper, quoted in John H. Britton, "Selma Woman's Girdle a Big Factor in Fight with Sheriff," *Jet*, February 11, 1965, 6-7. For analysis of the earlier shift from bourgeois

ideology of respectability to asserting respectability through demands for equal treatment, see Wolcott, *Remaking Respectability*, chapters 5 and 6.

35. Mrs. Septima Clark, "From a taped report at the Highlander Board of Directors' Meeting," May 14, 1965, box 2, folder 3, HRECP-WHS; Miss Bernice Robinson, "From a taped report at the Highlander Board of Directors' Meeting," May 14, 1965, box 2, folder 3, HRECP-WHS.

36. Clark interview with Walker, SOHP-UNC; Clark, *Ready from Within*, 68–69, quotation on 69; Clark, "From a taped report at the Highlander Board of Directors' Meeting."

37. Louise Shelton, Claudia Strong, Alice West, Addie Lily, and Annie Cooper taught handwriting clinics and attended CEP teacher training at Dorchester. For Clinic, see [CEP], "Report: Selma Handwriting Clinic, Selma, Alabama," [1965]. For Dorchester training, see [CEP], "Workshop Participants, Dorchester Center, February 22–26, 1965"; [CEP], "Workshop Participants, Dorchester Center, June 21–25, 1965," box 565, folder 2, series 10/10.2, SCLC-Emory. For Emma Jackson, see Branch, *Pillar of Fire*, 599.

38. "Free Adult Citizenship Classes," *Southern Courier*, August 6, 1965, 6; Alice West, "Citizenship School Semi-Annual Report," July 27, 1965, box 154, folder 21, series III/5, part 4, SCLC-MLK; Sallie Petties, "Citizenship School Report, July 1964–June 1965," July 28, 1965, box 154, folder 16, series III/5, part 4, SCLC-MLK; Sallie Petties, "Citizenship School Monthly Attendance and Record Sheet," July 1965, box 157, folder 36, series III/5, part 4, SCLC-MLK; Sallie Petties, "Citizenship School Monthly Attendance and Record Sheet," August 1965, box 157, folder 36, series III/5, part 4, SCLC-MLK; Mary Lee Strong, "Citizenship School Semi-Annual Report," July 29, 1965, box 154, folder 16, series III/5, part 4, SCLC-MLK; Ralph Gene Henry, "Citizenship School Semi-Annual Report," July 29, 1965, box 154, folder 18, series III/5, part 4, SCLC-MLK.

39. Nancy Brown, "Citizenship School Monthly Attendance and Record Sheet," box 156, folder 1, series III/5, part 4, SCLC-MLK. For Gee's Bend, see Ashmore, *Carry It On*, 1–3; Fleming, *In the Shadow of Selma*, xvii, 73–83; McCarty, *Reins of Power*, 120–121; Watters and Cleghorn, *Climbing Jacob's Ladder*, 161–162.

40. Sarah Lee Westbrook, "Citizenship School Report, July 1964–June 1965," July 22, 1965, box 154, folder 20, series III/5, part 4, SCLC-MLK. For occupation, see [Citizenship Education Program], "January, Refresher Workshop," 1966, box 565, folder 4, series 10/10.2, SCLC-Emory.

41. Jeffries, *Bloody Lowndes*, 60, 146–164; Ashmore, *Carry It On*, 154–159.

42. Hosea Williams and Fred V. Martin, "The Department of Voter Registration and Political Education Proposed Budget and Program," January 1, 1965–June 30, 1965, folder 31, series VI, VEPP-SRC. Student volunteer Maria Gitin documented Clark, Ponder, and Cotton's participation in SCOPE volunteer training. See Gitin, *This Bright Light*, 35, 42–44, 46.

43. Ashmore, *Carry It On*, 164, 12–13, 128, 126; Fleming, *In the Shadow of Selma*, 155–156. The Harrells attended CEP teacher training at the Dorchester Center in June 1964. See [Citizenship Education Program], "Dorchester Workshop Participants (Dorchester)," June 22–26, 1964, box 565, folder 2, series 10/10.2, SCLC-Emory.

44. Septima P. Clark, "Proposal for 1965–1970, Citizenship Education Program of Southern Christian Leadership Conference in cooperation with the Board of Homeland Ministries of the American Missionary Association," [1965], box 559, folder 2, series 10/10.2, SCLC-Emory. Proposal cited statistics through February 1965.

45. Annell Ponder to Citizenship Worker, August 6, 1965, box 551, folder 1, series 10/10.2, SCLC-Emory.

46. "Some Facts about Money," n.d., box 551, folder 1, series 10/10.2, SCLC-Emory.

47. Miss Annell Ponder, "Report of Activities—December 1965, January, February, March 1966," March 31, 1966, box 559, folder 17, series 10/10.2, SCLC-Emory.

48. [Citizenship Education Program], "Attendance at Precinct Meetings Is Key to Political Participation" and "The Precinct Worker's Job," n.d., box 551, folder 15, series 10/10.2, SCLC-Emory.

49. Emmett Peter Jr., "On the Outside Looking Out," *New Republic*, June 26, 1965. For discrimination within the USDA, including the Extension Service and county ASCS committees, see Daniel, *Dispossession*, chapters 4 and 5. For challenges to ASCS committees in Alabama, see Ashmore, *Carry It On*, 100–102, 206–209; Jeffries, *Bloody Lowndes*, 117–118, 125–131.

50. [Citizenship Education Program], "Lesson Plan—Consumer Education" and "Lesson Plan—Banking," n.d., box 559, folder 2, series 10/10.2, SCLC-Emory. Lesson plans included in "Proposal for 1965–1970, Citizenship Education Program of Southern Christian Leadership Conference."

51. Daphina Simpson, "Two Election Views in Perry County Town," *Southern Courier*, June 4–5, 1966; David M. Gordon, "Selma: Quiet after the Battle," *Southern Courier*, July 23, 1965, 4. Women for Constitutional Government organized subsequent protests at the University of Mississippi in 1962. The group argued that civil rights reform was the work of an overly aggressive federal government that overstepped constitutional powers and denied fundamental rights to white southerners. By early 1963, there were fifteen WCG chapters in southern states with programs to expand their reach nationwide. See McRae, *Mothers of Massive Resistance*, 208–215.

52. Edward R. Rudd, "Negro, White Lowndes Parents Wonder about School Integration," *Southern Courier*, August 15, 1965, 4; Edward M. Rudd, "Tense Lowndes Erupts as Minister Is Slain," *Southern Courier*, August 28–29, 1965, 1. See also Ashmore, *Carry It On*, 139; Jeffries, *Bloody Lowndes*, 81–83.

53. Rosie Mae Davis, "Citizenship School Semi-Annual Report," July 28, 1965, box 154, folder 16, series III/5, part 4, SCLC-MLK.

54. Ceola Miller, "Citizenship School Monthly Attendance and Record Sheet," July 1965, box 157, folder 32, series III/5, part 4, SCLC-MLK; Ceola Miller, "Citizenship School Monthly Attendance and Record Sheet," August 1965, box 157, folder 32, series III/5, part 4, SCLC-MLK.

55. Edward M. Rudd, "Freedom City, Alabama: Lowndes Families Start Tent Village," *Southern Courier*, January 8–9, 1966; Jeffries, *Bloody Lowndes*, 106–111; Martha Saulsberry, "Citizenship School Report, July 1964–June 1965," July 22, 1965, box 154, folder 19, series III/5, part 4, SCLC-MLK; "Wilcox Plans Big Housing Project," *Southern Courier*, August 28–29, 1965, 1.

56. Sallie Petties to Citizenship Staff, October 4, 1965, box 157, folder 36, series III/5, part 4, SCLC-MLK.

57. Moton, quoted in Aimee Isgrig Horton, "A Workshop for Volunteer Teachers in the Citizenship Education Program of the Southern Christian Leadership Conference, 1965," [1966], box 10, folder 9, MHP-WHS, quotations on 112, 133–134, emphasis in original.

58. Alvin Adams, "Selma Today: 10 Weeks after the March," June 10, 1965, *Jet*, 14–21; Annie Lee Cooper, SERF Application, [1965], box 148, folder 12, series II/3, SCLC-MLK.

59. Robinson, "From a taped report at the Highlander Board of Directors' Meeting."

60. Ashmore, *Carry It On*, 164; Edward M. Rudd, "Race Complicates Black Belt Anti-Poverty Plans," *Southern Courier*, October 16–17, 1965, 1. For Bradford committee, see Ashmore, *Carry It On*, 169; Ashmore, "Going Back to Selma," 310–322.

61. Ashmore, *Carry It On*, 168–169; Frank Prial to Robert Clampitt and Jack Gonzales, November 7, 1965, box 1, folder "Alabama OEO Programs (Compilation) 1964–1965," Inspection Reports 1964–67, Office of Economic Opportunity, Inspection Division, RG 381, National Archives and Records Administration, College Park (hereafter cited as NARA-CP); Edward M. Rudd, "Poverty Dispute in Selma," *Southern Courier*, November 13–14, 1965. See also Ashmore, "Going Back to Selma."

62. John Klein, "Civil Rights Leaders Disagree on Using Votes in Black Belt," *Southern Courier*, January 22–23, 1966, 1, 4. For LCFO, see Jeffries, *Bloody Lowndes*, 146–164.

63. David R. Underhill, "Political Confederation Lays Plans to Decide Who Gets Negro Vote," *Southern Courier*, April 2–3, 1966, 1, 4.

64. John Klein, "Dallas County Voters Start Third Party," *Southern Courier*, March 19–20, 1966, 6. See also Ashmore, *Carry It On*, 174–175.

65. "Voters Hard to Reach in County Like Perry," *Southern Courier*, April 30–May 1, 1966, 6; Robert E. Smith, "Hard Work, Hard Cash Needed to Be Sheriff, Candidates Told," *Southern Courier*, March 26–27, 1966, 1, 5; Ashmore, *Carry It On*, 179n51, 339; Student Non-Violent Coordinating Committee, "Report on Alabama Elections," May 6, 1966, box 1, folder 1A, SNCC-MLK. For DCIFVO, see also Ashmore, "Going Back to Selma," 321–324.

66. Louise Shelton, "District Supervisor Report," June 7, 1966, box 559, folder 18, series 10/10.2, SCLC-Emory. For runoff elections, see Michael S. Lottman, "Slim Chance for Negroes to Win Legislative Races," *Southern Courier*, May 7–8, 1966, 5; "A Fighter for the Vote: Albert Turner," *New York Times*, March 26, 1965, 23; James K. Batton, "Negro Stands Chance in Dixie Sheriff Race," *Detroit Free Press*, May 1, 1966, 19-D.

67. Michael S. Lottman, "Kirksey Is Only Negro to Win Outside Macon," *Southern Courier*, June 4–5, 1966, 1, 2; Daphina Simpson, "Two Election Views in Perry County Town," *Southern Courier*, June 4–5, 1966, 5.

68. Terry Cowles, "SCLC Moves Out of Ala.," *Southern Courier*, June 4–5, 1966.

69. Mrs. Addie Lily, letter to the editor.

70. Septima P. Clark, "Report of Interviews in Selma, Alabama—May 18–31, 1966," May 1966, box 545, folder 4, series 10/10.2, SCLC-Emory.

71. Bessie M. King, "Citizenship School Report," July 23, 1965, box 154, folder 20, series III/5, part 4, SCLC-MLK; Julia McKnight to Dear Sir, December 7, 1965, box 156, folder

27, series III/5, part 4, SCLC–MLK; Annell Ponder to Mrs. Caroline Saulsberry, March 15, 1966, box 156, folder 32, series III/5, part 4, SCLC–MLK; Caroline Saulsberry to Miss Ponder, April 5, 1966, box 156, folder 32, series III/5, part 4, SCLC–MLK.

72. [Mississippi Freedom Democratic Party], "The Congressional Challenge Is Defeated by a Majority Vote of the Democratic and Republican Party Members in Congress," [1965], reel 2, segment 2, part 1, MFDPC–WHS; Gray, quoted in Holsaert et al., *Hands on the Freedom Plow*, 236; "Opinions Given on the Unseat Attempt," *Hattiesburg (MS) American*, September 18, 1965.

73. *Connor et al. v. Paul B. Johnson*, n.d., reel 2–3, segment 37, CORE—Mississippi Freedom Democratic Party—Memoranda and Reports, 1964–1966, MFDPC–WHS. See Dittmer, *Local People*, 352.

74. [Citizenship Education Program], "Workshop Participants, Waveland, Mississippi," December 5–10, 1965, box 565, folder 3, series 10/10.2, SCLC–Emory; Bernice Robinson, "Field Report for October, November, December 1965," box 540, folder 8, series 10/10.2, SCLC–Emory; [Citizenship Education Program], "Mt. Beulah Workshop Participants," December 13–17, 1965, box 565, folder 3, series 10/10.2, SCLC–Emory.

75. Mrs. Victoria Gray, "Political Workshop in Sunflower," May 7, [1966], box 5, folder 28, Victoria Gray Adams Papers, University of Southern Mississippi, Hattiesburg (hereafter cited as VGAP–USM).

76. Gray, "Political Workshop in Sunflower," May 7, [1966].

77. Atlean F. Smith to Miss Annell Ponder, November 17, 1965, box 162, folder 37, series III/5, part 4, SCLC–MLK.

78. Mrs. Victoria Gray to Mrs. Dorothy Cotton, "Mississippi Report of Citizenship Education Program from April 1–November 30, 1966," [November 1966], box 1, folder 25, VGAP–USM; Gray, "Political Workshop in Sunflower," May 7, [1966].

79. Mrs. Victoria Gray to Mrs. Dorothy Cotton, "Mississippi Report of Citizenship Education Program from April 1–November 30, 1966"; Branch, *At Canaan's Edge*, 475–479.

80. Branch, *At Canaan's Edge*, 475–479; Mrs. Victoria Gray to Mrs. Dorothy Cotton, "Mississippi Report of Citizenship Education Program from April 1–November 30, 1966."

81. Mrs. Victoria Gray to Mrs. Dorothy Cotton, [1966], box 1, folder 25, VGAP–USM.

Chapter 8. The Citizenship Education Program's "Second Phase," 1966–1969

1. Leslie W. Dunbar to Reverend Martin Luther King Jr., June 21, 1966, box 553, folder 7, series 10/10.2, SCLC–Emory; Wesley Hotchkiss to Mr. Leslie Dunbar, Dr. Robert Green and staff of CEP, Dr. Truman Douglas, and Dr. Howard Spring, September 7, 1966, box 553, folder 7, series 10/10.2, SCLC–Emory; Leslie W. Dunbar to Dr. Wesley A. Hotchkiss, October 3, 1966, box 553, folder 7, series 10/10.2, SCLC–Emory.

2. In this later period, lines blur between active CEP involvement and related activities. I categorize activities as CEP-related if the report author had a direct connection to the program (for example: paid staff member or supervisor or teacher earning a stipend). This category also includes reports from local teachers who responded to requests for

information or contacted CEP staff members for assistance, seeing this as evidence of enduring connection between the local leader and the CEP network.

3. Scholarship examining anti-poverty programs and political action develops local case studies, or focuses on a formal organization or a specific issue. As a result, few studies examine a variety of local initiatives organized in a variety of communities. For case studies, see, for example, Germany, *New Orleans after the Promises*; Greene, *Our Separate Ways*; Ashmore, *Carry It On*; Orleck, *Storming Caesar's Palace*. For studies with a broader view, see de Jong, *You Can't Eat Freedom*; Orleck and Hazirjian, *War on Poverty*.

4. King, *Where Do We Go*, 188.

5. Branch, *At Canaan's Edge*, 548–551.

6. [Citizenship Education Program], "New CEP Administrator," *CEP News*, September 1965, box 153, folder 17, series III/2/ii, part 4, SCLC-MLK; Young, *Easy Burden*, 396.

7. Young, *Easy Burden*, 418.

8. Clark, *Ready from Within*, 120; Cotton, *If Your Back's Not Bent*, 185–186.

9. (Mrs.) Dorothy F. Cotton to Dr. Leslie Dunbar, May 2, 1967, box 552, folder 16, series 10/10.2, SCLC-Emory; Dorothy F. Cotton, "Proposal for Citizenship Education Program to the Marshall Field Foundation," [1967], box 552, folder 16, series 10/10.2, SCLC-Emory.

10. Cotton's view was consistent with contemporary discourse about a culture of poverty and federal anti-poverty programs that posited a cultural deprivation theory to explain conditions in low-income communities, particularly in low-income African American communities. For culture of poverty, see Harrington, *Other America*. For "cultural deprivation theory" in anti-poverty programs, see Raz, *What's Wrong with the Poor?*, chapter 2.

11. (Mrs.) Dorothy F. Cotton to Dr. Leslie Dunbar, May 2, 1967, box 552, folder 16, series 10/10.2, SCLC-Emory; Leslie W. Dunbar to Dr. Wesley A. Hotchkiss, November 22, 1967, box 553, folder 3, series 10/10.2, SCLC-Emory.

12. List of topics from workshop agendas for February 1967, August and September 1968, and February 1969, box 565, folder 7, series 10/10.2, SCLC-Emory.

13. Mrs. Victoria Gray, "Mississippi CEP Report," [1966], box 545, folder 4, series 10/10.2, SCLC-Emory; Aimee Isgrig Horton, "A Workshop for Volunteer Teachers in the Citizenship Education Program of the Southern Christian Leadership Conference, 1965," [1966], box 10, folder 9, MHP-WHS.

14. [Citizenship Education Program], "Citizenship Education Workshop, Dorchester Center, Liberty County, Georgia," February 13–17, 1967, box 565, folder 7, series 10/10.2, SCLC-Emory; Bernice Robinson, Memorandum to Dorothy F. Cotton, January 1967, box 560, folder 7, series 10/10.2, SCLC-Emory.

15. Bernice V. Robinson, "Field Report for June 12th thru July 31st, 1968," August 2, 1968, box 560, folder 7, series 10/10.2, SCLC-Emory; Bernice V. Robinson, "Field Report for August–September 1968," October 7, 1968, box 560, folder 7, series 10/10.2, SCLC-Emory.

16. (Mrs.) Septima P. Clark to Mr. Maxwell Hahn, October 5, 1966, box 543, folder 10, series 10/10.2, SCLC-Emory; Septima P. Clark to Mrs. Dorothy F. Cotton, "Month of January," [1967], box 560, folder 7, series 10/10.2, SCLC-Emory.

17. (Mrs.) Septima P. Clark to Mr. Maxwell Hahn, October 5, 1966.

18. Reba Maria Belle, "Citizenship School Report," July 17, 1965, box 154, folder 26, series III/5, part 4, SCLC–MLK; Citizenship Education Program, *CEP News*, September 1965, box 153, folder 17, series III/2/ii, part 4, SCLC–MLK; Ruth Paulding to Mrs. [Septima] Clark, April 16, 1965, box 543, folder 9, series 10/10.2, SCLC–Emory; Rev. Lewis H. Simmons, "Citizenship School Report," August 2, 1965, box 155, folder 7, series III/5, part 4, SCLC–MLK.

19. Minnie L. Butler, "Citizenship School Report, July, 1964–June, 1965," July 27, 1965, box 155, folder 40, series III/5, part 4, SCLC–MLK.

20. For MSSC infiltration, see "Office of Field Operations: Master Code, Center Name and Chairman List, as of July 26, 1966," n.d., SCR ID# 6-45-4-13-1-1-1 through SCR ID# 6-45-4-13-19-1-1, MSSCP–MDAH. See also Sanders, *Chance for Change*, 110–120.

21. Mrs. Victoria Gray, "Mississippi CEP Report," [1966], box 545, folder 4, series 10/10.2, SCLC–Emory; Mrs. Victoria Gray to Mrs. Dorothy Cotton, "Mississippi Report of Citizenship Education Program from April 1–November 30, 1966," [December 1966], box 1, folder 25, VGAP–USM. For conservative resistance to the War on Poverty in Mississippi, see Folwell, *War on Poverty*; Sanders, *Chance for Change*.

22. Articles of Incorporation for the Wilcox County Southern Christian Leadership Conference Incorporated, n.d., box 148, folder 16, series II/3, part 4, SCLC–MLK; [Wilcox County SCLC], "Rationale for Program Components," n.d., box 148, folder 17, series II/3, part 4, SCLC–MLK; "OEO Releases $500,000 in Anti-Poverty Funds," *Southern Courier*, November 26–27, 1966, 2; Wilcox County Southern Christian Leadership Conference, Inc., "Definition of Requirements for Students in This Anti-Poverty Program," n.d., box 543, folder 10, series 10/10.2, SCLC–Emory. See also Ashmore, *Carry It On*, 146–150; de Jong, *You Can't Eat Freedom*, 71–72. Text places undated documents before the May 1966 elections.

23. Septima P. Clark to Dorothy Cotton, "Month of January," [1967], box 560, folder 7, series 10/10.2, SCLC–Emory; SCLC Staff to our Friends, May 1967, box 106, folder 5, HRECP–WHS.

24. Septima P. Clark, "Report of Wilcox County–Southern Christian Leadership Conference Anti-Poverty Program," May 16–19, 1967, box 563, folder 10, series 10/10.2, SCLC–Emory. "Miss Brooks" is likely Ethel Brooks, who participated in voter registration activities in Coy and is photographed in CEP classrooms. See Gitin, *This Bright Light*, 189–190.

25. Annell Ponder, "Anti-Poverty Committee of Wilcox County Southern Christian Leadership Conference, Inc. seeks a refunding of CAP ALA 66-8604," n.d., box 563, folder 10, series 10/10.2, SCLC–Emory. This document is a draft of the APCWCSCLC's application for renewed funding with Ponder's handwritten comments. The request refers to volunteers arriving in the summer and prospective funding anticipated in February 1968. Ashmore and de Jong untangle complex relationships as local people created cooperatives and anti-poverty programs in Alabama's Black Belt after the Selma campaign. Both mention SCLC staff involvement in the migrant education program but do not support Ponder's broad claims of extensive SCLC influence in the area. Ashmore, *Carry It on*, 186–197, 208–216, 273–275; de Jong, *You Can't Eat Freedom*, 71–75, 94–112.

26. Mrs. Victoria Gray, "Mississippi CEP Report," [1966]; [Citizenship Education Program], "Citizenship Education Program Staff Meeting," June 5, 1967, box 556, folder 3, series 10/10.2, SCLC–Emory; Mrs. Victoria J. Gray Adams to Mrs. Dorothy F. Cotton, "Summary of Mississippi Activities in '67," January 5, 1968, box 567, folder 15, series 10/10.2, SCLC–Emory.

27. Robinson, quoted in Wigginton, *Refuse to Stand*, 297–301, quote on 299. Bernice Robinson resigned from Highlander effective October 31, 1963, and was listed as CEP staff in SCLC documents after this point. For resignation, see Bernice V. Robinson to Myles Horton, October 7, 1963, box 544, folder 16, series 10/10.2, SCLC–Emory. For Robinson on SCLC staff, see, for example, Citizenship Education Program, "Staff Meeting," September 16, 1964, box 544, folder 21, series 10/10.2, SCLC–Emory; Septima P. Clark, "Proposal for 1965–1970, Citizenship Education Program of Southern Christian Leadership Conference in cooperation with the Board of Homeland Ministries of the American Missionary Association," [1965], box 559, folder 2, series 10/10.2, SCLC–Emory.

28. Bernice Robinson, "Field Report for January 1966," February 16, 1966, box 545, folder 4, series 10/10.2, SCLC–Emory; Bernice Robinson, "Field Report for February 1966," [March 1966], box 545, folder 4, series 10/10.2, SCLC–Emory.

29. Honey, *To the Promised Land*, 116–117.

30. Martin Luther King Jr., "Where Do We Go from Here," August 1967, transcript accessed October 20, 2018, at the Martin Luther King, Jr., Research and Education Institute at Stanford University website, https://kinginstitute.stanford.edu/king-papers/documents/where-do-we-go-here-address-delivered-eleventh-annual-sclc-convention; King, *Where Do We Go*, 188.

31. Honey, *To the Promised Land*, 120–121; Branch, *At Canaan's Edge*, 640, 661; Fairclough, *To Redeem the Soul*, 358–359; Martin Luther King Jr., "Statement by Dr. Martin Luther King Jr.," December 4, 1967, accessed November 3, 2018, at the Civil Rights Movement Veterans website, https://www.crmvet.org/docs/6712_mlk_ppc_anc.pdf.

32. [Citizenship Education Program], "CEP Information Newsletter," December 1967, box 550, folder 20, series 10/10.2, SCLC–Emory.

33. [Southern Christian Leadership Conference], "Action Committee Meeting," February 11, 1968, box 572, folder 21, series 10/10.3, SCLC–Emory.

34. Clark interview with Hall, SOHP–UNC; Cotton, *If Your Back's Not Bent*, 194; Young, *Easy Burden*, 139.

35. [Southern Christian Leadership Conference], "Action Committee Meeting," February 11, 1968; [Citizenship Education Program], "Citizenship Education Program Bi-Annual Report," January 1968, box 559, folder 20, series 10/10.2, SCLC–Emory.

36. [Citizenship Education Program], "Citizenship Education Program Staff Meeting," June 5, 1967; [Citizenship Education Program], "List of Attending Participants—January 28th–29th, 1968," [January 1968], box 565, folder 5, series 10/10.2, SCLC–Emory; [Citizenship Education Program], "Citizenship Education Program Bi-Annual Report," January 1968.

37. Bernice Robinson, "Field Report for February–March," April 2, 1968, box 560, folder 7, series 10/10.2, SCLC–Emory; Rebecca F. Jenkins, "Report for December 31, 1968," January 7, 1969, box 568, folder 8, series 10/10.2, SCLC–Emory, an annual sum-

mary of activities for 1968; Victoria J. Gray Adams, "CEP Report for May, 1968," June 17, 1968, box 567, folder 15, series 10/10.2, SCLC-Emory.

38. Mrs. Victoria J. Gray Adams to Mrs. Dorothy F. Cotton, "Summary of Mississippi Activities in '67," January 5, 1968; Victoria J. Gray Adams to Mrs. Dorothy F. Cotton, "C.E.P. Report from January," February 14, 1968, box 567, folder 15, series 10/10.2, SCLC-Emory. This analysis draws on scholarship that roots black women's activism in their roles as mothers. See Orleck and Hazirjian, introduction to *War on Poverty*, 18–22; Orleck, *Storming Caesar's Palace*; Hamlin, *Crossroads at Clarksdale*; Tiyi M. Morris, *Womanpower Unlimited*; Naples, *Grassroots Warriors*.

39. Victoria J. Gray Adams to Mrs. Dorothy F. Cotton, "CEP Report for February–April 1968," April 25, 1968, box 567, folder 15, series 10/10.2, SCLC-Emory. Recent scholarship on War on Poverty programs documents similar patterns in local communities, where local activists confronted intransigent state and local political and economic systems that effectively blunted prospects for social justice. See Orleck and Hazirjian, *War on Poverty*; Ashmore, *Carry It On*; Orleck, *Storming Caesar's Palace*; Sanders, *Chance for Change*; de Jong, *You Can't Eat Freedom*.

40. [Citizenship Education Program], "CEP Information Letter," January 1967, box 550, folder 20, series 10/10.2, SCLC-Emory.

41. "County Water Supply Issue Raised by Ogeecheeton Trio," *Savannah Morning News*, April 12, 1968, 12B and 6B, woman's quotes on 6B; "hand pump" in Editorial, "Give Ogeecheeton Water," *Savannah Morning News*, April 14, 1968, 4B; "Ogeecheeton Razing Part of Project," *Savannah Morning News*, September 7, 1968; [Citizenship Education Program], CEP Information Newsletter, January 1967.

42. Honey, *Going Down Jericho Road*, chapters 13, 14, and 19; Bernice V. Robinson, "Field Report for April-May-June 11th," June 17, 1968, box 560, folder 7, series 10/10.2, SCLC-Emory; Cotton, *If Your Back's Not Bent*, 264–266.

43. "Sporadic Outbursts in the City," *Savannah Morning News*, April 5, 1968; "City Holds Curfew; Chiefs Urge Calm," *Savannah Morning News*, April 6, 1968; Barbara Dlugozima, "Open Doors to All: Toomey," *Savannah Morning News*, April 8, 1968; Victoria J. Gray Adams to Mrs. Dorothy F. Cotton, "CEP Report for February-April, 1968," April 25, 1968, box 567, folder 15, series 10/10.2, SCLC-Emory.

44. Mary Ellen Gale, "'We Are Going to Washington,'" *Southern Courier*, April 13–14, 1968. For SCLC's leadership succession agreements, see Branch, *At Canaan's Edge*, 197–198.

45. Mrs. [Rosa] Robinson to Mrs. [Dorothy] Cotton, February 1, 1969, box 569, folder 19, series 10/10.2, SCLC-Emory; [Southern Christian Leadership Conference], "Final Plans for the Washington Poor People's Campaign," n.d., box 572, folder 30, series 10/10.3, SCLC-Emory; Robinson, "Field Report for April-May-June 11th," June 17, 1968.

46. Young, *Easy Burden*, 481–485, quotation on 481; John Creighton, "Chaos in PPC," *Southern Courier*, June 15–16, 1968; Peake, *Keeping the Dream Alive*, 238–242.

47. "Floyd to Present Grant Application," *Savannah Morning News*, April 12, 1968; "Application to the Department of Housing and Urban Development for a Grant to Plan a Comprehensive Model Cities Program," April 15, 1968, box: Model Cities Reports, 1966–73, Georgia, GA 10–14, folder: GA 14 Savannah, General Records of the Depart-

ment of Housing and Urban Development, RG 207, NAACP, neighborhood boundaries on pp. 2–3 in part 2A.

48. Mrs. Rebecca Jenkins to Mr. Hosea L. Williams, "Report Daily," January 31, 1969, box 568, folder 8, series 10/10.2, SCLC-Emory; Mrs. Rebecca Jenkins to Mr. Hosea L. Williams, "Report Daily," February 28, 1969, box 568, folder 8, series 10/10.2, SCLC-Emory; Alma Middleton, "Citizenship School Monthly Attendance and Record Sheet," February 4, 1969, box 569, folder 9, series 10/10.2, SCLC-Emory; Bernice J. Green to Director, May 6, 1969, box 567, folder 16, series 10/10.2, SCLC-Emory.

49. "7 Are Named to Newberry EOC," *Greenville (SC) News*, January 22, 1966, 3; [VOLT], "Official Report of On-Site Findings, Newberry-Saluda Community Action, Inc., Newberry, South Carolina, CG-3223," March 19–21, 1969, box 11 of 20, folder: SC 3223-Newberry-Saluda Community Action, Inc., accession number 4NN-381-90-137, Community Action/Anti-Poverty Programs, Anti-Poverty Program Evaluation, Office of Economic Opportunity, National Archives and Records Administration, Southeast Region, Morrow (hereafter cited as NARA-SE). For teachers and students, see [Citizenship Education Program], "Participants at the August 19–23rd, 1963 Workshop at Dorchester," [August 1963], box 565, folder 1, series 10/10.2, SCLC-Emory; Mrs. Septima P. Clark, "Saturday, February 16th, 1963," [February 1963], box 559, folder 17, series 10/10.2, SCLC-Emory.

50. Vennie Reed to Dorothy F. Cotton, December 20, 1968, box 569, folder 17, series 10/10.2, SCLC-Emory; [VOLT], "Official Report of On-Site Findings, Newberry-Saluda Community Action, Inc."

51. Mrs. Marie Epps to the Staff, January 21, 1969, box 567, folder 5, series 10/10.2, SCLC-Emory; Marie Epps, "Citizenship School Monthly Attendance and Record Sheet," May 6, 1969, box 567, folder 5, series 10/10.2, SCLC-Emory.

52. Vennie Reed, "Citizenship School Monthly Attendance and Record Sheet," September 8, 1969, and May 1969, box 569, folder 17, series 10/10.2, SCLC-Emory.

53. Mrs. [Rosa] Robinson to Mrs. [Dorothy] Cotton, February 1, 1969, box 569, folder 19, series 10/10.2, SCLC-Emory.

54. Mrs. [Rosa] Robinson to Mrs. [Dorothy] Cotton, April 18, 1969, box 569, folder 19, series 10/10.2, SCLC-Emory; Blondell Conley, "Citizenship School Monthly Attendance and Record Sheet," March 19, 1969, box 566, folder 2, series 10/10.2, SCLC-Emory. Quotes about center from Robinson.

55. Ralph David Abernathy to Dr. Leslie Dunbar, September 20, 1968, box 553, folder 3, series 10/10.2, SCLC-Emory; Leslie W. Dunbar to Dr. Ralph David Abernathy, October 11, 1968, box 553, folder 3, series 10/10.2, SCLC-Emory.

56. Dorothy F. Cotton to the Rockefeller Foundation, January 28, 1969, box 553, folder 3, series 10/10.2, SCLC-Emory; [Dorothy Cotton], "Proposal for the Citizenship Education Program of the United Church Board for Homeland Ministries, Southern Christian Leadership Conference," [1969], box 559, folder 1, series 10/10.2, SCLC-Emory. In January and February 1969, Cotton sent the same form letter, proposal, and budget to Mary Reynolds Babcock Foundation, Carnegie Corporation, New World Foundation, Norman Fund, and Charles E. Merrill Trust.

57. Wesley A. Hotchkiss to Mrs. Dorothy Cotton, January 22, 1969, box 553, folder 3,

series 10/10.2, SCLC-Emory; Leland DeVinney to Ms. Cotton, February 26, 1969, box 553, folder 3, series 10/10.2, SCLC-Emory. Letters from the other five foundations follow the same pattern as this quoted letter.

58. Dorothy F. Cotton to Mrs. Bernice Green, February 12, 1969, box 567, folder 16, series 10/10.2, SCLC-Emory. Cotton sent similar letters to active teachers. Bernice J. Green to Director, May 6, 1969, box 567, folder 16, series 10/10.2, SCLC-Emory; Mrs. Ruth Mallard to Mrs. Dorothy T. Cotton, May 7, 1969, box 569, folder 3, series 10/10.2, SCLC-Emory, emphasis in original.

59. Dorothy F. Cotton to Dr. Wesley A. Hotchkiss, March 5, 1969, box 553, folder 3, series 10/10.2, SCLC-Emory; Nelson A. Rockefeller to Dr. Hotchkiss, May 20, 1969, box 553, folder 3, series 10/10.2, SCLC-Emory.

Epilogue

1. Andrew J. Young to Ralph David Abernathy, President, SCLC; Board of Directors, SCLC; SCLC Executive Staff, August 13, 1969, box 177, folder 20, series 3/3.2, SCLC-Emory; Peake, *Keeping the Dream Alive*, 265–266. For strike, see Estes, *Charleston in Black and White*, 22–34.

2. Peake, *Keeping the Dream Alive*, 259–261.

3. Faulkenberry, *Poll Power*, 118–123.

4. Peake, *Keeping the Dream Alive*, 269–276.

5. [Citizenship Education Program], "Workshop Participants, Dorchester Center," April 27–May 1, 1970, box 565, folder 5, series 10/10.2, SCLC-Emory.

6. Southern Christian Leadership Conference, "A Proposal for General Assistance," September 1971, box 205, folder 11, series 4/4.3, SCLC-Emory.

7. Documents show Ponder leaving in spring 1967. A February 1969 memorandum suggests that she returned to the SCLC. Her final departure date is not recorded. In a 1976 interview with Clark, Eugene Walker commented that Ponder lived in Atlanta, but "she won't answer the door." See [Citizenship Education Program], "Citizenship Education Program Banquet," October 27, 1966, box 106, folder 5, HRECEP-WHS; [Southern Christian Leadership Conference], "North and South: SCLC Staff News," March 1967, box 5(1), folder 5, BVRP-ARC; Annell [Ponder] to Dorothy [Cotton], February 11, 1969, box 560, folder 8, series 10/10.2, SCLC-Emory; Clark interview with Walker, SOHP-UNC.

8. Victoria J. Gray Adams, "CEP Report for May 1968, Temporary Resignation as Community Coordinator," June 8, 1968, box 567, folder 15, series 10/10.2, SCLC-Emory; Young, *Easy Burden*, 507–520; Clark, *Ready from Within*, 120–121; Charron, *Freedom's Teacher*, 345–347; Bernice Robinson to Leslie Dunbar, August 31, 1970, box 10, folder 3, BVRP-ARC; "Bernice V. Robinson Announces Her Candidacy for the S.C. State House of Representatives from Charleston County," [1972], box 13, folder 7, BVRP-ARC; Cotton, *If Your Back's Not Bent*, 276–277.

9. Workshop attendance figures compiled from attendance rosters from December 1961 to April 1970, archived in box 565, folders 1–5, series 10/10.2, SCLC-Emory. For cumulative class and student figures, see [Citizenship Education Program], "Citizenship Education Program Bi-Annual Report," January 1968, box 559, folder 20, series 10/10.2,

SCLC–Emory; Septima P. Clark, "Proposal for 1965–1970," Citizenship Education Program of Southern Christian Leadership Conference in cooperation with the Board of Homeland Ministries of the American Missionary Association," [1965], box 559, folder 2, series 10/10.2, SCLC–Emory.

10. Alma Middleton, "Citizenship School Attendance and Record Sheet," reports dated April 3, 1970, and July 7, 1970, box 569, folder 9, series 10/10.2, SCLC–Emory; Eddie Lou Holloway, "Citizenship School Attendance and Record Sheet," December 9, 1969, box 569, folder 9, series 10/10.2, SCLC–Emory; Grace Salley, "Citizenship School Attendance and Record Sheet," June 5, 1969, box 569, folder 9, series 10/10.2, SCLC–Emory; Vennie Reed, "Citizenship School Attendance and Record Sheet," November 6, 1969, box 569, folder 9, series 10/10.2, SCLC–Emory.

11. Ceola Hollis, "Citizenship School Monthly Attendance and Record Sheet," reports dated November 7, 1969, October 8, 1969, July 2, 1969, and August 5, 1970, box 567, folder 25, series 10/10.2, SCLC–Emory; Josefina B. Harvin, "Citizenship School Monthly Attendance and Record Sheet," May 12, 1970, box 567, folder 19, series 10/10.2, SCLC–Emory; Josefina B. Harvin, "Citizenship School Monthly Attendance and Record Sheet," March 6, 1970, box 567, folder 19, series 10/10.2, SCLC–Emory.

12. Thomas C. Cothran, "Wagener Woman Wins Her Diploma," *Aiken (SC) Standard and Review*, clipping sent with Holloway report, received by CEP on June 5, 1969, box 567, folder 26, series 10/10.2, SCLC–Emory; "14 Receive High School Equivalency Certificates," *Hattiesburg (MS) American*, April 20, 1970.

13. Oldendorf, "Highlander Folk School," 105–106; Charron, *Freedom's Teacher*, 347; Ealey Forrest interview, in author's possession; Rhynes Morrison interview, in author's possession; Tim Weiner, "Victoria Gray Adams, Civil Rights Leader, Is Dead at 79," *New York Times*, August 19, 2006; Nikki Davis Maute, "Freedom Summer Trail offers Glimpse of History," *Hattiesburg (MS) American*, March 25, 2004. For interpretations emphasizing CEP teachers' public service as evidence of lasting legacy, see Charron, *Freedom's Teacher*, chapter 9 and epilogue; Oldendorf, "Highlander Folk School," 101–111.

14. Clark, *Ready from Within*, 120–121; Charron, *Freedom's Teacher*, 345–347.

15. Bernice Robinson to Leslie Dunbar; "Bernice V. Robinson Announces Her Candidacy." In this cover letter, Robinson informed Dunbar that she was employed with the South Carolina Commission for Farm Workers as supervisor for the VISTA program.

16. Cotton, *If Your Back's Not Bent*, 276–277; Young, *Easy Burden*, 507–520.

17. Robinson, quoted in Wigginton, *Refuse to Stand*, 368–369.

Bibliography

Manuscript Collections

Adams, Victoria Gray. Papers. University of Southern Mississippi, Hattiesburg.
Clark, Septima Poinsette. Papers. Avery Research Center for the Study of African American History and Culture, Charleston.
Community Services Administration. Papers. RG 381. National Archives and Records Administration, College Park.
Community Services Administration. Papers. RG 381. National Archives and Records Administration Southeast Region, Morrow.
Department of Housing and Urban Development—Model Cities Program. Records. RG 207. National Archives and Records Administration, College Park.
Highlander Folk School Collection. Tennessee State Library and Archives, Nashville.
Highlander Research and Education Center. Papers. Social Action Collection. Wisconsin Historical Society, Madison.
Horton, Myles. Papers. Social Action Collection. Wisconsin Historical Society, Madison.
Mississippi Freedom Democratic Party. Collection. Martin Luther King, Jr. Center for Nonviolent Social Change, Atlanta.
———. Digital Collection. Wisconsin Historical Society, Madison.
Mississippi State Sovereignty Commission. Papers. Mississippi Department of Archives and History. http://mdah.state.ms.us/arlib/contents/er/sovcom/.
Model Cities Program. Records. National Archives and Records Administration Southeast Region, Morrow.
National Association for the Advancement of Colored People (NAACP). Papers [microfilm]. Athens-Clarke County Public Library, Athens.
Robinson, Bernice Violanthe. Papers. Avery Research Center for the Study of African American History and Culture, Charleston.
Southern Christian Leadership Conference. Collection. Martin Luther King, Jr. Center for Nonviolent Social Change, Atlanta.
———. Collection. Emory University, Atlanta.
Student Non-Violent Coordinating Committee. Collection. Martin Luther King, Jr. Center for Nonviolent Social Change, Atlanta.
———. [Microfilm]. Auburn Avenue Research Library, Atlanta.
Voter Education Project. Papers. Southern Regional Council Collection [microfilm]. Atlanta University Library, Atlanta.

Interviews

Adams, Victoria Gray. Interview with Charles Bolton. June 5, 1999. Recording in Oral History Digital Collections. University of Southern Mississippi Libraries, Hattiesburg.
Bailey, Charles L. Interview by author. December 15, 2005.
Baxter McGee, Willie. Interview by author. August 11, 2006.
Block, Margaret. Interview by author. August 7, 2006.
Bryan, Viola. Interview with J. Herman Blake. August 1967. Transcript in J. Herman Blake and Emily L. Moore. Papers. Emory University Library, Atlanta.
Clark, Septima Poinsette. Interview with Jacquelyn Dowd Hall. July 25, 1976. Recording and transcript in Southern Oral History Project. University of North Carolina Library, Chapel Hill.
———. Interview with Peter H. Wood. February 3, 1981. Recording and transcript in Southern Oral History Project. University of North Carolina Library, Chapel Hill.
———. Interview with Eugene Walker. July 30, 1976. Recording and transcript in Southern Oral History Project. University of North Carolina Library, Chapel Hill.
Connor, Peggy Jean. Interview with Richard Conville. September 11, 2001. Transcript in Oral History Digital Collections. University of Southern Mississippi Libraries, Hattiesburg.
Cooper, Neloweze. Interview by author. April 18, 2007.
Ealey Forrest, Pearlie Inez. Interview by author. March 15, 2006.
Gray, Victoria Jackson. Interview with KZSU Project South. 1965. Recording in Stanford University Library, Stanford.
Hagan, Booker T. Interview with author. December 15, 2005.
Hamer, Fannie Lou. Interview with KZSU Project South. 1965. Recording in Stanford University Library, Stanford.
Jenkins, Esau. Interview with Guy and Candie Carawan. 1963. Recording in Guy and Candie Carawan Collection #20008. Southern Folklife Collection. Wilson Library, University of North Carolina, Chapel Hill. https://finding-aids.lib.unc.edu/20008/#d1e534.
Johnson, Otis S. Interview with author. November 30, 2005.
Ladner, Dorie, and Joyce Ladner. Interview with Joseph Mosnier. September 20, 2011. Recording and transcript in Civil Rights Oral History Project Collection. Library of Congress Archive of Folk Culture, American Folklife Center. http://hdl.loc.gov/loc.afc/folklife.home.
Law, Westley Wallace. Interview with Clifford Kuhn and Tim Crimmins. November 15, 1990. Recording and transcript in Georgia Government Document Project Collection. Georgia State University Library, Atlanta.
Lockwood Romasco, Anne. Interview with author. October 1, 2006.
Rhynes Morrison, Greta. Interview with author. March 15, 2006.
Turnbow, Hartman. Interview with Susan Lorenzi Sojourner. N.d. Transcript in Oral History Digital Collections. University of Southern Mississippi Libraries, Hattiesburg.
Watkins, Hollis. Interview with John Rachal. October 30, 1995. Transcript in Oral History Digital Collections. University of Southern Mississippi Libraries, Hattiesburg.

Wine, Alice. Interview with Guy and Candie Carawan. 1963. Recording in Guy and Candie Carawan Collection #20008. Southern Folklife Collection. Wilson Library, University of North Carolina, Chapel Hill. https://finding-aids.lib.unc.edu/20008/#d1e534.

Wine, Alice and Isabel Simmons. Interview with Guy and Candie Carawan. 1960. Recording in Guy and Candie Carawan Collection, #20008. Southern Folklife Collection. Wilson Library, University of North Carolina-Chapel Hill. https://dc.lib.unc.edu/cdm/singleitem/collection/sfc/id/49484/rec/1.

Published Sources

Adams, Frank, with Myles Horton. *Unearthing Seeds of Fire: The Idea of Highlander.* Winston-Salem, N.C.: John Blair Publishing, 1975.

Adickes, Sandra. *The Legacy of a Freedom School.* New York: Palgrave Macmillan, 2005.

Anderson, James D. *The Education of Blacks in the South, 1860–1935.* Chapel Hill: University of North Carolina Press, 1988.

Arsenault, Raymond. *Freedom Riders: 1961 and the Struggle for Racial Justice.* New York: Oxford University Press, 2006.

Ashmore, Susan Youngblood. *Carry It On: The War on Poverty and the Civil Rights Movement in Alabama, 1964–1972.* Athens: University of Georgia Press, 2008.

———. "Going Back to Selma." In Orleck and Hazirjian, *War on Poverty,* 308–333.

Barkley-Brown, Elsa. "Negotiating and Transforming the Public Sphere: African American Public Life in the Transition from Slavery to Freedom." *Public Culture* 7 (1994): 107–146.

Barnett, Bernice McNair. "Invisible Southern Black Women Leaders in the Civil Rights Movement." *Gender and Society* 7 (June 1993): 162–182.

Bolster, Paul D. "Civil Rights Movements in Twentieth Century Georgia." Ph.D. diss., University of Georgia, 1972.

Bolton, Charles C. *The Hardest Deal of All: The Battle over School Integration in Mississippi, 1870–1980.* Jackson: University Press of Mississippi, 2007.

Boyte, Harry. "The Dorchester Center: An Interview with Dorothy Cotton, 1991." Center for Democracy and Citizenship, http://www.publicwork.org/pdf/interviews.

Branch, Taylor. *At Canaan's Edge: America in the King Years, 1965–68.* New York: Simon & Schuster, 2006.

———. *Parting the Waters: America in the King Years, 1954–1963.* New York: Simon & Schuster, 1988.

———. *Pillar of Fire: America in the King Years, 1963–65.* New York: Simon & Schuster, 1998.

Brown, Elsa Barkley. "Negotiating and Transforming the Public Sphere: African American Political Life in the Transition from Slavery to Freedom." *Public Culture* 7 (Fall 1994): 107–146.

Brown-Nagin, Tomiko. *Courage to Dissent: Atlanta and the Long History of the Civil Rights Movement.* New York: Oxford University Press, 2011.

Carawan, Guy, and Candie Carawan, eds. *Ain't You Got a Right to the Tree of Life? The People of Johns Island, South Carolina—Their Faces, Their Words and Their Songs.* Athens: University of Georgia Press, 1989.

Carmichael, Stokely, and Charles V. Hamilton. *Black Power: The Politics of Liberation in America*. New York: Random House, 1967.

Carson, Clayborne, ed. *The Student Voice, 1960–1965: Periodical of the Student Non-Violent Coordinating Committee*. London: Westport, 1990.

Charron, Katherine Mellen. "Teaching Citizenship: Septima Poinsette Clark and the Transformation of the African-American Freedom Struggle." Ph.D. diss., Yale University, 2005.

———. *Freedom's Teacher: The Life of Septima Clark*. Chapel Hill: University of North Carolina Press, 2009.

Chirhart, Ann Short. *Torches of Light: Georgia Teachers and the Coming of the New South*. Athens: University of Georgia Press, 2005.

Clark, Septima. *Echo in My Soul*. New York: E. P. Dutton & Co., 1962.

Clark, Septima, with Cynthia Stokes Brown. *Ready from Within: A First Person Narrative*. Trenton, NJ: Africa World Press, 1990.

Cobb, James C. *The Most Southern Place on Earth: The Mississippi Delta and the Roots of Regional Identity*. New York: Oxford University Press, 1992.

Collier-Thomas, Bettye. *Jesus, Jobs, and Justice: African American Women and Religion*. New York: Alfred A. Knopf, 2010.

Collier-Thomas, Bettye, and V. P. Franklin, eds. *Sisters in the Struggle: African-American Women in the Civil Rights–Black Power Movement*. New York: New York University Press, 2001.

Cooper, Melissa. *Making Gullah: A History of Sapelo Islanders, Race, and the American Imagination*. Chapel Hill: University of North Carolina Press, 2017.

Cotton, Dorothy F. *If Your Back's Not Bent: The Role of the Citizenship Education Program in the Civil Rights Movement*. New York: Atria Books, 2012.

Crawford, Vicki. "African American Women in the Mississippi Freedom Democratic Party." In Collier-Thomas and Franklin, *Sisters in the Struggle*, 121–138.

———. "'Be Ye Doers of the Word, Not Just Hearers Only': Faith and Politics in the Life of Victoria Gray Adams." *CrossCurrents* 57 (Summer 2007): 170–179.

Crawford, Vicki L., Jacqueline A. Rouse, and Barbara Woods, eds. *Women in the Civil Rights Movement: Trailblazers and Torchbearers, 1941–1965*. Bloomington: Indiana University Press, 1990.

Crosby, Emilye. *A Little Taste of Freedom: The Black Freedom Struggle in Claiborne County, Mississippi*. Chapel Hill: University of North Carolina Press, 2005.

Crosby, Emilye, ed. *Civil Rights History from the Ground Up: Local Struggles, a National Movement*. Athens: University of Georgia Press, 2011.

Daniel, Pete. *Dispossession: Discrimination against African American Farmers in the Age of Civil Rights*. Chapel Hill: University of North Carolina Press, 2013.

Danielson, Michael N., and Patricia R. F. Danielson. *Profits and Politics in Paradise: The Development of Hilton Head Island*. Columbia: University of South Carolina Press, 1995.

de Jong, Greta. *You Can't Eat Freedom: Southerners and Social Justice after the Civil Rights Movement*. Chapel Hill: University of North Carolina Press, 2016.

DeMuth, Jerry. "Tired of Being Sick and Tired." *Nation* 198 (June 1964): 548–551.

Dittmer, John. *Black Georgia in the Progressive Era, 1900–1920*. Urbana: University of Illinois Press, 1980.
———. *Local People: The Struggle for Civil Rights in Mississippi*. Urbana: University of Illinois Press, 1994.
Drago, Edmund L. *Initiative, Paternalism, and Race Relations: Charleston's Avery Normal Institute*. Athens: University of Georgia Press, 1990.
Draper, Alan. "Class and Politics in the Mississippi Movement: An Analysis of the Mississippi Freedom Democratic Party Delegation." *Journal of Southern History* 82 (May 2016): 269–304.
Erenrich, Susie, ed. *Freedom Is a Constant Struggle: An Anthology of the Mississippi Civil Rights Movement*. Montgomery, AL: Black Belt Press, 1999.
Eskew, Glenn T. *But for Birmingham: The Local and National Movements in the Civil Rights Struggle*. Chapel Hill: University of North Carolina Press, 1997.
Estes, Steve. *Charleston in Black and White: Race and Power in the South after the Civil Rights Movement*. Chapel Hill: University of North Carolina Press, 2015.
———. *I Am a Man! Race, Manhood, and the Civil Rights Movement*. Chapel Hill: University of North Carolina Press, 2005.
Fairclough, Adam. *A Class of Their Own: Black Teachers in the Segregated South*. Cambridge, MA: Harvard University Press, 2007.
———. *To Redeem the Soul of America: The Southern Christian Leadership Conference and Martin Luther King, Jr.* Athens: University of Georgia Press, 1987.
Faulkenberry, Evan. *Poll Power: The Voter Education Project and the Movement for the Ballot in the American South*. Chapel Hill: University of North Carolina Press, 2019.
Fields, Mamie Garvin, with Karen Fields. *Lemon Swamp and Other Places: A Carolina Memoir*. New York: Free Press, 1983.
Fleming, Cynthia Griggs. *In the Shadow of Selma: The Continuing Struggle for Civil Rights in the Rural South*. New York: Rowman & Littlefield, 2004.
Folwell, Emma. *The War on Poverty in Mississippi: From Massive Resistance to New Conservatism*. Jackson: University Press of Mississippi, 2020.
Ford, Tanisha C. *Liberated Threads: Black Women, Style, and the Global Politics of Soul*. Chapel Hill: University of North Carolina Press, 2015.
Franson, Jerome. "Citizenship Education in the South Carolina Sea Islands, 1954–1966." Ph.D. diss., Vanderbilt University, 1977.
Fraser, Walter J., Jr. *Charleston! Charleston! The History of a Southern City*. Columbia: University of South Carolina Press, 1992.
———. *Savannah in the New South: From the Civil War to the Twenty-First Century*. Columbia: University of South Carolina Press, 2018.
Frederickson, Kari. *The Dixiecrat Revolt and the End of the Solid South, 1932–1968*. Chapel Hill: University of North Carolina Press, 2001.
Gaines, Kevin K. *Uplifting the Race: Black Leadership, Politics, and Culture in the Twentieth Century*. Chapel Hill: University of North Carolina Press, 1996.
Garrow, David J. *Bearing the Cross: Martin Luther King, Jr., and the Southern Christian Leadership Conference*. New York: Random House, 1986.
Germany, Kent. *New Orleans after the Promises: Poverty, Citizenship, and the Search for the Great Society*. Athens: University of Georgia Press, 2007.

Giddings, Paula. *When and Where I Enter: The Impact of Black Women on Race and Sex in America*. New York: William Morrow & Company, 1984.
Gilkes, Cheryl Townsend. *If It Wasn't for the Women: Black Women's Experience and Womanist Culture in Church and Community*. New York: Orbis Books, 2001.
Gill, Tiffany M. *Beauty Shop Politics: African American Women's Activism in the Beauty Industry*. Urbana: University of Illinois Press, 2010.
Gillette, Michael L. *Launching the War on Poverty: An Oral History*. New York: Oxford University Press, 2010.
Gilmore, Glenda Elizabeth. *Defying Dixie: The Radical Roots of Civil Rights, 1919–1950*. New York: W. W. Norton, 2008.
———. *Gender and Jim Crow: Women and the Politics of White Supremacy in North Carolina, 1896–1920*. Chapel Hill: University of North Carolina Press, 1996.
Gitin, Maria. *This Bright Light of Ours: Stories from the 1965 Voting Rights Fight*. Tuscaloosa: University of Alabama Press, 2014.
Gomez, Michael A. *Exchanging Our Country Marks: The Transformation of African Identities in the Colonial and Antebellum South*. Chapel Hill: University of North Carolina Press, 1998.
Grady-Wills, Winston A. *Challenging U.S. Apartheid: Atlanta and Black Struggles for Human Rights, 1960–1977*. Durham, N.C.: Duke University Press, 2006.
Graves, Brian. "Between 'Preservation' and 'Progress': A Cultural History of Gullah Landownership and Commercial Development on James Island, SC." *Southern Studies* 18 (Fall/Winter 2011): 66–86.
Green, Laurie B. *Battling the Plantation Mentality: Memphis and the Black Freedom Struggle*. Chapel Hill: University of North Carolina Press, 2007.
Greene, Christina. *Our Separate Ways: Women and the Black Freedom Movement in Durham, North Carolina*. Chapel Hill: University of North Carolina Press, 2005.
Hale, Jon N. "Early Pedagogical Influences on the Mississippi Freedom Schools." *American Educational History Journal* 34 (2007): 315–329.
———. *The Freedom Schools: Student Activists in the Mississippi Civil Rights Movement*. New York: Columbia University Press, 2016.
Hall, Jacquelyn Dowd. "The Long Civil Rights Movement and the Political Uses of the Past." *Journal of American History* 91 (2005): 1233–1263.
Hamlin, Françoise N. *Crossroads at Clarksdale: The Black Freedom Struggle in the Mississippi Delta after World War II*. Chapel Hill: University of North Carolina Press, 2012.
Harrington, Michael. *The Other America: Poverty in the United States*. New York: Macmillan, 1962.
Harris, Leslie M., and Daina Ramey Berry, eds. *Slavery and Freedom in Savannah*. Athens: University of Georgia Press, 2014.
Harwell, Debbie Z. *Wednesdays in Mississippi: Proper Ladies Working for Radical Change, Freedom Summer, 1964*. Oxford: University of Mississippi Press, 2014.
Herd-Clark, Dawn. "Dorchester Academy: The American Missionary Association in Liberty County, Georgia, 1867–1950." Ph.D. diss., University of Florida, 1999.
Hersh, Jenny, and Sallie Ann Robinson. *Daufuskie Island*. Charleston: Arcadia Publishing, 2018.

Higginbotham, Evelyn Brooks. *Righteous Discontent: The Women's Movement in the Black Baptist Church, 1880–1920.* Cambridge, MA: Harvard University Press, 1993.

Holland, Endesha Ida Mae. *From the Mississippi Delta: A Memoir.* Chicago: Lawrence Hill Books, 1997.

Holsaert, Faith S., Martha Prescod Norman Noonan, Judy Richardson, Betty Garman Robinson, Jean Smith Young, and Dorothy M. Zellner, eds. *Hands on the Freedom Plow: Personal Accounts for Women in SNCC.* Urbana: University of Illinois Press, 2010.

Honey, Michael K. *Going Down Jericho Road: The Memphis Strike, Martin Luther King's Last Campaign.* New York: W. W. Norton, 2007.

———. *To the Promised Land: Martin Luther King and the Fight for Economic Justice.* New York: W. W. Norton, 2018.

Horton, Aimee Isgrig. *The Highlander Folk School: A History of Its Major Programs, 1932–1961.* Brooklyn, N.Y.: Carlson Publishing, 1989.

Horton, Myles, and Paulo Freire. *We Make the Road by Walking: Conversations on Education and Social Change.* Philadelphia: Temple University Press, 1990.

Horton, Myles, with Judith and Herbert Kohl. *The Long Haul: An Autobiography.* New York: Teachers College Press, 1998.

Jeffries, Hasan Kwame. *Bloody Lowndes: Civil Rights and Black Power in Alabama's Black Belt.* New York: New York University Press, 2009.

Jones, Jacqueline. *Labor of Love, Labor of Sorrow: Black Women, Work and the Family, from Slavery to the Present.* New York: Basic Books, 1985.

Jones-Branch, Cherisse. *Crossing the Line: Women's Interracial Activism in South Carolina during and after World War II.* Gainesville: University Press of Florida, 2014.

Jones-Jackson, Patricia. *When Roots Die: Endangered Traditions on the Sea Islands.* Athens: University of Georgia Press, 1989.

Joyner, Charles. *Down by the Riverside: A South Carolina Slave Community.* Urbana: University of Illinois Press, 1984.

Kahrl, Andrew W. *The Land Was Ours: African American Beaches from Jim Crow to the Sunbelt South.* Cambridge, MA: Harvard University Press, 2012.

Katagiri, Yasuhiro. *The Mississippi State Sovereignty Commission: Civil Rights and States' Rights.* Jackson: University of Mississippi Press, 2001.

Kelley, Robin D. G. "'We Are Not What We Seem': Rethinking Black Working-Class Opposition in the Jim Crow South." *Journal of American History* 80 (June 1993): 75–112.

King, Martin Luther, Jr. *Where Do We Go from Here: Chaos or Community?* Boston: Beacon Press, 1967.

Lau, Peter. *Democracy Rising: South Carolina and the Fight for Black Equality since 1865.* Lexington: University Press of Kentucky, 2006.

Lee, Chana Kai. *For Freedom's Sake: The Life of Fannie Lou Hamer.* Urbana: University of Illinois Press, 1999.

Levine, David P. "The Birth of Citizenship Schools: Entwining the Struggles of Literacy and Freedom." *History of Education Quarterly* 44 (2004): 388–414.

———. "Citizenship Schools." Ph.D. diss., University of Wisconsin–Madison, 1999.

———. "Learning for Liberation: The Citizenship Education Program and the Freedom Struggle." *American Educational History Journal* 38 (2011): 75–92.

Lewis, John, with Michael D'Orso. *Walking with the Wind: A Memoir of the Movement*. New York: Simon & Schuster, 1998.

Ling, Peter. "Local Leadership in the Early Civil Rights Movement: The South Carolina Citizenship Education Program of the Highlander Folk School." *Journal of American Studies* 29 (1995): 399–422.

Ling, Peter J., and Sharon Monteith, eds. *Gender and the Civil Rights Movement*. New Brunswick, NJ: Rutgers University Press, 2004.

Littlefield, Valinda W. "'I Am Only One, but I Am One': Southern African-American Women Schoolteachers, 1884–1954." Ph.D. diss., University of Illinois–Urbana-Champaign, 2003.

Martin, Gordon A., Jr. *Count Them One by One: Black Mississippians Fighting for the Right to Vote*. Jackson: University Press of Mississippi, 2010.

McCarty, Clinton. *The Reins of Power: Racial Change and Challenge in a Southern County*. Tallahassee: Sentry Press, 1999.

McDonald, Laughlin. *A Voting Rights Odyssey: Black Enfranchisement in Georgia*. New York: Cambridge University Press, 2003.

McGuire, Danielle L. *At the Dark End of the Street: Black Women, Rape, and Resistance—a New History of the Civil Rights Movement from Rosa Parks to the Rise of Black Power*. New York: Random House, 2010.

McMillen, Neil. *Dark Journey: Black Mississippians in the Age of Jim Crow*. Urbana: University of Illinois Press, 1990.

McRae, Elizabeth Gillespie. *Mothers of Massive Resistance: White Women and the Politics of White Supremacy*. New York: Oxford University Press, 2018.

Mills, Kay. *This Little Light of Mine: The Life of Fannie Lou Hamer*. New York: E. P. Dutton, 1993.

Morris, Aldon D. *The Origins of the Civil Rights Movement: Black Communities Organizing for Change*. New York: Free Press, 1984.

Morris, Tiyi M. *Womanpower Unlimited and the Black Freedom Struggle in Mississippi*. Athens: University of Georgia Press, 2015.

Moye, J. Todd. *Let the People Decide: Black Freedom and White Resistance Movements in Sunflower County, Mississippi, 1945–1986*. Chapel Hill: University of North Carolina Press, 2004.

Naples, Nancy A. *Grassroots Warriors: Activist Mothering, Community Work, and the War on Poverty*. New York: Routledge, 1998.

Newman, Mark. *Divine Agitators: The Delta Ministry and Civil Rights in Mississippi*. Athens: University of Georgia Press, 2004.

Ntiri, Daphne W. "Adult Literacy through a Womanist Lens: Unpacking the Radical Pedagogy of Civil Rights Era Educator, Bernice Robinson." *Journal of Black Studies* 45 (March 2014): 125–142.

Oldendorf, Sandra B. "Highlander Folk School and the South Carolina Sea Island Citizenship Schools: Implications for the Social Studies." Ph.D. diss., University of Kentucky, 1987.

———. "The South Carolina Sea Island Citizenship Schools, 1957-1961." In Crawford, et. al., *Women in the Civil Rights Movement*, 169-182.

Orleck, Annelise. *Storming Caesar's Palace: How Black Women Fought Their Own War on Poverty*. Boston: Beacon Press, 2005.
Orleck, Annelise, and Lisa Gayle Hazirjian, eds. *The War on Poverty: A New Grassroots History, 1964–1980*. Athens: University of Georgia Press, 2011.
Payne, Charles M. *I've Got the Light of Freedom: The Organizing Tradition and the Mississippi Freedom Struggle*. Berkeley: University of California Press, 1995.
Payne, Elizabeth Anne, Martha H. Swain, and Marjorie Julian Spruill, eds. *Mississippi Women: Their Histories, Their Lives*. Vol. 2. Athens: University of Georgia Press, 2010.
Peake, Thomas R. *Keeping the Dream Alive: A History of the Southern Christian Leadership Conference from King to the Nineteen-Eighties*. New York: Peter Lang, 1987.
Perman, Michael. *Struggle for Mastery: Disfranchisement in the South, 1888–1908*. Chapel Hill: University of North Carolina Press, 2001.
Powers, Bernard E. *Black Charlestonians: A Social History, 1822–1885*. Fayetteville: University of Arkansas Press, 1994.
Pratt, Robert A. *Selma's Bloody Sunday: Protest, Voting Rights, and the Struggle for Racial Equality*. Baltimore: Johns Hopkins University Press, 2017.
Price, Margaret. *The Negro and the Ballot in the South*. Atlanta: Southern Regional Council, 1959.
Raines, Howell. *My Soul Is Rested: Movement Days in the Deep South Remembered*. New York: G. P. Putnam & Sons, 1977.
Ransby, Barbara. *Ella Baker and the Black Freedom Movement: A Radical Democratic Vision*. Chapel Hill: University of North Carolina Press, 2003.
Raz, Mical. *What's Wrong with the Poor? Psychiatry, Race, and the War on Poverty*. Chapel Hill: University of North Carolina Press, 2013.
Robnett, Belinda. *How Long? How Long? African American Women in the Struggle for Civil Rights*. New York: Oxford University Press, 1997.
Roche, Jeff. *Restructured Resistance: The Sibley Commission and the Politics of Desegregation in Georgia*. Athens: University of Georgia Press, 1998.
Russell, Clare. "A Beautician without Teacher Training: Bernice Robinson, Citizenship Schools, and Women in the Civil Rights Movement." *The Sixties: A Journal of History, Politics, and Culture* 4 (2011): 31–50.
———. "More than Mrs. Robinson: Citizenship Schools in Lowcountry South Carolina and Savannah, Georgia, 1957–1970." Ph.D. diss., University of Nottingham, 2010.
———. "Upheaval in Savannah: The Protest Cycle of a 'Short' Civil Rights Movement." *Journal of Contemporary History* 47 (2012): 773–792.
Sanders, Crystal R. *A Chance for Change: Head Start and Mississippi's Black Freedom Struggle*. Chapel Hill: University of North Carolina Press, 2016.
Schulman, Bruce J. *From Cotton Belt to Sunbelt: Federal Policy, Economic Development, and the Transformation of the South, 1938–1980*. New York: Oxford University Press, 1991.
Shaw, Stephanie. *What a Woman Ought to Be and Do: Black Professional Women Workers during the Jim Crow Era*. Chicago: University of Chicago Press, 1996.
Sojourner, Sue [Lorenzi], with Cheryl Reitan. *Thunder of Freedom: Black Leadership and the Transformation of 1960s Mississippi*. Lexington: University Press of Kentucky, 2013.

Spencer, Robyn C. *The Revolution Has Come: Black Power, Gender, and the Black Panther Party in Oakland*. Durham, NC: Duke University Press, 2016.
Sturkey, William. *Hattiesburg: An American City in Black and White*. Cambridge, MA: Harvard University Press, 2019.
Sullivan, Patricia. *Days of Hope: Race and Democracy in the New Deal Era*. Chapel Hill: University of North Carolina Press, 1996.
———. *Lift Every Voice: The NAACP and the Making of the Civil Rights Movement*. New York: New Press, 2009.
Swain, Martha H., Elizabeth A. Payne, and Marjorie Julian Spruill, eds. *Mississippi Women: Their Histories, Their Lives*. Vol. 1. Athens: University of Georgia Press, 2003.
Telfair Academy of Arts and Sciences. "*. . . We Ain't What We Used to Be.*" Savannah: Telfair Academy of Arts and Sciences, 1983.
Theoharis, Jeanne. *The Rebellious Life of Mrs. Rosa Parks*. Boston: Beacon Press, 2013.
Theoharis, Jeanne, and Komozi Woodard, eds. *Freedom North: Black Freedom Struggles Outside the South, 1940–1980*. New York: Palgrave Macmillan, 2003.
———. *Groundwork: Local Black Freedom Movements in America*. New York: New York University Press, 2005.
Thornton, J. Mills. *Dividing Lines: Municipal Politics and the Struggle for Civil Rights in Montgomery, Birmingham, and Selma*. Tuscaloosa: University of Alabama Press, 2002.
Tjerandsen, Carl. *Education for Citizenship: A Foundation's Experience*. Santa Cruz: Emil Schwarzhaupt Foundation, 1980.
Tuck, Steven G. N. "'A City Too Dignified to Hate': Civic Pride, Civil Rights, and Savannah in Comparative Perspective." *Georgia Historical Quarterly* 79 (1995): 539–559.
———. *Beyond Atlanta: The Struggle for Racial Equality in Georgia, 1940–1980*. Athens: University of Georgia Press, 2001.
Tuuri, Rebecca. *Strategic Sisterhood: The National Council of Negro Women in the Black Freedom Struggle*. Chapel Hill: University of North Carolina Press, 2018.
Tyson, Timothy B. *Radio Free Dixie: Robert F. Williams and the Roots of Black Power*. Chapel Hill: University of North Carolina Press, 1999.
Umoja, Akinyele Omowale. *We Will Shoot Back: Armed Resistance in the Mississippi Freedom Movement*. New York: New York University Press, 2013.
Vinovskis, Maris A. *The Birth of Head Start: Preschool Education Policies in the Kennedy and Johnson Administrations*. Chicago: University of Chicago Press, 2005.
Wall, James Bowers. "'Settling Down for the Long Haul': The Black Freedom Movement in Southwest Georgia, 1945–1995." Ph.D. diss., University of Georgia, 2018.
Watters, Pat, and Reese Cleghorn. *Climbing Jacob's Ladder: The Arrival of Negroes in Southern Politics*. New York: Harcourt, Brace & World, 1967.
Webb, Sheyann, and Rachel West Nelson, with Frank Sikora. *Selma, Lord, Selma: Girlhood Memories of the Civil-Rights Days*. Tuscaloosa: University of Alabama Press, 1980.
White, Deborah Gray. *Too Heavy a Load: Black Women in Defense of Themselves, 1894–1994*. New York: W. W. Norton, 1999.
Williams, Heather Andrea. *Self-Taught: African American Education in Slavery and Freedom*. Chapel Hill: University of North Carolina Press, 2005.

Williams, Rhonda W. *The Politics of Public Housing: Black Women's Struggles against Urban Inequality*. New York: Oxford University Press, 2004.
Wigginton, Eliot, ed. *Refuse to Stand Silently By: An Oral History of Grass Roots Social Activism in America, 1921–64*. New York: Doubleday Publishing, 1991.
Wolcott, Victoria W. *Remaking Respectability: African American Women in Interwar Detroit*. Chapel Hill: University of North Carolina Press, 2001.
Young, Andrew. *An Easy Burden: The Civil Rights Movement and the Transformation of America*. New York: HarperCollins, 1996.

Index

Page numbers in *italics* refer to illustrations.

Abernathy, Ralph D., xi, 83, 177, 180, 183–84
Abernethy, Thomas, 142
Adams, Robert C., 49
Adams, Victoria Gray. *See* Gray, Victoria Jackson
African American women. *See* Black women
Agricultural Stabilization and Conservation Service (ASCS), 139, 154
Alabama Christian Movement for Human Rights (ACMHR), 89, 105
Alabama Democratic Conference, Inc., 157
Allen, Thomas, 85
American Missionary Association (AMA), 67, 73, 75
Anderson, H. C., 138
Anderson, Helen V., 126–27, 132, 135–36, 138, 144, 175, 186
Arnold, Carl, 122, 127
Avery Institute (Charleston), 15, 16

Baggs, Earl M., 73
Baker, Ella, xii, 47–48, 126, 202n48–49
Ball, John, 112, 113
Barber, George, 132
Baxter (McGee), Willie, 111, 144
Belle, Reba Maria, 168
Bennette, Bernita, 55
Bennette, Fred C., 210n33
Bevel, James L., 90, 130, 145, 148, 150; biography, 98–99, 119; and CEP, 98–101, 103–7, 110, 115–16; SCLC field secretary, 93, 98
Birmingham campaign (1963), 89, 105, 110, 114–15, 119–20
Black, Adell, 88

Black, Lewis, 167
Black beauty business, 2, 5, 44, 63, 116, 121; of Addie Lily, 150; of Atlean Smith, 107, 135; of Bernice Robinson, 4, 12, 13, 17–18, 27; of Mary Lee Davis, 39; of Peggy Jean Connor, 127; of Vera Mae Pigee, 97–98; of Victoria Jackson Gray, 118, 120–21, 123
Black civil rights movement, xi–xii, 2–4, 7–11, 182, 187. *See also* Birmingham campaign; Montgomery bus boycott; Selma campaign; Freedom campaigns
Blackwell, Alice, 108, 132, 135, 138–39, 144, 148
Blackwell, Randolph, 137, 165, 166
Blackwell, Robert, 105
Black women, xi–xii, 2–5, 9, 13, 187, 213n4
Bligen, Lula, 45, 201n38
Block, Margaret, 101, 128, 132
Block, Samuel T. "Sam," 101, 105, 106, 215n25
Bloody Sunday (1965), 148, 158. *See also* Selma campaign
Board of Concerned Members of Wadmalaw Island, 36
Boles, Dorothy, 89
Boynton, Amelia, 145
Bradford, Ernest M., 157
Bradshaw, Adline, 88
Branton, Wiley, 83, 90
Brewer, Allene, 36–38, *38*, 44–45, 49–50, 62–63, 106, 186
Brewer, U. L., 37
Brooks, Ethel, 170, 234n24
Brooks, John M., 55
Brown, Arthur "Joe," 18
Brown, Bettye, 108
Brown, Cisero, 90
Brown, G. C., 21

Brown, Lonnie, 147
Brown, Nancy, 147, 151, 152
Brown, Solomon, 45
Brown v. Board of Education, xi, 4, 5, 34, 43, 121
Bryan, Viola, 40, 199n19
Bryant, William, 65
Burns, Willie J., 113, 135
Butler, Minnie L., 169
Byrd, Mary Lois, 64

Calhoun, John H., 60, 205n28, 210n33
Calhoun County Improvement League, 168
Campbell, Ruth Ratliff, 126, 127, 128, 132, 134, 222n24
Carmichael, Stokely, 157, 161
Carnegie, Alma Mitchell, 112, 113, 160, 218n54
Carnegie, Charlie, 112
Carter, Dover, 59–60
Carter, James, 147
Charleston Committee for Day Care, 186
Chatham County Crusade for Voters (CCCV), 52, 55–57, 66, 70–71, 176–78, 207n4
Child Development Group of Mississippi (CDGM), 144, 169
Citizens Committee of Charleston, 168
Citizens Councils, 22, 54, 96, 102, 104
Civil Rights Act of 1964, xi, 139, 141, 153–54
Civil Rights movement. *See* Black civil rights movement
Clark, Jim, 145, 148, 150
Clark, Septima Poinsette, 3–5, 9, 13, 78, 84, 171; and Bernice Robinson, 13–14, 18–19, 25–26, 68–69; biography, 14–19, 22–23, 185, 186; on class divisions, 158–59; and CEP after Voting Rights Act, 141, 153, 160, 167–70; and CEP connection to SCLC, 47–49, 53, 67–72, 74–77, 91, 174; and CEP expansion in Alabama Black Belt, 146–47, 149–51; and CEP expansion in Mississippi, 93, 96–97; and CEP expansion in South Carolina and Alabama, 33–46, 50, 62; and CEP expansion in southeastern Georgia, 57, 62–63, 65–66, 68–71; on direct action, 137; Dorchester teacher training, 72, 74–79, 81, 122–23; and Esau Jenkins, 12, 19, 24–25; health, 66, 165; and Freedom Schools, 131–32; Highlander, first connections with, 23–27, 30–32; jailed, 43–44; Johns Island Citizenship School, 26–27; and Myles Horton, 24–26, 50, 200n24; and SCOPE, 229n42; teaching methods, 29–31, 33, 39–42, 62–63, 65, 153; Viola Bryan on, 199n19
Collier, Henry M., 203n9
Committee of One Hundred, 127
Community Action Agency, South Carolina (CAA), 179
Confederation of Alabama's Political Organizations (COAPO), 157
Congress of Industrial Organizations (CIO), 23
Congress of Racial Equality (CORE), 82, 93, 105–6, 117, 125, 152, 161
Conley, Blondell, 180
Connor, Peggy Jean, 126–28, 132, 136, 138, 144, 160, 186
Cooks, Stoney, 184
Cooper, Annie Lee, 150–51, 156, 158–59, 229n37
Cooper, Evans B., 205n25
Cooper, Neloweze, 205n25
Cotton, Dorothy F., 78, 84, 170, 233n10; and Alice Blackwell, 138; biography, 74, 186, 229n42; CEP administrative work, 81, 122, 129, 137, 166; CEP expansion efforts, 75–76, 91, 93, 96–97, 146–47; CEP, head of, 163–67, 179, 180–82, 184–85, 237n56; and gender bias, 9, 174; and Martin Luther King, Jr., 74, 120, 164, 166, 173, 177; and MFDP, 160; and Saint Augustine direct action campaign, 137; and Savannah direct action campaign, 90; SCLC liaison to CEP, 74; and Septima Clark, 74–75; singing, 74, 77, 97; teaching philosophy, 1, 77–78, 167, 169, 176; on Vera Mae Pigee, 97; and Winona assaults, 115, 219n66
Council of Federated Organizations (COFO), 157, 224n54; establishment of, 93, 118–19; Freedom Summer, 131–35, 137, 139, 152; Freedom Vote, 119, 123, 125–28, 139; in Greenwood, MS, 105–7, 118; splintering of, 119, 138, 140, 143
Crawford, Vicki, 123
Crusade for Citizenship, 47–48
Current, Gloster, 206n44

Daise, Tony, 45
Dallas County Economic Employment Opportunity Committee (DCEEOC), 157
Dallas County Independent Free Voters Organization (DCIFVO), 158
Dallas County Voters League (DCVL), 145, 158
Daniels, Jonathan, 155
Davis, Celeste, 99, 100, 106
Davis, Eloise, 113
Davis, Lenard, 99, 100
Davis, Mary Lee, 39, 97
Davis, Patt J., 158
Davis, Rosie Mae, 155–56
Democratic Party, 48, 136, 138, 165; Democratic National Convention, 4, 18, 119, 136, 140; Democratic primaries, 18, 60, 193n24. *See also* Mississippi Freedom Democratic Party (MFDP); Progressive Democratic Party (PDP)
Dennis, Dave, 105
Devine, Annie, 138, 160, 161
Diggs, Mary, 128
Doar, John, 128
Dorchester Center, 78, 83, 119, 168, 229n37, 229n43; and CEP in Alabama, 145, 156; CEP move to, 67–69, 72, 74–76, 80–81; and CEP in Mississippi, 92–93, 97–99, 102–4, 110–13, 126–27, 144–45; and Dorothy Cotton, 1, 76, 166, 167, 181; end of, 175, 180–81, 184–85; and Victoria Jackson Gray, 118, 122, 126
Dorrough, Charles, 99, 100
Downing, Virgil, 112
Dunbar, Leslie W., 163–66, 180, 181, 239n15

Ealey (Forrest), Pearlie, 61, 63–65, 71, 79–81, 85, 90, 186
Ealey, W. C., 210n38
Ebenezer Baptist Church (Atlanta), 173
Economic Opportunity Act, 141, 143, 226n8
Edisto Island Voters Association, 37, 45
Edmund Pettus Bridge, 10, 148, 150. *See also* Selma campaign
Eichelberger, Essie, 179
Elmore, George, 18
Elmore County Civic League (Wetumpka, Alabama), 80
Elmore v. Rice, 18

Emil Schwarzhaupt Foundation, 23, 24, 66, 68, 70, 192n8
Epps, Marie, 179
Evers, Medgar, 114

Fairley, J. C., 121
Farmer, James, xi
Farmers Home Administration (FHA), 139
Farm Security Administration (FSA), 111
Federal Housing Administration, 156
Field Foundation. *See* Marshall Field Foundation
Forman, James, 66
Foster, Earnestine, 110
Francis Bartow Homes community center, 90
Freedom Days, 125–28, 139
Freedom Rides, 4, 82, 96, 98, 105
Freedom Schools, 119, 131–35, 170, 175, 216n39
Freedom Summer, xii, 4, 119, 133–36, 139–40, 221n16, 224n48; aftermath, 136–38, 140–42, 152, 162; beginning of, 131–33, 139. *See also* Freedom Days; Freedom Schools
Freedom Vote, 119, 123–25, 128, 129, 138–39, 221n16
Freeman, Rosemary, 114
Frieda Foundation, 181

Gardner, Eddie, 64
Georgia Voters League, 60, 61, 210n33
Gilbert, Ralph Mark, 53
Gitin, Maria, 229n42
Goram, Adel, 86, 87
Gould, John Henry, 127
Gould (son of John Henry Gould), 127
Graves, Isaiah, 39
Graves, Sylvia, 39, 40
Gray, Anthony, 120, 123
Gray, Ethel, 144
Gray, Victoria Jackson (Victoria Gray Adams), 219n70, 222n28; biography, 117–18, 120–24, 128, 132, 134–42, 184–86, 220n2; in CEP teacher training, 118, 122; leadership role in Mississippi, 141–44, 159–61, 167, 169, 172, 175–77
Green, Bernice, 181
Green, Robert L. "Bob," 160, 165, 166
Greene, Susie, 78–79, 81

Grimball, Ethel Jenkins, 37; biography, 33, 35, 197n2; and CEP, 35–38, 45, 50, 62–63, 106, 186
Grimball, Juanita, 33, 34, 35, 197n2
Guyot, Lawrence, 122, 127

Hahn, Maxwell, 40, 80
Hall, Mamie, 211n43
Hamer, Fannie Lou: biography, 99–101, 103, 114–15, 132–33, 139; and CEP, 107, 110, 114–15, 190n13; and Freedom Days, 126–27; and Freedom Summer, xii; in MFDP delegation, 136; run for office, 132–33, 138; voter registration attempt, 100, 101, 103; Winona assault, 114–15, 136
Harrell, Daniel, Jr., 152, 156, 169, 229n43
Harrell, Juanita, 152, 229n43
Harris, Chessie, 45
Hattiesburg Ministers' Project, 126
Hayes, Curtis, 102
Hayes, Ralthus H., 112–13, 128, 139, 160, 172
Head Start program, 144, 162, 164, 168–69, 186
Henry, Aaron, 97–98, 123–26, 138
Henry, Ralph, 151
Hercules Powder Works, 120, 127
Hialeah Heights Civic Club, 185
Hicks, Fred, 100
Highlander Folk School: and CEP, origin of, 3–5, 8–10, 12–14, 23–35, 37, 39–53; and CEP, move away from, 9, 47–50, 53, 66–77, 198n4, 235n27; and communism, 23, 34, 43, 46, 49, 98, 102; and funding issues, 23, 31–32, 34, 53, 56–57, 67–70; Monteagle property, closing of, 75–76; and SGCV, 56–57, 61–67, 70–71. *See also* Horton, Myles
Holland, Ida Mae, 106, 108, 109, 216n39
Hollis, Ceola, 185
Holloway, Eddie Lou, 185, 186
Horton, Aimee Isgrig, 75, 167
Horton, Myles: and communism, 23, 34, 43, 46, 49, 98, 102; desegregation beliefs, 14, 23–24, 43; and founding of CEP, 4, 12–14, 23–32, 34–35, 40–41, 43–53; and Freedom Schools, 131; and funding issues, 23, 31–32, 34, 53, 56–57, 66–70, 80; legal challenges, 34, 43–44, 47, 53, 56–57, 67, 75; moving CEP to SCLC, 9, 34, 47–50, 66–70, 75–76, 198n4; and SGCV, 56–57, 61, 66–67, 70; and SNCC, 101, 102, 198n4. *See also* Highlander Folk School
Horton, Zilphia, 24
Hotchkiss, Wesley "Wes," 67, 69, 75–76, 163–65, 175, 180
Hughes, Ollie M., 128
Hunter, Janie, 20

Jackson, Ellis, 144
Jackson, Emma, 151
Jackson, Jimmy Lee, 147–48, 151
Jackson, Leonia, 151, 158
James, Lonnie, 87
James Island Improvement League, 172
Jenkins, Arthur, 36
Jenkins, Esau, 102, 168, 175, 194n32, 195n44; biography, 12–13, 19–22, 24, 33, 51, 72; CEP, founding of, 4, 12–13, 24–35, 39, 46, 50–51, 57
Jenkins, Marie, 25
Jenkins, Rebecca, 177, 178
Jim Crow. *See* Segregation
Johns Island Citizens Club, 24, 25
Johns Island Progressive Club, 12, 20, 24, 33, 65, 72; store, 26, 29, 168
Johnson, June, 114
Johnson, Lyndon B., 142, 148
Johnson, Otis S., 54, 55, 56, 203n7, 212n59
Johnson, Paul, 160, 169
Johnson, S. L., 147
Johnson, Virginia, 147
Jones, Daisy P., 88, 89
Jones, Frances, 40
Jones, Sidney A., 56, 203n9

Katzenbach, Nicholas, 152
Kennedy, John F., 48, 82, 131
King, Bessie, 159
King, Edwin, 123
King, Martin Luther, Jr., xi, 4, 9, 180; assassination, 9, 177, 182; Birmingham campaign, 89; and CEP at SCLC, 47–49, 68, 73–74, 83, 92, 163, 202n48; at Dorchester, 83; and Highlander Folk School, 47, 49, 74; inner circle, 92, 120, 162, 166; March on Washington, 119; Meredith March, 161; Montgomery bus boycott, 9, 46; and MSSC, 97–98, 112; People to People tour, 97–98; Poor People's Campaign, 162, 164, 173–74, 177–78, 181–82, 184; reputation of,

87; Selma campaign, 4, 146, 148; and Septima Clark, 137; and Winona assaults, 115
Knoxville's Associated Council, 76
Ku Klux Klan, 22, 59, 60, 65, 85, 155

Ladner, Dorie, 121, 220n9
Ladner, Joyce, 121, 220n9
Lafayette, Bernard, 174
Lane, Eddye, 132
Lane, Mary, 138–39, 144
Law, Westley Wallace, 52–55, 59, 90, 206n44; and Hosea Williams, 55, 71, 82, 88, 207n4, 212n59
Levison, Stanley, 181
Lewis, Curtis, 177
Lewis, John, xi, 66, 98, 126, 148
Lewis, P. H., 158
Li, Mew Soong, 170
Lily, Addie, 150, 158, 229n37
Lockwood (Romasco), Anne, 49, 62, 75, 205n33
Lona, Ethel, 87
Long, Herman, 67, 68
Lowndes County Christian Movement for Human Rights (LCCMHR), 152
Lowndes County Freedom Organization (LCFO), 157
Luchion, Bennie J., 168
Luckett, Leonia, 110–11, 217n49
Lynd, Theron, 122, 123, 125, 128

Macanic, James L., 57, 61
Mack, Anderson, 36, 39, 45
Mack, Benjamin, 175
Mack, Virginia, 55
Madison County Voters League, 46
Mallard, Robert, 59, 60
Mallard, Ruth, 181
March on Washington, 115, 119, 178
Marcus, McKinley, 128
Marlow, W. D., 100, 103
Marshall Field Foundation: CEP funding, 9, 40, 153, 163–67, 175, 180–81, 184; CEP funding increase, 80–81, 92; CEP reporting to, 81, 91; CEP to SCLC transfer, 48, 67–68, 70, 73; Highlander funding, 23, 75; SGCV funding, 70
McDonald, Joe, 99, 100
McDonald, Rebecca, 99–100, 103, 106, 133
McKaine, Osceola, 18

McKnight, Julia, 159
McLaurin, Charles, 99, 103
Meredith, James, 161
Meredith March (Mississippi), 161, 165
Mesher, Shirley, 152
Middlebrook, Harold, 152, 157
Middleton, Alma, 185
Miller, Ceola, 156
Mincy, Mollie Grace, 207n52
Mingo, Fred, 210n38
Mississippi Action for Progress (MAP), 169
Mississippians United to Elect Negro Candidates, 172
Mississippi Freedom Democratic Party (MFDP): and CDGM, 169; and CEP, 119, 131–45, 159–60; congressional challenge, 138, 141–43, 159–60; DNC challenge, 4, 10, 119, 136, 138, 140; Freedom Summer, 4, 119, 131–36, 139–40, 175
Mississippi Freedom Labor Union (MFLU), 139
Mississippi State Sovereignty Commission (MSSC), 96, 97, 100, 112–13, 124, 169
Mitchell, Ozell, 112, 218n54
Model Cities Program, 178, 186
Montgomery bus boycott, xii, 4, 9, 12, 34, 46
Montgomery Improvement Association, 46
Moore, Amzie, 99, 101, 102, 125, 126
Moore, L. B., 48
Moses, Robert "Bob," xi, 93, 99, 101–2, 105–6, 126
Moton, Ella Mae, 156
Moving Star Hall (Johns Island, South Carolina), 20, 26, 31

Nash, Diane, 99, 100
Nashville sit-in movement, 98, 101
National Association for the Advancement of Colored People (NAACP), xii, 213n2; and Bernice Robinson, 18–19, 22; and CCCV, 55–56, 66, 70–71, 207n4; and COAPO, 157; and COFO, 93, 138; Ella Baker, 48; and Esau Jenkins, 19–20; and Hosea Williams, 53–57, 62, 66, 70–71, 73, 82–83, 87–90; John H. Calhoun, 60, 210n33; Liberty County, Georgia, 59; Medgar Evers, 114–15; Mississippi, 96–99, 112–15, 121, 125, 127, 220n9; Montgomery County, Georgia, 59–60; Roy Wilkins, 82; and Septima Clark, 16, 18–19, 22, 25;

NAACP—*continued*
  Savannah, 52–54, 70–71, 83, 90, 94, 175, 177–78; and SGCV, 70, 73, 82–83, 87–89; South Carolina, 18, 20, 22, 35, 94; and SRC's VEP, 82, 85; Women's Auxiliary, 54–55; W. W. Law, 52–55, 59, 82, 90; Youth Council, 53–54, 97, 220n9
National Council of the Churches of Christ (NCCC), 67
Nixon, Isaac, 59–60
Nixon, Richard M., 183, 184
Norwood, David J., 61, 63, 64, 85

Office of Economic Opportunity (OEO), 157, 164, 168–69, 173, 179–80, 184
O'Neal, John, 122, 127

Parks, Rosa, xii, 34
Perry County Voters League (PCVL), 147
Petties, Sallie, 149–51, 156
Pierce, Cassie, 88–89
Pigee, Vera Mae, 97–98, 105, 107, 116, 122, 138
Pilcher, Pinkie, 130, 132, 138, 144
Political Action Committee of Charleston County, 172
Ponder, Annell, 9, *84*; biography, 83, 136, 185, 229n42, 238n7; CEP field supervisor, 83–84, 87; and CEP in Mississippi during Freedom campaigns, 118, 125–26, 129–37, 138, 139–41, 224n47; and CEP Mississippi expansion, 93–94, 106–11, 113–17; and CEP, new phase of, 141, 149, 154, 159–60, 165, 171, 234n25; Winona assaults, 114–15, 125
Poor People's Campaign, 164, 174–78, 182
Progressive Democratic Party (PDP), 18, 123
Promise Land School (Johns Island), 15, 16, 37
Pughsley, Melvina, 211n40

Quarterman, Ralph, 59
Quilloin, Carolyn, 203n8

Racial uplift ideas, 6–7, 16, 19, 30–31, 49, 65, 78
Ratliff, J. H., 127
Reagan, Ronald, 187
Reconstruction, 6, 96, 145, 186
Redding, Daisy Pearl, 211n40

Red Scare, 23, 43
Reeb, James, 148
Reed, Vennie, 179–80, 185
Reese, Frederick D., 157
Resurrection City. *See* Poor People's Campaign
Rhynes, Greta, 60, 64–65, 71, 79, 90, 186
Riggs, Clara Nell, 85–86
Riggs, Lou Anna, 85–86
Ritter, E. D., 64
Roberts, Carolyn, 57, 90
Robinson, Bernice Violanthe, 9, 29, *78*, 122, 180, 200n19; beauty business, 4, 12, 13, 17–18, 27, 97; biography, 12–14, 17–19, 28, 185–86, 235n27, 239n15; CEP, founding of, 4, 12–13, 26–32, 40–41; CEP Georgia expansion, 52–53, 56–57, 61–63, 65–71; on CEP legacy, 187; and CEP, second phase, 167–68, 172–73, 175; CEP South Carolina and Alabama expansion, 33–36, 38–44, 47, 49–51; CEP, training role, 47, 49, 62–63, 71–72, 77, 107–8, 167; curriculum design, 27–31, 33–34, 36, 38–42, 49; Highlander, first connections with, 25–26; Johns Island CEP, 4, 12, 26–30; and King's assassination, 177–78; and NAACP, 18–19, 22; on Selma, 150, 156; and Septima Clark, 13–14, 18–19, 68–69; and SCLC CEP transition, 66–70, 74–76; SNCC workshop, 102–3
Robinson, Ernest, 203n8
Robinson, H. C., 125
Robinson, Rosa, 178, 180
Roby, Harold, 138
Rockefeller, Nelson A., 181
Rodgers, Lois Lee, 101, 103, 110, 125, 130–31
Rountree, George, 86
Russell, Jesse J., 112, 139
Rustin, Bayard, xi

Salley, Grace, 185
Sanford, Walter, 211n40
Saulsberry, Caroline, 159
Saulsberry, Martha, 156
Scarbrough, Tom, 97–98, 100
Schlei, Norbert A., 143, 226n8
Schwarzhaupt Foundation. *See* Emil Schwarzhaupt Foundation
Seay, Solomon S., Sr., 43, 46
Segregation, xi–xii, 5–8, 14; challenges

against in education, xi–xii, 22–23, 34, 43; and economic opportunity limitations, 17, 36; in education, 15, 36, 41, 45, 53, 65, 95; federal legislation against, 11, 132, 138–39, 141–42, 166; and first class citizenship ideas, 7–8, 13; Freedom Riders against, 96; Highlander against, 14, 23, 43; and power of education against, 2, 7, 78, 86–88, 166, 173; Savannah protests against, 89–90; and Winona assaults, 114
Selma campaign, 4, 10, 234n25; aftermath, 150, 155–59, 162, 169; and CEP, 140–42, 145–48, 150, 155–59, 162, 169; marches to Montgomery, 10, 140, 148, 150, 158
Selma Emergency Relief Fund (SERF), 156
Shaw, Ethel, 109
Shelton, Louise, 158, 229n37
Simmons, Lewis H., 168
Simpson, Euvester, 114
Slavery, 6, 8, 20, 145, 151, 166, 173; in CEP curriculum, 111
Smalls, John, 20
Smalls-Mack, Ida, 88
Smith, Atlean, 107, 135, 139, 160
Smith, James, 73
Smitherman, Joe, 157
Smith v. Allwright, 6, 18, 127, 193n24
Sojourner, Sue (Lorenzi), 218n54, 224n54
Southeastern Georgia Crusade for Voters (SGCV): and CEP, 61–66, 71, 73, 76, 83–91; founding of, 61–62, 66; funding, 61, 66–68, 70, 73, 82–83, 87–88, 90–91. *See also* Williams, Hosea
Southern Christian Leadership Conference (SCLC), 162, 183–84, 202n48, 213n2, 215n25, 234n25, 238n7; and ACMHR, 89, 105; in Alabama, 110, 119, 145, 147–48, 150, 152, 157–59; CEP incorporated into, 2–5, 9, 47–49, 51, 53, 66–76, 198n4; CEP expansion of under, 76–77, 80–84, 88, 91; and CEP second phase, 163–67, 169–71, 173–78, 180–82; and COFO, 93, 138, 143; and Ella Baker, 47–48; and Martin Luther King, Jr., 9, 49; in Mississippi, 97–98, 101, 104–7, 110–18, 122–24, 133–39; Poor People's Campaign, 164, 174–78, 182; and SGCV, 73, 82–84, 90; and SRC's VEP, 82–84; uniform, 129–30
Southern Courier, 151, 157, 158
Southern Regional Council's Voter Education Project (VEP), 73, 82–91, 97, 101, 104–5, 131
Southland Sewing Center, 180
Southwest Alabama Farmers Cooperative Association (SWAFCA), 171
Southwest Alabama Self-Help Housing (SWASH), 171
Stephens, Anna Laura, 211n38
Stroman, Emogene, 56–57, 62
Strong, Claudia, 229n37
Strong, Mary, 144, 151
Student Non-Violent Coordinating Committee (SNCC), 213n2, 213n4, 215n25, 217n39, 220n9; in Alabama, 145, 147–50, 152, 155–57; and CEP, 101–7, 110–13, 117; Charles McLaurin, 99; and COFO, 93, 125; founding of, xii, 48, 202n49; James Bevel, 98–99; James "Jimmy" Travis, 93, 106; John Lewis, 98, 148; Jonathan Daniels, 155; in Mississippi, 4, 101–7, 110–13, 117, 122, 125; Myles Horton workshop, 101–2; and SRC's VEP, 82, 101, 104; uniform, 130; and Victoria Jackson Gray, 118
Summer Community Organization and Political Education (SCOPE), 152, 229n42
Surney, Jeff, 100
Surney, Lafayette, 103
Systematic Training and Redevelopment (STAR), 186

Tattnall County Christian Citizens League, 85
Thompson, Ethel Lee, 139
Thompson, James G., 135, 139
Till, Emmett, 63, 111
Tillman, Lizzie, 86
Tjerandsen, Carl, 192n8
Travis, James "Jimmy," 93, 105–6
Troupe, Mary, 211n43
Tucker, David, 106
Turnbow, Hartman, 112–13, 136
Turner, Albert, 147, 152
Tyson, Joan, 203n8

United Church Board of Homeland Missions (UCBHM), 67–69, 163, 164
United Presbyterian Church in the United States of America (UPCUSA), 126
United States Department of Agriculture (USDA), 143, 154

Vastine, Anna, 28
Volunteers in Service to America (VISTA), 186, 200n19, 239n15
Voter Education Project (VEP). *See* Southern Regional Council's Voter Education Project (VEP)
Voting Rights Act of 1965, xi, xii, 187; CEP, impact on, 141, 153–55, 157, 159–62, 164, 181; and Richard Nixon, 183, 184; and WCG, 155

Wadmalaw Improvement Committee, 35
Walker, Eugene, 238n7
Walker, Merdis, 211n43
Walker, Wyatt Tee, 48, 74, 120
Wallace, George, 146, 147, 148
Waring, J. Waties, 18
War on Poverty, 142, 143, 144, 169, 226n8, 236n39
Watkins, Hollis, 102, 112
Wesley, John Daniel, 112
West, Alice, 150, 151, 159, 229n37
West, Alonzo, 159
West, James, 114
Westbrook, Sarah, 152
Wheeler County Crusade for Voters, 86
Whitmire Leadership Club, 172
Wilcox County Civic and Progressive League (WCCPL), 147
Wilcox County SCLC, Inc., 156
Wilkins, Roy, 82
Williams, Alberta, 176
Williams, Dollie Mae, 87, 211n43
Williams, Hope, 168
Williams, Hosea, 129; biography, 55–57, 90, 119, 152, 157–58; Bloody Sunday, 148; and CCCV, 52, 55–57, 66, 70–71; and CEP, 52, 57–62, 66, 70–71, 73, 82–90; and NAACP, 53–57, 62, 66, 70–71, 73, 82–83, 87–90; Savannah campaign, 89–90; and SGCV, 61–62, 66, 70, 73, 82–84, 87–89; and SNCC workshop, 102; and VEP, 83–84, 88, 90; and W. W. Law, 55, 71, 82, 88, 90, 207n4, 212n59. *See also* CCCV; SGCV
Williams, Juanita (Terry), 55, 56, 57, 71
Willis, Viola, 85
Wine, Alice, 21–22, 29, 195n44
Wine, Lee Grant, 21, 194–95n43
Winona jail assaults, 114–15, 125, 136
Women for Constitutional Government (WCG), 155, 230n15
Wood, James, 48
Woods, John Bradley (J. B.), 220n7
Woods, Lenon E., 121, 220n7
Wright, Marian, 174
Wright, Mercedes, 55

Young, Andrew J., xi, 78, 119, 122, 210n33; biography, 67, 74, 120, 185, 186; CEP director at SCLC, hired as, 9, 66–67, 69–70, 74–76; CEP, expanding of, 76–83, 86, 91–93, 96–98, 104–7, 147; fundraising, 80–81, 83, 92; Highlander, distancing from, 75–76; and Martin Luther King, Jr., 9; on Resurrection City, 178; and Robert L. "Bob" Green, 165; Saint Augustine campaign, 137; on SCLC gender dynamics, 174; SCLC proposal, 183–84; and SGCV, 83–84, 90; and Winona assaults, 115, 219n66

Deanna M. Gillespie is professor of modern United States history at the University of North Georgia.

SOUTHERN DISSENT

Edited by Stanley Harrold and Randall M. Miller

The Other South: Southern Dissenters in the Nineteenth Century, by Carl N. Degler, with a new preface (2000)

Crowds and Soldiers in Revolutionary North Carolina: The Culture of Violence in Riot and War, by Wayne E. Lee (2001)

"Lord, We're Just Trying to Save Your Water": Environmental Activism and Dissent in the Appalachian South, by Suzanne Marshall (2002)

The Changing South of Gene Patterson: Journalism and Civil Rights, 1960–1968, edited by Roy Peter Clark and Raymond Arsenault (2002; first paperback edition, 2020)

Gendered Freedoms: Race, Rights, and the Politics of Household in the Delta, 1861–1875, by Nancy D. Bercaw (2003)

Civil War on Race Street: The Civil Rights Movement in Cambridge, Maryland, by Peter B. Levy (2003)

South of the South: Jewish Activists and the Civil Rights Movement in Miami, 1945–1960, by Raymond A. Mohl, with contributions by Matilda "Bobbi" Graff and Shirley M. Zoloth (2004)

Throwing Off the Cloak of Privilege: White Southern Women Activists in the Civil Rights Era, edited by Gail S. Murray (2004)

The Atlanta Riot: Race, Class, and Violence in a New South City, by Gregory Mixon (2004)

Slavery and the Peculiar Solution: A History of the American Colonization Society, by Eric Burin (2005; first paperback edition, 2008)

"I Tremble for My Country": Thomas Jefferson and the Virginia Gentry, by Ronald L. Hatzenbuehler (2006; first paperback edition, 2009)

From Saint-Domingue to New Orleans: Migration and Influences, by Nathalie Dessens (2007)

Higher Education and the Civil Rights Movement: White Supremacy, Black Southerners, and College Campuses, edited by Peter Wallenstein (2008)

Burning Faith: Church Arson in the American South, by Christopher B. Strain (2008; first paperback edition, 2020)

Black Power in Dixie: A Political History of African Americans in Atlanta, by Alton Hornsby Jr. (2009; first paperback edition, 2016)

Looking South: Race, Gender, and the Transformation of Labor from Reconstruction to Globalization, by Mary E. Frederickson (2011; first paperback edition, 2012)

Southern Character: Essays in Honor of Bertram Wyatt-Brown, edited by Lisa Tendrich Frank and Daniel Kilbride (2011)

The Challenge of Blackness: The Institute of the Black World and Political Activism in the 1970s, by Derrick E. White (2011; first paperback edition, 2012)

Quakers Living in the Lion's Mouth: The Society of Friends in Northern Virginia, 1730–1865, by A. Glenn Crothers (2012; first paperback edition, 2013)

Unequal Freedoms: Ethnicity, Race, and White Supremacy in Civil War–Era Charleston, by Jeff Strickland (2015)

Show Thyself a Man: Georgia State Troops, Colored, 1865–1905, by Gregory Mixon (2016)

The Denmark Vesey Affair: A Documentary History, edited by Douglas R. Egerton and Robert L. Paquette (2017; first paperback edition, 2022)

New Directions in the Study of African American Recolonization, edited by Beverly C. Tomek and Matthew J. Hetrick (2017; first paperback edition, 2022)

Everybody's Problem: The War on Poverty in Eastern North Carolina, by Karen M. Hawkins (2017)

The Seedtime, the Work, and the Harvest: New Perspectives on the Black Freedom Struggle in America, edited by Jeffrey L. Littlejohn, Reginald K. Ellis, and Peter B. Levy (2018; first paperback edition, 2019)

Fugitive Slaves and Spaces of Freedom in North America, edited by Damian Alan Pargas (2018; first paperback edition, 2020)

Latino Orlando: Suburban Transformation and Racial Conflict, by Simone Delerme (2020)

Slavery and Freedom in the Shenandoah Valley during the Civil War Era, by Jonathan A. Noyalas (2021; first paperback edition, 2022)

The Citizenship Education Program and Black Women's Political Culture, by Deanna M. Gillespie (2021; first paperback edition, 2023)

www.ingramcontent.com/pod-product-compliance
Lightning Source LLC
Chambersburg PA
CBHW020833160426
43192CB00007B/636